History of Spain and Portugal

Samuel Astley Dunham

Copyright © BiblioLife, LLC

This historical reproduction is part of a unique project that provides opportunities for readers, educators and researchers by bringing hard-to-find original publications back into print at reasonable prices. Because this and other works are culturally important, we have made them available as part of our commitment to protecting, preserving and promoting the world's literature. These books are in the "public domain" and were digitized and made available in cooperation with libraries, archives, and open source initiatives around the world dedicated to this important mission.

We believe that when we undertake the difficult task of re-creating these works as attractive, readable and affordable books, we further the goal of sharing these works with a global audience, and preserving a vanishing wealth of human knowledge.

Many historical books were originally published in small fonts, which can make them very difficult to read. Accordingly, in order to improve the reading experience of these books, we have created "enlarged print" versions of our books. Because of font size variation in the original books, some of these may not technically qualify as "large print" books, as that term is generally defined; however, we believe these versions provide an overall improved reading experience for many.

ANALYTICAL AND CHRONOLOGICAL TABLE

OF THE
HISTORY OF SPAIN AND PORTUGAL.

BOOK III. — *continued.*

THE PENINSULA DURING THE DOMINATION OF THE MOHAMMEDANS.

SECTION II. — *continued.*
CHRISTIAN SPAIN.

CHAP. II.
NAVARRE.
About 885—1512.

A.D.		Page
	The Origin and early History of Navarre wrapt in great Obscurity; various Hypotheses	1
	The first Hypothesis stated	2
	——————— confuted	3
	Authority of the Monk Vigila, the Continuator of the Chronicle of Albelda	4
	Exposition of fabulous Sovereigns	4
	On what Power was Navarre anciently dependent?	5
	Disputes for the Supremacy by the Kings of Asturias and France	6
	The first Count Sancho Iñigo, probably a Vassal of the French King	7
885—891.	GARCIA I. the first King	8
891—905.	Interregnum	8
905.	SANCHO I. surnamed Abarca, son of Garcia	9
905—908.	He invades France, but is recalled by an Irruption of the Arabs, whom he defeats	9
908—921.	His subsequent Conquests, and Retirement to the Monastery of San Salvador de Leyre	10
	He issues from his Convent to punish the Audacity of the Misbelievers; and prevails	11

ANALYTICAL AND CHRONOLOGICAL TABLE.

A.D.		Page
925.	His Death and Character	11
925—970.	GARCIA II., Son of Sancho: his Exploits and Death	12
970.	SANCHO II., surnamed el Mayor: Confusion of Kings	12
970—1035.	Sancho the most powerful Prince of his Age and Country	13
	His Division of his States	14
1035—1037.	GARCIA III. succeeds his Father Sancho in the Throne of Navarre	15
1037—1054.	His Exploits and Death	15
1054.	SANCHO III.	16
1054—1076.	His peaceful Reign and tragical Death	16
	Disputes for the Crown between Castile and Aragon: Success of the latter	17
1076—1134.	SANCHO IV., PEDRO I., and ALFONSO I., being also Kings of Aragon, their Exploits must be looked for in the History of that Kingdom	17
1134.	Disputes consequent on the Death of Alfonso, who died without Issue, and left his Dominion to the Knights of St. John and the Temple	18
	The Navarrese elect GARCIA IV.	18
1134, 1135.	His Disputes with Ramiro, the new King of Aragon	18
1136—1150.	His Transaction with the King of Portugal and the Emperor Alfonso	19
1150.	SANCHO V., Son of Garcia	20
1150—1180.	His Transactions with Aragon and Castile	20
1190—1195.	His Alliance with Richard Plantagenet, and subsequent Death	21
1194.	SANCHO VI., Son of the preceding Monarch	22
1194—1234.	His Transactions with the Christians and Moors	22
1234.	He dies, and with him ends the *Male* Line of the House of Sancho Iñigo	23
	Perplexity of the Navarrese about the Choice of a Successor: it at length falls on Thibault, a Nephew of the late King	23
	THIBAULT I.	24
1236—1240.	Assumes the Cross, and proceeds to Syria: Disasters of the Crusaders: his Return	24
1247—1253.	His Disputes with the Bishop of Pamplona	26
1253—1270.	THIBAULT II., Son of the former, joins the Crusade of St. Louis, visits Tunis, and dies at Trapani, in Sicily	27
1270—1274.	HENRI, Brother of the deceased King	27
1274, 1275.	JEANNE I., Daughter of Henri, removed by her Mother into France, of which she became the Queen	28
1276—1284.	Navarre governed by a French Viceroy	29
1284—1328.	Navarre a Province of France during Four Reigns	30
1328.	JEANNE II., Daughter of Louis Hutin, and her Husband PHILIP of Evreux	31
1328—1342.	Their Residence chiefly in France	31
1343—1349.	Death of Philip at Xeres de la Frontera; of Jeanne at Paris	32
1349.	CHARLES II., (the *first* of this Name was King also of

ANALYTICAL AND CHRONOLOGICAL TABLE.

A.D.		Page
	France) surnamed *le Mauvais*, or the Bad, Son of Jeanne	32
1349—1352.	His Alliance with Pedro the Cruel	32
1352—1360.	His strange Intrigues, &c. in France	33
1361—1370.	Renews his Alliance with the King of Castile: the Duplicity of his Behaviour to the rival Brothers	35
1371, &c.	Subsequent Transactions with King Enrique	37
1377—1384.	His suspicious Intelligence with the English Monarch	37
1387.	His Death	38
	CHARLES III., the *Noble*, his Son	39
1387—1402.	Dissatisfaction of the new Queen	39
1403.	He obtains the Restitution of some Domains in France	39
1403—1425.	His pacific Reign and Death	40
1425.	BLANCHE, his Daughter, and her Husband, JUAN of Aragon	40
1426—1434.	The new King foments the Troubles of Castile	40
1435, 1436.	His Transactions in Italy	41
1441—1446.	Death of Blanche, who bequeaths the Sceptre to her Son Charles, Prince of Viana: Juan refuses to lay it down	41
1451—1454.	Navarre distracted by rival Factions	42
	Charles raises the Standard of Revolt; is defeated, imprisoned, and released	43
1454—1458.	Injustice of Juan: continued Disputes with his Son: he becomes King of Aragon	43
1459, 1460.	Second Reconciliation between them	44
1460.	Renewed Dissensions, and Imprisonment of Charles	45
1461.	He is released through the armed Intervention of the Inhabitants of Barcelona, who proclaim him their Sovereign	46
	Perfidy of Father and Son: Death of the latter	46
	Vindication of the former, and of his Queen, from the Charge of procuring the Death of Charles	47
	Disputes respecting the Succession, which properly belonged to the Princess Blanche, Sister of Charles	48
	Juan retains Possession of the Navarrese Crown	48
1461—1464.	Persecution of Blanche: her violent Imprisonment and mysterious End	49
1469—1479.	Internal Dissensions: Violence of the two Parties which afflicted the Kingdom	50
1479.	Accession and sudden Death of LEONORA, Daughter of Juan	52
1479—1483.	FRANÇOIS PHŒBUS, her Grandson, succeeds: his brief Reign	52
1483.	CATHERINE, his Sister	53
1484, &c.	She is married to Jean d'Albret, a French Lord	53
1494—1512.	Unprincipled Ambition of Fernando, King of Aragon	54
1512.	He Invades and subdues Navarre, which he annexes to his Crown	55
	This violent Usurpation characterised	56

A 4

CHAP. III.

COUNTS OF BARCELONA.

801—1162.

A.D.		Page
	Barcelona, the only Independent Sovereignty of Catalonia	57
	Fabulous Exploits of Otgar and his Nine Companions	57
777—801.	Disputes of the Mohammedans and the Franks for the Possession of Catalonia: Success of the latter, and Foundation of the Lordship of Barcelona	58
801—820.	BERA, first Count; his Rapacity and Banishment	60
	Hostilities between the Mohammedans and Franks	60
820—830.	BERNARDO, the second Count: Invasion of the Arabs and Subjugation of Barcelona	61
824—832.	Intrigues, &c. of Bernardo in France	61
833—836.	Barcelona recovered, and Bernardo restored	62
836—844.	His reprehensible Policy, and violent Death by the Hands of the French King	63
844, 845.	Steps of Wilhelm, his Son, to avenge his Death	64
846—850.	ALEDRAN is expelled and restored	65
850—858.	His subsequent Disasters	66
858—872.	WIFREDO I., his Administration, and tragical End	66
872—884.	SALOMON, his Government, and Assassination by young Wifredo	67
884.	WIFREDO II. Son of Wifredo I., surnamed the Warlike	68
884—912.	His Transactions with France, and his great Conquests over the Arabs	68
912—928.	MIRO, Son of Wifredo II.	69
928—967.	SENIOFREDO, Son of Miro	70
967—993.	BORELLO, Cousin of the late Count; his troubled Government	70
993—1017.	RAYMUNDO I., Son of Borello	71
1017—1035.	BERENGARIO I., Son of Raymundo	72
1035—1076.	RAYMUNDO II., Son of Berengario; his vigorous and fortunate Administration	72
1076—1082.	RAYMUNDO III., Son of Raymundo II.	73
1082—1110.	RAYMUNDO IV., Son of the late Count, his Transactions in France	74
1108—1131.	His other Exploits, and End	76
1131—1137.	RAYMUNDO V., Son of the late Count; his Marriage with the Heiress of Aragon, and Administration of that Kingdom	77

CHAP. IV.

ARAGON.

1035—1516.

Fabulous History of this Kingdom		78
Its limited Dimensions, and probable Dependence on the Asturian King		79

ANALYTICAL AND CHRONOLOGICAL TABLE.

A.D.		Page
1035—1063.	Ramiro I., the first King	80
1063.	Sancho I. Son of Ramiro	80
1063—1076.	His Successes over the Mohammedans, and his Election to the Throne of Navarre	81
1076—1094.	Continued Successes, and his Death before Huesca	81
1094—1104.	Pedro I., Son of Sancho, King of Aragon and Navarre. Victory over the Moors	82
1104.	Alfonso I., Brother of Pedro, succeeds to both Kingdoms	83
1104—1118.	His great Conquests over the natural Enemy	84
1119—1130.	Other Victories	85
1131—1134.	His Defeat, Death, and Character	86
	He dies without Issue, and bequeaths his Dominions to the Religious Orders	88
1134.	Ramiro II., Brother of the late King, forced from the Cloister to the Throne	88
1134—1137.	His Disputes with the new King of Navarre, and Resignation	88
1137.	Petronilla, Daughter of Ramiro, and her Husband Count Raymundo	89
1137—1140.	Treaty with the Grand Master of the Templars	89
1140—1153.	Disputes of Raymundo with Navarre	89
1162—1163.	Death of Raymundo, and Abdication of Petronilla	90
1163—1196.	Alfonso II., Son of Petronilla and Raymundo	90
1196—1204.	Pedro II., Son of Alfonso, his Disputes with his Mother, and base Submission to the Roman See	91
1204—1208.	Extraordinary Relation concerning the Birth of his Son Jayme	92
1206—1212.	Transactions with the Moors	94
1209—1213.	With Simon de Montfort, and the Albigenses of France	94
1213.	His last Campaign, and Death	95
	Jayme I, his Son, surnamed *el Conquistador*, or the Conqueror	97
1213—1226.	Troubles during his Minority	97
1228—1235.	Conquest of the Balearic Isles	99
1232—1239.	Conquests in Valencia: Memorable Reduction of the Capital	102
1239—1245.	Persecutions sustained by the vanquished Mohammedans	104
1229—1276.	His domestic Character. Marriage of his Son Pedro to Constanza, Daughter of Manfred, King of Sicily. Dissensions between his Sons	105
1276.	His Death and Character	108
	Pedro III., Son of Jayme	108
1276—1280.	His Transactions with his rebellious Barons	109
	Memorable Events in Sicily. Oppressive Government of the French. Pedro solicited to claim the Throne	109
1281.	He prepares to assert the Claim. his Designs favoured by Accident: Massacre of the odious French	111
1282.	He invades Sicily, and is joyfully recognised by the Inhabitants	113

A. D.		Page
1283.	Opposition of Pope Martin to his Title: his Transactions with the dethroned Charles	114
1284.	The French vainly penetrate into Catalonia	115
1285.	Death of Pedro, who leaves Aragon to Alfonso, and Sicily to Jayme, his Sons	115
	ALFONSO III. dethrones his Uncle, the King of Majorca	116
1286.	Factious Conduct of many Aragonese Nobles, who compel him to make dangerous Concessions	116
1286—1291.	His Transactions with the Pope and the French: his unmanly Desertion of the Sicilians	117
	He dies without Issue, and is succeeded by his Brother, the King of Sicily	119
1291—1295.	JAYME II. also betrays the Sicilians, by surrendering them to their former King	120
	They proclaim Frederic, his Brother, and prepare for a vigorous Defence	120
1300.	Jayme joins the League against them; but, after some partial Successes, returns Home	121
1309—1319.	Strange Conduct of his Son, the Infante Don Jayme, who renounces the Rights of Primogeniture	122
	Reflections on that Event	123
1309—1312.	Persecution of the Templars	124
1321—1326.	Affairs of Sardinia	124
1327.	Death of Jayme	125
1327—1336.	ALFONSO IV., Son of Jayme, his Efforts to reduce the Sardinians fruitless	126
	Domestic Dissensions: his Death	126
1336—1349.	PEDRO IV., Son of Alfonso, disputes with his Step-Mother	127
1336—1347.	Discontent of his Barons	128
1347.	Their Insolence and Rebellion: Civil War: Scenes at Saragossa	130
	The Rebellion continues in Valencia: Intrepidity of the King; his ultimate Triumph	132
1348—1374.	Transactions with Castile,—with Pedro the Cruel and Enrique of Trastamara	134
1338—1349.	Duplicity and Violence of Pedro towards his Kinsman, the King of Majorca, whom he dethrones	137
1340—1386.	Affairs of Sardinia	140
1377—1384.	Policy of this Monarch in regard to Sicily	142
1382—1387.	His Ambition at once insatiable and senseless	143
1387.	His Death and Character	143
	During his Reign, the Era of Cæsar is abolished in Aragon and Castile	144
	JUAN I., Son of Pedro	145
	His Dispute with his Step-Mother Sibella	145
1387—1389.	He patronises the Troubadours, and is indignantly reproved by his Subjects	145
1389—1395.	Troubles in Sardinia and Sicily: Death of Juan while hunting	146

… ANALYTICAL AND CHRONOLOGICAL TABLE. xi

A.D.		Page
1395.	Martin, Brother of Juan, then in Sicily	147
	The Count de Foix, Son-in-law of the late King, unsuccessfully strikes for the Crown	147
1396.	Martin returns and establishes his Authority	147
1397—1409.	Troubles in Sardinia: Death of the Sicilian King, only Son of Martin	148
1410.	Various Candidates for the Throne: Death of Martin	149
1410—1411.	Dreadful Troubles consequent on the King's Death, and the disputed Succession: Murder of the Archbishop of Saragossa	150
1411—1412.	Disagreement between the three great States — Aragon, Catalonia, and Valencia	152
1412.	Nine Arbitrators chosen to elect a King	153
	The Choice falls on Fernando of Castile	154
	Reflection on this Election	155
	Fernando I. is acknowledged in Spain and Sicily	155
1413.	The Count d'Urgel, one of the late Candidates, troubles the Kingdom, but loses his Liberty	156
1414—1416.	Transactions of Fernando in Italy: his Death	156
1416—1429.	Alfonso V., Son of Fernando; his Firmness	157
1417—1420.	Affairs of Corsica and Sardinia: his Treaty with Joanna Queen of Naples	158
1420—1423.	He aids her with his Troops: her characteristic Fickleness	160
1426—1435.	He again interferes in the Affairs of Naples, and is made Prisoner by the League	161
1435—1443.	His Release, and subsequent Exploits against his Enemies, whom he humbles	163
1443—1458.	His Peace with the Pope, who grants him the Investiture of Naples	164
1458.	His Death: in Naples he is succeeded by his bastard Son, Fernando; in Spain by his Brother, Juan of Navarre	165
1458—1473.	Juan II., his Transactions with the rebellious Catalonians, and with France	165
1473—1476.	Perfidy of Louis XI. in regard to Roussillon	168
1476—1479.	Internal Troubles	169
1479.	Fernando II., Son of Juan, also King of Castile	170
1479—1483.	He recovers Roussillon and Cardaña	170
1492—1495.	Affairs of Naples, which is invaded by the French: Abdication of the King	170
1495—1498.	The Spanish King sends an Armament to expel the French: Success of his Captain	171
1498—1500.	He agrees to divide the Country with France	172
1501—1504.	The Royal Robbers dispute about the Prey: Subjugation of the whole by Fernando	173
1504—1508.	Envious Fortune of Fernando's great Captain, Gonsalo de Cordova	174
	Introduction of the Inquisition into Aragon: Murder of the Chief Inquisitor in the Cathedral of Saragossa	175

CHAP. V.

PORTUGAL.
1095—1516.

A.D.		Page
1095.	Early Condition of Portugal; the Fief conferred on Count Henri	176
	Nature of the Authority held by the Count, a Subject of great Dispute	177
1095—1112.	Administration of the first Count	178
1112—1128.	Administration of *Teresa*, the Widow of Count Henri	178
1128—1137.	War of his Son Count *Alfonso* with the King of Leon	179
1137.	The great Battle of Ourique, with its fabulous Circumstances: Alfonso proclaimed King	180
	Alfonso I., his Conquests over the Moors: Recovery of Santarem and Lisbon	182
1152—1163.	Continued Successes of the King; Giraldo the Dauntless	183
1166—1179.	The Wars of Alfonso with the Christians and Moors: Accident at Badajoz	185
1180—1181.	Heroism of Don Fuas Roupinho: Miraculous Legend concerning him	186
1184—1186.	Death and Character of the Lusitanian King; his reputed Sanctity	187
1186.	Sancho I., Son of Alfonso	188
1188—1202.	Transactions of the new King with the Moors and Alfonso of Castile	188
1203—1211.	His Disputes with the Church	189
1211—1216.	Alfonso II., Son of the late King, endeavours to evade his Father's Will: War with the Sovereign of Leon	190
1217—1219.	Transactions with the Mohammedans: Miraculous Legend: Tragical Fate of two Moorish Lovers	191
1220—1223.	Disputes of Alfonso with the Church	192
1223.	Sancho II., Son of Alfonso	193
1228—1240.	His Successes over the Moors	193
1220—1245.	His Disputes with the Clergy, and his consequent Deposition by the Council of Lyons	194
1245—1248.	He is compelled to retire into Castile, where he ends his Days	195
1248.	Alfonso III., Brother of the deposed Sancho	195
1241—1254.	His Conquests in the Algarve, and his Treaty with the Castilian King	196
1255—1262.	He commits Bigamy: Claim of his lawful Wife, and his base Ingratitude	198
1263—1279.	His Disputes with the Church, and Oppression over his People	199
1270.	Dinis, his Son, effects a Reconciliation with his powerful Enemy the Pope	200
1286—1298.	His Transactions with Castile	200
1299.	Rebellion of his Son Don Alfonso: Open Warfare between them, and subsequent Reconciliation	201

ANALYTICAL AND CHRONOLOGICAL TABLE. xiii

A.D.		Page
1299—1323.	Second Dispute; disgraceful Scene at Santarem	203
1325.	Death and Character of Dinis	204
	ALFONSO IV., surnamed the Brave	205
1325, 1326.	The Vengeance with which he pursues his natural Brother	205
	His Neglect of Public Business, and repeated Expostulations of his Ministers	506
1327—1339.	His numerous Transactions with Castile, and his first Dissatisfaction with that Power	206
1340—1350.	He assists in the Campaigns against the Mohammedans of Spain and Africa	209
1340—1355.	Guilty Connection of his Son Don Pedro with Iñes del Castro: Tragical Fate of that Lady	210
1355.	His real Character	212
	Pedro arms to revenge her Death; but is reconciled with his Father	212
1356, 1357.	Last Acts and Death of Alfonso	213
1357—1360.	PEDRO I.: the Vengeance with which he pursues the Murderers of Iñes	214
1361.	The studied Pomp with which he buries her Remains	215
1362—1367.	His internal Administration: his whimsical Regard for Justice	216
1367.	FERNANDO I., son of Pedro, his bad Character	218
1360—1382.	His Disputes with Castile	218
1372—1378.	Acts and Character of the new Queen: her bloody Perfidy	222
1370—1372.	His Negotiation for a Wife: he falls in Love with a married Woman, whom he divorces from her Husband, and marries: Indignation of his Subjects	219
1379—1382.	Criminal Intrigues of Leonora with Andeiro; her bloody Design	224
1382, 1383.	Her unblushing Effrontery: Death of King Fernando	226
	Deplorable Character of his Reign	227
1383.	INTERREGNUM. Leonora, Regent for her Daughter, the Queen of Castile, whom the Nation refuses to acknowledge	223
	Don Joam, bastard Brother of the late King, and Grand Master of Avis, aspires to supreme Power: he murders Andeiro: Insurrection of the Mob in his Favour: he accepts the Regency	228
1383—1385.	His first Measures: Violence of his Partisans: his crooked Policy	231
1384, 1385.	The War with Castile: he defends the Country, and is proclaimed King	233
1385—1403.	JOAM I.; his Transactions with Castile	234
1404—1411.	He rewards some of his People with a needy Hand: his Great Constable, Nuno Alvares Pereira	235
1411—1415.	His five Sons urge him to undertake an Expedition to Ceuta	236
1416, 1417.	Heroism of the Governor Don Pedro de Menezes, in de-

ANALYTICAL AND CHRONOLOGICAL TABLE.

A.D.		Page
	fending the new Conquest against the African Moors: Destructive Irruption into the Neighbourhood	240
1417—1420.	Various Assaults on Ceuta	243
1420—1433.	Internal Administration of the King: Anecdote of his Zeal for Justice	244
1419—1430.	First Maritime Discoveries of the Portuguese, who penetrate to Sierra Leone: Travels of the Infante Dom Pedro	245
1433.	DUARTE, eldest Son of Joam: his disastrous Reign	247
1435—1437.	Preparation for an Expedition to Africa	247
1437.	Unsuccessful Assault on Tangier: the Christian Army enveloped by the Moors: Heroism of the Portuguese: Treaty, and the Infante Fernando retained as an Hostage	248
1437—1443.	Unsuccessful Attempts to procure the Liberation of Fernando: his Ill-usage by the Moors: his Resignation, Death, and reputed Sanctity	253
1438.	Duarte endeavours to solace his People: he dies of the Plague	256
	ALFONSO V., Son of Duarte, a Minor	256
1438, 1439.	Regency of Leonora, the Queen Mother: Opposition to her Authority: Intrigues of the King's Uncle, Don Pedro, to obtain the Regency: Commotion of the Mob at Lisbon: he obtains the Object of his Ambition	257
1440—1445.	Intrigues of Leonora to regain her lost Power: her fickle Conduct, and ultimate Retirement into Castile	260
1446—1449.	Alfonso reaches his Majority: is made to entertain Suspicions of his Uncle, whom he at length abhors; Pedro retires from Court: his continued Persecution by the unprincipled Princes of Braganza: his Death decreed by the King	262
1449.	Affecting Scene at Coimbra, and at the Monastery of Alcobaça: Pedro's Intention to oppose his Enemies: His Death in the Field, and that of his Friend, Don Alvaro	266
1450—1456.	Sensation produced by Don Pedro's Death: Tardy Repentance of the King: Sudden Death of the Queen	268
1457—1459.	Alfonso fits out an Armament from the African Coast; he takes the Fortress of Alcacer-Seguer: Heroism of its Commander, Dom Duarte de Menezes	269
1464.	Unsuccessful Attempt on the Fortress of Tangier; Defeat of the Christians; Conquest of Arsilla	271
1471.	The King of Fez endeavours to wrest the new Conquest from the Christians: his Repulse with heavy Loss	272
	Tangier abandoned by the Moorish Inhabitants, and entered by the Christians	273
1474—1479.	Transactions of Alfonso with Castile: his Visit to Louis XI. King of France: Perfidy of that Monarch: his Return, and Reception by the Infante Joam	275
1481.	Death and Character of Alfonso	275

A.D.		Page
	JOAM II. - - -	- 276
	His Reformation in the Business of Administration; he subjects the Nobles to the Power of the Crown	- 276
1481, 1482.	Opposition to his Measures by a Portion of that Body, especially by the House of Braganza -	- 278
1482, 1483.	Treasonable Conduct of the Duke of Braganza: Discovery of his Guilt: his Trial, Execution, and Character	279
1483.	Still more criminal Conduct of the Duke de Viseo, who heads a Conspiracy for the Assassination of the King: Disclosure of an Accomplice -	- 282
	Fruitless Attempts of the Conspirators: Vigilance of Joam: Death of the Duke by the royal Hand -	- 283
1484.	Execution of other Conspirators -	- 284
1482—1486.	Maritime Enterprise of the Portuguese under the Reign of Joam: Settlement on the Coast of Guinea: Punishment of three Seamen	- 285
1486.	Two Travellers despatched to visit the East	- 287
1486—1490.	Discovery of Congou: Intercourse with the Natives: Progress of the Christian Religion: Causes of its Decline: Melancholy Fate of a Mohammedan Prince	- 287
1487.	Discovery of the Cape of Good Hope by Bartolomeo Dias	- 291
1487—1491.	Hostilities of Joam with the Moors of Fez: Triumph of the Christians -	- 291
1490—1495.	Marriage and tragical Death of Prince Alfonso, only Son of Joam: Grief of the King: he transfers his Affection to his natural Son: his Death -	- 292
1495.	Character of Joam: some of his more remarkable Sayings: his jealous Vindication of the national Honour	- 295
	MANUEL, Brother of the Duke de Viseo, and Cousin of the late King - - -	- 298
1495—1500.	He perseveres in the Maritime Enterprise of his great Predecessor - - -	- 298
	First Voyage to India by the celebrated Vasco de Gama: Transactions with the African and Hindoo Princes	- 298
1500, 1501.	Second Voyage under Cabral: Transactions with the Africans of Mozambique: Hostilities with the King of Calicut: a commercial Intercourse opened with the Hindoos - - -	- 300
1502—1504.	Second Voyage made by Vasco de Gama: the Moors of Mozambique: Hostilities in the Indian Seas and on the Coast of Malabar: Vindictive Spirit of the King of Calicut: Heroic Defence of Cochin -	- 301
1506—1509.	Departure of another Armament under Lope Soares: Francisco de Almeida named Viceroy of the Indies: Transactions with the Africans, Hindoos, the Cingalese, and People of Ormuz: the Portuguese Flag waves from Ormuz to Siam: Tragical Fate of the Viceroy	- 304
1509—1515.	Administration of the Great Albuquerque: Loss and Reconquest of Goa: Affairs in Malacca, Malabar, and the Arabian Sea: Death and Character of the Viceroy	- 307

xvi ANALYTICAL AND CHRONOLOGICAL TABLE.

A.D.		Page
1515—1521.	The Successors of Albuquerque: *Lope Soares;* his Incapacity, and consequent Want of Success; Troubles throughout the whole Line of Portuguese Settlements: Administration of *Siqueira* no less unfortunate	309
1519—1521.	Dissatisfaction of Fernando de Magalhanes with the Portuguese King; offers his Services to the King of Spain; departs on an Expedition to discover a Western Passage to India: Its remarkable Result: his Death in the Philippine Islands	311
1501—1513.	Affairs of North-western Africa: Irruptions of the Moors into the Territories of the Portuguese: Conquest of Saphir: Siege of Arsilla by the King of Fez: Exploits of Ataide, Governor of Saphin, and of a Moorish Ally, Yahia ben Tafut: Honourable Fidelity of the latter: Conquest of Azamor by the Duke of Braganza	313
1510—1519.	Origin of the celebrated Family of Xerifs; their Fanaticism and vast Designs: their Defeat by the Portuguese: Continued Successes of the Christians; Hostilities of the two People: Unsuccessful Attempt to construct a Citadel at the Mouth of the Marmora	318
1515—1521.	Uniformity of the War: Death of the illustrious Yahia ben Tafut, and of the dauntless Ataide	321
	Activity of the Xerifs: they lay the Foundation of Sovereignty in the Valley of Fez: they prepare to recover Azamor, and proceed to the Court of the King of Morocco: Assassination of that Monarch, and Proclamation of the elder Xerif	321
1521.	Death and Character of Manuel	322

APPENDIX.

A.	Division of Sancho's Dominions	325
B.	Fable respecting the Re-building of Palencia	325
C.	The Possessed Princess	326
D.	Chivalry of Count Raymundo	327
E.	Origin of the Word Æra	328
F.	Miraculous Escape of Dom Fuas Roupinho	329

THE HISTORY OF SPAIN AND PORTUGAL.

BOOK III. CONTINUED.

THE PENINSULA DURING THE DOMINATION OF THE ARABS.

SECTION II.

CHRISTIAN SPAIN, CONTINUED.

CHAP. II.

NAVARRE.

ABOUT 885—1512.

No historical subject is wrapt in greater obscurity than the origin and early history of the kingdom of Navarre. Whether during a great portion of the eighth and ninth centuries the country was independent or tributary; and if dependent, whether it obeyed the Franks, the Asturians, or the Arabs, or successively all three, are speculations which have long exercised the pens of the peninsular writers. The natives, as might naturally be expected, stoutly contend for their ancient freedom, and do not scruple to assert that the foundation of their kingdom is coeval with that of the Asturian state by Pelayo. On the other hand, the Castilians maintain that until the latter half of the ninth century this mountainous region was subject, with a slight interruption, to the successors of that prince; while the French, and such as follow their authorities, affirm that a full century after the time of Charlemagne, Navarre, as well as Catalonia, owned the paramount sway of the Carlovingian sovereigns.

According to the first of these three hypotheses, the first king of Navarre was Garcia Ximenes, the contemporary of Pelayo. The occasion of his election is stated to have been singular. A number of the natives, among whom were two hundred persons of distinction, attended the last obsequies of a holy hermit. The degraded state of the surrounding country,—degraded through its subjection to the insolent misbelievers,—the indignities they were made continually to endure; the tale of new wrongs, and the apprehension of greater, roused their patriotism, and caused them to elect on the very spot a ruler who should lead them against the abhorred strangers. The choice fell on Garcia Ximenes, one of the most valiant as well as powerful of the native lords. His domains were, at first, very circumscribed, comprising only the mountains of Sobrarve and a few neighbouring places; but by his valour he recovered a considerable territory from the Arabs. He was succeeded, continue the advocates of this hypothesis — for it is no better,—by several sovereigns, who swayed the sceptre with the usual alternations of glory and failure, until 905, when the darkness involving the history of this kingdom begins to be dissipated.*

---

* Joannes Vasæus Hispaniæ Chronicon, pp. 617—706, &c. Alfonsus à Carthagena, Anacephalæosis, cap. 69. Lucius Marineus Siculus, de Rebus Hispaniæ, lib. viii. (apud Schottum.) Hispania Illustrata, tom. 1. Garibay, Compendio Historial, tom. iii lib. 2. Morales, Coronica General, tom. iv. Mariana, Historia Genealogica, tom. i. lib. 8. Favyn, Histoire de Navarre, lib. i. et ii. Moret, Anales del Reyno de Navarra, tom. i. lib. iv. Hermilly, Préface du Traducteur, tom. iii. of Ferreras, Sandoval, Père d'Orleans, Davalos, Blancas, and a multitude besides. These authors, following the archbishop Rodrigo Ximenes, have so confounded the names of Garcia's successors, that we cannot find our way through the labyrinth.

But the acts and even the existence of these kings rest on authority too disputable to be followed: a MS. history of San Juan de la Peña; the rule of San Salvador de Leyre; some royal epitaphs, and a series of diplomas and privileges, have been triumphantly adduced as evidence of the antiquity so obstinately advocated. But criticism has shown that these instruments are of comparatively modern composition;—invented, according even to some orthodox catholics, by certain monks, for ends sufficiently obvious. That the *epitaphs* of San Juan de la Peña are also modern, is apparent both from their containing *Arabic* numerals and the *Christian* computation (the Spanish *era* was not abolished in Navarre until the fourteenth century), and from express mention of the church of San Juan, a structure known to have been erected in later times. The *privileges* of the same order are no less suspicious: the style in which they are written sufficiently exposes the fabrication: besides most of them,—that for instance of Garcia Sanchez bearing the date of 959, and that of Charles the Noble in 1412,—so confound events, persons, and times, that it is impossible to receive them as any other than monastic impostures. The other instruments have been proved to be no less apocryphal. That the Arabs ever possessed Navarre is at least doubtful. A passage in Sebastian [*] has been adduced to show that at all times Alava, Biscay, &c. were possessed by the native inhabitants: Rodrigo of Toledo [†] has a much stronger one to the same purport. So that all *positive* testimony hitherto adduced betrays, instead of confirming, the system it ought to support. The *negative* is no less entitled to attention, and is no less fatal to

---

[*] "Alava namque Biscaya, Aizone et Urdunia, à suis incolis reperiuntur semper possessæ, sicut Pampilonia," &c. — *Sebast. Chron.* p. 482. (apud Florez, xiii.)

[†] "Sarraceni enim totam Hispaniam occupaverunt, gentis Gothicæ fortitudine jam contritâ, nec alicub iresistente, exeptis paucis reliquis quæ in montanis Asturiarum et Biscagiæ, Alavæ, Guipiscoæ, Ruchoniæ (which was certainly in Navarre Proper) et Aragoniæ remanserunt, quas ideo Dominus reservavit, ne lucerna sanctorum in Hispaniis eoram Domino extingueretur." — *Rodericus Toletanus*, lib. i. cap. i. (apud Schottum Hisp. Illust. tom. ii.)

the antiquity in question. If monarchy existed in Navarre at so remote a period, we might reasonably expect to find some *incidental* mention, at least, of the fact in the old chronicles. Yet the continuator of Joannis Biclarensis, who wrote in 724; Isidorus Pacensis, who finished his work in 753; the monk of Albelda and Sebastian of Salamanca, who come down to the latter half of the ninth century, say not one word of the Navarrese kingdom. On the contrary, from one passage of Sebastian in which he speaks of the expedition of Alfonso III. to punish the *revolted* Alavese, we may infer, not only that no monarchy was yet established, but that the country, or at least a portion of it, was subject to the Asturian kings.[*]

From the preceding statement it is evident that no reliance is to be placed on authorities pretended to be prior to the monk Vigila, who made some additions to the Chronicle of Albelda. He is the first writer from whom we derive the slightest information respecting the existence of kings in Navarre, and the manner in which that information is conveyed, is not of the most satisfactory description. " Era 943 surrexit in Pampilona rex nomine, Sancio Garseanis." He does not here tell us whether Sancho was the *first* king or not. In another passage, however, which is evidently an interpolation or addition,— probably by the same Vigila,— we are informed that, Sancio Rex filius *Regis* Garseanis regnavit annos XX."[†]

Admitting, then, that Garcia the father filled the royal dignity, we must also admit that he is the first king of Navarre. There is nothing in authors nearest to the period that affords us the slightest ground for

---

[*] Yepes, Cronica General de la Orden de San Benito, tom. iii. passim. Diccionario Geografico-Historico de España, por la Real Academia de Historia, section i. tom. ii. art. Navarra. Masdeu, Historia Critica de España, tom. xv. Illustracion 7. Additio ad Joannem Biclarensem (apud Florez España Sagrada, tom. vi. p. 422, &c.). Isidorus Pacensis (apud eundem viii. 282, &c.). Monachus Albeldensis, necnon Sebastianus Salmanticensis (apud eundem xiii. 468, &c.) Garibay, Morales, Mariana, Favyn et Moret ubi supra.

[†] Chronicon Albeldense, pp. 450. and 463. (apud Florez, España Sagrada, tom. xiii.)

assuming that the dignity existed there prior to the latter half of the ninth century. They, indeed, who follow the archbishop Rodrigo, and the vast store of monastic charters—the only authorities for the pretended antiquity of this monarchy—may easily find room for six or eight successive kings before the time of Garcia. But these kings are deservedly rejected by the best historians of Spain: by Zurita, Oihenart, Mondejar, Ferreras, Masdeu, &c. There can be no doubt that they have been inconsiderately multiplied. Thus the father of this royal line, the count of Bigorre, had two names, *Sancho Iñigo.* Agreeably to the Spanish system of patronymic derivation, Garcia his son was sometimes called Garcia *Sanchez*, at others Garcia *Iñiguez:* by the advocates of Navarrese antiquities, this double name is easily made to represent two distinct sovereigns. In many other cases, subsequent to the reign of Garcia, we find the same confusion. Thus, any one who minutely enters into an examination of the subject will soon be convinced, that Garcia el Tembloso and Sancho el Mayor are identical with Garcia Sanchez, and Sancho Garces, though by most historians these two kings have been invariably multiplied into four. A line of rulers so numerous, their names so carefully recorded, were reasonably admitted as demonstration of a very respectable antiquity.*

As, then, there appears no foundation for the ancient independence of Navarre, on what power was she dependent—on the Asturians or the Franks?

The chroniclers who lived nearest to this period, the monk of Albelda and bishop Sampiro, are so meagre

---

* Ximenes, Rerum in Hispania Gestarum, lib. iv. cap. 21.; lib. v. cap. 11, 12, &c. (apud Schottum, tom. ii.) Lucas Tudensis, Chronicon Mundi (apud eundem, tom. iv.). Risco, España Sagrada, tom. xxxii. cap. 18, 19. Masdeu, Historia Critica, tom. xii. et xv. " Los documentos," says this last judicious writer, " que se alegan en favor de los reyes añadidos no merecen atencion, pues son memorias forjadas para ilustrar la historia de algunos monasterias, principalmente los de San Salvador de Leyrey San Juan de la Peña."—Yepes Cronica General de la Orden de San Benito, tom. i. et iii. Briz Martinez, Historia de San Juan de la Peña, lib. i. cap. i. &c.

that they afford us no information on the subject beyond incidental obscure hints, which may be forced to mean any thing or nothing, according to the predilection of the writer. One, however, who has no predilections to gratify, may observe, that from the general tendency of the hints, an *impression*,—he would not be justified in using a stronger term,—rests on his mind, that in the reign of Alfonso el Casto, at least, perhaps, in that of Alfonso I., the country was dependent on the Asturias. If, as Sebastian of Salamanca intimates, (and what better authority can be found?) the Arabs had not settled in Navarre prior to his days, we may infer that it was previously governed by *local* counts, vassals of Pelayo himself, or at least of his immediate successors. But leaving these speculations, it seems undoubted, that in just dread of the Mohammedan domination, the inhabitants of these regions, as well as those of Catalonia, applied for aid to the renowned emperor of the Franks; and that he, in consequence, in 778, poured his legions into Navarre, and seized Pamplona. It seems no less certain, that from this period he considered the country as a fief of his crown; and that his pretensions, whether founded in violence or in the voluntary submission of the natives, gave the highest umbrage to the Asturian kings: the feudal supremacy thenceforth became an apple of discord between the two courts, each striving to gain the homage of the local governors. There is, however, reason enough for inferring that this supremacy generally rested with the Carlovingian dynasty. In 806, on the occasion of a revolt,—whether through the arts of Alfonso el Casto, or through a desire for independence, is doubtful,—Pepin passed the Pyrenees with a considerable force, received the submission of the people, and divided the country into new governments, both for its better defence against foreign aggression, and as the means of more effectually quelling domestic commotions. Thus things remained until the time of Alfonso III., who, for the reasons stated on a former occasion, endeavoured to secure peace both with

Navarre and France by marrying a princess related to both Sancho Iñigo, count of Bigorre, and to the Frank sovereign*, and by consenting that the province should be held as an immovable fief by that count. This Sancho Iñigo, besides his lordship of Bigorre, for which he was the vassal of the French king, had domains in Navarre, and is believed, on apparently good foundation, to have been of Spanish descent. He is said, however, not to have been the first count of Navarre; that his brother Aznar held the fief before him, nominally dependent on king Pepin, but successfully laying the foundation of Navarrese independence.† If the chronology which makes Sancho succeed Aznar in 836, and the event itself, be correct, Alfonso only confirmed the count in the lordship. In this case, the only remaining difficulty is to determine whether the fief was held from Charles or Alfonso. It will, however, if not vanish, at least be weakened, when we consider, that though the Castilian chroniclers are silent on this subject, those of France expressly assert that it was held from the former: the silence of the one party is surely more than counterbalanced by the positive testimony of the other. But whichever of the princes was acknowledged for the time the lord paramount of the province, there can be little doubt that both governor and people were averse to the sway of either; both had long aspired to independence, and that independence was at hand. The son of this Sancho Iñigo was Garcia, father of Sancho Garces, and the first king of Navarre; the first, at least, whom for reasons before given, historic criticism can admit.‡

* Non multo post universam Galliam simul cum Pampilonâ causâ cognationis secum associat, uxorem ex illorum prosapiâ generis accipiens, nomine Xemena ex qua quatuor filios genuit, &c. — *Chron. Samp.* See vol. ii p. 133.

† There is, perhaps, reason to doubt whether Aznar was ever in Spanish Vascony, whether his fief was not wholly confined to the country north of the Pyrenees. See Risco, España, Sagrada, tom. xxxii. cap. 18. There is nothing but inextricable confusion throughout this period.

‡ Sebastianus Salmanticensis (apud Florez, xiii. 484, &c.). Samplrus Astoricensis (apud eundem, xiv. 438, &c.). Monachus Silensis (apud eundem, xvii. 292, &c.). Eginhardus, Annales Regum Francorum, Vita Caroli Magni, necnon Vita Ludovici Imperatoris (apud Duchesne His-

885 to 891.

The precise period when GARCIA I. (*Sanchez Iniguez*) began to reign is impossible to be determined. Considering, however, the deep silence of the contemporary monk of Albelda, who concludes his history in 883, as to the foundation of the monarchy, that event must be referred to a period subsequent. All that we know by inference is, that in 891, or in the following year, he was killed in battle with the Arabs, who invaded his dominions, and that he left an infant, Sancho. Whether from this period to 905, there was an interregnum, or whether the government was exercised by one Fortuño Garces; whether this Fortuño Garces was the uncle or elder brother of the infant prince; whether even such a person as Fortuño Garces existed; or, finally, if he did exist, whether he may not be identical with some other prince of his line,—Fortuño being possibly an adjunct applied by later times *,—are problems of which we need not expect the solution. Until less apocryphal documents are adduced in support of

toriæ Francorum Scriptores Coactanei, tom. ii. *variis locis*). Annales. Bertiniani, p. 164. necnon Chronicon Moisiacense, p. 147. (apud eundem, tom. iii.) The evidence of these writers, as regards the ancient dependence of Navarre on the Carlovingian princes, is too firm to be shaken. The objections of Risco (España Sagrado, tom. xxxii. cap. 18. and 19.) are certainly without foundation — as far, we mean, as Sancho Iñigo is concerned.—Zurita, Anales de Aragon, lib. i. cap. 5. Marca, Limes Hispanicus, lib. iii. Oihenart, Notitia Utriusque Vasconiæ, liv. xi. chap. 9. Rodericus Toletanus Rerum in Hispania Gestarum, lib. iv. cap. 6, &c. (apud Schottum Hispania Illustrata, tom. ii.) This writer seems to have had few guides beyond monastic charters and tradition.—Favyn, Histoire de Navarre, lib. xi. Moret, Anales del Reyno de Navarra, tom. i. lib. 4. to 6 The most learned, the most elaborate, and the most prejudiced of guides.— Ferreras, Histoire Générale d'Espagne, tom. ii. et iii. with Hermilly's Preface to the latter. Masdeu, Historia Critica de España, tom. xv. Illustracion 7. et tom. xii. (in regno, Alonso el Magno) as obstinate in prejudice as the very worst of his class.

* If we believe the Rule of San Salvador de Leyre, (apud Yepes, Coron.) Fortuño resigned the sceptre to his brother Sancho, and entered the cloister. But the worthy monk, who wrote the following note, is bungling enough to expose his own imposition:—" Post cujus obitum (of Garcia Iniguez) venit Fortunius Garseanes de Corduba, et inveniens ipsum mortuum in Lumberri, transtulit corpus ejus ad monasterium Legerense, et regnavit annis 57. Postquam senuit, fuit effectus monachus in monasterio Legerensi, et regnavit pro eo *filius* ejus Sancius Garseanes, cum uxore sua domina Todâ reginâ; et venerunt ambo ad dictum monasterium, ut a prædiato Fortuño acciperent gratiam et benedictionem; quos quum benedixisset, dedit Sancio *fratri* suo," &c. Thus, in the very same sentence, Sancho is made the son and brother of Fortuño! The *dates* are not less blundering. Finally, the monastery was not founded at the period in question. Such are the authorities followed by Garibay, Morales, Marianâ, Favyn, Moret, and a host besides!

his actions, and even of his existence, criticism must refuse him a place among the kings of Navarre. We must be satisfied with knowing that, in 905, Sancho assumed the reins of sovereignty. Perhaps the expression, "*Surrexit in Pampilonia rex Sancho,*" may legitimately bear the construction that his accession had been preceded by an interregnum.*

SANCHO I. (*Garces Abarca*), was fortunate enough to extend the dominions left him by his two predecessors, and to wield their sceptre with greater glory than either. In 907, he led an army into Gascony — for what purpose does not clearly appear — and during his absence the city of Pamplona was invested by the Arabs. The inhabitants, being unprepared for a siege, were in the deepest consternation: they despatched messengers to acquaint their king with their critical situation. Sancho was naturally solicitous to return, and save his capital; but he had scarcely issued orders to that effect, when a heavy fall of snow blocked up the passes of the Pyrenees, and in the estimation of all men rendered that return impossible. Yet he was undismayed; he resolved to attempt the passage, though his followers loudly exclaimed that thus "to combat nature" was the very height of rashness. He caused them, we are told, to bind to their sandals undressed skins and the rough bark of trees, so that they might safely tread the slippery declivities: at the same time, he ordered his horsemen to lead their beasts by the hand, and commence the perilous ascent on foot. The courage with which he himself set the example, his patience under fatigue, his cheering exhortations to all about him, redoubled their energy, enabled them to persevere, and finally to surmount every difficulty. But the passage was not effected without considerable loss; some, overcome by cold and fatigue, lay down to rise no more; some fell into fathomless pits; others down

905 to 908.

---

* The same authorities, with the addition of the Diccionario Geografico Historico de España, art. Navarra. This article does little credit to the *judgment*, however honourable to the ingenuity, of its author, Señor Traggia.

abrupt precipices, and were seen no more. At length, after a rapid nocturnal march, they appeared at daybreak before the city; which still held out, but the surrender of which was hourly expected by the assailants. The joy of the besieged, on the arrival of their deliverers, was boundless. While the aged, the women, and children, watched the furious attack of their king on the surprised ranks of the misbelievers, most of whom were half dead by the severity of the weather, all capable of bearing arms left the place to assist their heroic countrymen. The carnage of the Arabs was frightful: such as escaped into the mountains were known by their footsteps, were pursued, and put to death; few of the vanquished survived that day.*

908 to 921. During several succeeding years, Sancho nobly followed up this splendid success. He reduced some important fortresses on both banks of the Ebro, and recovered Rioja: in 914 he conquered the country from Tudela to Najera: the following year he took Tarragona and Agreda, and seized on the mountainous district surrounding the sources of the Duero. In fact, his successes were as solid as they were brilliant; and we may lament, with one of the peninsular historians, that they have been handed down to us in so meagre a manner.† Many of his conquests he fortified against the threatened irruptions of the Arabs: among these was Pamplona, the works of which he carefully strengthened. His prudent foresight was justified by the sequel. In 920, whether through impaired health, or devotion, or both, he retired to the monastery of San Salvador de Leyre, leaving to his son, whom he had previously placed over Rioja, the government of his states. The following year Abderahman III., at the instance of the Mohammedans of Saragossa, poured a formidable army into Rioja, and recovered several of the fortified places. The infante Sancho

* Though no mention of this battle is to be found in contemporary Castilian writers, it ought not to be rejected: it rests on the authority of the Archbishop Rodrigo, Rerum in Hispania Gestarum, lib. iv.
† Ferreras, iii. 26., Hermilly's translation.

consequently prepared for defence, and obtained from Ordoño II., king of Leon, a powerful aid, which that king headed in person. On this occasion the monarch of Navarre did not leave the cloister, but he despatched orders to all his vassals to join his son with all the forces they could raise. The hostile armies met at Val-de-Junquera, near Salinas de Oro. The result was fatal to the Christians, who were signally routed, two of their bishops and many princes remaining in the power of the misbelievers. Ordoño returned to Leon,—doubtless, to defend his own dominions,—while the infante threw himself within the walls of Pamplona. The Mohammedan general, however, molested neither, but pursued his way into Gascony, which he ravaged. On his return he was surprised with one division of his army in the mountain defiles by the troops of the king, who had now taken the field: the general himself was taken prisoner, and was poignarded by a woman. Not satisfied with the destruction of his enemy, and the immense plunder which had been brought from southern France, Sancho marched against the other division that had passed the Pyrenees by another route, and completely cut it to pieces. No Mohammedan remained in the whole kingdom north of the Ebro, for the fortresses which Abderahman's general had reduced were recovered with facility. The following year, while Sancho was suffering under severe illness, his son recovered Rioja. In the reduction of the two strongest fortresses in that province, Najera and Viguera, the infante was aided by his cousin of Leon; and the good understanding between the two crowns was increased by the marriage of Ordoño with doña Sancha, princess of Navarre.

Don Sancho did not long survive this last success 925. of his arms. He reigned, say the chroniclers, near twenty years, so that his death must have taken place about 925. He was one of the most valiant princes of his age, and his numerous religious foundations prove him to have been one of the most devout. The salutary severity with which he administered justice, and the vigour with which he extirpated the robbers who infested his dominions, were no less useful to his people than his warlike deeds.*

925 to 970. GARCIA II. (*Sanchez*) surnamed *El Tembloso*, or the Trembler, from the involuntary dread which he experienced at the commencement of any battle,—a dread, however, which speedily yielded to his latent courage,—ascended the throne in 925. Of this prince very little is known, and that little has often been confounded with the actions of his successors. In 951, on occasion of the dispute between Ordoño III. of Leon, and Sancho, brother of that prince, he, with his brother-in-law, Fernan Gonsalez, count of Castille, espoused the cause of the rebel †; but legitimacy triumphed, and Sancho sought refuge for a time in Navarre. In 956 he again received Sancho, who had been expelled from the court of Leon; and afterwards entered into an alliance with Abderahman to restore the exile to the throne. On this occasion he marched an army into Castile, to overawe the movements of the rebellious Fernan Gonsalez, whom he defeated and took prisoner, but whom he afterwards released in consideration of the affinity between them. Garcia died in 970.‡

970 to 1035. SANCHO II., surnamed *El Mayor*, according to Rodrigo was but five years old when he ascended the throne. If this be true, he was probably the grandson, not the son, of the deceased king; and as the realm would necessarily be governed by a regent, that regent may have been ranked among the lawful sovereigns of

---

* Chronicon Albeldense, pp. 464. et 450. (apud Florez, tom. xiii.) Sampirus Astoricensis, p. 449. (apud eundem, tom. xiv.) Monachus Silensis (apud eundum, xvii. 301.). Chronicon Burgense, p. 308. et Annales Compostellani, p. 318. (apud eundum, tom. xxiii.) Rodericus Toletanus, Rerum in Hispania Gestarum, lib. v. cap. 23, &c. (apud Schottum Hispania Illustrata, tom. ii.) Vasæus, Chronicon Hispaniæ, p. 722. necnon Lucius Marineus Siculus, de Rebus Hispaniæ, lib. viii. Hieronymous Blancas, Rerum Aragonensium Commentarii, p. 618, &c. (omnes apud eundem, tom. l. et iii.) Zurita, Anales de Aragon, lib. i. cap. 9. Moret, Anales de Navarra, lib. viii. cap. 1—5. Diccionario Geografico Historico de España por la Real Academia de Historia, section l. tom. ii. art. Navarra, *aliiscum*.
† See vol. ii. p. 139. ‡ The same authorities.

the country. However this be, it is certain, that nothing can exceed the obscurity which covers the reigns of this period. In preference to the very questionable documents which have been already exposed, and which, without any support in authentic chroniclers, multiply the Navarrese kings, we will follow the authority of the *Annales Compostellani* and of the Chronicon Silense. From 905 to 1035, the former exhibit the names of three sovereigns only, while Moret and others give us a catalogue of half a dozen.* That the number of sovereigns has been greatly exaggerated may be more than suspected from the instance of two Sanchos; of whom one, represented as the grandson of the prince, who reigned from 905 to 925, is said to have reigned from 970 to 994. The very instruments quoted for the separate existence of these kings call both *Sancho*, give both the surname of *Abarca*, and both a wife named *Urraca*, and make both sons of *Garcia*.

Sancho el Mayor was the most powerful prince of his age and country. Besides Navarre and Sobrarve, he held the lordship of Aragon, (then however confined within narrow limits, as Saragossa and most of the province were subject to the Mohammedans,) and in 1026 in right of his wife Muña Elvira, princess of Castile, he became king of that country. The marriage of his son Fernando, to the heiress of Leon, gave him uncontrolled influence in the affairs of that kingdom,—an influence which, as observed in a former chapter†, he was not slow to vindicate even by force of arms. By his conquests, too, he considerably extended his dominions, especially on the Pyrenean frontier: among

---

* "Era 943 (A. D. 905) surrexit in Pamplona Rex nomine Sancius Garsia, et obiit era 967," (A. D. 927; this is an error of one year or more,) "post quem filius ejus Rex Garsias regnavit annis 35," (an error of the transcriber; it ought to be 45, according to the Chronicles of Burgos and Albelda,) "et obiit 1008" (this number is correct enough). "Post eum regnavit Sancius filius ejus 65 annis et obiit era 1073." *Annales Compostellani*, p. 318. (apud Florez, tom. xxiii.) "Porro Sancius Rex *in senectute bonâ*, plenus *dierum* — hac vita decessit era 1073." Chron. Silense, p. 313. (apud eundem, tom. xvii.) At 70 years a man can scarcely be said to have attained a *good old age*, and to be *full of days;* Sancho might be 20 at his accession instead of 5.

† See vol. ii. p. 149.

these was the lordship of Ribagorza, which had generally been dependent on the French crown, and to which indeed he had some claim in virtue of his consanguinity with a house that had long given governors to that province. He was thus, at the period of his death in 1035, virtually master of all Christian Spain except Catalonia.

1035. By most historians of the peninsula Sancho has been blamed for not laying the foundation of one Christian monarchy, in other words, for dividing his dominions among his four sons. In leaving Navarre and Biscay to his eldest son Garcia, Castile to Fernando, Ribagorza to Gonsalo, and Aragon to Ramiro[*], he certainly committed an act of great impolicy; but it may be doubted, whether, if even he had left them united under the sceptre of the eldest, the integrity of the whole would have been long preserved. In those ages, when the principle of succession was not regularly adopted; when successful rebellion on every side presented an example too alluring to fail of imitation; and when authority, however sanctioned by religion, was disregarded, if unsupported by a degree of power necessary to make it respected, the excluded brothers would doubtless have struggled for a share of the monarchy, and would probably have triumphed. Besides, however disastrous his policy, he must not be blamed with undue severity, for not rising superior to his age. The fable related by Alonzo el Sabio, Zurita, and others, as the cause of the division[†], has been as much despised by the reflecting as that which led to the rebuilding of Palencia.[‡] These times, as is evident from the interminable mass of monastic legends, are full of wonders.[§]

---

[*] Ramiro became the first sovereign of Aragon. See the history of that kingdom.
[†] See Appendix A.
[‡] See Appendix B.
[§] Pelagius Ovetensis, p. 470, &c. Annales Compostellani, p. 318. (apud Florez España Sagrada, tom. xiv. et xxiii.) Monachi Silensis Chronicon (apud eundem, xvii. 312, &c.). Chronicon Burgense, p. 308. Chronicon Compostellanum, p. 326. Anales Toledanos i. p. 383., &c. (apud eundem, tom. xxiii.) Ximenes, Rerum in Hispania Gestarum, lib. v. cap. 24. usque ad lib. vi. cap. 6. (apud Schottum Hispania Illustrata, tom. ii.) Vasæus,

GARCIA III., at the time of his father's death, was absent on a pilgrimage to Rome. Ramiro of Aragon, who was discontented with the boundaries assigned him, thought this a favourable opportunity for removing them to a greater distance: he invaded Navarre, the greater part of which he occupied with facility. Before the fortress of Tafalla, however, which he invested, he was detained until the arrival of the royal pilgrim, who not only expelled him from his conquests, but pursued him into his own dominions. But Garcia was either averse to profit by the advantage thus acquired, or he preferred lending his immediate aid to his brother Fernando of Castile, whose dominions were then invaded by Bermudo of Leon. The triumph of Fernando, who by the death of the Leonnese king inherited that crown, has been related in the proper place.*

1035 to 1037.

But this service either made no impression on the heart of Fernando, or Garcia's own ambition led to the hostilities which followed. The manœuvres which each adopted to gain possession of the other,— manœuvres disgraceful alike to their fraternal and knightly characters, — and the death of Garcia, in 1054, at the battle of Atapuerca, are to be found in another place.† This latter prince left few to regret his loss, except the monks, whose monasteries he had enriched. He was more courageous than prudent, too stern to be loved by his subjects, and two reckless to command the respect of his neighbours. He made some conquests from the Mohammedans, among which was Calahorra (1045); but he lost Rioja, which was annexed to Castile, and which, though sometimes re-occupied in the subsequent

1037 to 1054.

Hispaniæ Chronicon, p. 723. Lucius Marineus Siculus, de Rebus Hispaniæ, lib. viii. p. 365. Roderius Santius, Historia Hispanica, pars iii. (omnes apud eundem, tom. i.) Alonso el Sabio, Chronica de España, part iii. Moret, Anales de Navarra, lib. xi. cap. 1—4. Zurita, Anales de Aragon, lib. i. cap. 18. Yepes, Cronica General de la Orden de San Benito, tom. iii. et vi. (in variis locis.) Diccionario Geografico Historico, por la Real Academia de Historia, section i. tom. ii. art. Navarra.

* See vol. ii. p. 150. Ferreras, tom. iii. p. 179. would delay the invasion of Navarre by Ramiso to 1042, on the faith of a monastic document cited by Moret. We follow the archbishop Rodrigo.

† See vol. ii. p. 152.

reigns by the Navarrese princes, was always recovered by their powerful neighbours. The Ebro again became the boundary of the two kingdoms.*

1054 to 1076.
SANCHO III., eldest son of Garcia, was quietly permitted, by the victor Fernando, to be proclaimed in the very camp. Nor, whatever may be stated by the writers of Navarre and Aragon, from the monk of San Juan de la Peña downwards, was he ever disturbed in his possessions by the king of Leon and Castile. As little proof is there, that Sancho, the successor of Fernando, molested his cousin of Navarre. It is allowed that Alfonso, the successor of Sancho, afterwards the famous conqueror of Toledo, was too much occupied in fighting the Moors, to dream of incommoding his Christian relatives. Hence the reign of Sancho III. appears to have been passed in peace. But if he had no enemies from without, unfortunately he had them within his own kingdom, and in his own family. In 1076, his brother, don Ramon, and his sister, Doña Ermesinda, conspired against his life. From the meagre relation of the chroniclers, it is difficult to say what motive could induce the princess to approve so horrid an act: as the children of Sancho were in their infancy, the guilty object of Ramon is evident enough. Some of the courtiers, in hope of favour from the expected successor, were drawn into the plot. The king was fond of the chase, and the conspirators resolved to assassinate him during one of his frequent excursions into the neighbouring mountains. Accordingly one fine morning in June, while the royal party scoured the valleys between Funes and Milagro, in pursuit of a stag, the king, accompanied by the Infante, and by several of the conspirators, whom Ramon had purposely drawn round his person, ascended a high rock, that he might have a wider view of the animating scene. While eagerly

* The same authorities. It is amusing to see how Moret attempts to shake the authority of the monk of Silos, and Rodrigo of Toledo, and to pervert history in favour of Don Garcia. Still worse is Traggia (Dic. Geog. Hist. art. Navarra), the least scrupulous of writers where a system or the national honour is concerned.

watching the sport, they stabbed him in the back, and precipitated him from the eminence: his body was dashed to pieces by the fall. This tragical deed the people at length rose to avenge; but the assassins had escaped to the court of the Moorish king of Saragossa.

Ramon derived no advantage from this deed of blood: the kingdom refused to be ruled by a fratricide, whom it indignantly expelled. The choice of a successor promised to be attended with some difficulty. While the inhabitants of Biscay and Rioja, at the instance of prince Ramiro, another brother of Sancho, declared for Alfonso of Leon and Castile, those of Navarre Proper were generally in favour of Sancho Ramirez, second king of Aragon. The former led an army into Rioja, was proclaimed at Calahorra and Najera, and from that moment the sovereignty of the country between those important places remained in the crown of Castile. Sancho was no less active: with a considerable force, he entered Navarre, and was proclaimed at Pamplona. There appeared great probability of a war between the two candidates, neither of whom bestowed a thought on the legitimate rights of the orphan infante; but peace was at length made between them, on the condition that each of the royal robbers should retain the spoils he had seized. One account says, that Sancho Ramirez agreed to do homage to Alfonso for Navarre Proper; but there appears no foundation for the statement.*

As the three next sovereigns of Navarre, SANCHO IV., who reigned from 1076 to 1094, PEDRO I., from 1094

1076 to 1134.

* Pelagius Ovietensis, p. 471, &c. (apud Florez, España Sagrada, tom. xiv.). Monachi Silensis Chronicon, p. 318, &c. (apud eundem, tom. xvii.). Chronicon Burgense, p. 309. Annales Complutenses, p. 313. Annales Compostellani, p. 319. Chronicon Compostellanum, p. 327. Chronicon de Cardeña, p. 370. Anales Toledanos, i. p. 384. (apud eundem, tom. xxiii.). Rodericus Toletanus, Rerum in Hispania Gestarum, lib. vi. (apud Schottum, Hisp. Illust. tom. ii.). Rodericus Santius, Historia Hispanica, part iii. Alfonsus à Carthagena, Anacephalæosis, cap. 72, &c. Lucius Marineus Siculus, De Rebus Hispaniæ, lib. viii. p. 365, &c. (omnes apud eundem, tom. i.). Blancas, Rerum Aragonensium Commentarii, p. 623. (apud eundem, tom. iii.) Zurita, Anales de Aragon, lib. i. cap. 17, &c. Moret, Anales de Navarra, lib. xi. xiv. Yepes, Cronica General de la Order de San Benito, tom. vi.; cum multis aliis.

VOL. III. C

to 1105, and ALFONSO I., from 1105 to 1134, were all kings of Aragon, their actions must be related in the history of that country. The last-named prince dying without issue, made a singular will, by which he bequeathed his dominions to the knights of St. John and of the Temple, and passed a heavy denunciation on any one of his barons who should seek to set aside his last dispositions. But no sooner was he laid at rest, than his menace was disregarded; and, as the Navarrese and Aragonese would not agree in the choice of a common sovereign, the former raised Garcia Ramirez, a scion of their royal house, to the vacant dignity; while the latter threw their eyes on Ramiro, brother of Alfonso, who, though a monk, was forced from the cloister to the palace.

1134, 1135. GARCIA IV. no sooner ascended the throne than he was disturbed by the ambition or policy of Ramiro, who aspired to the re-union of the two kingdoms. The animosity of the two princes was, for a moment, prevented from openly breaking out by the approach,— whether friendly or hostile has been much disputed,— of Alfonso VIII., of Leon and Castile, surnamed the Emperor, who made both tremble for their respective dignities.* On the departure of the emperor, who had received the homage both of Garcia and Ramiro, an homage, however, which neither of them intended to be of long continuance, they resumed their hostile attitude; but their respective subjects, in dread of the fatal consequences which their division might bring on the two kingdoms, especially in the vicinity of enemies so active and enterprising as the Moors, interfered, and forced them to be reconciled. Each was to remain master of his present possessions; but Garcia was to consider himself a feudatory of the Aragonese.

1136 to 1150... Scarcely was this reconciliation effected, when Garcia leagued himself with Alfonso, prince of Portugal, against

* See the reign of this prince, Vol. II.

the emperor, whose ambition began to fill both with apprehension: the former aimed at the recovery of Rioja; the latter, at an independent sovereignty. While the Portuguese prince invaded Galicia, where his generals obtained some partial success, Alfonso made an irruption into Navarre, which he laid waste, and did not leave until Garcia acknowledged his supremacy and sued for peace. In 1140, however, the latter again entered into an alliance with the Portuguese king, and for the same reason — jealousy of the emperor's power. Again was Navarre invaded; while the king, confiding in the fortifications of Pamplona, carried the war into the territories of Aragon, against Raymundo, count of Barcelona, the ally of Alfonso, and, in virtue of a marriage with the daughter of Ramiro, actual sovereign of Aragon. Though he triumphed over Raymundo, from whom he took abundance of spoil, that spoil was scarcely divided among his followers, when the active emperor reached the field, and the Navarrese fled without striking a blow, or carrying away any portion of their plunder. Before the end of the year, however, peace was made between them, chiefly through the interference of their respective prelates, and strengthened by the marriage of Alfonso's son, Sancho, with the infanta Blanche of Navarre. But as Garcia, in 1143, again armed, to humble his enemy don Ramiro, the Castilian displeased at this attack on his brother-in-law, made formidable preparations to punish his disobedient vassal. Again, through the instrumentality of the prelates and nobles, was peace made between them, — the emperor, being anxious to fall on the Mohammedans, — and confirmed by the marriage of Garcia with a natural daughter of Alfonso. But Garcia and Raymundo were never on good terms; and it required all the influence of their common friend to prevent them from inflicting hostilities on each other. By engaging them in the same cause, — war with the Moors, — he turned their warlike inclinations to the common good of Christendom.

Garcia died in 1150 — some authors say, through the

fall of his horse. We only know with certainty that his death was sudden.*

1150 to 1180. SANCHO V., son of the deceased king, was no less subject than his father to the hostilities of the prince of Aragon, and no less eager to return them. But the emperor, though war was frequently and loudly proclaimed by both parties, and though some indecisive irruptions into the Navarrese territory followed, continued to exert his beneficial influence for the restoration, if not of harmony, at least of outward tranquillity. Soon after his death, which happened in 1157, don Raymundo, as usual, commenced hostilities; but, as usual also, without result; since both kings, terrified at the inroads of the Almohades, began to perceive the necessity of peace, unless both of them were to fall a sacrifice to these formidable Africans. But though Sancho had married a daughter of Alfonso, he was not always disposed to remain on good terms with that emperor's successor in Castile, who bore the same name as himself. Towards the end of that monarch's short reign, he made an irruption into Rioja; but, meeting with a vigorous repulse, he retired to his own dominions. During the minority of Alfonso IX., knowing how much Castile was weakened by civil dissensions, he again penetrated into that province, where his arms, meeting with no serious opposition, were successful: the following year it was recovered. Such were nearly all the wars of this period; the success of one day being neutralised by the disasters of the next. But those princes were incapable of profiting by the lessons of experience. In 1172, while Alfonso

* Chronica Alfonsi Imperatoris, lib. i. et ii. (apud Florez, España Sagrada, tom. xxi.). Ximenes, De Rebus Hispaniæ, lib. vii. cap. 1—6. Lucas Tudensis, Chronicon Mundi, p. 103, &c. (ambo apud Schottum, Hispania Illustrata, tom. ii. et iv.). Annales Compostellani, p. 322. Anales Toledanos, i. p. 588, &c. (ambo apud Florez, tom. xxiii.). Rodericus Santius, Historia Hispanica, pars iii. cap. 31. Alfonsus à Carthagena, Anacephalæosis, cap. 77. (ambo apud Schottum, tom. i.). Zurita, Anales de Aragon, tom. i. lib. 2. cap. 1.—10. Blancas, Rerum Aragonensium Commentarii, pp. 645—648. (apud Schottum, tom. iii.) Moret, Anales de Navarra, tom. ii. lib. xviii. Traggia, art. *Navarra*, in the Diccionario Geografico-Historico de España, tom. ii.
We quote this last-named writer, to censure in the strongest terms his wicked perversion of historical facts in favour of a blind prejudice. His statements are continually, and, what is worse, knowingly, at variance with the contemporary writers of Castile.

of Aragon was opposing the Africans in Andalusia, Sancho cast a covetous, and ungenerous as covetous, eye on the possessions of the absent monarch, which he invaded. His wanton and senseless ambition was injurious only to himself: it recalled the valiant Alfonso; who, having prevailed on the Castilian king to join him, invaded Navarre, and ravaged the country up to the gates of Pamplona. The two following years witnessed the same obscure and indecisive operations. In 1176 the kings of Castile and Navarre agreed to refer their differences, which concerned the restitution of some Castilian fortresses seized during the minority of the former prince, to Henry Plantagenet, king of England. The English monarch could entertain no unfavourable sentiments towards the father-in-law of his son [*]; yet he condemned him to surrender five fortresses, in consideration, however, of a considerable sum of money, and of two or three small fortified places, or rather castles, in return, which rightly belonged to Sancho. It does not appear that the award was put into force, though, in 1179, the two kings agreed to a peace, on conditions not much unlike those proposed by Henry.

In 1191, Sancho conferred his daughter, the princess Berengaria, on Richard I. of England, who had succeeded his father. As the Plantagenet had already departed for the Holy Land, the infanta was despatched to the Isle of Cyprus, where she was received by her affianced husband, and where the marriage ceremony was performed. By favour of this marriage, as well as by a preceding one, which had been contracted between another princess of Navarre with an elder brother of Richard, Sancho hoped to have a powerful and near ally, — the English possessions in France then extended almost to the Pyrenees, — to aid him whenever he should be in danger of becoming a prey to his neighbours. From the succour, too, which he himself sent to the seneschal of that province, when invaded, the following year, by the count of Toulouse,—

[*] See the following paragraph.

800 men at arms assisting to repel the assailant, — we may infer that the obligation was mutual. This king did not long survive the marriage of his daughter. He died in 1194.

1194 to 1234. Sancho VI. had but just seized the reins of government, when he entered into an alliance with the kings of Castile and Leon against the Moors, who were then ravaging Andalusia. The impetuosity of the Castilian, which impelled him to risk an action before the arrival of his allies, and his consequent defeat near Alarcos, have been already related.* His ill humour with his allies, who had advanced to Toledo, led to some hostilities between the three, even though the conquering Aben Yussef was reducing several of the Christian fortresses. After the marriage, however, of doña Berengaria, infanta of Castile, with the king of Leon, those two princes were at liberty to unite in defence of their country and religion. But Sancho, for a time, stood aloof from the confederacy: in dread of Yacub ben Yussuf's power, or rather through jealousy of his two neighbours, he entered into an alliance with the misbeliever, and even sought an interview with their emperor.† Whether, as the national writers affirm, he only claimed, as the reward of neutrality, the hand of Aben Yusuf's daughter, or whether — a far more probable supposition — he eagerly hoped to profit by the anticipated overthrow of his hateful neighbours, certain it is that his conduct drew on him the execration of all good men, and the severest reprimands of the pope, and that he was forced — perhaps from the failure of his negotiations with the African he was no longer indisposed — to join the Christian coalition. If he was wrong-headed and obstinate in his errors, or even crimes, he was a valiant soldier‡; and his conduct at

---

* See Vol. II. p. 41.

† This fact is not only mentioned by the Arabian writers, but it rests on the unquestionable authority of one who took a prominent part in the events of those times, — the archbishop Rodrigo. It appears that Sancho was not treated with much respect by Yacub.

‡ "Fortis viribus, armis strenuus, sed voluntate propria obstinatus." — *Rod. Tolet.*

the great battle of the Navas de Tolosa* partly redeems him from the deep stain he had contracted by his humiliating negotiations with Yacub. But he was deservedly punished; for during his absence in Africa Biscay, Alava, and Guipiscoa, which Sancho el Mayor had joined to the crown of Navarre, were reduced by Alfonso of Leon.

With don Sancho, who died in 1234, ended the male line of the house of Sancho Iñigo, founder of the sovereignty. The accidental death of his son, which several years preceded his own, caused him to nominate as his successor king Jayme I. of Aragon. From his valour he was surnamed *the Brave;* but this appears to be the only title he possessed to the respect of posterity. Towards the close of his long reign, he laboured under some bodily infirmities, which, probably, by superinducing reflection, made him more observant of his duties, both as a Christian and a sovereign.†

THIBAULT I.‡ On the death of Sancho, the Navarrese were perplexed about the choice of a successor. On the one hand, they had done homage to Jayme of Aragon, as their future king; on the other, they were unwilling to sacrifice their national existence by a union with the neighbouring kingdom. In this emergency, the states assembled at Pamplona are said to have made an extraordinary request to king Jayme,— that he would relieve them from their homage, and

---

* See Vol. II. p. 41.
† Chronicon Conimbricense, p. 334. Annales Compostellani, p. 323. Anales Toledenos i. p. 395. (omnes apud Florez, España Sagrada, tom. xxiii.). Rodericus Toletanus, De Rebus Hispaniæ, lib. vii. et viii. (apud Schottum, Hispania Illustrata, tom. ii.). Lucas Tudensis, Chronicon Mundi, pp. 107—116. (apud eundem, tom. iv.). Rodericus Santius, Historia Hispanica, pars iii. cap. 32—36. Alfonsus à Carthagena Anacephalæosis, cap. 78—83. Franciscus Tarapha, De Regibus Hispania, p. 360. (omnes apud eundem, tom. i.). Zurita, Anales de Aragon, tom. i. lib. ii. (in regno don Alonso el Segundo et don Pedro el Segundo.). Moret, Anales de Navarra, tom. ii. lib. xviii.—xx. Blancas, Rerum Aragonensium Commentarii, p. 648, &c. (apud Schottum, tom. iii.). Traggia, art. *Navarra*, in the Diccionario Geografico-Historico de España, tom. ii.
‡ As Thibault was a French prince, we prefer the orthography of this nation to that of the Spaniards, who distort the name into *Teobaldo*. Nor would we substitute the English *Theobald*. As the rulers of Navarre were mostly French from the time of this prince, we shall in future retain the French orthography.

permit them to choose another ruler,—and that the magnanimous monarch immediately conceded it. However this be, they elected Thibault, count of Champagne, son of the infanta Sancha, sister of the late king.

1236 to 1240.
Of Thibault we know little beyond his expedition to Palestine. In the second year of his reign, he assumed the cross, resolved, like so many other princes of his age, to assist in recovering the holy sepulchre from infidel hands. That he might pursue his purpose without embarrassment, the pope prevailed on his feudal lord, St. Louis, who was preparing to invade his French dominions, to disarm, and procured pledges from the kings of Castile and Aragon, that they would not take advantage of his absence to injure his possessions. Accordingly, in 1238, he passed over into France to join the dukes of Bretagne and Burgundy; the counts of Bar, Vendome, Montfort, and other crusaders. As the French king could not depart with them, they proceeded to the choice of a generalissimo: it fell on Thibault, both on account of his superior dignity to the rest, and of his martial character. The following year the French princes hastened into Provence, for the purpose of embarkation; but as there was not a sufficient number of vessels to convey so great an armament, it was agreed that, whilst a portion only proceeded by sea, the rest should travel by land, by way of Hungary, Thrace, and Asia Minor. The disasters which befell the latter, of whom two thirds perished through fatigue, hunger, pestilence, or intemperance, are well known. Fortunately for the Navarrese king, he was one of those who embarked at Marseilles, and safely reached Syria. But he had little reason to congratulate himself on the success of the expedition: he found nothing but jealousy or open opposition among the crusaders. The imperial generals refused to attack the caliph of Egypt, with whom their master had concluded a truce: the Templars, who had allied themselves with the caliph of Damascus, were no less in-

active. Thibault assembled the chiefs of his party, and it was determined that siege should be laid to Ascalon, a dependency of the Egyptian crown. But the rashness or avarice of the duke of Bretagne proved fatal to their views. That prince, without acquainting the rest with his purpose, made a predatory sally into the territories of the caliph, and returned with abundant booty. The example was too tempting not to be followed: some other chiefs speedily assembled their forces, and proceeded towards Gaza, which they hoped to take by surprise. But the caliph of Egypt, who had spies every where, being acquainted with the design, silently threw a strong body of troops into the fortress, or placed them on the neighbouring heights. Unsuspicious of the snare laid for them, the holy warriors marched all night, and at break of day arrived before Gaza. Their consternation at finding the eminences occupied was great; but, though fatigued with their arduous march, and so much inferior in number, they prepared to resist the meditated attack of the misbelievers. They fought under every disadvantage: the sand on which they stood afforded no ground for a secure footing either for themselves or horses; they could not move backwards or forwards without extreme difficulty; and they were constantly exposed to the arrows or sabres of the enemy, whose detachments continually harassed their flanks; and, by superior dexterity, as well as knowledge of the localities, evaded their indignant attempts at revenge. If they prepared to fall back, the Arabian cavalry was instantly in their rear; if they made a vigorous stand, it was immediately beyond their pursuit. In the meantime the arrowy showers from the heights did not fall in vain; and the Christians began to faint as much through want of food and water as through fatigue. Nor did night bring a relief to their sufferings: they were constrained to remain under arms, to repel the never-ceasing attacks of their sleepless foes. On the morning of the following day, their prospect of escape was totally precluded by the arrival of the Egyptian caliph in person, at the head of a considerable army. They were surrounded; most of them were cut to pieces; the rest compelled to surrender: among the former were the counts of Bar and Clermont; among the latter, the count of Montfort: the duke of Burgundy was the only chief who escaped, and that through the generous devotion of the count de Montfort. The disastrous news soon reached the camp of Thibault, and the other crusaders who were lying before Ascalon: it produced unmixed dismay; yet the dissensions of the Christians were too inveterate to rouse them to the necessity of union. The French princes resolved to return, without considering that the disasters of the crusade were mostly owing to themselves; that the most pressing considerations of honour, religion, and even humanity, compelled them to remain; in opposition to the entreaties and remonstrances of their confederates they embarked—Thibault among the rest—at the port of St. Jean d'Acre, and, followed by the curses of their abandoned comrades, safely reached France.

1247 to 1253. The only incident worth notice in the remaining life of Thibault is his quarrel with one of his bishops. Conceiving that the fortress of San Estefan, which belonged to the see of Pamplona, might be usefully employed in the defence of the kingdom, he seized it by force, and treated the remonstrances of the prelate, don Pedro, with indifference. As usual, the latter had recourse to ecclesiastical thunder: the king was excommunicated, and the realm laid under an interdict until he had made satisfaction to the church; when the ecclesiastical censures were removed. He seems, however,—such is the superstition of the period,—to have entertained serious doubts whether the bishop's authority had sufficiently absolved him; and he undertook a journey to Rome, to demand a general absolution from the pope. He died in 1253, leaving the guardianship of his youthful son and kingdom to his friend don Jayme of Aragon.*

THIBAULT II. found a generous and powerful protector in the Aragonese king, who, whenever his presence was required by the interests of his French possessions, preserved his kingdom in peace. In 1258, while at Paris, in attendance on his feudal lord, he married the princess Isabelle, daughter of St. Louis. This connection with the house of France was unfortunate: he had no issue by it; and it had the mischievous effect of making him assume the cross, in conjunction with his father-in-law. Having procured a wife for his brother Henri, in whom he placed his hopes of succession, in 1270 he embarked with St. Louis. A tempest, or rather a succession of tempests, forced the Christian fleet to the African coast. The crusaders invested Tunis, which they were unable to reduce: the plague broke out in their camp, and carried off St. Louis, with many chiefs, and a multitude of knights. The siege was ignominiously raised: Thibault, accompanied by Philip, son and heir of St. Louis, and by Charles, king of Sicily, sailed to that island, and landed at Trepani; where fatigue and anxiety brought the Navarrese king to the grave.†

1253 to 1270.

HENRI, the brother of Thibault II., did not long enjoy the sceptre. By the princess Blanche, daughter of

1270 to 1274.

---

* Zurita, Anales de Aragon, tom. i. lib. iii. (in regno don Jayme el Conquistador). Moret, Anales de Navarra, tom. iii. lib. xxi. Bernardinus Gomecius Miedes, De Vita et Rebus Gestis Jacobi Primi, passim (apud Schottum, Hispania Illustrata, tom. iii.). Traggia, art. *Navarra* in the Diccionario Geografico-Historico de España, tom. ii. Michaud, Histoire des Croisades, passim.

It is not very creditable to our literature that we cannot boast of one good history of the crusades: that of Mills is contemptible; Michaud's (in 8 vols. 8vo.) is infinitely superior, and for that very reason, perhaps, has not been translated into English. It is, however, too copious, and is not without considerable errors. The desideratum can only be supplied by an European scholar,—by one at least extensively versed in the contemporary literature of Germany, Italy, and France.

† The same authorities, with the addition of Malaspina, Historica Sicula, p. 806. (apud Carusium, Bibliotheca Historica Regni Siciliæ, tom. li.). Gulielmus de Nangiaco, Monachus S. Dionysii, Gesta Sancti Ludovici IX. Francorum Regis, p. 435, &c. (apud Duchesne, Rerum Francorum Scriptores Coætanei, tom. v.) Gullelmus Carnotensis, Capellanus ejusdem Regis, de Vita et Actibus, &c. Ludovici IX. p. 466, &c. (apud eundem in eodemque tomo). Bouges, Histoire Ecclésiastique et Civile de la Ville et Diocèse de Carcassonne, p. 192.

Robert count d'Artois, and niece of St. Louis, he had son and daughter. The former, however, while but a infant, one day made a sudden spring from the arms of the nurse, and, by falling from a high window, was dashed to pieces on the ground below: the terrified nurse threw herself after the infant. The afflicted father now caused the princess Jeanne to be recognised as his successor. To preserve the crown in his family, and the independence of the nation, his design was to marry the infant princess to a son of our Edward I. but death surprised him before she had attained her fourth year.

1274, 1275. JEANNE was unanimously proclaimed sovereign of the kingdom; and the administration, during her minority confided to the queen-mother and a Navarrese noble don Pedro Sanchez de Monteagudo. The power thus intrusted to this subject gave umbrage to the rest of the Navarrese nobility; and not merely intrigues, but open force, was resorted to, for the purpose of procuring his deposition. One of the discontented lords sought the aid of Castile, which was ready enough to interfere, and thereby to acquire increased influence in the state. Besides, Fernando, infante of Castile, had for some time looked upon the princess as a suitable match for his eldest son. Unfortunately for him, don Pedro of Aragon, whom neither party had solicited to interfere, entertained the same views in favour of *his* son. Under the pretence of supporting their respective partisans, but in reality to gain possession of the heiress, each of the princes prepared to arm. The affrighted Blanche, who destined both her daughter and the crown to a French noble, precipitately fled from Pamplona with her important charge; and, on arriving at Paris, placed herself, the young princess, and the Navarrese kingdom, under the protection of Philip III. Her flight only added fuel to domestic strife. Deprived of their external supports, the two parties now struggled for the regency. The citizens of Pamplona had recourse to arms to decide the question; but, after a parley, the chiefs of the two parties agreed to an outward reconciliation — perhaps to divide the supreme power between them. Yet the intestine commotion, arising from the collision of the two factions, kept the country in a state of continual excitement: its laws became powerless; anarchy and violence alone reigned. Hearing of these melancholy news, Blanche, at the instance of the French king, sent Eustace de Beaumarchais, seneschal of Toulouse, — an officer of considerable valour, — to administer the affairs of the kingdom.

The salutary severity of the new governor soon quelled commotion, but did not reconcile the people to a foreign yoke. Nor was the well-known purpose of Blanche, of uniting her daughter to the heir of Philip, at all agreeable to the majority of the Navarrese. They were split into three parties: the most numerous was in favour of a union with Aragon; another for that of Castile; the last and least influential approved the policy of the queen-mother. Blanche did not much trouble herself about the opinions of the Navarrese, but finally arranged the conditions of the marriage with the French king. The party, however, which was opposed to the step, sought to be revenged on the governor, whose innovations — whether of a beneficial or dubious tendency does not appear — exasperated such of the people as were more than usually tenacious of their ancient customs. In 1278, a popular insurrection forced him to seek shelter in the castle of Pamplona. He lost no time in acquainting Philip with his situation; while the chief of the rebels, don Garcia de Almoravides, sought the aid of Alfonso el Sabio, and even occupied the passes into Navarre to oppose the arrival of the French troops. Philip immediately directed the count d'Artois, father of Blanche, to march with the troops which lay at Toulouse and Carcassonne, to the succour of Beaumarchais. On reaching the foot of the Pyrenees, the count found the passes occupied; but he effected a passage through another opening into Aragon, and marched on Pamplona, which he invested. On the other side advanced

1276 to 1284.

Alfonso of Castile, not less eager to dispute with France the superiority over the kingdom. When the latter found, however, that the count's army had greatly the advantage in numbers (it was 20,000 strong), he quietly returned, leaving the Frenchmen in undisturbed possession of the field. Though don Garcia had, for a moment, made a vigorous defence, he was no sooner acquainted with the retreat of his protector than he secretly fled from the city, accompanied by several barons of his party. The citizens now consented to capitulate; but, while the conditions were arranging, a body of French troops, in opposition, we are told, to the commands of their officers, scaladed the walls, and inflicted a terrific carnage on the defenceless people; sparing neither sex, the old nor the young, and using the women with a brutality worse than death. "Even the Saracens," says an historian, "could not have done worse." The terror caused by this massacre effectually secured the submission of the kingdom; nor was there any disturbance when, in 1284, the queen gave her hand to her affianced husband, — in other words, when Navarre became a province of France. The internal dissensions in Castile, and the wars which the kings of Aragon waged in Sicily, were extremely favourable to the views of Philip.

1284 to 1328. During the next four reigns, Navarre has no history distinct from that of France, by whose sovereigns it was governed. On the death of Jeanne, in 1305, the sceptre devolved on her son, LOUIS HUTIN, who, in 1314, succeeded to the French crown. In 1316 he died, and PHILIP reigned until 1322. His death made way for CHARLES I., the youngest son of Jeanne, on whose demise, in 1328, Navarre again obtained its separate sovereign. Of these French princes, Louis was the only one who ever visited the Peninsula, and that visit was before his elevation to the throne of France. The Navarrese nobles, at the commencement of each reign, were compelled to visit Paris to do homage to their sovereign; though their doing so was a direct violation of the constitution. To Charles, the last of these princes, the states refused to swear allegiance, unless, in conformity with ancient custom, he submitted to be crowned in Pamplona; yet their refusal did not prevent his governing through his viceroy. Charles had, indeed, no lawful claim to the crown, which belonged to Jeanne, daughter of Louis Hutin, and granddaughter of the queen of that name. If the Salique law excluded her from the throne of France, her right to that of Navarre was indisputable; and, on the death of Charles, in 1328, the states assembled at Pamplona immediately recognised it. It was first opposed by Philip de Valois, the new king of France, who was naturally loath to forego his sovereignty over the country; but some concessions extorted from the count of Evreux, husband of Jeanne, obtained his consent to her proclamation.*

JEANNE II., with her husband PHILIP (who had the title of king), arrived at Pamplona in 1329, and were immediately crowned. The spectacle of a coronation was new to the Navarrese, who testified unbounded joy at the prospect of having their sovereigns again among them. But the residence of the queen and her husband in the kingdom appears to have been but temporary, or, at most, occasional; since, in the obscure events of this time, we frequently meet with the names of the viceroys who treated with the courts of Aragon and Castile. Unfortunately this natural joy was accompanied, or but immediately preceded, by a horrid, yet far from uncommon species of excess — the indiscriminate massacre of the Jews. Wherever that extraordinary people abode, they were sure to attract the hostility of their Christian

1328 to 1343.

---

* Gulielmus de Nangiaco, Gesta Philippi III. Audacis Regis Franciæ, p. 516, &c. (apud Duchesne, Rerum Francorum Scriptores Coætanei, tom. v.), Zurita, Anales de Aragon, tom. i. lib. iv. et v. Miedes, De Vita et Rebus Gestis Jacobi I., necnon Blancas, Rerum Aragonensium Commentarii, p. 656, &c. (apud Schottum, Hispania Illustrata, tom. iii.). Lucius Marineus Siculus, De Rebus Hispaniæ, lib. ix. (apud eundem, tom. i.). Moret, Anales de Navarra, tom. iii. lib. xxiii. xxiv. Ferreras, Histoire Générale d'Espagne, by Hermilly, tom. iv. passim. Traggia, art. *Navarra*, in Diccionario Geografico-Historico de España, tom. ii.

These concessions embraced the lordships of Champagne and Brie.

neighbours — partly, no doubt, by their usurious and dishonest dealings, but chiefly, perhaps, by their peculiar tenets, and their reputed exposure to the wrath of heaven. The first year of her reign was peaceful: but, about 1334, a desultory warfare — the cause and progress of which we should vainly attempt to discover — desolated the frontiers of Navarre and Castile. In 1336, however, peace was restored, and all animosity was so far forgotten, that, in 1343, Philip marched with a considerable reinforcement to aid Alfonso XI. of Castile, who was then investing Algeziras.* By that monarch he was received with extraordinary honours; but the operations of the siege, though the place was pressed with vigour, were fatiguing; and in a short time he was seized with an illness serious enough to alarm his friends. Having retired to Xeres de la Frontera, his disorder grew worse, and he breathed his last: his corpse was conveyed by his afflicted troops to Pamplona.

1349. Jeanne died at Paris in 1349, leaving a numerous issue by her husband Philip. Her eldest daughter professed in a convent at Paris; her second was given to don Pedro, infante of Aragon; her third, the princess Blanche, was intended for Jean duke of Normandy, eldest son of Philip de Valois; but that monarch became the successful rival of the young prince, and married Blanche himself; two others were married to the count de Foix and the viscount de Rohan. Of her younger sons one was created count de Longueville, the other count de Beaumont, by the French king: her eldest succeeded her in the throne of Navarre.†

1349 to 1352. CHARLES II., surnamed *le Mauvais*, or *the Bad*, who was in France on his mother's death, returned to his kingdom the following year, to be crowned at Pamplona. On this occasion he exhibited the natural sternness of his disposition, by the severity with which he

---
* See Vol. II. p. 86.
† The same authorities, with the addition of the Castilian chroniclers of the period. Here, however, we part with Moret, whose Annals end in 1349. With all his prejudices, he is by far the best historian of his native kingdom, and among the very best of Spain.

punished the leaders of a partial insurrection, who, under the usual pretext of procuring a guarantee for the national liberties, aimed at anarchy and plunder. His next care was to confirm the good understanding subsisting between Navarre and Castile, an object no less desired by Pedro the Cruel: for this purpose both monarchs had an interview at Burgos, in 1351. Perhaps, as their dispositions were kindred, they were the more inclined to remain at peace with each other. It is certain that don Pedro showed him more respect than to any other monarch of the age, and that he bent before the commanding character of the Castilian.

In 1352 Charles passed into France, to promote his interests with his feudal lord, the monarch of that country. The following year he received the hand of Jeanne, eldest daughter of king Jean. Emboldened by this alliance, he solicited the restitution of the lordships of Champagne and Brie, which had been compulsorily surrendered by the count of Evreux, his father, and which he justly considered as his rightful inheritance. In his pretensions he was opposed by the constable of France, whom he resolved to assassinate. Knowing that the constable's usual abode was the castle of L'Aigle, near Rouen, he commissioned four of his creatures to perpetrate the deed. Under a disguise, and accompanied by a trusty band of soldiers, they hastened to the castle, scaled the walls at midnight, surprised their victim, whom they murdered in bed, and effected their escape. As a defence against the certain vengeance of the French king, he leagued himself with Edward III. of England, and other enemies of France. He did more; though by his lordship of Evreux, and other possessions, he was among the chief vassals of Jean, he loudly exclaimed against the war (and still more against the forced contributions to support it), which that monarch had declared against England. As he was too powerful to be openly punished, he was seized, under the mask of hospitality, at the table of

1352 to 1360.

the dauphin; his companions were put to death, and himself consigned to close confinement in a fortress. This proceeding was the more treacherous on the part of Jean, as he had assured Charles of pardon, and even given one of his sons, the duke d'Anjou, as hostage for his royal faith. At the same time he sent a body of troops to seize Evreux, and the other domains of his son-in-law; but so vigorous was the defence made by the subjects of Charles, that the royal forces were defeated, and, with the aid of the English, a good portion of Normandy was laid waste. This resistance, however, did not procure the liberation of Charles; perhaps it added to the rigour of his confinement. But after the celebrated defeat of the French king at Poitiers, and the troubles encountered by the new regent, the Navarrese nobles, especially Philip, brother of the king, entertained the design of releasing Charles from captivity. Having disguised themselves as coal-men, they went to the castle of Arleux, in Cambresis, where the royal prisoner then lay, scaled the walls by night, and bore him away, — no doubt with the connivance of the governor, in great triumph, — to Amiens. There he collected troops, resolved to have justice done him by the new regent, Charles. Knowing the fermentation that had long subsisted in the minds of the Parisians, and their recent efforts for the abolition of feudal abuses, he saw that by espousing their cause he should be greatly strengthened, and in a condition, if not to dictate to his father-in-law, at least to treat with him on equal terms. Through his queen he obtained a safe conduct from the regent, and hastened to Paris, where the states were then assembled. He fixed his quarters in the monastery of St. Germain des Prés, where he was visited by many of the discontented nobles, and not a few deputies. Seeing the influence which he might safely exercise, he convoked a meeting of the citizens for St. Andrew's day, in a square near the monastery.

Here, having ascended a scaffold, where the French kings were accustomed to witness the jousting of their knights, he harangued 10,000 of the inhabitants with great vehemence, and, we are told, with considerable eloquence. The burden of his discourse was the justice of God[*]: he earnestly expatiated on the sufferings he had been made to endure, and represented the present misfortunes of the royal house of France as the consequence, alike of its cruelty towards him and its disregard of the people. In short, by artfully blending his own case with theirs, he won their favour, and by exaggerating his sufferings, their compassion. Seeing the success of his manœuvre, the royal orator would soon have proceeded to other means of annoyance had not the regent, by the advice of some prudent counsellors, solicited an interview with him, and granted all his demands. Of these, the chief were, the full pardon of all his followers; the restoration, to the true heirs, of the property of all those who had been put to death at the time of his arrest; the payment of a considerable sum, as an indemnification for his imprisonment and the sequestration of his revenues, and the surrender of certain castles in Normandy until the money was paid.[†]

Charles returned into Navarre in 1361. He was soon invited by his old ally Pedro to an interview at Soria. As before, he was treated with marked distinction by the Castilian; who, however, requested him, in virtue of the alliance which they had before contracted, and which they now renewed, to aid in the war that Pedro was about to wage with the king of Aragon. He had no wish to commence hostilities against that prince,

[*] Justus Dominus et justitiam dilexit, — a very effectual text for his purpose.
[†] Froissart, Chronicles of England, &c., by Johnes, vol. iv. passim. But the French events of this period are to be found most minutely described in the "Collection des Mémoires relatifs à l'Histoire de France depuis la Fondation de la Monarchie jusqu'au treizieme Siècle," collected and edited by Guizot, in 29 vols. 8vo. *Paris*, 1820—1826; in the "Collection des Chroniques Nationales Francaises, écrites en Langue Vulgaire," by Buchon, 48 vols. 8vo. *Paris*, 1825—1830; and in the "Collection des Mémoires relatifs à l'Histoire de France depuis la Regne de Philippe Auguste jusqu'à Henri IV." in 52 vols. 8vo. *Paris*, 1825—1830.

but being in the Castilian's power, and with the fate of the murdered Moorish king before him[*], he promised his aid; besides, he had reason to expect that the preservation or amplification of his domains in France might bring him into collision with the monarch of that country, and that in the support of his pretensions he might rely on the co-operation of Pedro. Hence, early in the following year, while his ally was advancing on Calatayud, he himself seized Sos and Salvatierra, and invested Jaca. And on the expulsion of Pedro from Castile in 1366, he readily entered into a league with the prince of Wales for the restoration of his ally. For his promised aid on this service he was to receive Alfaro, and the whole country as far as Navarrete. Scarcely was this engagement formed, when Enrique, now king of Castile, sought an interview with him; and as the condition of his refusing a passage through his dominions to the army of the Black Prince, gave him a considerable sum of money, and promised him Logroño. On hearing of this new treaty, Pedro offered him both Logroño and Vittoria if he would allow the invaders an unobstructed passage. This proposal he accepted with the same facility as the preceding one: and on the entrance of the English prince into his kingdom he artfully caused himself to be arrested by sir Oliver Mauny, one of Edward's generals, and placed in confinement. By this manœuvre, he wished Enrique to understand, that he had endeavoured to obstruct the invader's march, and that his imprisonment was the penalty of his good faith. He little expected that what commenced in jest with the Breton knight would end in earnest, for Oliver refused to release him unless he paid a ransom. Charles, however, was not to be duped. On the pretext that he had no money in that place, but that if Oliver would accompany him to Tudela it should be raised, he no sooner reached that city than he made his gaoler a prisoner, whom, however, he afterwards

---

[*] See Vol. II. p. 93.

exchanged for one of his brothers, then a hostage to the Bretons. During the contest of the two brothers, he resolved not to wait for the places which had been promised him, but to seize them by force. With great facility he obtained possession of Salvatierra, Vittoria, and Logroño, which he strongly garrisoned. In short, all his actions were characterised by the basest perfidy or cupidity. Yet it may be doubted whether he was not, on the whole, the best peninsular sovereign then living, — at least among the Christians: in neither of these qualities was he more infamous than the two Pedros of Portugal and Aragon; and he was certainly both less dishonourable and less cruel than the brother kings of Castile.

In 1371 Charles forsook his correspondence with the English to league himself more closely with his national lord and kinsman the king of France. In one interview with the latter at Vernon, he ceded the cities of Nantes, Meulon, and Longueville, and his rights over Champagne and Brie, in exchange for the lordship of Montpellier. Soon after his return, however, being unprepared to resist Enrique, who armed to recover Vittoria and Logroño (Salvatierra had been already recovered), he was constrained to concede them, on receiving an indemnification for the expense he had incurred in strengthening their fortifications. The subsequent marriage of a daughter of Enrique with the son and heir of the Navarrese king preserved peace between the two crowns. 1371.

But the ambition of Charles was too restless and too unscrupulous to allow him to remain long at peace. In 1377 he is said to have made a secret agreement with our Edward III., in virtue of which he was to surrender his Norman domains for others which were situated in Gascony, and consequently bordering on Navarre. Whether such an agreement were ever made is doubtful, but it is certain that some suspicious communication existed between the two kings, and that it reached the ears of the French monarch, who caused 1377 to 1384.

prince Charles, son and heir of the Navarrese king, then at Evreux, to be arrested. Two of that prince's attendants, too, were put to the torture; under the pain of which, one of them confessed, not only that such an agreement had been made, but that the king of Navarre had plotted the assassination of the French monarch. Though the latter of these accusations rests on no authority beyond a confession thus painfully extorted,— in other words, on none whatever,—the two confidential agents were put to death, the French possessions of Charles were declared forfeited to the crown, were immediately occupied by the dukes of Bourbon and Burgundy, and the prince retained a prisoner. The indignant king of Navarre now sought the alliance of England with greater eagerness than before, and joined with the duke of Lancaster, uncle to Richard II., against France. Enrique of Castile was under too great obligations to the French monarch not to take that monarch's part against his neighbour, though his daughter had married that neighbour's son, and though the son-in-law, at this moment, was a prisoner in Paris. The war turned to the advantage of the Castilian, so that Charles was glad to sue for peace, which he easily obtained, on the condition of his abandoning his alliance with England. Juan I., the successor of Enrique, not only restored the places which his generals had reduced, but in 1382, procured from his ally the French king the release of prince Charles, his brother-in-law. The prince returned the obligation by aiding the Castilian monarch in the wars with Portugal and the English, which have been detailed in a former chapter.*

1387. Charles died in 1387. His character, which has been unnecessarily darkened by the French historians, must be sufficiently known from his actions.†

* See Vol. II. p. 237, &c.
† To the French authorities before quoted, add, Rodericus Santius, Historia Hispanica, pars iv. cap. 14—20. Alfonsus à Carthagena, Anacephalæosis, cap. 78—90. Franciscus Tarapha, De Regibus Hispaniæ, p. 565, &c. (omnes apud Schottum, Hispania Illustrata, tom. i.) Zurita, Anales de Aragon, tom. ii. lib. 7—10. Blancas, Rerum Aragonensium Commentarii, p. 668, &c. (apud Schottum, tom. iii.) Traggia, art. *Navarra*, in Diccionario Geografico-Historico de España, tom. ii.

Of CHARLES III., surnamed the *Noble*, we know little. Soon after his accession, his queen Leonora, a princess of Castile, under the pretence of seeking benefit by a change of air, obtained his permission to visit her nephew's court, and, when there, long refused to return to him. The reason she alleged for the refusal was, if true, a sufficient one: she attributed her illness to poison, administered to her by a Jew leech. By the protection which Enrique III. extended to her during several successive years, and by the guarantees he required from the husband for his aunt's future security in case of her return, we may infer that he at least believed her statement; nor is it easy to conceive that she could forsake her husband's court and kingdom without some powerful cause. Her intriguing character, however, in times when intrigue and violence alone were dominant in Castile*, at length so irritated her nephew, that, with the advice of his council, he determined on her return to Pamplona, on the condition of a solemn oath from Charles, not only that her life and liberty should be secure, but that she should be treated with the affection due to her conjugal character. In 1395 the oath was taken at Tudela, in presence of the archbishop of Toledo and other prelates, and the queen was consigned to her husband. In little more than a year after her return she was delivered of a son (she was already the mother of four daughters), a blessing which the national chronicles ascribe to his piety in rebuilding the cathedral of Pamplona. In 1398 he caused the infant prince to be acknowledged his successor; but, in 1402, Providence recalled its own gift, and his hopes of succession again rested in his female offspring.

1387 to 1402.

Charles, who could not behold without regret the loss of his hereditary domains in France, in 1403 went to the court of that kingdom to solicit their restitution. With great difficulty he obtained the territory of Nemours, with the title of duke; an annual pension of

1403.

---

* See the reign of Enrique III. in Vol. II.

12,000 francs, and a sum of 200,000 crowns, as an indemnity for the loss of his revenues during so many years.

1403 to 1425. The long reign of Charles was pacific, a blessing owing as much to his disposition as to his alliances with the courts of Aragon and Castile. In 1423 he caused his grandson of the same name, son of his daughter Blanche and Juan of Aragon, to be declared his successor after that princess, and to be styled prince of Viana. He died of apoplexy, in September, 1425,— an event which filled his subjects, by whom he was beloved, with lamentation.*

1425. BLANCHE, and JUAN I., her husband, to whom she abandoned the cares of government, were immediately proclaimed sovereigns of Navarre. The sceptre was now, for the first time since the death of Sancho VI. in 1234, in the hands of a prince who, both by descent and birth, could properly be called a native of the Peninsula.

1426 to 1434. The long reign of this prince was passed in fomenting the troubles of Castile, of which he continued a vassal, both as grand-master of a military order, and as the owner of spacious domains in that kingdom. Those troubles have been sufficiently explained in a former chapter†, and need not be repeated here. The part which both he and his brother Alfonso, king of Aragon, took in them, during the feeble reigns of Juan II. and a part of Enrique IV., would afford little entertainment and no instruction to the reader. It must be sufficient to observe, that much of his time was passed in that kingdom, which, as a residence, he appears to have preferred to his own; that, whether in peace or war, whether the ally or enemy of those helpless sovereigns, he was equally sure of exercising a considerable, seldom a salutary, influence; that his turbulent activity knew no bounds, and that he was the scourge alike of friend and foe. In 1430 his domains, as well as his brother Alfonso's in Castile, were confiscated by the justly

---

* The same authorities. † See the reign of Juan II. in Vol. II.

incensed Juan; but in the truce which immediately followed, he consented to award them in compensation.

In 1435 Juan embarked for Sicily to prevail on his brother, Alfonso of Aragon, who was also king of that island, to return and aid him against the Castilian. Alfonso, however willing to join his royal brother in harassing their cousin, was at that time too busily occupied in vindicating his claims on the kingdom of Naples to return.* Even Juan for a moment forgot his old enmities, and agreed to accompany the expedition about to sail from Messina for the Italian coast. In a naval battle before Gaëta, however, both kings were taken prisoners by the fleet of the duke of Milan, by whom they were treated with distinction — not so much as prisoners, as honoured guests, and were speedily released, without ransom. The king of Navarre returned to Spain, with instructions from his brother to manage a peace with the Castilian, that both might be more at liberty to pursue the still meditated conquest of Naples. Accordingly, the following year (1436), it was concluded by the plenipotentiaries of the three powers (Castile, Aragon, and Navarre), on conditions which none of the three could reasonably condemn.

In 1441 died queen Blanche, who, as sole proprietary sovereign of the state (she was still without male issue), left the sceptre to her grandson, the prince of Viana. In her will, however, she recommended the prince not to assume the government without the consent and benediction of his father, who was then in Castile, occupied as usual in fomenting the troubles of that distracted kingdom. Juan had no disposition to lay down a dignity which he had resolved to retain during life. In 1444 he entered into a second marriage with doña Juana, daughter of the admiral of Castile, one of the chiefs of the disaffected party, or at least of the one hostile to the constable don Alvaro de Luna. In his baneful activity he was the support of the infante

* See the history of Aragon.

Enrique, so long as that prince was disposed to make war on his father Juan II.; but whenever the latter returned to his duty, he took part with any nobles who were ready to embarrass the king. No less eagerly did he espouse the quarrels of his brother Alfonso, whenever that monarch was at war with Castile.*

1451 to 1454.
But the king of Navarre was not always at liberty thus to carry the scourge of war into the Castilian's territory. Two parties, actuated by hereditary hostility towards each other, began to agitate his kingdom, and to sow disunion between him and his son. Louis de Beaumont, the constable, and Philip de Navarre, marshal of the realm, had long burned with hatred to each other, and the feeling descended to their respective partisans; the former, who were called the *Beaumonts*, espoused the interests of the prince of Viana; the latter, who were denominated *Agramontese*†, adhered to the father. The Beaumonts urged their favourite to assume the reins of government, to which, since his mother's death, he had an undoubted claim. In 1452, after the birth of Fernando his brother, the offspring of Juan's second marriage, Charles openly raised the standard of revolt, and had the satisfaction to see Pamplona, Olite, Tafalla, and

* Pedro Lopez de Ayala, Cronicas de los Reyes de Castilla (in regno don Juan Segundo). Rodericus Santius, Historia Hispanica, pars iv. cap. 29—33. Alfonsus à Carthagena, Anacephalæosis, cap. 92. Lucius Marineus Siculus, De Rebus Hispaniæ, lib. xii. Franciscus Tarapha, De Regibus Hispaniæ, p. 566. (apud Schottum, Hispania Illustrata, tom. i.). Blancas, Rerum Aragonensium Commentarii, p. 70, &c. (apud eundem, tom. iii.) Zurita, Anales de Aragon, tom. ii. lib. 11—15. Paternio Catinensis, Sicani Reges, p. 148, &c. Traggia, art. *Navarra*, in Diccionario Geografico-Historico de España, tom. ii.

† " Je rends ici le nom tel que je la trouve en Espagnol. Le Père Charenton ecrit *Gramonts* dans sa traduction de Mariana, et il parait par l'Histoire des Grands Officiers de la Couronne, que de cette famille est sortie par les femmes l'illustre maison de Gramont, aujourd'hui si connue en France."— *Note of Hermilly to Ferreras*, vi. 604.

Had Père Charenton, or Hermilly, looked into original authorities, instead of copying from countrymen, neither would have shown such inexcusable ignorance:— " Omnes igitur fere Navarræ nobiles divisi sunt in partes duas, quorum alii Lusam, alii Agramontem, *oppidum* possident."— *Lucius Marineus Siculus*, lib. xiii.

The same excellent writer further tells us that the two towns were but three miles distant from each other, and had for ages been inimical. The constable and marshal placed themselves at the head of the two parties:— why does not Ferreras, like this author, use the term Lusitanians (from Lusa), and Agramontese?

Aylon, declare for him. The king was then in Aragon, which he governed during his brother's absence in the wars of Italy; but he hastily assembled troops and passed into Navarre. Though he found that his son, who had first received a reinforcement of cavalry from Castile — for Juan II. was not slow in supporting a rebellious son against a father who had so often raised *his* son against *him* — was superior in force, the Navarrese king prepared for battle. There were some, however, in both camps, who beheld this unnatural strife with indignation, and who laboured to effect a reconciliation between father and son. But one condition, — that relating to a peace which the prince had shortly before made with Castile, — was so unpalatable to the king, that all negotiation was ended, and the battle commenced. It ended in the defeat of the prince, who was taken prisoner and consigned to a fortress. There he remained about a year, and there he would have long continued to remain, notwithstanding the remonstrances of the Castilian king, or even of the Aragonese states, had not the Navarrese armed for his deliverance. The king was forced to yield, — he evidently bore no affection to his son, — to confirm Charles in the principality of Viana, and abandon to him half the royal revenues.

A reconciliation thus forcibly effected was not likely to be lasting; in fact, it was agreeable to neither party: the father wished to punish the rebellious son, the son to obtain what he considered his undoubted heritage; hence in 1455 both prepared to renew the contest. This was not enough for Juan. Divesting himself of every sentiment, not merely of nature, but of common justice, he caused his son to be set aside from the succession, and declared that it should rest in his daughter Leonora, wife of the count de Foix, and her issue. He very well knew that the crown was not his to bequeath; that his present retention of it was unlawful; and that in conformity both with the testament of his deceased queen, and the fundamental laws of the kingdom, it ought already to be on the brow of his son.

1454 to 1458.

The following year (1456) the prince was again defeated by the king, and compelled to seek refuge in France. From Paris he passed without delay to Rome, to interest the pope in his behalf; but his strongest hopes were directed to his uncle, king Alfonso, who was then at Naples. By that monarch he was received with affection, and his manners made him popular both with the Neapolitans and Sicilians. During his absence Juan, in an assembly of the states at Estella, exposed the reasons of his exclusion from the throne, as well as that of his sister Blanche, who had been separated from Enrique of Castile, on the ground of impotency[*], and who had had the misfortune, like him, to displease the tyrannical father. The inhabitants of Pamplona were so indignant at this injustice, that they elected Charles their king, and solicited aid from Enrique (now king of Castile). To end these disgraceful transactions, king Alfonso despatched one of his nobles from Naples, with instructions to bring about a reconciliation on any terms. Unfortunately, however, this monarch died without legitimate issue, in 1458, leaving his brother, the king of Navarre, heir of all his dominions in Spain, with the Balearic Isles and Sicily; and no one remained influential enough to finish the friendly work which he had begun.

1459 to 1460. Charles returned to Spain in 1459; but after despatching messages to his father, entreating an oblivion of the past, and his recognition as heir to the throne of Aragon, he sailed for Majorca; the place, indeed, which Juan had appointed for his abode. While here the treaty of reconciliation between them was effected. By it the son was restored to his principality, and the revenues he formerly enjoyed, and was allowed to reside in any portion of his father's dominions, except Navarre and Sicily. Blanche, too, who had made herself obnoxious by supporting her brother, was restored to her appanage, and a full pardon was secured to all who had

---

[*] See Vol. II. p. 257.

taken part in the recent disturbances. The prince now embarked for Barcelona, but Juan, who was there, on hearing of his approach, retired to Saragossa. This step appears to have been disapproved by the king's counsellors, who prevailed on him to return to the Catalonian capital. He was met on the way by the prince, whom he received with apparent satisfaction.

Had the misunderstanding ended here, well it would 1460. have been for the reputation of both father and son; but where no affection existed apparently on either part, where tyranny on the one side, and disobedience on the other were become habitual, and where each took a secret pleasure in thwarting the projects of the other. even outward harmony could not long exist. The league in Castile opposed to Enrique IV., was favoured by the kings of Aragon and Portugal. To strengthen their alliance, they agreed to marry the infanta Catalina, daughter of the Lusitanian, with the prince of Viana. The prince himself approved the projected match; but the arrival of a secret agent from Enrique IV., with the offer of the infanta Isabel, sister of that monarch, and at the same time of the throne of Navarre, which the Castilian troops were to procure for him, turned his head. His judgment must have been deplorably weak to have been captivated by such an offer: he ought to have known that it could never be realised, that Enrique was too busily occupied with domestic troubles to have either the time or the means of efficiently aiding him. The negotiation soon reached the ears of Juan, who at first disregarded it; but the expostulations and remonstrances of the queen, the malignant enemy of her step-son, roused his dormant hostility. He sent for Charles to Lerida, where the states were then holding, arrested him with two of his advisers, and gave orders for his trial. Incensed at this harsh treatment of one whom they hoped to see proclaimed their future sovereign, the states of Aragon and Catalonia earnestly solicited his liberation. In vain; the prince was removed, under a strong guard, to the fortress of Aytona.

1461. In accordance with the secret treaty, Enrique in person invaded Navarre, invested and reduced Viana, but laid siege in vain to Tudela. No sooner had he retired than the inhabitants of Barcelona armed to effect the liberation of their favourite prince; they were joined by many of the Aragonese, who were highly offended at the stern manner in which the king had repulsed their application. The aid of 1000 lances from Castile gave them new courage. The insurrection promising to become general and serious, the queen herself now solicited Juan to release the prince. The request was granted: the Catalonians were informed that he should be delivered into their hands; and the queen went to Morella, whither the captive had been transferred, to open the prison gates. He was conducted in triumph to Barcelona, which refused to admit the queen. In the excess of their joy the mob insisted on the trial of all the prince's enemies; but they were at length satisfied with demanding that he should be immediately declared successor to the throne; that he should be appointed the perpetual and irrevocable governor of Catalonia, whence the king's creatures should be banished; that all who had served his interests should not only escape without punishment, but be declared good subjects. These demands were ungrateful to the king; but as he was occupied in the Castilian troubles and the Navarrese war, and knew that if he were not, his means would be inadequate to suppress the insurrections, he authorised the queen to grant them. All Catalonia now recognised the prince as count; proclaimed him heir to the throne of Aragon, Navarre, and Sicily; and *Te Deum* was lustily sung in the cathedral of Barcelona.

1461. No sooner was this treaty signed, than Juan, alarmed at the preparations of Castile, proposed to the new count an interview at Jaca. They met, and Charles was easily induced to promise his aid in the defence of Navarre. Both agreed that the king of France should be solicited to procure peace from Enrique. Immediately afterwards, however, Juan himself obtained it from the Castilian.

king, whose troops evacuated Navarre. This treaty, to which the prince had been no party, and with the provisions of which he was unacquainted, afforded him no little uneasiness. Believing that his interests had been sacrificed by the two monarchs, and knowing that his father had destroyed his hopes with respect to the infanta Isabel, he formed the resolution of leaguing himself closely with the French monarch, when death surprised him in his capital of Barcelona. In the excitement of the public mind we need not be surprised that this unexpected event was ascribed to an extraordinary cause, — to poison administered by his physician at the instigation of the queen. Nothing, however, is more certain than that his death was natural, however it might be hastened by the agitation of his mind.* His last illness continued for some days; and it is impossible not to believe that, if he had any reason — and he was suspicious enough — to consider his approaching end premature, he would not have made a declaration to that effect, especially as he was surrounded by none but his own creatures, and consequently by none that were not his father's enemies. In his testament he left his father a thousand florins; and as the rightful sovereign of Navarre, he bequeathed that crown to his sister Blanche, the next in order of succession. The madness of party rage went farther than charging its idol's death on the queen: to render both her and the king odious, the deceased count was unblushingly proclaimed a martyr; and miracles were said to have been wrought by his intercession and relics. Though he was known to have been a rebel, to have been not very scrupulous in the fulfilment of his engagements, and to have left three illegitimate children †,

---

* " De pura desesperacion y angustia de espiritu, y de turbacion del animo, adolesció de suerte que le sobrevinó una fiebre con dolor de costado; de que luego se tuvo por muy peligroso — la dolencia fue de manera que murio li veinte y tres del mismo mes (September) en la fiesta de Santa Tecla, en edad de cuarenta años," &c.—*Zurita*, iii. 97.

† Don Felipe, the eldest, was created a count; don Juan Alfonso took holy orders, and became bishop of Huesca; doña Anna married a Castilian noble.

there was at one time some intention of applying to the pope for a bull of canonisation. Yet as he was evidently persecuted through life for the sake of his younger brother, Fernando; as he was sometimes treated cruelly, and always harshly, after his father's second marriage, it is impossible not to feel great compassion for his fate.*

1461 to 1464.

On the death of Charles, two sovereigns were anxious to gain possession of Navarre: first, Enrique of Castile, who proclaimed himself the protector of his wife, the princess Blanche, but who in reality aimed only at his own advantage; second, Louis XI., who contended that in the failure of male issue the fief should return to the house of France, or at least that Blanche should marry some French prince. But Juan was no less resolved to retain the sovereignty during his own life, and to transmit it at his death to his second daughter, the countess de Foix, or her issue. To disarm Louis he proposed a marriage between his grandson Gaston de Foix, and the princess Magdeleine, sister of that monarch. The proposal was readily accepted by Louis; and it was at the same time agreed that Blanche should renounce the crown, or take the veil, and if she refused to do either she should be consigned as a prisoner to the charge of the count and countess de Foix. That unfortunate princess had long been rigorously guarded by her unnatural parent, who feared, and not without reason, that if allowed to remain at liberty, she would soon be carried off by the Beaumonts and proclaimed

---

* Lucius Marineus Siculus, De Rebus Hispaniæ, 13, &c. (apud Schottum, Hispania Illustrata, tom. i.). This writer, as the historian of the emperor Charles V., could scarcely be expected to be impartial: he is very severe on the prince. Rodericus Santius, Historia Hispanica, pars iv. cap. 36 & 37. Alfonsus à Carthagena, Anacephalæosis, cap. 93. Tarapha, De Regibus Hispaniæ, p. 566. (apud eundem, eodemque tomo.) Blancas, Rerum Aragonensium Commentarii (in regno Joannis II. apud eundem, tom. iii.). Zurita, Anales de Aragon, tom. iii. lib. xvi. et 17. Paternio Catinensis, Siculi Reges, p. 151. Traggia, art. *Navarra*, in Diccionario Geografico-Historico de España, tom. ii.

"Hic Vianensis princeps," says the abbot of Casino (adnotationes in Paternionem, p. 153.) "expertus est genitorum durum et inflexibilem. Crimen est in patrem arma sumere, sed culpâ non vacat, filium, qui matris morte legitimus erat Navarræ rex, non solum titulo et administratione propriâ hereditatis exspoliari," &c. "Quanta," concludes the abbot, "est in eorum animos qui mulieres perdite amant imbecilitas! quale imperium in eosnon obtinent superbæ fœminæ!"

sovereign. In consequence of this most iniquitous agreement, and of the daily request of the countess Leonora, who was worthy of such a father, Juan now devised the means of securing the innocent Blanche. Both being at Olite, he informed her that she must accompany him across the Pyrenees, to be given in marriage to the duke de Berri, brother of the French king. But she had heard of the treaty which excluded her from the throne, and she refused to move: she was arrested and conveyed to Roncesvaux. While there she caused a protestation to be secretly prepared, in which she declared that she was carried away by violence; that she should soon be forced to renounce her rights over Navarre in favour either of her sister and issue, or of prince Fernando; and that she protested beforehand against the validity of such an act. As she proceeded in these wild regions her apprehensions increased, not merely for her liberty, but for her life. At St. Jean Pied de Port she supplicated by writing the king of Castile, the count de Armagnac, the constable of Navarre, and other friends, to arm for her liberty, empowering them to marry her to whatever king or prince they judged proper. Every thing continuing to wear a still more ominous appearance, her next step was to make a full and entire cession of her dominions in favour of Enrique. In a letter written to that prince she conjured him to have pity on one who had formerly stood towards him in the dear relation of a wife, — a letter, says Ferreras, which even at this day would melt the hardest heart. But neither her innocence nor her misfortunes could avail her in this world; she was consigned to the care of a suitable instrument of guilt; was closely confined in the solitary castle of Orthes in Bearne, and was not again heard of until the autumn of 1464, when her funeral rites were performed in the cathedral of Lescar. That a damning deed was perpetrated within the walls of that fortress is the unanimous opinion of all contemporary and succeeding writers. By most of these her death is believed to have been occasioned by poison, administered by the command of her own sister. If this virtuous, and through life unhappy princess, had no avenger on earth, it is some consolation to know that the justice of heaven slumbered not: we shall soon see in what manner the sceptre, the prize of this dark murder, was wrested from the house of Foix, and how deep a curse seemed to rest upon its members.

1469 to 1478.
After the death of Charles and of Blanche the condition of Navarre was deplorable. In 1469 the count de Foix, enraged that the government was not confided to him by his father-in-law, invaded the kingdom, but was speedily expelled by the archbishop of Saragossa, an illegitimate son of Juan. This was not the only mortification of the count: the same year he lost his son Gaston de Foix, who was killed, whether accidentally or by design is doubtful, in a tournay at Bourdeaux. By the princess Magdeleine the young prince left a son named Phœbus, and a daughter named Catherine, who in the sequel swayed the sceptre of Navarre. Anarchy and violence now reigned triumphant: the two parties, the Beaumonts and the Agramontese, became more implacable than ever; the chief of one, don Pedro de Peralta, assassinated in open day the bishop of Pamplona, though that prelate was the intimate friend of the countess Leonora, then at Tafalla. In short, owing to the character of the king, whose authority, even had he been present, would have been disputed by a considerable party, there was no government; for though Leonora, from her evident proximity to the throne, was courted by many nobles, her commands were seldom obeyed, while her intrigues were frequently thwarted. In 1471, through the earnest and repeated remonstrances of some barons, and above all of his daughter, Juan went to Olite to arrange the affairs of this distracted kingdom. It was then agreed that he should have the title of king during life; that the three estates should do homage to the countess and count de Foix as heirs to the crown, and that they, as perpetual viceroys, should exercise the

chief authority throughout the kingdom whenever the king was absent; and that there should be a full pardon for all political offenders, a restitution of all property violently or arbitrarily obtained, and an oblivion of all injuries. This last provision might be very excellent in itself, but where there was no power to insure its observance it was sure to be inoperative. The countess herself had soon experience of this truth. Intending to pass to Pamplona, which had long been held by the Beaumonts in opposition both to her and the Agramontese, she acquainted the count de Lerin, chief of that faction, with her purpose, and at the same time told him that, in consequence of the treaty which had just been concluded, she should be accompanied by the marshal don Pedro, chief of the Agramontese. The Beaumont replied that she should be welcome, but advised her to leave don Pedro behind. The countess persisted, and as there were many of the Agramontese faction in the city, the marshal secretly bribed one of them to open a gate on a certain night. At the time appointed he arrived before it, escorted by a strong body of cavalry. As the man was not immediately at his post the horsemen grew impatient, and endeavoured to break it open: the noise awakened one of the Beaumonts, who had time to give the alarm; the bell sounded from the tower of St. Firmin; the partisans leaped from their beds, put on their armour and hastened to the gate, which in the interim had been opened for the enemy. A bloody combat ensued, which ended in the expulsion of the Agramontese: the marshal fell; and such of his faction as could be found were hanged or cut down. The countess lost no time in acquainting both her husband and father with this audacious tragedy. The former, who was in his hereditary domains, collected troops; but — such was the retributive justice of heaven for the murder of Blanche — a sudden death seized him in the Pyrenees. Bereft of her chief support, of one whose name had hitherto strengthened her government, Leonora was henceforth more obnoxious than ever to the violence of the Beaumonts, and less able to preserve peace between the factions. In 1476 Juan and Fernando, who, with Isabel, had ascended the Castilian throne, met at Tudela to restore order in the realm, and their presence had the effect of suspending the open hostility of the factions; but they had scarcely returned when both the Beaumonts and the Agramontese flew to arms. Sometimes they suspended their quarrels, not from regard to Leonora's authority, but from their own mutual exhaustion. Such, with little intermission, continued to be the condition of the country, which was fast declining to a state of hopeless dependence, and on which the neighbouring powers cast an expectant eye, each only prevented from seizing the tempting and defenceless prey through fear of the other.*

1479. On the death of Juan in 1479, LEONORA was proclaimed sovereign of the kingdom. Her empire, the object for which she had incurred such a heavy load of guilt, was exceedingly fleeting: her father died on the 19th January; on the 10th of the following month she herself was a corpse. She had barely time to make a will, in which she declared Phœbus, the offspring of her son Gaston and the princess Magdeleine, heir to the throne. In the same act she placed the kingdom under the protection, — not of her brother Fernando, now king of Aragon and Castile, the nearest relation by blood, but — of the French monarch.

1479 to 1483. FRANÇOIS PHŒBUS, who was very young on his grandmother's death, was not permitted by the princess Magdaleine to pass the Pyrenees until 1482. The civil wars of the two rival factions, which now raged

---

* Zurita, Anales de Aragon, tom. iv. (in regno don Juan II.). Hernando del Pulgar, Chronica de los Señores Reyes Catolicos, Fernando y Isabel, parte segunda, passim. Blancas, Rerum Aragonensium Commentarii, p. 703, &c. (apud Schottum, Hispania Illustrata, tom. iii.). Franciscus Tarapha, De Regibus Hispaniæ, p. 567. (apud eundem, tom. i.). Rodericus Santius, Historia Hispanica, cap. 37, &c. (in eodem tomo). Lucius Marineus Siculus, De Rebus Hispaniæ, lib. xviii. (in eodem tomo). Mariana, De Rebus Hispanicis, lib. xxiv. (apud eundem, tom. iv.). Ferreras, Histoire Générale d'Espagne, by Hermilly, tom. vii. Traggia, art. *Navarra*, in Diccionario Geografico-Historico de España, tom. ii.

with greater fury than ever, justified her maternal caution. On Fernando's engaging to furnish a number of troops, sufficient to insure tranquillity at the period of his arrival, he at length crossed the mountain barrier from his hereditary fief of Foix with a considerable army, was civilly, rather than joyfully, received by his new subjects, and was crowned at Pamplona. His first care was to restore harmony between the factions; he made a decree, that whoever should ever name the rallying words *Beaumont* and *Agramont*, should be severely punished. The crafty sovereigns of Castile immediately proposed to him a matrimonial connection; but his mother, alarmed for the interests of France, and resolved that he should marry no one but a Valois, speedily hurried him over the Pyrenees. If she thereby averted the odious match, she could not avert the destiny which hung over the house of Foix: the king suddenly died at Pau, in about two months after his coronation.

CATHERINE, the sister of Phœbus, was immediately proclaimed sovereign; and as speedily was an embassy sent to the mother Magdeleine by the Castilian sovereigns, who proposed the marriage of the infante Juan with that princess. Magdeleine civilly declined the offer, pretending that she could do nothing in such a business without the consent of the French king. The subject, however, was speedily turned into a source of contention by the rival factions; the one shouting for a Castilian, the other for a French husband. To remove this pretext of strife, the princess was given the following year by her brother, the king of France, to JEAN D'ALBRET, whose estates bordered on those of Navarre. The information was mortifying to Fernando and Isabel; and though they contrived to gain possession of Tudela, one city was a poor compensation for the loss of a kingdom. The queen and king of Navarre, however, were not crowned until 1494. 1483.

During the following years, though Fernando was busily occupied in his wars with France, he never lost sight of Navarre; nor abandoned the resolution of 1494 to 1512.

seizing it whenever a favourable opportunity should occur. Under the pretext of defending the country against the probable invasion of the French, he obtained permission to introduce Castilian soldiers into some of the fortresses, especially Viana and Sanguesa; nor would he surrender them when the danger was removed. His money was no less usefully expended in procuring the favour of such nobles as had influence in the councils of the realm: in fact, Fernando would have stooped to any measure, however dishonourable, capable of aiding his ambitious views. Unfortunately for the independence of the country, it was the policy of the Navarrese king to oppose and exasperate his brother of Castile: in almost every dispute of Fernando with the kings of France or the emperor he took the part of the former. Nor need this surprise us: the lion of Castile held violent possession of his fortresses, and by every act showed a disposition to spring on the remainder of the prey. It was hoped that the marriage of Fernando with a princess of the house of Foix, niece to Louis, would render him more considerate towards the interests of his new kindred; but the hope was vain. Their hostility towards him in banishing his creature, the chief of the Beaumonts, and compelling Viana to surrender, at a time when he was wholly occupied in securing his second regency (1507), sunk deep into his heart: and when, in 1512, Jean d'Albret, at the instigation of France, not only refused a passage for his army into that kingdom, but leagued with Louis, his greatest enemy, he determined to strike the blow which he had so long meditated,—to seize on the whole country, and unite it with his hereditary estates.

1512. In July, 1512, the duke of Alba, general of Fernando, marched from Vittoria direct on Pamplona[*]; the queen had retired into France; and Jean d'Albret, instead of encouraging his subjects, by his presence, to

[*] At this period, the duke of Dorset embarked in Biscay with a few thousand English to assist in the conquest of Guienne; but, on finding that the expedition was to reduce Navarre, he refused to aid the Castilians, and speedily re-embarked.

hold out, prepared to follow the example. Before his departure he assembled the chief inhabitants of that capital, exhorted them to make a vigorous resistance, and promised them soon to return from France with a formidable army. He had scarcely reached the Pyrenees, when the duke of Alba arrived before the place, which was summoned to surrender, and which did surrender without firing a shot. The inhabitants, who had neither guns nor ammunition, perceived that resistance would be hopeless; and they had no wish, by an attempt at defence, to exasperate the enemy, and probably sustain all the horrors of a forcible entry. Fernando now marched with reinforcements, and most of the fortresses of the kingdom surrendered to him, or his martial son, the archbishop of Saragossa. It was not, however, to be expected that France would tamely witness the usurpation of the Spaniard. A formidable army, under the dukes de Longueville and Valois, and accompanied by the expelled king, speedily crossed the frontier, and laid siege to Pamplona. But in a few days, owing partly to the want of provisions in the camp of the invaders, and partly by the destructive assaults of the Spaniards, who yet refrained from a general action, the siege was raised, and the French army returned into Guienne. Its inglorious departure was followed by the submission of the whole kingdom to Fernando. The succeeding year king Jean made another effort to regain the throne, but with as little success. From the bloodstained house of Foix the sceptre had for ever departed; nor could all the armies of France, during the reigns of the emperor Charles, and his son Philip, restore it to the descendants of Jean. Both Catherine and her husband died in 1516.*

1513.

* Zurita, Historia del Rey Hernando el Catolico, tom. ii. lib. x. Aelius Antonius Nebrissensis, De Bello Navariensi, lib. i. et ii. (apud Schottum, Hispania Illustrata, tom. i.). Blancas, Rerum Aragonensium Commentarii, p. 704. (apud eundem, tom. iii.), necnon Mariana, De Rebus Hispaniæ, lib. xxix xxx. (apud eundem, tom. iv.) Petrus Martyr Anglerius, *Epistolæ* (as quoted by Ferreras, tom. viii.). Ferreras, Histoire Générale d'Espagne, by Hermilly, tom. vii. passim. Traggia, art. *Navarra*, in Diccionario Geografico-Historico de España, tom. ii.

The conquest of Navarre by this great prince, however necessary to the tranquillity of Spain, can be characterised in no other terms than as an act of unblushing rapacity; yet attempts have been made to justify it, and by writers who would not willingly be considered the advocates of a criminal abuse of power. According to one authority[*], the king of Navarre was excommunicated by the pope as a schismatic, — as one of the league formed by the emperor and France against the papal pretentions to the duchy of Ferrara[†], — and bulls, absolving the Navarrese from their oath of allegiance, deposing Jean, and conferring the kingdom on the first that took possession of it, were sent to Fernando; in other words, that the enterprise was sanctioned by the head of the church in gratitude for the aid which, in conjunction with the Venetians, he afforded the successor of St. Peter. In the estimation of such writers as Garibay, Antonio de Nebrija, and Mariana, who allow the pope an indirect authority over kings, who subject the temporal to the spiritual power, the title of Fernando to the kingdom is every way sufficient. As such a title, however, will not be admitted at this day even beyond the Pyrenees, the conquest must be designated as one of the most flagitious transactions of a lawless age.

[*] Petrus Martyr Anglerius, Ep. 409.
[†] The wars of this period may be found in Guicciardini, Istoria d'Italia, and in Zurita, Historia del Rey Hernando el Catolico.

CHAP. III.

COUNTS OF BARCELONA.*

801 — 1162.

Among the numerous lordships of Catalonia, that of Barcelona being the only one which at any time exhibited the attributes of sovereignty, is the only one that can be admitted into the present compendium. The rest were either dependent on it, or on the French kings, prior to the mersion of all in the crown of Aragon.

The exploits of Otgar and his nine companions, who are said to have made considerable conquests in the Tarraconensian province, or the country lying between the Ebro and the Pyrenees, prior to the irruption of Charlemagne in 778, are evidently fabulous. That a German or Northman, named Otgar and surnamed Catalo, governor of Guienne for king Pepin, being filled with grief at the miserable state of this province under the misbelievers, assembled nine bold companions, each with a resolute band, and passed the mountain barrier; that during a ten years' war he reduced most of the fortified places, restoring liberty to Christianity and its worshippers; that from him the province changed its name from Tarragona to *Catalonia;* that his nine companions were so many barons, each with a separate government, but subject to their chief; that on the death of Otgar while pressing the siege of Ampurias he was succeeded

---

* The reader will find this chapter very meagre, owing to the want of authentic materials. Catalonia, prior to the sixteenth century, is lamentably deficient in *native* historians; and of these not one is contemporary. The anonymous monk of Ripol lived half a century after the junction of Barcelona with Aragon. If, however, like Pere Tomich and Diago, we were disposed to admit fables, or to chronicle dry ecclesiastical transactions, we could easily make a respectable-sized folio.

by one of the barons; that on the approach of a vast Mohammedan army, the Christian knights, foreseeing the impossibility of resistance, reluctantly retired to the fastnesses of the Pyrenees, where they remained until the army of Charlemagne, which they joined, made its celebrated irruption into the province; are so many inventions which have no foundation in ancient authorities, which are read for the first time in one of the fifteenth century, and which are at variance with the statements of the Frank writers of the period.*

777. The arrival of Ben Alarabi, styled Mohammedan governor of Saragossa, or an embassy from him, at the court of Charlemagne, who was then at Paderborn, and his offer to become a vassal of the emperor on the condition of his being protected against the resentment of Abderahman I. king of Cordova, have been already related.† We are assured that Gerona, Huesca, Saragossa, and even Barcelona, submitted to the invader, their Mohammedan governors doing homage to him as obedient vassals. His success, however, was but transient; for in 781 Abderahman easily recovered these places, and was again acknowledged as undisputed master of all Aragon and Catalonia. In 785 Gerona again submitted to Louis king of Aquitaine, son of the emperor, who convinced that the Moorish vassal had been perfidious in the surrender of the place to Abderahman, nominated a Christian count to the government. In 796 the French generals, by the command of Louis, returned to the Peninsula, where they collected booty and captives in abundance. Though they undertook no siege, their arrival is said to have so terrified Zeyad wali of Barcelona, that he became a vassal of the emperor. The following year they repeopled and fortified Vique, Cardona, and other places. The wali of Huesca imitated the example of Zeyad, and the latter went to the court of

* Mossen Père Tomich, Historias e Conquestas dels excellentissims e Catholics Reys de Arago, e de lurs antecessors los Comtes de Barcelona, &c. p. 19. &c. Lucius Marineus Siculus, De Rebus Hispaniæ, lib. ix. (apud Schottum, Hispania Illustrata, tom. i.). Zurita, Anales de Aragon, lib. i. cap. 3. Marca, Limos Hispanicus, lib. iii. cap. 5.
† See Vol. I. p. 254.

Charlemagne at Aix-la-Chapelle to renew his homage in person. But Zeyad in 799 again transferred his allegiance to the king of Cordova. This perfidy so irritated Louis that another Frank army laid waste Catalonia, took and destroyed Lerida, and laid siege to Barcelona. Though the city was vigorously invested, it made a noble defence during two years. That it was not relieved by Albakem will create no surprise, when we recollect that he was long harassed by domestic rebellion*, and, therefore, unable to oppose the enterprises of the Franks. In the second year of the siege, indeed, an Arabian army left Cordova for the purpose, and at the express solicitation of Zeyad; but the approach of a single division of the Christian army compelled it to remain inactive. The place was now pressed with renewed vigour by Rosteing count of Gerona; so that Zeyad, convinced that resistance was hopeless, departed for Gothic Gaul, with the intention of again recognising Charlemagne as lord paramount of Catalonia. No sooner, however, did he appear before Louis than he was arrested as a traitor and sent to the emperor, who condemned him to a rigorous exile. The king of Aquitaine now hastened to an easy conquest. After six weeks more of frequent assault and a close investment, the inhabitants consented to surrender both the city and its governor, (Omar, a relation of Zeyad,) on the condition of their being allowed to retire wherever they pleased. The condition was accepted; Louis made a triumphant entry; the Christian worship was restored in all its splendour; a Christian garrison was left in the place, and a count nominated— a native of Gothic Gaul, named Bera.†

801.

* Vol. I. p. 262, &c.
† Annales Francorum Fuldenses, p. 539. (apud Duchesne, Historiæ Francorum Scriptores Coætanei, tom. ii.) Annales Bertiniani Rerum Francorum, p. 165. (apud eundem, tom. iii.). Eginhardus, Annales Regum Francorum (apud eundem, ii. 251.). Rodericus Toletanus, Historia Arabum, cap. 25. (apud Schottum, Hispania Illustrata, tom. ii.). Lucius Marineus Siculus, De Rebus Hispaniæ, p 372. (apud eundem, tom. i.) Zurita Anales de Aragon, lib. i. cap. 3. Marca, Limos Hispanicus, lib. iii. cap. 15. et 16. Baluzius Tutelensis, Marca Hispanica (ad calcem Marcæ, lib. iv. col. 341—346.) Diago, Historia de los victoriossissimos antiguos Condes de Barcelona, lib. i. Condé, by Marlés, Histoire de la Domination des Arabes, &c. tom. i. p. 232. &c.

801 to 820. BERA.—Of this count's admistration we have nothing in detail, but are informed that it was characterised by great rapacity and cruelty. That he was not much worse in this respect than the other counts of Catalonia may be inferred from the complaints of the people, and from the edict in favour of the oppressed promulgated by Charlemagne in 812. In it Bera and the other governors were strictly enjoined to discontinue their vexations, of which the archbishop of Arles was commissioned to enquire into the extent, and do justice towards the sufferers. But the count was at length accused by one Sunila, a Barcelonian of distinction, not only of rapacity but of treason—of holding a secret understanding with Alhakem. As the latter part of this accusation rested on no other foundation than the assertion of Sunila, the question of his innocence or guilt was decided in 820 by a single combat between the accuser and the accused before the emperor Louis. Bera was vanquished, was therefore convicted of the crime, and subject to the last penalty; but by the clemency of the emperor death was mitigated into banishment to Rouen.

During the period of Bera's sovereignty hostilities were not unfrequent between the Mohammedans and Franks. In 802 Louis assembled a great army at Barcelona, took Tarragona, and laid waste the country in the neighbourhood of Tortosa. At the same time a division of his army under Bera, Borello count of Ossuna, and other generals, passed the Ebro, and destroyed the Mohammedan possessions as far as the gates of Villarabia. An army of the enemy however, headed by Alhakem in person, soon forced them to retreat. The following year they renewed their attempts on Tortosa, but without effect; though by their own writers they are represented as victors in a battle on the banks of the Ebro, it is admitted that the advantage was dearly bought. In 804, however, the king of Aquitaine reduced the place, after a bloody siege of forty days; but his generals failed before Huesca. In the sequel both places were recovered; and though in 809 Louis vigorously assailed Tortosa, he was compelled to raise the siege, and retreat before prince Abderahman, son of the Mohammedan king. If Huesca and Saragossa soon afterwards acknowledged Charlemagne as their liege superior, both were speedily recovered by the arms of Alhakem. Such was the ordinary fortune which attended the wars of this period; such the alternations of success and failure, that neither party could justly boast of a decided issue. Both at length agreed to a peace, or perhaps a truce.*

On the deposition of Bera, BERNARDO, son of Wilhelm, count of Narbonne, was intrusted with the fief of Barcelona. War was now declared by the Franks against Alhakem; but though the Christian historians award the success to the generals of Louis, it is certain that so long as that king lived such success is very doubtful. On the accession of Abderahman the troubles which internally agitated the Mohammedan kingdom, afforded a good opening for the warlike counts to resume their irruptions. They crossed the Segro, say the Frank historians, penetrated considerably into the kingdom of Toledo, and returned laden with abundant spoil. The same historians do not tell us,—which, however, is the fact,— that the invaders were soon forced to retreat, and that Barcelona itself was recovered by the Arabs. The government of the Franks was also weakened by the differences of their counts: one of these, Aizo, forcibly dispossessed another dignitary, and entered into an alliance with Abderahman. The Arabian king lost no time in improving the opportunity. Having effected a junction with the rebel, he speedily reduced Manresa, Cardona, Salsona, and other fortresses. In fact, the domination of the Franks was now confined to some places at the foot of the Pyrenees. [826 to 830.]

For some years no efforts were made to recover these lost conquests. The dissensions, which even during the life of Louis prevailed among his sons, afforded the Franks little opportunity for prosecuting the war with [830 to 832.]

---

* Authorities, the histories in Duchesne, Marca, Baluzius, Diago, Zurita, and Condé by Marlés.

the Mohammedans. During these years we frequently find Bernardo at the court of Louis. In 829 he was made grand chamberlain, was intrusted with the education of Charles, afterwards surnamed the Bald, and received as a partner in the empire; a fortune which rendered him peculiarly obnoxious to the fierce sons of the monarch. His familiarity with the empress Judith was made a pretext for the persecution raised against him, and he found it necessary to fly from the imminent danger which surrounded him. He took shelter in Spain; but in 831, after the empress had been declared innocent, he again appeared at court, and was absolved. It would appear, too, that he was restored to the dukedom of Septimania, a dignity which he had probably held in conjunction with the lordship of Barcelona. The imprudent part, however, which he took in fomenting the undutiful conduct of Pepin, king of Aquitaine, whom he encouraged to arm against Louis, led in 832 to his deprivation of his various dignities. In revenge he caused Burgundy to declare in favour of Pepin. Indignant at his audacity, Lothaire, brother and rival of Pepin, and the enemy of Bernardo, violated the sanctity of the cloister by seizing the nun Gerberg, the count's sister, and drowning her in the Arar, on the pretence of her being a witch. A brother and cousin of his were consigned to an untimely end, and another relative banished.

833 to 836. From the tenor of history it is certain that the city of Barcelona again declared for the Christian emperor. It may be doubted, however, whether he held the dignity immediately after the recovery,—the time and circumstances of which are wholly unknown,—of this important place. From a passage in the life of Ludovicus Pius by the anonymous astronomer, it appears that in 836 he had a rival in power, Berengario by name, from whom he took either by stratagem or open force the city of Thoulouse. As this Berengario is styled marquis of Gothia, or duke of Septimania, a government which at this period was apparently comprehended in that of

Barcelona, and subject to it, there is strong presumption for suspecting that he had superseded Bernardo, and that the latter in revenge deprived him of his dignity, perhaps of his life.* It is, indeed, possible that count Berengario might only hold the separate government of Thoulouse; for which reason we do not positively rank him among the counts of Barcelona. Where the obscurity is so great and opinion so divided, he must be a bold writer who will venture to decide. Though inclined to the opinion that Berengario was invested with the forfeited fiefs of Bernardo (forfeited in 832), both in Catalonia and Gothic Gaul, as the point is not and cannot be settled, our attention must be confined to facts, or to circumstances which are so reputed.

Whatever might be the dignity held by Bernardo from 832 to 836, there seems little doubt that from the latter year to the period of his death he was count of Barcelona, and from 840, at least, he was certainly duke of Septimania.† He did not long survive his restoration to power. By the death of Louis in 840, Catalonia and Gothic Gaul fell to Charles, the youngest son of that emperor. Indignant that in the division of the empire no portion was left for him, Pepin, son of the rebellious prince of that name, no sooner heard of his grandfather's death than he seized on Aquitaine. Bernardo formed the party of the son as he had formed that of the father, and when summoned by Charles, his new sovereign, to do homage in person for his fief, he at first refused to appear, but not without assigning the most plausible pretexts he could for neglecting to obey. Soon hearing, however, that these reasons were unsatisfactory to Charles, he hastened to disarm by his presence that prince's anger. His arrest was resolved; he

836 to 844.

---

* Sed et causa Gothorum ibidem ventilata est: quorum alii partibus Bernardi favebant, alii ducebantur favore Berengarii Humroci quondam comitis filii. Sed Berengario immaturâ morte præpreto, apud Bernardum potestas Septimaniæ quam maxima remansit.—*Astronomus Vita Ludovici Pii.*

† Masdeu, (Historia Critica de España, tom. xv. Illustracion 12.) not only recognises Berengario as count of Barcelona during the four years there mentioned, but makes another count of the name of Bernardo succeed in 836. There is no foundation for the existence of the latter Bernardo.

fled; his domestics were laden with fetters, and his movable property seized. Feeling that he was unequal to contend with so powerful a prince, he forsook, or pretended to forsake, Pepin, gained the advisers of Charles, and again waited on the king. He threw himself at the royal feet: protested that he always had been, and would always remain, faithful; that the enemies of his sovereign should also be his, and offered to do battle with any one who should gainsay him. Charles believed, and pardoned him. In the wars which followed he remained neuter; but when in 843 on a new division between the two brothers, Catalonia again fell to Charles, he began to aim at independence. However cautious his proceedings, they reached the ears of his superior, who concealed his resentment, but meditated a detestable revenge. Being summoned to attend a convocation of the states at Thoulouse, he reluctantly obeyed. On entering the assembly, as he knelt to do homage, Charles seized him with the left hand, and with the right plunged a poniard into his heart.* What makes this tragedy the more striking is the common belief of the times that the victim was the father of the murderer, who is said to have kicked the body, exclaiming, " Such is thy punishment for defiling the bed of my father thy liege lord!" †

844 to 845. Wilhelm, the son of Bernardo, resolved to revenge this treacherous deed. The incursions of the Scandinavians, who now began to ravage the province of Neustria, seemed to afford him a propitious opportunity for

* Another account says, that Bernardo was arrested and legally tried. The Annales Fuldenses says, that he was unsuspectingly killed by the king.
† Eginhardus, Annales Regum Francorum, p. 272. &c. (apud Duchesne, Historiæ Francorum Scriptores Coætanei, tom. ii.). Annales Francorum Fuldenses, p. 546, &c. (in eodem tomo). Annales Bertiniani Regum Francorum, p. 184—269. (apud eundem, tom. iii.). Nithardus, De Dissensionibus Filiorum Ludovici Pii, lib. i. p. 360., lib. ii. p. 256., lib. iii. p. 371. necnon, Astronomus, Vita Ludovici Pii, p. 305, &c. (apud eundem, tom. ii.). Rodericus Toletanus, Historia Arabum, cap. 26, 27. (apud Schottum, Hispania Illustrata, tom. ii.). Zurita, Anales de Aragon, lib. i. cap. 4. &c. Diago, Historia de los victoriosissimos antiguos Condes de Barcelona, lib. ii. cap. 1 —4. Marca, Limes Hispanicus, lib. iii. c. 16. &c. necnon, Baluzius Tutelensis, lib. iv. col. 346—354. (ad calcem ejusdem operis). Condé, as spoiled by Marlés, Histoire de la Domination, &c. tom. i.
The empress Judith, accused of adultery with Bernardo, was forced into a monastery immediately after the death of Louis in 841.

his purpose. Having collected a few troops, he surprised Toulouse, where his family had doubtless many partisans; but the city being invested by Charles, he contrived to effect his escape, and to reach the court of Abderahman. The Arabian king promised to aid him in the recovery of his father's fief, on the condition of vassalage; and caused troops to be immediately collected for the purpose. At the head of his Mohammedan allies, and of such Christians as choosed to join him, he returned into Narbonensian Gaul, where his followers committed great excesses. To damp his party in Catalonia, at least, Charles intrusted the fief of Barcelona and Gothic Gaul to —

ALEDRAN, an officer of great valour, and made peace with Abderahman. But, though thus deserted by his ally and constrained to flee before the French generals, Wilhelm was not discouraged. He was still at the head of some followers, whose predatory excursions supplied him not merely with necessaries, but with wealth. With the latter, and still more with the aid of his secret creatures, in 848 he obtained possession of both Ampurias and Barcelona—by cunning, say the Annalists, rather than by force.* It appears that his presence before the town, at the head of his lawless band, was the signal for the delivery of the place: the gates were opened and the governor fled. Not satisfied with this success, he next aspired to the possession of all Catalonia. In one expedition he reduced and made prisoners two of the counts. In another, being reinforced by the troops of Abderahman, he advanced against Gerona. The governors of the frontiers collected troops and hastened to oppose him. They vanquished him, and compelled him to a hasty retreat. During his absence from the capital, the two captive counts, who had partisans in Barcelona, and who were aided by those of Aledran, formed a con-

846 to 850.

---

* " Impuriam et Barcinonam *dolo* magis quam *vi* cepit." — *Annal Bertin.*
" Isto anno (848), Wilhelmus, filius Bernardi, ducis Barcinonem urbem Hispaniæ munitissimam, cepit *per dolum,* expulso Aledranno custode illius urbis et Limotis Hispanici." — *Chronicon Fontanellense.*

spiracy against him, and stabbed him on his return to the city. The Frank domination was now re-established, and the exiled count restored to his dignity.

850 to 858. But Medran had little reason to congratulate himself on that event. First, because Narbonensian Gaul had been severed from his government to amplify the fief of the count of Toulouse; and, secondly, because in 852 the Jews betrayed the city to the Mohammedans. Having made great carnage among the Christians, and plundered the place, they consumed the greater part of it by fire and returned. We are not told why they did not retain a place so formidable by its fortifications; nor do we henceforth find any mention of the count. Whether he fell with the multitude of Christians on this occasion *, or whether he continued to hold the fief, as generally supposed, for some years longer, must remain in utter darkness. All we certainly know is, that in 858 the dignity was held by another.†

858 to 872. WIFREDO I. (or HUNFRIDO) is first mentioned as count in 858, on the occasion of a visit made by two French monks in quest of relics. From the relation of their journey we incidentally learn that he himself was not present, but that they were received with courtesy by the *viscount* (vice-count); hence we may infer that he was occupied in Gothic Gaul, probably not yet severed from the Spanish March. He, however, is mentioned as the last marquis of Gothia, his dominions north of the Pyrenees being, about 865, separated from the lordship of Barcelona, and incorporated with that of Toulouse. This division he appears to have anticipated; for, in 863, he seized by open force on Toulouse and other places, under the pretext that they belonged to the fief of Barcelona. But by Charles the Bald he was deprived of his usurpation, and thenceforth regarded with suspicion. Of this circumstance advan-

* "Interfectisque pene omnibus Christianis, et urbe vastata, impune redierunt."—*Annal. Bertin.*
† Fragmentum Chronici Fontanellensis (apud Duchesne, Historiæ Francorum Scriptores, ii. 388.). Annales Bertiniani (apud eundem, iii. 204—211.). Marca, Limes Hispanicus, lib. iii.; necnon, Baluzius, ad calcem ejusdem, lib. iv.

tage was taken by one count Salomon, a Frank, who aspired to the fief, and who was not very scrupulous about the manner in which the present possessor might be deprived of it. By his malicious representations, the king commanded Wifredo to appear at Narbonne. The count, accompanied by his son, a youth of tender years, obeyed the mandate. On reaching Narbonne, in a popular affray, a Frank had the audacity to pull him by the beard: he drew his sword and plunged it into the heart of the offender. He was immediately seized by the by-standers, was placed under arrest by the royal officers, and ordered to be conducted before the king: on the way, however, the soldiers of his escort pretended to quarrel, probably at the instigation of Salomon; and, in attempting to restore harmony between them, he received a mortal wound. As he alone fell on this occasion, his death has not been considered accidental. The king, who is said to have been affected by the catastrophe, confided his son to the care of his friend the count of Flanders, to be educated as became his birth and according to the custom of the times.*

SALOMON obtained the object of his ambition; but his government, of which no record remains, was not of long duration. The manner in which he lost both it and life, as related by the oldest authority for his actions, the anonymous monk of Ripol, has an improbable and even romantic air. As the young Wifredo who had been consigned to the care of the count of Flanders, grew in years, he became passionately fond of the count's daughter; and it soon appeared that his love was returned with more ardour than virtue. The countess discovered the situation of her daughter, but was so far moved by the tears and protestations of the delinquent as not to reveal it to the count. After some reflection, like a prudent mother, she sought an interview

872 to 884.

---

* Annales Bertiniani (apud Duchesne, Historiæ Francorum Scriptores, lii. 216, &c.). Monachus Rivipullensis, Gesta Comitum Barcionensium, cap. 1. (ad calcem Marcæ Hispanicæ, col. 539.) Lucius Marineus Siculus, De Rebus Hispaniæ, lib. ix. p. 373. (apud Schottum, Hispania Illustrata, tom. i.) Diago, Historia de los victoriosissimos Antiguos Condes de Barcelona, lib. ii. cap. 4. & 5.

with Wifredo, and required an oath from him,— an oath which he willingly took,— that if fortune ever put him in possession of his father's fief, he would make the victim of his passion his wife. She also insisted that he should leave Flanders and return to Barcelona, where his mother and kindred resided. In a mean disguise, that of a poor pilgrim, assumed to escape detection, he bade adieu to a home in which he had been so long and affectionately fostered, and journeyed on foot towards Spain. He entered Barcelona at nightfall, and hastened to his mother's house, who immediately recognised him by his hairy skin. His kindred were secretly assembled; a conspiracy was formed to restore him, and, by so doing, to revenge the death of the elder Wifredo. Hearing one day that the count was riding out through the city unattended, Wifredo, accompanied by some of his relations, hastened to the place, drew his sword and ran it through the governor's body. To the astonished crowd whom this deed assembled he declared who he was, and how he had revenged his murdered father; and, amidst the acclamations of all, was raised to the vacant dignity.

884 to 912. WIFREDO II., continues the Monk, lost no time in fulfilling the pledge he had given the countess of Flanders. He despatched an embassy to that court, acquainted his benefactor with what he had done, and demanded the hand of his promised bride. The count not only readily acquiesced, but went to the French king and represented that what his son-in-law had done was only in pursuance of a purpose commendable in that age, — revenge,— and procured not only Wifredo's pardon, but the confirmation of his dignity. Having received this unexpected intelligence, the new governor hastened to the court of Charles, to whom his manners rendered him agreeable. While there, news reached him that the Mohammedans were laying waste Catalonia. To repel them he demanded troops from the emperor; but Charles could spare none, and merely advised him to return and oppose them with all his might. Being thus disap-

pointed in the royal aid, and seeing that the whole means of resistance were to be furnished by himself alone, he is said to have required, that if, through his unaided arms, the misbelievers should be expelled from Catalonia, he and his descendants in perpetuity should enjoy the fief independent of the French sovereigns,—in other words, the uncontrolled sovereignty of the province,— and we are told that the request was granted.*

How little soever of this relation be true, it is certain that Wifredo the Warlike entirely cleared Catalonia of the infidels, and that from his time the province began to show little respect for the feudal rights claimed by the French kings. We have no details of the wars which he so successfully waged against the enemy. He is no less celebrated as the founder of the monastery of Ripol, which he is said to have erected in 888, out of gratitude to Our Lady for the happy issue of his wars. He died in 912, leaving to Miro, his eldest son, his new sovereignty, comprehending the lordships of Barcelona, Besalu, Rousillon, Gerona, Cerdaña, and Urgel, but placing over the last another of his sons, Suniario, on the condition of faith and homage to Miro. A third son professed in the monastery of Ripol, and was afterwards bishop of Urgel.†

Of MIRO, who reigned about sixteen years, history is wholly silent. In his last testament he fell into the usual impolicy of the age,—of dividing his dominions among his sons. To Seniofredo, the eldest, he left Barcelona ; to Oliva, Cerdaña ; and to Miro, the youngest, Gerona. As the three princes were too young to govern, he confided the regency of the three states to his uncle Suniario, count of Urgel.

912 to 928.

Of SENIOFREDO little more is known. He did not

---

* Some parts of the obscure relation we know to be true from contemporary authorities ; of the rest we will not attempt to separate the probable from the marvellous.

† Monachus Rivipullensis, Gesta Comitum Barcionensium, cap. ii. Marca, Limes Hispanicas, lib. iii. cap. 30. Baluzius, Marca Hispanca, col. 382. Lucius Marineus Siculus, De Rebus Hispaniæ, lib. ix. p. 374. (apud Schottum, Hisp. Illustr., tom. i.). Zurita, Anales de Aragon, lib. i. cap. 8. Diago, Historia de los Condes de Barcelona, lib. ii. cap. 6—15. — See Appendix (C).

928 to 967. assume the sovereignty until 950: perhaps the uncle was too fond of power to resign it until necessity demanded the sacrifice. He is represented as a prince of great devotion. In 963 he went on a pilgrimage to visit the tombs of the apostles Peter and Paul at Rome. In 967 he died without issue, leaving his lordship to his cousin Borello, son of Suniario, count of Urgel. The reason assigned for the exclusion of his brother Oliva is singular. The latter, we are told, had an impediment in his speech, and could not utter a word until he had first dug up the soil with his hands like a goat. Hence his surname of Capella. It is more probable that his real appellation was Cabreta, which signfies a digger, because when angry he could not articulate until he had stamped his foot on or into the ground. But this defect was not, perhaps, the cause of his exclusion: Zurita, with greater appearance of reason, though without citing any authority, assigns it to his wickedness. He continued, however, to hold Besalu and Cardeña as a fief of Barcelona.

967 to 993. BORELLO was not permitted to exercise so peaceful a sovereignty as his two immediate predecessors. The first seventeen years appear to have been passed in tranquillity, since during the whole of that period we hear of no action of his except a voyage to Rome, undertaken as much to settle the ecclesiastical government of his state as through devotion. In 984 he began to tremble at the prowess of the formidable Almansor, who appeared intent on reducing all Spain to the Mohammedan yoke. After a destructive course through the states of Leon and Castile, this great general entered Catalonia. Near Moncada he annihilated the little army of Borello; who with difficulty escaped to the mountains of Manresa. The victor now marched on Barcelona, which he speedily stormed, and demon like, not only butchered a number of the inhabitants, but destroyed by fire a great part of the town. In this vast conflagration perished the public archives and private titles. Though the count was not present to defend the

city, the preservation of which he probably considered as hopeless, he soon issued from his mountain refuge, to rescue not only it, but Catalonia from the infidel grasp. To form a considerable body of cavalry, he caused proclamation to be made, that all horsemen who aided him with lance and sword should enjoy the privileges of nobles. He also applied for aid to the king of France, promising, that, in the event of triumphing over the Arabs, he would hold his lordship as an hereditary fief of the French crown. Though Louis promised the aid solicited, we have no proof that it was granted. The privileges, however, offered by the count, soon attracted a considerable number to his standard. He now marched on Barcelona, in which Almansor had left a garrison, and which he speedily recovered. Of his subsequent actions no record remains. We only hear, in general terms, that he laboured to repair the disasters inflicted by the Mohammedans, whom he at length succeeded in expelling from the province.*

Of RAYMUNDO I., the eldest son of Borello, history is almost silent. In the tenth year of his government, Catalonia being again invaded by the misbelievers, he and his brother Ermengaudo, count of Urgel, made a noble stand against them. In 1089 both armed in behalf of the usurper Mohammed, king of Cordova, against Suleyman, the Berber chief, whom his own troops had declared king.† In a battle which took place about ten leagues from Cordova, Ermengaudo and three Catalonian bishops (of Barcelona, Vique, and Gerona,) fell mortally wounded; but, in the end, victory declared for Raymundo and his allies — a victory which placed Mohammed on a slippery throne. This campaign added to the martial fame of Raymundo, and caused his name to be held in respect by the princes who were

993 to 1017.

* Monachus Rivipullensis, Gesta Comitum Barclonensium, cap. 7. Lucius Marineus Siculus, De Rebus Hispaniæ, lib. ix. p. 375. Marca Hispanica, lib. iv. Zurita, Anales de Aragon, lib. i. cap. 10. Diago, Historia de los victoriosissimos antiguos Condes de Barcelona, lib. ii. cap. 19—25. Condé, by Marlés, Histoire de la Domination, &c. tom. ii. p. 47. &c. See also Vol. I. of this history, reign of Hixem II.
† See Vol. I. p. 302.

now fiercely contending for the fragments of the ruined empire of Abderahman. He died in 1017.

1017 to 1035. BERENGARIO I. is still more summarily dismissed by the meagre chroniclers of the province. By the monk of Ripol he is characterised as one who performed nothing worthy of mention, and who was every way inferior to his father.* He died in 1035.

1035 to 1076. RAYMUNDO II. was a prince of much more vigour than his father. His victories over the Moorish king of Saragossa made his name renowned throughout all Spain. By the same monk of Ripol, twelve Mohammedan kings are said to have been tributary to him. Though this is an exaggeration, yet in those days when a Mohammedan ruler of every city styled himself king, it is less outrageous than might at first view be imagined. The districts which he conquered he divided among his barons and knights, to be held by the usual feudal tenure. He was the first sovereign of all Catalonia. Nor is he less celebrated for his abolition of the old Gothic laws, which had hitherto governed the province, and for substituting others which are called the *Usages of Catalonia;* and the observance of which he rendered obligatory on all the counts and viscounts subject to his jurisdiction.

993 to 1017. But the sovereignty of Raymundo was not confined to Catalonia or his conquests in Aragon: he obtained considerable possessions beyond the Pyrenees, through his marriage with Almodis, daughter of the count de la Marche Limosine. In 1070, Rengarde, countess of Carcassonne, and sister of Almodis, sold to Raymundo, to his countess, and their son Raymundo Berengario, all her rights over and interest in the lordships of Conflans, Comenge, Carcassonne, Narbonne, Minerve, and Toulouse; and that of Razés was soon added. Two of them, Carcassonne and Razés, Raymundo soon granted, as a convertible fief, to the viscount de Beziers; who in return sold him the seignorial rights which the latter possessed, or might possess, in certain of those lord-

---

* "Nihilique ibi boni gessit; immo in omni vita sua parentelæ probitate fuit inferior."— *Gesta Comit. Barcion.*, cap. 9.

ships. The sovereignty of Carcassonne was conferred on his son Raymundo, who assumed the title of count. The young prince became exceedingly popular among his new subjects, who flocked to his standard whenever his state was invaded by the count de Foix who, in virtue of a relationship with the ancient house of Carcassonne, laid claim to the rights which Rengarde had sold. Though not the oldest, Raymundo was the best beloved son of the count of Barcelona, and the destined heir to that sovereignty. For his favour he was as much indebted to his own qualities, which are represented as excellent, as to his being the only-son of Almodis. — Raymundo II. died in 1077, during the festivities consequent on the marriage of his favourite son with a daughter of Robert Guiscard, count of Apulia. In his last will he left, we are told, the joint sovereignty of his states in Spain to two of his sons (the third had the lordship of Toulouse), Berengario, and Raymundo: but the former only is acknowledged by the monk of Ripol.*

RAYMUNDO III., surnamed the Hairy, had scarcely grasped the reins of government, when he was exposed to the intrigues of his elder brother, Berengario, who could not tamely witness his own exclusion from the rights of primogeniture. The two brothers soon regarded each other as enemies; the efforts of some courtly reptiles added to their animosity; and though Raymundo, in the hope of procuring peace, abandoned to Berengario the tribute paid by the Moorish king of Saragossa, deadly hatred took possession of the latter. Open hostilities appear to have been averted through the friendly interference of the pope, who despatched a legate for the purpose. In 1081 the princes

1076 to 1082.

* Monachus Rivipullensis, Gesta Comitum Barcionensium, cap. xi. Lucius Marineus Siculus, De Rebus Hispaniæ, lib. ix. p. 376. (apud Schottum, Hispania Illustrata, tom. i.). Baluzius, Marca Hispanica, lib. iv. passim. Zurita, Anales de Aragon, lib. i. cap. 16. 20. Diago, Historia de los victoriosissimos Antiguos Condes de Barcelona, lib. ii. cap. 25—65. Bouges, Histoire Ecclésiastique et Civile de la Ville et du Diocèse de Carcassonne, partie i. p. 88, &c.
This powerful sovereign is the one whom, by the fabulous chronicle of the Cid, Ruydias is made so frequently to humble. See Appendix (H), in Vol. II.

were induced to give hostages to each other for the preservation of outward peace. But the hopes of the Catalonians, that their princes would combine in the meditated war against the Mohammedans, were disappointed by the tragical death of Raymundo, who was assassinated between Barcelona and Gerona,—no doubt at the instigation of Berengario.* The fratricide in vain endeavoured to grasp the fruit of his crime. After a long struggle, being expelled from Catalonia by the barons and prelates, who espoused the interests of the infant son of Raymundo, and stung by intolerable remorse, he departed on a pilgrimage for the Holy Land, and died in Jerusalem, or on his return.†

1082 to 1111. Of Raymundo IV., prior to his reaching his majority, we hear nothing, until the rebellion of a vassal, the viscount de Carcassonne, brings him into notice. Bernard Atto, viscount de Beziers, and on the maternal side descended from the house of Carcassonne, seeing the troubles in Catalonia consequent on the murder of Raymundo III., resolved to profit by them. Arriving in Carcassonne, he offered to the inhabitants to defend them against the usurper Berengario, and all other enemies, and to hold the lordship as the liege vassal of young Raymundo, until that prince reached an age fit to govern. The offer was accepted; and Bernard swore on the holy gospel to resign the trust on the majority of the lawful heir. By the council of Barcelona he was confirmed in the temporary possession of the fief. His administration was onerous; to carry on the war with the count de Foix, who aspired to the dignity he held, and who, in 1090, inflicted on him a disastrous defeat,

---

* Baluzius (Marca Hispanica, lib. lv.), Diago (Historia de los Condes de Barcelona lib. ii. cap. 70.), and Ferreras (Hist. Générale, 111—253.), contend that Raymundo was not murdered by Berengario, and that his assassins were unknown. They found their statement on a pasage of Malaterra (Rerum Gestarum Rober'l Guiscardi, &c., lib. iii.), which states that the surname of Raymundo (caput stupæ,) arose from the many wounds he received on the head. We follow the monk of Ripol, a Catalonian, and, therefore, likely to be much better informed than the Sicilian.

† Bouges (Histoire de Carcassonne, p. 94.) says, that Berengario was condemned to lose both eyes and tongue, and that the sentence was executed prior to his expulsion from Catalonia.

he loaded the people with exactions. These seem to have been borne with patience, in the hope that they would be ended in a few years. But Bernard had no intention of resigning his usurped power; and when summoned, in 1104, by Raymundo, who had assumed the reins of government, to fulfil his pledge, he flatly refused. The indignant inhabitants—indignant as well through his mal-administration, as from affection to the memory of Raymundo III.—sent a deputation to Barcelona to do homage to the new count, as their only lawful sovereign. They did more: they took up arms, and expelled him. To resume the lordship, he solicited and obtained the aid of the count de Toulouse, whose vassal he offered to become. Carcassonne was soon invested; but the inhabitants having received some succours from count Raymundo, resolved to hold out. After a siege of some months, however, being discouraged, alike by the loss of their best defenders, the want of provisions, and by the non-arrival of reinforcements from Barcelona, they consented, in 1110, to admit Bernard, on condition of his swearing to respect their privileges. But the cruelties inflicted on them by Roger, the son of Bernard, who, probably in his father's absence, threw into prison, or tortured, or mangled, such as had been most conspicuous in the defence, again compelled them to lay their grievances before Raymundo. The wars of this prince with the Mohammedans had hitherto prevented him from hastening to the aid of his oppressed vassals; but, in 1111, he put his troops into motion, passed the Pyrenees, and marched on Carcassonne. Bernard prepared for an obstinate defence. The city had again the prospect of a harassing siege, when the nobles and prelates of the lordship proposed terms of accommodation, to which both parties turned a favourable ear. Bernard agreed to hold the country as a fief of Barcelona, and to aid Raymundo in all his wars as became a good vassal.

The people, however, continued to be dissatisfied with the successful viscount, whose exactions pressed heavily upon them; and their complaints to his superior of Barcelona were both loud and frequent. Having once interfered without effect, the latter left them and their governor to settle the disputes between themselves. Again did they expel him from the capital; again did he return with troops and invest it. This time the siege continued three years; a fact sufficiently indicative of their deep-rooted hostility to him: nor even, when reduced to extremities, would they consent to surrender the place until they had obtained certain conditions, of which the observance was guaranteed by the count of Barcelona.

1108 to 1117. During this rebellion of Bernard, Raymundo had experienced no slight vexation from the Mohammedan arms. In 1108, they laid waste most part of Catalonia, and forced him, we are told, but on authority somewhat disputable, to solicit the aid of the French king. However this be, it is certain that he succeeded in clearing the province of the misbelievers. His power daily increased. In 1111 the lordship of Besalu devolved to him by inheritance; in 1112 he married the only daughter and heiress of Gilbert count of Provence, to whose estates he soon succeeded *; in 1117, the fief of Cerdaña reverted to him by the death of the hereditary owner without heirs. But for much of his prosperity he was no less indebted to his arms than to his good fortune. In 1116 he hired a fleet for the conquest of Majorca, on which he embarked a considerable body of troops, furnished him by his vassals both of Catalonia and southern France. This fleet was chiefly supported by the maritime states of Pisa and Genoa, at the request of pope Pascal II. Of all the exploits of Raymundo, this was the most useful; as the Balearic Isles, ever since the decline of the kingdom of Cordova, had been the retreat of Mohammedan pirates, whose extirpation both policy and humanity demanded. The expedition was crowned with complete success; though that success was stained by

* According to Pere Tomich, and Lucius Marineus Siculus, Raymundo received the fief of Provence as the reward of his chivalry in behalf of an empress. See Appendix D.

the indiscriminate carnage made of the inhabitants, — of women and children, and the aged as well as the armed men. This conquest, however, was not enduring.

Raymundo died in 1131. In his last illness he assumed the habit of the Templars. He left two sons; Raymundo, who succeeded him in Catalonia, and Berengario, who inherited Provence.[*]

RAYMUNDO V., was a prince well fitted to tread in the steps of his father. He wisely preserved a good understanding with Alfonso the emperor, who had married his sister, and whom he acknowledged as his liege lord; and still more wisely did he solicit the hand of doña Petronilla, daughter and heiress of Ramiro the Monk, king of Aragon. At first, indeed, Ramiro was more inclined to bestow the princess on the eldest son of Alfonso, and thereby lay a foundation for the union of the two crowns; but the Aragonese opposed their union with Castile and Leon, — in other words, their extinction as a nation, — and declared for the count of Barcelona, whose valour was already well known in Spain. The king was easily induced to approve the match; in 1137 it was arranged at Balbastro, in an assembly of the states. Raymundo was there affianced with the princess, and declared heir to the throne, if even she died before arriving at a marriageable age. Ever jealous of their national honour, the Aragonese stipulated that the name of their country should, in the public documents, precede that of Barcelona; that Raymundo should be styled, not king, but prince of Aragon and count of Barcelona; that when he advanced to battle, the standard should be intrusted to a knight of their own nation. In the same

1131 to 1137.

---

[*] Monachus Rivipullensis, Gesta Comitum Barcionensium, cap. xv. xvi. Baluzius Tutelensis, Marca Hispanica, lib. iv. (sub propriis annis.) Chronicon Barcionense, col. 754. (apud eundem). Lucius Marineus Siculus, De Rebus Hispanica, lib. ix. p. 367. (apud Schottum, Hispania Illustrata, tom. 1.) Bouges, Histoire Ecclésiastique et Civile de Carcassonne, p. 180, &c. Chronicon Fossæ Novæ, p. 67. (apud Carusium, Bibliotheca Historica Regni Siciliæ, tom. i.). Zurita, Anales de Aragon, lib. i. Malaterra, Rerum Gestarum Roberti Guiscardi, lib. iii. (apud Carusium, tom. ii. necnon, apud Schottum, tom. iii.). Diago, Historia de los Condes de Barcelona, lib. ii. cap. 69—113.

The Spanish historians are ill acquainted with the transactions of Raymundo in France.

assembly, Ramiro resigned the royal dignity in favour of his son-in-law, and retired to the cloister. From this moment until his death, Raymundo governed Aragon with supreme authority, and Catalonia became inseparably united with that kingdom, or rather merged in it. His administration and warlike exploits will be found in the next chapter.*

CHAP. IV.

ARAGON.

1035—1516.

THE origin and early history of Aragon being the same with that of Navarre †, on which it was long dependent, need not be investigated here. The statements of writers who contend for the fabulous kingdom of Sobrarve, the root of both sovereignties; of those who assign the origin of both to Garcia Ximenes, in 716, or of Aragon, in the ninth century, to the Navarrese Iñigo Arista, are not worth the trouble of refutation, since they rest on wholly monastic documents known to be apocryphal. The reasoning of such writers is about equal to the authority they adduce. The founders of Fortaleza de Panno, says the abbot Briz Martinez, were in number 200; the electors of Garcia Ximenes 300; and those of Iñigo Arista 600. What follows proves the Pythagorean virtue of numbers. The city built by the 200 fell, because 2 is a pèrfidious number, fatal to *unity*. But the election of Garcia could not fail to have a prosperous issue; for what number is more mighty than 3? If, however, 3 be excellent, 6 must be *doubly* so, as containing a two-

* The same authorities.
† See the history of that kingdom in chapter ii. of the present volume.

fold portion of the same virtue! The series of counts, beginning with Aznar or Asinarius, is not less fabulous than that of the kings. Undoubtedly there were local governors with that title at an early period, who, prior to the establishment of the Navarrese monarchy, were dependent either on the Asturian kings, or on the Mohammedans of Aragon. Whether they were natives or Arabians, Christians or Mussulmans, can never be determined.

Nothing can better expose the provincial vanity of the writers who advocate the ancient monarchy of this region, than its insignificant dimensions. In the time of Sancho el Mayor, the lordship of Aragon formed only an inconsiderable angle of the present country of that name, comprising the north-western extremity, and bounded by a line drawn from the Pyrenees above Jaca, passing somewhat west of that city by San Juan de la Peña, and diverging westwards to the Val de Anso, near the banks of the river Aragon. It comprehended the most eastern portion of territory inhabited by the ancient Vascones, and this reason gives some countenance to the hypothesis that it followed the fate of Vasconia; — that from the reign of Alfonso I. it obeyed the Asturian kings. Notwithstanding the contiguity of the inhabitants to the Mohammedan possessions of Jaca, Huesca, and Saragossa, their position amidst the fastnesses of the Pyrenees might secure them against the attacks of the misbelievers. However this be, certain it is that the date of Aragonese independence must be assigned to 1035, the period when Sancho el Mayor divided his states among his sons; and when, as before related, Aragon fell to Ramiro.*

---

* See the reign of Sancho el Mayor in the history of Navarre. See also, Anales Toledanos, p. 384. (apud Florez, España Sagrada, tom. xxiii.) Monachus Silensis, p. 312. &c. (apud eundem, tom. xiv.). Monachus Rivipullensis, cap. 19. (ad calcem Marcæ, Limes Hispanicus, vol. 548.). Ximenes, De Rebus Hispaniæ, lib. v. cap. 26 (apud Schottum, Hispania Illustrata, tom. ii.) Moret, Anales de Navara, tom. i. lib. xi. Zurita, Anales de Aragon, lib. i. cap. 14. Briz Martinez, Historia de la Fundacion y, Antiguedades de San Juan de la Peña, y de los Reyes de Sobrarbe, Aragon, y Navarra, lib. i. cap. i. Lucius Marineus Siculus, De Rebus Hispaniæ, lib. viii. (apud Schottum, tom. i.) Blancas, Rerum Aragonensium Commentarii, in variis locis (apud eundem, tom. iii.). Masdeu, Historia Critica de España, tom. xii. (sub propriis annis) et tom. xv. Illustracion 8.

1035 to 1063.   RAMIRO I. was no sooner in possession of the throne than, in concert with the Moorish kings of Saragossa, Tudela and Huesca, he invaded the dominions of his brother Garcia, then absent on a pilgrimage to Rome. While pressing the siege of Tafalla, the royal devotee returned, vanquished, and expelled him from his new conquests. During Garcia's life, the war was as frequently renewed; but its progress was desultory, and its issue indecisive. Not so Ramiro's wars with the Mohammedans, which, though scarcely mentioned by writers nearly contemporary, must have been successful, since he extended his sway along the southern base of the Pyrenees, over the lordships of Sobrarbe, Ribagorza, and a great part of Pallas. The kings, too, of Tudela, Saragossa, and Lerida, were his tributaries: we are even told that he compelled the second of these hereditary governors to receive a Christian bishop into that city. His authority over the two first is apparent from the acts of the council, which, in 1060, he convoked at Jaca. But scarcely had the ecclesiastics separated, when Sancho of Castile appeared before Saragossa with a numerous army, and forced the Mohammedans to do him homage, on the ground that his father, Fernando, had been recognised as lord paramount over that state. Highly indignant at this irruption, Ramiro, who was then pressing the siege of Grado in Ribagorza, advanced against the invader: in the battle which ensued he was vanquished and slain. This tragical event happened in the year 1063, in the month of May.*

1063 to 1076.   SANCHO I. (RAMIREZ) was no less successful than his father in warring against the Mohammedans; who, after

* Monachus Silensis Chronicon (in regno Santii ii.), necnon Anales Toledanus, p. 384 (apud Florez, España Sagrada, tom. xvii. et xxiii.). Rodericus Toletanus, De Rebus Hispanicis, necnon Lucas Tudensis, Chronicon Mundi, sub propriis regnis (apud Schottum, Hispania Illustrata, tom. ii. et iv.). Lucius Marineus Siculus, De Rebus Hispaniæ, lib. viii. p. 366., necnon Blancas, Rerum Aragonensium Commentarii, p. 623. (apud eundem tom. i. et iii.). Monachus Rivipullensis, cap. 19. (ad calcem Marcæ, Limes Hispanicus, col. 548.). Zurita, Anales de Aragon, lib. i. cap. 17. et 18. Moret, Anales de Navarra, tom. i. lib. xii. &c.

Notwithstanding the statements of the Aragonese writers to the contrary, it does not appear that the successor of Ramiro took any means to avenge his death on the Castilian king.

the catastrophe just related, had fortified Huesca and Balbastro, and set their Christian masters at defiance. Having joined his forces with those of Ermengaudo count of Urgel, he invested Balbastro. Though during the siege he lost this courageous ally, and though the Mohammedan kings sent powerful detachments to relieve it, in 1065 he forced the place to surrender, and converted it into a bishop's see. To protect his kingdom against the incursions of his natural enemy, he erected several fortresses along the southern frontier; and, by his subsequent irruptions into the hostile territory, inflicted great injury on the Mohammedans. It was doubtless owing as much to his military fame as to the contiguity of his state, that, on the tragical death of Sancho III. of Navarre, in 1076, he was elected king of that country. His proclamation at Pamplona, and his subsequent war with his competitor the king of Leon and Castile, have been related in a former chapter.*

During the following years of his reign, don Sancho steadily pursued his great object, — the extension of his boundary at the expense of the misbelievers. To defray the expenses of his continual wars, he at length laid hands on the revenues of the church, convinced that they could not be better employed than in so pious a use. But not all the valour he had so often exhibited, nor the religious foundations he had erected, nor the devotion with which he had removed the relics of St. Indaletius from Almeria to the monastery of San Juan de la Peña, could atone with the ecclesiastics of his kingdom for his present sacrilege. He encountered so much opposition, that he was glad not only to forego his pretensions, but to escape the thunders of the church by submitting to public penance before the high altar in the cathedral of Roda. To efface the remembrance of his reputed crime, he resolved to exhibit more zeal than ever in the cause of Christianity. Having reduced, one by one, the Mohammedan fortresses, between the Pyrenees and the Cinca, in 1089 he invested Monzon; a place strong

1076 to 1094.

* See the History of Navarre.

alike by nature and art, and situated on the eastern bank of that river. After a siege of some weeks it fell into his power. His next exploit was the reduction of several towns belonging to the Moorish king of Huesca. He carried his triumphant standards to the Ebro, on the northern banks of which he fortified Castellar, as a position whence future operations might be undertaken against the king of Saragossa, the most powerful of the rulers of Aragon. Huesca itself, being now the only considerable city from the Pyrenees to the Ebro, and from Navarre to the Cinca, which defied his power, in 1094 he invested that formidable place. The siege was pressed with vigour; but one day having approached too near the walls with the view of reconnoitring, while raising his hand to show a point where the assault might be made, he was mortally wounded by an arrow in his right side, which the action exposed. Being carried to his tent, he exacted an oath from his two sons, Pedro and Alfonso, that they would not raise the siege, but remain before the place until it capitulated or was taken by storm. Having received the necessary sacraments, he himself drew the arrow from the wound and breathed his last.

1094 to 1104. PEDRO I., the eldest son of the deceased king, was immediately proclaimed in the camp. According to Rodrigo of Toledo the siege was continued without intermission, and the place reduced in six months. That the city continued to be invested is not improbable; but ancient writers agree in deferring its capitulation two years, until 1096. As Abderahman, the Moorish king of Huesca, obtained promises of aid both from the neighbouring king of Saragossa and from king Alfonso of Leon and Castile, Pedro appears to have left his troops before the place and hurried over his dominions to press the march of reinforcements. On his return with a considerable force, he had reason to congratulate himself on his precaution: the king of Saragossa, at the head of a great army, and the Christian count of Najera, Alfonso's vassal, with a brave body of Castilians, were in motion. On the eve of the battle, the Christian count is said to have entreated him to retire from the city, as resistance to such a force was hopeless. But he boldly advanced to the attack, which on both sides was impetuous, and which raged during many hours, — until the count of Najera was taken prisoner, perhaps also till night separated the combatants. But though the Moors retired in order to their tents, and though the troops of king don Pedro remained under arms the whole of the night, in the expectation of a new attack, the former had suffered too severely to risk another field. Under cover of the darkness, they fled with precipitation. The number of slain was prodigious: the following morning it was increased by a hot pursuit, which was continued as far as Almudevar. This great battle was fought in November, 1096, in the plain of Alcoraz, not far from Huesca.* It was followed by the surrender of that important city, and, consequently, by the destruction of the Mohammedan power between the Ebro, the Cinca, and the Pyrenees. Some fortresses they still possessed east of that river; but they had no longer the means of combined defence.—The victor died in 1104.†

ALFONSO I., brother of the deceased Pedro, who now succeeded to the thrones of Aragon and Navarre, was of a genius even more military than his predecessors.

1104 to 1118.

---

* Zurita (1 — 32) quotes the history of San Juan de la Peña to show that in this great battle St. George performed the same service to Aragon as Santiago had done for Castile. He appeared on horseback, having behind him, *en croupe*, a German knight, who was occupied that very day in the siege of Antioch. En memoria desta tan grande y señalada vitoria mando el Rey edificar en aquel mismo lugar una iglesia a honra y gloria de San Jorge, patron de la cavalleria Christiana: y escriven los autores modernos que entonces tomo el Rey por sus armas y devisas la Cruz de San Jorge en campo de plata, y en los quadros del escudo quatro cabeças roscas, por quatro reyes y principales caudillos que en esta batalla murieron.

† Rodericus Toletanus, De Rebus Hispanicis, lib. vi. cap. 1. (apud Schottum, Hispania Illustrata, tom. ii.). Annales Compostellani, p. 320. (apud Florez, España Sagrada, tom. xxiii.). Annales Toledanos, p. 385. (in eodem tomo). Annales Complutenses, p. 314. (in eodem tomo). Monachus Rivipullensis cap. 19. (ad calcem Marcæ, Limes Hispanicus). Lucius Marineus Siculus, De Rebus Hispaniæ, lib. viii. p. 367. (apud Schottum, tom. i.). Zurita, Anales de Aragon, tom. i. lib. i. cap. 18 — 36. Blancas, Rerum Aragonesium Commentarii, p. 630. (apud Schottum, tom. iii.). Abu Abdalla, Vestis Acu Picta (apud Casiri, Bibliotheca Arab. Hisp. ii.—219.). Condé, by Marlés, Histoire de la Domination, &c. tom. ii.

Unfortunately for the interests of his kingdom and of his own fame, his marriage with an unprincipled woman, Urraca, daughter of Alfonso of Leon and Castile, and the dissensions to which that marriage gave rise, long averted the destruction of his misbelieving enemies.*

Alfonso began his career of conquest by the reduction of such places north of the Ebro as were still occupied by the Mohammedans. How long he was engaged in this preparatory warfare, — whether it was conducted by his generals during his unfortunate wars in Castile and Leon, or by himself, during the intervals of those wars, — cannot be determined. All that we certainly know is, that in 1114 he passed the Ebro and laid siege to Saragossa. Convinced that the fall of this place would but occasion their own, the Mohammedans of Tudela armed, harassed the camp of Alfonso, intercepted his provisions, and always fled when any considerable force was drawn out to oppose them. A council of war was held, and, in pursuance of its deliberations, a division of the army sent to surprise Tudela. The general intrusted with this enterprise executed it with success. Arriving in the adjoining mountains, he despatched a small body of his cavalry to draw the enemy from the place, while he himself, with his chief force, remained in ambush. The Moors issued forth, the horsemen fled as if in a panic fear; and, when both pursuers and fugitives were out of sight, the main body advanced towards the walls, broke open the gates, and gained possession of the place. When the Mohammedans returned from the pursuit, they had no alternative but submission. It appears that Alfonso was satisfied for the present with the advantage thus gained, since Saragossa did not capitulate until 1118, and since a siege of four years is improbable. We have before related how he had previously defeated and slain the enterprising Abu Giafar, king of Saragossa, and how Abdelmelic, surnamed Amad Dola, the son and successor

* See Vol. II. page 161, &c.

of that prince, had done him homage for that kingdom.* But its entire destruction was resolved. If Alfonso thus suspended the great object he had so long in view, he did so only to attain it by surer means. While pursuing his conquests around the capital, and circumscribing the dominions of the Mohammedan king to the walls of that city, he was also collecting troops from Bearne and Gascony, as well as from his own states. Having routed and slain Mezdeli, the wali of Granada, and defeated the generals of the Almoravides, among whom was Temim, brother of the emperor Ali †, in the spring of 1118 he vigorously assailed Sarragossa; but it was valiantly defended, and the assaults were repulsed with some loss. The French allies, hopeless of its reduction, and, consequently, of the plunder they coveted, abruptly returned home. Though weakened by this dishonourable desertion, he no less persevered, declaring that he would not remove until the city was his. In consternation at the evident firmness of his purpose, the besieged implored the aid of their brethren of Tortosa, Valencia, and even Andalusia. In vain: he prevented the arrival of reinforcements, and at length compelled the city to surrender. The following year he made it the capital of his kingdom.

This great hero was far from being satisfied with these important successes. In 1120 he overthrew, near Daroca, an amazing force of the Almoravides, leaving 20,000 dead on the field. The same year he reduced Taragona, and many other fortresses in its neighbourhood; he next obtained Calatayud, one of the most important cities south of the Ebro. Its fall, as well as the terror of his recent victory, occasioned the surrender of all the fortified places on the banks of the Xalon, among which was Daroca. Almost every year continued to witness his success. Though he assailed Lerida in vain, or perhaps spared the city in consideration of a tribute, he made destructive irruptions into Valencia, and even

1119 to 1130.

* See page 23. of Vol. II. † See pp. 24. and 32. of Vol. II.

into Andalusia. In the latter province he was joined by 10,000 Christian families, whose ancestors had remained under the Mohammedan yoke ever since the invasion by Tarik, and who were anxious—doubtless through fear of the consequences that might follow the discovery of their secret correspondence with him—to settle in his dominions. He placed them in the conquests which he had won from the Moors. In 1128 he obtained another glorious victory over his enemy on the confines of Valencia. But though these victories were thus signal, and redounded to the glory of the Christian name; though these irruptions were always recompensed by ample booty, from 1124 to 1134 he made few conquests. His hostilities appear to have been too rapid to have any permanent effect. At times, indeed, his attention was so much distracted by the affairs of Leon*, that he must have intrusted the conduct of these wars to his generals. In 1130, too, he passed the Pyrenees from Navarre and assailed Bourdeaux; which, after a long siege, he reduced. His motive for this act of hostility was probably to punish the injuries inflicted by the duke of Aquitaine on the count of Bigorre, and his other allies in the south of France. His absence encouraged the Mohammedans of Lerida, Tortosa, and Valencia to harass his frontiers: they even defeated two of his generals.

1131 to 1134. On his return, the following year, he prepared for new campaigns. In 1133 he invested and obtained Mequinencia, an important Moorish fortress on the confines of Catalonia, and on the banks of the Ebro. He next laid siege to Fraga, situated on the Cinca, a few leagues from Mequinencia. The place was well defended, both by art and the valour of the inhabitants. Aben Gama, governor of Valencia, endeavoured to dislodge the besiegers, but was repulsed with heavy loss. The inhabitants now proposed terms of capitulation; which Alfonso, incensed at their resistance, indignantly rejected. Despair urged them to new efforts. Owing

* See the reigns of Urraca and her son Alfonso VIII. in Vol. II.

to their pressing solicitations, Aben Gama, having received from Africa a reinforcement of 10,000 Almoravides, and collected all that could bear arms in his own state, again advanced to relieve Fraga. Though the Christian king had despatched a strong body of his cavalry in search of provisions, and though he was greatly inferior in numbers, he did not hesitate to accept the engagement. It was long and desperately continued; but in the end the Christians were completely defeated: thousands of the Aragonese lay extended on the plain. Whether the king himself fell on this day, as is affirmed by three ancient authorities, or whether, as we are informed by another and a contemporary, he fled to the monastery of San Juan de la Peña, where grief in a few days put a period to his life, is doubtful.* After the battle the Moors ravaged the surrounding country.

Thus fell the conqueror of Tudela, Saragossa, Tarragona, Calatayud, Daroca, Mequinencia, and most of the country south of the Ebro—the victor in many battles, who, from his warlike habits, was surnamed *el Batallador*; and, from the extent of his sway while king of Leon and Castile, *el Emperador*. Spain cannot boast of a more valiant prince: he was the first, since the conquest by the Arabs, who carried the Christian ensigns into Andalusia. He is also praised for his devotion; but, if some of the Castilian chroniclers are to be believed, during his wars with Urraca and the young Alfonso he committed many atrocities. †

1134.

---

* The Monk of Ripol, Archbishop Rodrigo, and the anonymous writer of the Anales Toledanos I., say that he fell on the field; the author of the Chronicle of Alfonso the Emperor, that he died in the monastery.

We know not on what authority Zurita makes him escape from the battle, and fall, some time afterwards, while attempting, with only 400 horsemen, to repel an inroad of the Moors. It seems to be little preferable to that which sends him, through pure vexation at his defeat, on a pilgrimage to the Holy Land, which makes him return after the lapse of many years, and gives him a more disgraceful death than would have happened to him on the battle field.

† Chronica Adefonsi Imperatoris, p. 321. 342. (apud Florez, España Sagrada, tom. xxi.). Monachus Rivipullensis, cap. 20. (ad calcem Marcæ, Limes Hispanicus, col. 549.). Anales Toledenos i. p. 387, 388. (apud Florez, tom. xxiii.). Chronicon Burgense, p. 309. (in eodem tomo). Annales Compostellani, p. 321. (in eodem). Anales Complutenses, p. 314. (in eodem). Rodericus Toletanus, De Rebus Hispanicis, lib. vii. cap. 1. 3. (apud Schottum, Hispania Illustrata, tom. ii.). Lucas Tudensis, Chronicon Mundi, p. 103. (apud eun-

In his last will, made some time previous to his death, Alfonso, who had no issue, had bequeathed his dominions to two military orders, — to the knights of St. John at Jerusalem, and to the Templars. But neither Navarre nor Aragon paid the least attention to this disposition. The nobles of both kingdoms having met to choose a common sovereign, unfortunately disagreed in the choice, and separated: at length the Aragonese elected the brother of their deceased king, Ramiro the Monk, whom they married to a princess of Aquitaine; while the Navarrese, no less desirous to restore their royal house, elected Garcia Ramirez.*

1134 to 1137. RAMIRO II. was no sooner in possession of the throne than he was visited by Alfonso of Leon, whose dubious conduct was well calculated to alarm him.† Being at length rid of this dangerous ally, he laid claim to Navarre, on the pretence that it had long formed part of the same kingdom, and could not be dismembered; and Garcia no less actively armed to assert his right to Aragon. A reconciliation being effected in the manner before related ‡, both kings were at liberty to pursue other objects. Garcia seems to have hoped, that as his rival was old, he should succeed, in default of heirs, to the sister kingdom; but before the expiration of the year the queen of Aragon was delivered of the princess Petronilla. It was probably through disgust with the never-ceasing pretensions of Garcia, as well as from conscience which stung him for breaking his vows, that, in the third year of his reign, he resolved to marry his infant daughter, resign his dignity to his son-in-law, and return to the cloister. The choice, as related in the

---

dem tom. iv.). Lucius Marineus Siculus, De Rebus Hispaniæ, lib. viii. p. 368. (apud eundem tom. i.). Zurita, Anales de Aragon, lib. i. cap. 36. 52. Moret, Anales de Navarra, lib. xv. cap. 1. 4. et lib. xvii. cap. 1. 9. Blancas, Rerum Aragonensium Commentarii, p. 630. 644. (apud Schottum, tom. iii.). To these Christian authorities must be added Abu Abdalla, Vestis Acu Picta, sive Regum Almoravitarum Series, necnon Reges Almohaditæ (apud Casiri, Bibliotheca Arab. Hisp. ii. 216. &c.) Condé, by Marlés, Histoire de la Domination, etc. tom. ii.

* See the History of Navarre in chapter II. of the present volume.
† See the reign of Alfonso VIII. in Vol. II. section II. Chap. I.
‡ See the corresponding period in the History of Navarre.

last chapter, fell on Raymundo count of Barcelona, who, under the title of Prince of Aragon, entered on the supreme government of the kingdom. Whether Ramiro continued to be styled king until his death, in 1157, is doubtful; but that his daughter is frequently styled *sovereign*, and that Raymundo *never* assumed the regal title, are clear from ancient documents.

PETRONILLA. In 1140 the grand master of the Templars arrived in Spain, to claim the kingdom in virtue of the testament made by king Alfonso. The modesty of the demand roused the wrath of the people. As, however, the chief nobles of Aragon had sworn to enforce its observance, and as the poor grand master had undertaken a long and perilous voyage to vindicate the rights of the order, he and Raymundo at length agreed that the absurd claim should be abandoned, and that, in lieu of it, the knights should receive ample domains in Aragon, on the tenure of military service against the misbelievers. For this purpose a college, with a prior at its head, was established in the kingdom, having commanderies in four or five great towns; and the jurisdiction of all other places which might be recovered by its arms from the common enemy, was guaranteed to the order. 1137 to 1140.

As Raymundo was brother-in-law to Alfonso, he had little difficulty in obtaining from that emperor the restitution of some places in Aragon still held by the Castilian troops, under the condition, however, of homage. Like Ramiro, he also aspired to the incorporation of Navarre with his kingdom, but without success. Finding that his own force was insufficient to contend with so warlike a prince as don Garcia, he entered into an alliance with the emperor Alfonso, the iniquitous object of which was a partition of the Navarrese dominions. But while Alfonso was investing Pamplona, Raymundo, in 1140, was signally defeated by the Navarrese king. In his hostile irruptions, during the following years, he was equally unsuccessful. In 1146, through the interference of the emperor Alfonso, both princes agreed to suspend their 1140 to 1153.

quarrels, and aid their ally of Leon and Castile in warring against the Mohammedans. All three were present at the siege and reduction of Baëza and Almeria. These important conquests, which were the right of Alfonso, appear to have excited the emulation of Raymundo. The following year he invested and took the important city of Tortosa: for the success of this enterprise he was considerably indebted to his new subjects, the Templars, and to the Genoese fleet, which had assisted in the capture of Almeria. Next Lerida and Fraga, which had withstood the assaults of Alfonso I., yielded to the prince of Aragon. Finally, in 1153, he had the glory to free all Catalonia from the Mohammedans.

1162. In 1162 Raymundo went to Turin, to do homage in person for Provence, which he had received as a fief from the emperor Frederic Barbarossa. But death surprised him within a few leagues of that city. His administration was fortunate for Aragon, the interests of which he zealously advanced. In his last will he left both it and the lordship of Barcelona to his eldest son Alfonso; to his second son, Pedro, the lordship of Cerdaña and Narbonensian Gaul. No sooner did intelligence of his death reach Saragossa, than the queen Petronilla assembled the states of Aragon and Catalonia at Huesca, where the testamentary dispositions were confirmed. In 1163 she resigned her regal title to her son, though she lived until 1173.*

1163 to 1196. ALFONSO II. took possession of the government at a tender age, for which reason the three first years of his reign are barren of events. In 1167, on the death of his cousin, the count of Provence, to whom his father

* Chronica Adefonsi Imperatoris, passim (apud Florez, España Sagrada, tom. xxi.). Anales Toledanos, l. p.389. (apud eundem tom. xxii.). Anales Toledanos, ii. p. 404. (apud eundem eodemque tomo). Monachus Rivipullensis, Gesta Comitum Barcionensium, cap. 21. (ad calcem Marcæ, Limes Hispanicus, vol. 249.). Rodericus Toletanus, De Rebus Hispanicis, lib. vii. cap. ii. (apud Schottum, Hispania Illustrata, tom. ii.). Lucas Tudensis, Chronicon Mundi, p. 104. &c. (apud eundem tom. iv.). Lucius Marineus Siculus, De Rebus Hispaniæ, lib. viii. p. 368. &c. et lib. x. p. 578. &c. (apud eundem tom. i.). Blancas, Rerum Aragonensium Commentarii, p. 648. (apud eundem tom. iii.). Zurita, Anales de Aragon, lib. ii. cap. 1. 19. Moret, Anales de Navarra, lib. xviii. Diago, Historia de los victoriosissimo santiguos Condes de Barcelona, lib. ii. cap. 119. 147.

had granted that fief in perpetuity, he re-united that lordship to Aragon; and he soon succeeded, by inheritance, to that of Roussillon. He was no less ambitious to extend his dominion by conquest over the Moors. From 1168 to a few years before his death, he gained several fortresses south of the Ebro, lying towards the Valentian frontier, from the enemy. Of these the most important was Teruel. In 1177 he assisted Alfonso IX., of Castile, whose niece he had married, to reduce Cuenza; and for this service he was exempted from the homage which his predecessors paid to the Castilian king for their possessions on the western side of the Ebro. That he obtained no farther successes over the Africans must be attributed partly to the unfortunate defeat of the Castilian king at Alarcos*, and partly to his own dissensions with the king of Navarre;—dissensions, however, which are too obscure to be noticed. He did not long survive that defeat. He died in 1196, leaving Aragon, Catalonia, and Roussillon to his eldest son, Pedro, and Provence to the second son, Alfonso. In his reign the Spanish era was suppressed in Catalonia, and the Christian substituted. This country was the first in Spain to set the example.†

PEDRO II., in the first year of his reign, had some disputes with his mother respecting some fortresses left to her as a dowry by the late king. As these fortresses were situated on the frontier, and exposed to the irruptions of the Mohammedans, he probably trembled for their security while in the hands of a woman; he therefore proposed to exchange them for others in the interior of the kingdom. The refusal of doña Sancha led to a disgraceful rupture between mother and son, which was at length ended through the interference of the Castilian king, who persuaded her to comply with the reasonable wishes of Pedro. In this transaction we may applaud the policy, however we condemn the want of filial respect of the king. But for another act he is justly exposed to the censure of posterity. In 1203 he

1196 to 1204.

* See Vol. II. p. 41.   † See Appendix (E).

embarked for Rome, to be crowned by the pope. He was received with great pomp by the sacred college; was solemnly anointed by one of the number, and presented with the crown, the globe, and sceptre, by the hands of Innocent. On this occasion he not only did homage as a feudatory of the church, but, by a public instrument, engaged that Aragon should for ever remain a fief of the Holy See, and be considered the property of the successors of St. Peter. To render the humiliation more complete, he agreed for himself and his heirs to pay an annual tribute to his liege lord, and to all succeeding chiefs of the catholic world.* This disgraceful scene excited the indignation of the royal barons; who, on his return, fiercely upbraided him for his treacherous sacrifice of the national honour. He replied, that he had surrendered only his own rights, not those of his people. But as the monarch was the representative of the national power, as, by virtue of his office, he was a personification of the nation itself, the fallacy did not impose on the barons, however it might delude the weak-minded Pedro. In 1205 the states assembled at Saragossa, protested against the act, as derogatory to the honour of the nation, as injurious to the people, and, consequently, as remaining without effect.

1204 to 1208. In 1204 Pedro married Maria, daughter and heiress of the count de Montpellier. Whether through dissatisfaction with his conduct towards his bride, which is represented as unjustifiable, or through his disregard of their privileges, the people of that lordship refused, in 1205, to admit him within their capital. Incensed at their disrespect, the following year he applied to the pope for a dissolution of his marriage (probably it had not then been consummated); but it does not seem that his application was well received. If even he had canonical grounds for it, he appears to have soon abandoned them; for in 1207, or in 1208, his queen was delivered, at Montpellier, of a son — afterwards the famous don Jayme

* The instrument of Pedro's homage is to be found in the appendix of Zurita under the corresponding year.

el Conquistador. If any faith is to be placed in the best of Jayme's biographers*, the debitum conjugale would never have been paid, but for the artful ingenuity of the queen. The king, says this writer being of an amorous temperament, and in love with a fair attendant of Maria, employed one of his chamberlains to make certain overtures. The agent being discovered and gained by the queen, returned to his master, who was then in the neighbourhood of Montpellier, and told him that he might prosecute his object as soon as he pleased, as it was fully secured. He accordingly hastened to the place, and supped with the queen, but was somewhat disappointed to find that the lady he expected did not appear. Considering, however, that she would not be wanting to the appointment, he desired to be shown to his apartment. In the middle of the night the queen crept softly to his bed; and, at day-break the morning following, she so managed that several of her household were admitted, to swear as witnesses of the fact. In process of time the queen was delivered of a son.—The circumstance which led to the imposition of the royal infant's name is represented as no less extraordinary. His mother resolved to call him after one of the twelve apostles. To decide which should have the preference, she caused twelve candles, all equal in size and weight, and each named after one of the apostles, to be lighted; declaring that the matter should be determined by the candle which burnt the longest. When all the rest were consumed, that of St. James was still burning: accordingly the name of Jayme was imposed at the baptismal font. But the birth of a son did not diminish the hatred of Pedro, nor prevent him, at a subsequent period, from resuming his application to the papal court; but Innocent, after a patient examination of the grounds on which it was made, refused to grant him the relief he solicited.

* Bernardus Gomecius Miedes, De Vita et Rebus Gestis Jacobi Primi, lib. i. Though there is nothing improbable in the relation, we do not vouch for its truth.

1206 to 1212. Like his predecessors, Pedro was frequently at war with the Moors. In 1206 he took the important fortress of Montalvan. He had also the glory of assisting in the campaign of 1212 against the emperor of Morocco, and of contributing to the defeat of the Moors on the immortal plains of Tolosa.*

1209 to 1213. But if the king of Aragon was thus valiant against the enemies of Christianity, he did not exhibit equal zeal against the Albigenses, who were now exceedingly numerous in the south of France, especially in his French domains. In the crusade headed by the famous Simon de Montfort, he afforded no aid to the catholic cause; though he frequently and fruitlessly interfered to reconcile the chiefs of the two parties. Carcassonne was one of the strongholds of this heresy. In 1209 it was accordingly invested by the crusaders. Both the viscount, a relative of Pedro's, and the inhabitants, offered a brave resistance, and implored aid from the Aragonese king. His aid he was not unwilling to grant; but whether he feared openly to oppose the crusaders with the papal legate at their head, or distrusted his own means of resistance, he contented himself with exhorting the besieged to hold out, and with again interceding in behalf of the viscount Raymund. No attention was paid to his entreaties or remonstrances; the siege was prosecuted with new vigour, and the place surrendered. At first the chiefs of the catholic league deliberated whether it should not be rased to its foundation: in the end they resolved to preserve, and to place a governor over it; and their choice ultimately fell on Simon de Montfort. The intelligence was disagreeable to Pedro, who refused to receive the homage of the new viscount. Montfort is known to have been of a stern, rapacious, and remorseless disposition; and, probably, the complaints respecting his administration, which daily reached the ears of Pedro, might be one cause of this refusal. In 1211, however, being at Montpellier, he was reluctantly persuaded not only to receive the viscount's

* See Vol. II. Section I. Chap. II. page 45—47.

homage, but to sanction the proposal of a marriage between his son Jayme and a daughter of Simon; he even delivered the young prince into the hands of the viscount, both as a pledge of his sincerity, and that the infante might be educated according to the manner of the times under so renowned a leader. But that sincerity was suspected by the crusaders, when, on his return to Aragon, he gave one of his sisters in marriage to the count of Toulouse, the head of the Albigenses,—the more still when he married another to the son of that baron.

After the campaign, immortalised by the victory of 1213. Las Navas de Tolosa, Pedro was urgently pressed by his brother-in-law, and by his relatives the counts of Bearn and Foix, all protectors of the Albigenses, to arm in their behalf. Though he had some reason to be dissatisfied with the crusaders, who had seized several fortresses belonging to the appanage of his sisters, and had shaken his own domination in France; and though he now passed the Pyrenees with a considerable army, his object was rather to act as a mediator than as a belligerent. But the proposals which he submitted to the papal legates on the part of the chiefs of the Albigenses were, after a mature deliberation, rejected. The ground of this rejection was the faithless characters of the counts of Toulouse and Foix, who had evidently made Pedro their dupe. He then declared that he could not forsake his kindred and allies. At the head of a great combined army of Aragonese, Catalonians, and French, he advanced against Muret, a fortified town on the Garonne, about two leagues from Toulouse. The besieged soon acquainted the count de Montfort with their situation, and implored relief. The latter, who was then at Saverdun, within a few miles of Muret, seeing that a contest was inevitable, and impressed with the inferiority of his force, made his will, confessed, and received the sacraments of the church. He then marched to the besieged place, forced the lines, and threw himself into it. On the morning of September 12th, the crusaders prepared for battle. To encourage them, the bishop of Toulouse, on horseback, with a mitre on his head, and the cross in his hands, approached them, and held out for their idolatrous worship this symbol of man's salvation. Hundreds flocked around to touch it with their lips. The bishop of Commenges, seeing how much time was wasted by this display of devotion, took the cross from the the hands of his brother prelate, ascended an eminence, and gave his benediction to the assembled multitude. He impiously added, "whoever falls in this battle, provided he has humbly confessed his sins to a priest, or even has the disposition to confess them as soon as the battle is over, shall enter eternal life without passing through purgatory! For this I will be your surety in the day of judgment! depart in the name of Christ!" The little army then issued from the gates, and the struggle commenced. The van, headed by the count de Foix, was soon dispersed. Montfort now hastened to the place where he perceived the floating standard of Aragon, knowing that he should there find the king. Pedro manfully defended himself; but he was soon overpowered by the furious charge of the crusaders, and he fell among a heap of slain. The victors inflicted a horrible carnage among the fugitives, showing mercy to none. There seems to have been great cowardice among the Albigenses on this eventful day: more perished in the pursuit than on the field. The royal corpse was discovered, and buried with suitable honours by the Templars.*

* Rodericus Toletanus, De Rebus Hispanicis, lib. viii. (apud Schottum, Hispania Illustrata, tom. ii.). Monachus Rivipullensis, Gesta Comitum Barcionensium, cap. 24. (ad calcem Marcæ, Limes Hispanicus, col. 552.). Chronicon Barcionense, col. 755. (apud eundem). Chronicon Vlianense, col. 759. (apud eundem). Lucas Tudensis, Chronicon Mundi, p. 110, &c. (apud Schottum, tom. ii.). Annales Compostellani, p. 323. (apud Florez, España Sagrada, tom. xxiii.). Anales Toledanos, p. 395—398. (in eodem tomo). Lucius Marineus Siculus, De Rebus Hispaniæ, p. 380. (apud Schottum, tom. i.). Rodericus Santius, Historia Hispanica, cap. 35. (in eodem tomo). Bernardinus Gomecius Miedes, De Vita et Rebus Gestis Jacobi Primi, lib. i., necnon Blancas, Rerum Aragonensium Commentarii, p. 650. (apud eundem, tom. iii.). Zurita, Anales de Aragon, lib. ii. cap. 19—63. Moret, Anales de Navarra, lib. xx. Bouges, Histoire Ecclésiastique et Civile de la Ville, &c. de Carcassonne, pp. 136—153. Petrus Monachus Cisterciensis, Historia Albigensium, p. 554, &c. (apud Duchesne Historiæ Francorum Scriptores Coætanei, tom. v.). Præclara Francorum Facinora, variaque ipsorum Certamina, &c. (apud eundem, eodemque tomo, p. 666 &c.).

As JAYME I, the most celebrated sovereign in the ancient annals of Aragon, was only six years of age on his father's death, troubles could not fail to distract his minority. At first, Simon de Montfort refused to surrender him to his subjects, — doubtless through fear of losing a royal husband for his daughter, but the pope, at the instance of the Aragonese nobles, interfered, and commanded the victor to deliver the infante into the hands of the cardinal Pietro de Mora. The count reluctantly obeyed, especially as he perceived the Aragonese were arming in good earnest to recover their prince. By the papal legate, don Jayme was conducted to Lerida, where an assembly of the states was convoked. In that assembly, the young prince was recognised as *dominus et hæres* of the realm, and his education was confided to the provincial master of the Templars in the castle of Monzon. The administration of the kingdom during his minority rested in his uncle don Sancho, count of Roussillon, assisted by two colleagues, — one for the affairs of Aragon, the other for those of Catalonia. The choice of Sancho was the very worst that could have been made: he was known to have aspired openly to the crown; and though the hope was entertained that by investing him with the power, he would be satisfied without the title, of king, they who thus trusted in his moderation must have been ignorant alike of his character and of human nature. He soon renewed his attempts to procure his nephew's exclusion. The party increased so rapidly, that the grand master, alarmed for the interests of his ward, consulted with the staunch adherents of royalty; and the result was a resolution to convoke, at Monzon, a general meeting of the states. At the time appointed (September 1216,) some prelates, barons, and many deputies assembled, and did homage to Jayme, as king of Aragon and count of Barcelona. No sooner was Sancho acquainted with this proceeding than he began to raise troops, with the undisguised view of forcibly seizing the crown. As the castle of Monzon was justly considered too insecure a residence for the young king, his loyal barons conducted him first to Huesca, and then to Saragossa, where he was joyfully received by the people. This step, and the unpopularity of his government, which is represented as rapacious, seems to have disconcerted the rebel uncle; who now wished to secure, as long as possible, the continuance of his power. But the year following (1218), in an assembly of the states at Lerida, he was persuaded or compelled to resign the regency, in consideration of ample revenues secured to him both in Aragon and Catalonia. But though Jayme was under the especial protection of the pontiff, and the supreme authority thus transferred to his royal council, his youth and consequent weakness encouraged some of his lawless nobles to set at defiance both him and the laws. In 1220, two of them not only forsook their allegiance, but threw themselves into the fortress of Albaracin, where they successfully repelled all his efforts to reduce them. It was probably as much with the view of fortifying their young monarch by the alliance of Castile, as of securing a heir to the throne, that his counsellors now married him to the infanta Leonora, daughter of Alfonso VIII., and sister of the princess Berengaria. But tranquillity long continued a stranger to Aragon. In 1222, two barons raised troops, and made war on each other with as much ceremony as greater potentates. The king himself, for some time, was but a machine in the hands of another of his uncles, Fernando, whose creatures spied all his steps and indirectly opposed all his views. One day, however, he effected his escape, and retired to Teruel, where he assembled his cavaliers to accompany him in a meditated irruption into Valencia. Though some thousands hastened to join him, and he laid siege to Peñiscola, the place resisted all his assaults. One good effect, indeed, resulted from his preparations; they so much alarmed the Mohammedan governor, that he made haste to acknowledge Jayme as his liege lord: but this unexpected advantage was nearly counterbalanced by the disobedience of an Aragonese chief. Though, on the submission of the governor, Jayme ordered his barons to retire from the Valencian territories, one of these absolutely refused to obey, and continued to lay waste the country. The incensed king marched to chastise the daring leader, who fled farther into the interior, still intent on his predatory occupation. A detachment of the royal troops being sent in pursuit of him, at length overtook him, and he was pierced to the heart by the lance of the leader. Though the king lamented the catastrophe, and caused suitable honours to be paid to the corpse, the kindred of the deceased, among whom was the bishop of Saragossa, immediately armed to avenge his death. They were joined by don Fernando, uncle of Jayme, and by the viscount de Bearne, and were enabled to raise a considerable force. By artfully representing themselves as the advocates of liberty and correctors of abuses, they prevailed on several towns to declare for them. The king marched to oppose them, and triumphed. While besieging Cellas, the inhabitants of Huesca, evidently with a perfidious design, invited him to enter and take possession of the city. Full of confidence in their honour, he appeared among them with few attendants; but a sedition arose which would probably have proved fatal to him, had not he and his little band valiantly fought their way through the multitude and escaped. This attempt appears to have raised the fears or indignation of many among the confederates, who began to reflect that in opposing their lawful sovereign they were only aiding the ambition of the unprincipled Fernando, and who, therefore, chose the part of submission. Their example constrained many more; and though the cities of Huesca, Saragossa, and Jaca for a time held out, they ended by joining the royal cause.*

Though the Balearic isles, or at least the chief of those isles, Majorca, had been reduced by Raymundo III., count of Barcelona, the Mohammedan pirates had regained

1228 to 1235.

* Authorities; Rodrigo of Toledo, Lucas of Tuy, the monk of Ripol, Rodericus Santius, Lucius Marineus Siculus, Miedes, Zurita, Blancas, &c. nearly in the places last quoted.

possession of them, and resumed their savage descents on the coast of Catalonia. Amidst the troubles which had recently afflicted the kingdom, and while destitute of a fleet, the Aragonese had neither the inclination nor the means to think of the re-conquest. The Catalonians, who suffered most by the pirates, whose ships were sometimes captured by them, demanded redress, but in vain. The king himself, who despatched an envoy for the same purpose, had no better success: instead of obtaining satisfaction, the royal messenger was ordered to quit Majorca without delay. No sooner, however, was internal peace restored, than pressing solicitations were made to Jayme to prepare an armament for the destruction of these piratical strongholds. For this purpose, at the close of the year 1228, he convoked the states of Barcelona, in which the expedition was unanimously decreed. The preparations were pushed with ardour,— the crusade was proclaimed,— from Genoa and Provence a fleet was procured to transport the forces,— and 18,000 men were embarked on 150 vessels. After a tempestuous passage, which made most of the crusaders repent leaving their domestic hearths*, the armament appeared off the port of Palmera. In utter ignorance where a landing might be most safely attempted, and where the enemy was to be found, the king at first hesitated what to do. He was soon released from his anxiety by a Moorish mariner, who swam towards the fleet from the shore, was taken on board the royal vessel, and was able to give him all the information he required.† He learned that the islands contained 42,000 men capable of bearing arms, and that 10,000 were already drawn up beyond a moun-

---

* Miedes (vi. 432.) discovers a two-fold admirable efficacy in sea-sickness: " Quin etiam milites, qui mare nunquam intrarant atque tempestatis insolentes erant, fluctuum agitatione et conflictu expavescentes admodum, Deo et Virgini matri sese verè et ex animo commendabant." — " Is quippe sacer atque omnino salutaris est fructus, qui excipitur ex marina tempestato: *nam ea quidem non modo sanando corpori utilis est, vomitione, ut solet, omnem e ventriculo bilem excernens, sed ab intimo quoque animo impietatem omnem expectorat.*"

† " Beno te animo rex esse volo" was, we are told, the salutation of the man, " ventura enim est insula in potestatem tuam; itaque quippe fore augurata est mea mater, quæ magicis instructa artibus omnium insularum habetur sapientissima."— *Miedes.*

tain which appeared in sight; as succours were also daily expected from Tunis, he was advised to land without delay. The disembarkation was effected at midnight, yet not without opposition from a small body of islanders who watched the operation, and were easily dispersed. The day following, as the Christians advanced they encountered the forces of the Moorish king, ready to receive them. The battle immediately commenced: it was for some time disputed with equal bravery; but reinforcements arriving in aid of the islanders, the assailants began to give way. At this critical moment the king advanced with his guards and furiously assailed one wing of the enemy. His example was followed by the Christians around him. The Moors at length retired towards the capital, in little fear of a pursuit; for both parties had suffered so much, that though the honour of the day remained with the invaders, they were unable to profit by it. The capital was soon after invested; and though the defence was obstinate, the assaults were not less so. Seeing that however protracted the resistance, it would ultimately be vain, the Moorish king at length made overtures of vassalage and of a large tribute; but they were rejected by the council of Jayme, the members of which, like their sovereign, were resolved to force an unconditional surrender. The city was taken by storm: a great number of the besieged fled at one gate, while the Christians entered at another*, the royal Moor with one of his sons being taken prisoner. The victor having purified the grand mosque, and confided the defence of the place to a Christian garrison, returned to his kingdom. The governors whom he left pursued the Mohammedans into the interior of the island. As many took refuge in caves, and refused to come out, fires were kindled at the mouth, the smoke of which soon forced them from their hiding-places. But many escaped

---

* St. George was the first to enter. "Fue publico en aquellos tiempos y muy confirmados por los mismos Moros, que se vio al entrar la ciudad que yva el primero un caballero anciano armado en blanco, caballo y sobre conseñales blancas; y se creyo segun se escrive en la historia del rey, que fue el glorioso San Jorge," &c.— *Zurita,* iii. 132.

the pursuit of the invaders, united their scattered bands, and surprised one of the towns. They were joined by such as had submitted; and their appearance was formidable enough to bring king Jayme a second time to the island. They again fled to the mountains, and were pursued like wild beasts; but their old haunts, which were mostly unknown to the Christians, a second time procured them safety. Besides, Minorca and Iviça were still in possession of the pirates. In 1232, Jayme headed a third expedition: Minorca immediately submitted, and the example was now followed by the mountaineers of Majorca itself. But no attempt was made on Iviça until 1235, when it was subdued by his generals. The conquest, which was now perfected, surrounded the name of don Jayme with glory, and prepared the way for one of much greater magnitude,— that of Valencia.*

1232 to 1239.
The decline of the empire of the Almohades, and the successes obtained by Fernando III. over the princes of Andalusia, were sufficient to excite the emulation of so enterprising a monarch as don Jayme. In 1232, he convoked his states at Monzon to deliberate on the invasion of Valencia. The project was approved, and the following year was appointed for its execution. As in the case of Majorca, a crusade was solemnly proclaimed;

* Rodericus Toletanus, De Rebus Hispanicis, lib. ix., necnon Lucas Tudensis, Chronicon Mundi, p. 114, &c. (apud Schottum, Hispania Illustrata, tom. ii. et iv.). Monachus Rivipullensis, Gesta Comitum Barcionensium, cap. 26. Chronicon Barcionense, necnon Chronicon Vliauense, col. 755—759. (ad calcem Marcæ, Limes Hispanicus). Miedes, De Vita et Rebus Gestis Jacobi Primi, lib. 4—7. (apud Schottum, Hispania Illustrata, tom. iii.). Lucius Marineus Siculus, De Rebus Hispaniæ, p. 382, &c. (apud eundem, tom. l.). Zurita, Anales de Aragon, lib. iii. tom. i. Blancas, Rerum Aragonensium Commentarii, p. 651, &c. (apud Schottum, tom. iii.) cum multis aliis.

With some pious Spaniards this expedition is more memorable from the miracle recorded of St. Raymundo de Peñafort than from its success. The saint, who was the royal confessor, having long and vainly endeavoured to reclaim the king from lewdness, whose indignation his honest zeal seems to have incurred, he wished to return to the Continent; but found that rigorous orders had been given that no vessel should be furnished him. Nowise dismayed at this prohibition, and trusting, like Peter of old, to the power of our Lord, the saint spread his cloak or pall on the water, made his pastoral staff into a mast, stepped fearlessly on this novel bark, and sailed gloriously along to Barcelona! The miracle, continues the legend, effected what his exhortations had never been able to do — the king's conversion. — *Nicolas Antonius, Bibliotheca Vetus*, lib. viii. cap. 4.

This miracle is as prodigious, though not quite so poetical, as that of the Anglo-Saxon ecclesiastic, who one day hung his garment on a sunbeam.

and, early in the spring of 1233, numbers of adventurers from Provence and Narbonne flocked to the frontiers of Valencia The campaign opened by the siege of Buriana, which, after a gallant defence, submitted. Its fall constrained that of several fortresses in the neighbourhood. In 1234, Moncada was rapidly reduced During the three following years Jayme seems to have been occupied in his preparations for the entire conquest of the Moorish kingdom and capital; though his generals triumphed in one action at least over a formidable body of the misbelievers, he himself did not take the field until 1238. To meet the approaching storm, the Mohammedan king solicited aid from the sovereign of Tunis, and prepared for a desperate defence As the Christians advanced, Almenara and other places, convinced how fruitless resistance must prove, capitulated, on the condition of their property, freedom, and religion being guaranteed. At length, with the powerful reinforcements which reached him from all parts, Jayme crossed the Guadalaviar, seized on Ruzafa, where he entrenched his camp, and drew his lines of circumvallation around the city of Valencia. A Tunisian fleet soon arrived off the coast, but, seeing the place so closely invested, the Mohammedans, in despair of throwing relief into the city, removed to sea. The departure of this long-expected ally was the death-blow to the hopes of the king of Valencia, especially as the progress of the siege was rapid, as the walls were much shaken by the battering-engines, and as provisions began to fail. He now demanded a safe conduct for his nephew, whom he sent to the Christian camp, to procure favourable terms from the enemy. Jayme would grant no other than a permission to the inhabitants to retire within five days with their moveable substance. The condition was a hard one, but it was accepted by the Moorish king, who, at the command of the Christian, even hoisted the standard of Aragon on the towers of the city On the expiration of the time the place was delivered up to don Jayme, and 50,000 Mohammedans with the king left its walls never to return: the victor triumphantly entered, was present, as usual, at the purification of the grand mosque, which was converted into a cathedral; and, as usual also, the deserted houses and fields were divided among the soldiers.

1239 to 1245. By a treaty solemnly made between Jayme and the Moorish king, the latter was guaranteed in the possession of the whole country south of the Xucar; but scarcely had the former left the new conquest, than the grand master of the Templars invested and took Cullera, while another division of the Aragonese reduced another fortress belonging to the dethroned Moor. The inhabitants armed and advanced against the faithless assailants, but without success. Their complaints, however, of Christian perfidy were so loud and so just, that Jayme was compelled to notice them. He affected great indignation towards his generals, and even threatened to punish them; but they escaped with impunity — a fact which must strengthen the suspicion that hostilities had been recommenced with his full connivance. So far was he from restoring the profits of this iniquity, that the following year he led an army in person against the important fortress of Bayren; which, in opposition to the entreaties or remonstrances of the Moorish king, he persisted in reducing. Its fall was followed by that of other places in the neighbourhood. This success incited him to greater acts of perfidy. He marched against Xativa, turned a deaf ear, as before, to the expostulations of justice and honour, and reduced the alcalde of the place to subjection. During the following five years he persevered in his career of spoliation, and incorporated, one by one, a considerable number of towns and fortresses with his kingdom: among these were Xativa, Viar, and Denia.

1247 to 1276. It cannot be matter of surprise that the insulted, betrayed, and oppressed Mohammedans should be eager to throw off the yoke under which they groaned. In 1247 they rose, chose a leader, and seized several fortresses. Jayme had now an excuse for proceeding to greater rigour—for decreeing their expulsion from the kingdom of Valencia. He caused the fatal mandate to be translated into Arabic, and to be distributed throughout the country. A month only was allowed the persecuted people to collect their moveable property and to depart. In vain did they beseech him to recal his mandate, and offer a large sum of money for permission to remain. Seeing that nothing was to be obtained from his humanity or justice, they arose in a body to resist his decree. But this desperate effort was of little avail: the places which they surprised were quickly recovered, and the inhabitants escorted to the frontiers of Murcia. Owing, however, to some domestic troubles, and to the resistance offered by some fortresses, the expulsion of the whole body was necessarily deferred. In 1252, four years after the promulgation of the decree, he issued a second, which allowed them a respite of twelve months prior to their final departure. At the expiration of this period most of them were pitilessly driven across the frontier: many took up their abode under the enlightened sway of Mohammed ben Alhamar, and many took refuge in Murcia, which continued subject to Mohammedan kings until its conquest by the Castilians. But many also must have remained; for, in 1268, we find that a considerable number more were expelled; and eight years afterwards they were powerful enough to rise a third time, and defeat two of the royal barons; nor could Jayme vindicate his authority before his last illness assailed him.—The share which he took in the re-conquest of Murcia for his son-in-law, the king of Castile, has been already related.*

If we except these brilliant conquests, there is little in the actions of Jayme to command our respect. In 1229, his marriage with Leonora of Castile was declared null, on account of their being within the forbidden

1229 to 1276.

---

* See Vol. II. p. 64. Monachus Rivipullensis, Gesta Comitum Barcionensium, cap. 26, necnon Chronicon Barcionense, col. 755., et Chronicon Vlianense, col. 759. (omnes ad calcem Marcæ, Limes Hispanicus). Anales Toledanos, ii. p. 408. (apud Florez, España Sagrada, tom. xviii.). Miedes, De Vita et Rebus Gestis Jacobi Primi, lib. vii. p. 14. (apud Schottum Hispania Illustrata, tom. iii.). Lucius Marineus Siculus, De Rebus Hispaniæ, p. 382, 383. (apud eundem, tom. i.). Blancas, Rerum Aragonensium Commentarii, p. 652. (apud eundem, tom. iii.). Zurita, Anales de Aragon, tom. i. lib. iii. Condé, by Marlés, Histoire de la Domination, &c., tom. ii.

degrees of consanguinity; but the infante Alfonso, the issue of this connection, was at the same time declared legitimate. As he was not of a temperament to remain long without a queen, in 1235 he received the hand of Yoland, an Hungarian princess. On her death, in 1252, he secretly married doña Teresa Vidaurre; but with the third wife he appears soon to have been disgusted: in the sequel he made pressing applications to the pope for the dissolution of the marriage. The reason on which he founded his prayer for relief was the reported leprosy of the queen — the real one was a criminal intercourse with a princess whom he wished to marry. To Pedro, the issue of the second marriage, he proposed to leave Catalonia; a proposal highly resented by prince Alfonso, and not very agreeable to the Catalonians themselves: hence the divisions which began to distract his family, and which embittered his domestic peace. In 1258, his states remonstrated against the partition of the monarchy, as prejudicial to all their interests, and as injurious to the eldest son, Alfonso; but the remonstrance was without effect. In 1260, Alfonso, who had never been loved by him, suddenly died, and the favourite son, Pedro, became his lawful heir. The same year he arranged the marriage of this son with Constança, daughter of Manfred, king of Sicily — a marriage, as we shall perceive in the next reign, followed by momentous events. As Manfred was obnoxious to the pope, and under the ban of the church, and as that pope was raising up a crusade in France to dethrone him, this union was exceedingly unpalatable to the papal see; which endeavoured, but in vain, to prevent the alliance of the two princes. But Pedro was doomed to give Jayme no less vexation than Alfonso, and from the same cause. The infante, in the apprehension that Valencia would be left to his younger brother Jayme, made a secret protestation, before some barons assembled at Barcelona, against the dreaded dismemberment. But if the king ever seriously intended to dissever Valencia, he soon dissipated the public apprehension by a new testament, which secured Pedro in the undivided possession of Aragon, Catalonia, and Valencia, and which conferred the Balearic isles, with the lordships of Conflans, Roussillon, and Montpellier, on the second son, Jayme. He hoped that by this step the animosity which had so long distinguished the two brothers would cease. But his domestic peace was now wounded in another quarter. By one of his mistresses he had another son, Fernando Sanchez, who possessed more than a due portion of his affection, and whom he had laden with riches. Jealous of the empire reserved for Pedro, and mortified at his own exclusion, Fernando laboured to sow dissension between the king and his eldest brother. Alarmed for the possible consequences, Pedro knowing that expostulations or remonstrances would not avail him, took up arms to punish the perfidious delator. Fernando summoned his kindred by his mother's side to his defence: both parties acquired considerable strength by the accession of many turbulent barons; so that civil war would have been inevitable, had not the king to avert it hastily convoked his states at Saragossa. The factions were ordered to disarm; an order with which the two brothers were constrained to comply: but their internal hatred still continued to embitter the peace of the father. In 1272, they again broke out into open hostility. On this occasion, one of Fernando's confidential advisers having fallen into the hands of Pedro, was thrown by that prince into the river. Not satisfied with this deed of violence, Pedro planned a darker — the assassination of his brother. Fortunately his creatures could not effect an entrance into the apartments of the intended victim before the latter was apprised of their errand, and was enabled to escape: nor was it without considerable difficulty that the king could pacify his eldest son, who long cherished the murderous design. If to these harassing cares we add frequent revolts of his barons, who, under the pretence of defending their privileges, aimed at annihilating his power, we shall find, that however splendid the reign of this conqueror, his lot was far from enviable. In 1274, wishing to punish some of his nobles who had refused to accompany him the preceding year into Valencia, he proceeded to seize their fortresses: they flew to arms, and were joined by his favourite son, Fernando Sanchez. To appease them, he convoked his states at Lerida; but they refused to hear his proposals. Nothing now remained but to reduce them by force. While he quelled the tumult in Catalonia, Pedro, his eldest son, pursued Fernando, who had sought refuge in the castle of Pomar. Seeing the impossibility of long resistance, Fernando one day disguised himself as a shepherd, and issued from the gates: he was taken by the soldiers of Pedro, and by that prince's order was immediately drowned in the river Cinca. Jayme, whom this rebellion had completely estranged from his son, is said to have testified an unnatural joy on hearing of the horrid catastrophe.

1276. Don Jayme died in 1276, in Valencia, whither he had advanced to chastise a partial insurrection of his Moorish subjects; who, being aided by the king of Granada, had defeated two of his barons. He is little deserving the high character given him by the peninsular historians. If magnanimity can be reconciled with perfidy, devotion with unbridled lust and barbarous cruelty, their encomiums may be just. His immoderate passion for women, his disregard in its gratification of any tie of honour or religion, or decency, are notorious. In 1246, the bishop of Gerona being so honest as to reprove his excesses, or so imprudent as to betray his confidence, was punished by the loss of the offending member, the tongue. The Catalonian prelates instantly excommunicated him; but he was absolved by the pope, on the condition of his finishing, at his own expense, the monastery of St. Boniface, near Morella. On another occasion (the year before his death), he forcibly carried off a married woman who had the misfortune to please him; and when the pope reprimanded him for the unhappiness he introduced into so many families, and the scandalous example he afforded his subjects, the hoary sinner complained with bitterness that he had surely a right to do as he would. One cause of the favour with which his memory is regarded, is his having assumed the cross, and actually embarked for the Holy Land; but a storm by which he was assailed off the coast of Sicily, effectually cooled his devotion: with great difficulty he gained a French port, and immediately returned to his dominions, resolved never again to trust himself on the treacherous deep.*

Pedro III. lost no time in restoring tranquillity in Valencia; but scarcely was this object effected, when many of his rebellious barons, whose constant end was the curtailment of the royal prerogative and the oppression of the poor, broke out into an open insurrection. He reduced them to obedience. In two years they again rebelled, but with no better success: they were invested in the fortress of Balaguer, which was at length compelled to surrender, and were for some time detained prisoners.

1275 to 1280.

But the most important transactions of Pedro were with Sicily. On the death of Manfred, who had usurped that kingdom, to the prejudice of Conradin, his nephew, the true heir, and who fell at Benevento, in battle with Charles of Anjou, whom the pope had invested with the fief, the French prince took undisturbed possession of the Two Sicilies. When Conradin had attained his sixteenth year, knowing the hatred borne to the French rule by the Sicilies, and that the Ghibelline faction was at his command, he resolved to vindicate his rightful claims. Despising the papal thunders, which had consigned him, while living, to every ill that life can suffer, and, when dead, to the goodly fellowship of Dathan, Abiram, and the devil, he invaded Italy, passed, in contempt of the church, through the city of Rome, where he was hailed

* The same authorities as last quoted, with the addition of Alexander Abbas Coenobii Telesini, De Rebus Gestis Rogeri Siciliæ Regis (apud Schottum, Hispania Illustrata, tom. iii., necnon apud Muratorium, Rerum Italicarum Scriptores, tom. v. p. 607, &c.) The text of this author is beyond all comparison more correct in the invaluable collection of Muratori than in that of Schott. Also, Nicolaus de Jamsilla, Historia de Rebus Gestis Frederici II. ejusque Filiorum Conradi et Manfredi, cum Supplemento Anonymi, De Rebus Gestis ejusdem Manfredi, &c. (apud eundem, tom. viii. p. 489, &c.).

with enthusiasm, and proceeded towards Naples. He was defeated by his formidable adversary; was taken prisoner in the retreat; was tried, condemned, and executed at Naples. The Ghibellines, and all who revered the rights of blood, now turned their eyes towards Constança, daughter of Manfred and queen of Aragon, while the Guelphs, and all who recognised the papal supremacy over the kingdom, continued the zealous assertors of the rights of Charles, the pope's feudatory.* But the tyrannical government of Charles, his rapacity and injustice; the heavy exactions which he made the people to endure; his contemptuous disregard of their complaints; the haughtiness of his French counsellors, soon made him hateful to the whole body of his subjects. Not even the remonstrances of one whom he professed to regard as his liege superior, and from whom he had received the investiture of the Two Sicilies, had any effect on him: he exhibited, however, great eagerness for revenge on the prelates and nobles who had dared to complain of his administration to the papal see. All this, says Saba Malaspina, the Sicilians might have borne; but when the French to tyranny the most atrocious added lust the most unbridled; when they began by violence to attempt the chastity of virgins and matrons, and sully the honour of families even the most distinguished, then human endurance had its limit. The oppressed inhabitants despatched messengers with renewed complaints to Nicholas III., to Michael Palæologus emperor of Constantinople, and, above all, to Pedro of Aragon, whom they regarded in right of Constança as lawful ruler, and whom they urged to expel the tyrant without delay.†

* The best and fullest account of these transactions is to be found in Anonymus, et Saba Malaspina, Historia Sicula (apud Carusium, Bibliotheca Historica Regni Siciliæ, tom. ii. p. 784, &c.); and in Nicolaus Specialis Rerum Sicularum, libri viii. (ad calcem Marcæ, Limes Hispanicus). A good history of Sicily and Naples, though one of the most interesting subjects in the whole range of histories, is a great desideratum in English literature.

† Anonymus, et Saba Malaspina, Historia Sicula (apud Carusium, Bibliotheca Historica Regni Siciliæ, tom. ii. p. 677, &c.). Anonymus, Historia Sicula, p. 380, &c. (apud eundem, tom. ii.) Matthæus Spinellus, Ephemerides Neapolitanæ, sive Diarium Rerum Gestarum in Regno Neapolitano (apud Muratorium, Rerum Italicarum Scriptores, tom. vii. p. 1035,&c.) Nicolaus de Jamsilla, Historia Frederici II., cum Supplemento Anonymi, De Rebus

Pedro was overjoyed at this opportunity of extending his dominions; but to fight against the pope, the king of France, brother to Charles of Sicily, and the whole party of the Guelphs, was too momentous an undertaking to be lightly commenced. He first secured a considerable sum from the Greek emperor, to whom the Sicilian usurper was obnoxious; he next collected a fleet, assembled his barons, gave liberty to his rebel subjects, whom he had placed in confinement; but took care to conceal his purpose. It seems, however, to have been divined both by the pope and the French king, who, alarmed at the extent of his preparations, demanded for what object they were intended. By pretending that his expedition was to be directed against Barbary, and by even sending an ambassador to the pope (Martin IV.), soliciting an indulgence for all who joined him in warring against the infidels, he hoped to lull the suspicions of Europe. But Martin, who was not to be deceived, contumeliously dismissed the ambassador. This circumstance did not discourage Pedro, whose armament was prosecuted with an alacrity inspired by the hope of success. An accident, which, operating like a spark on the inflammable temper of the Sicilians, forced them into open insurrection, hastened his departure. The inhabitants of Palermo, according to ancient custom, resorted to the church of Santo Espiritu, outside the walls of the city, to celebrate the solemnities of Easter: on the way they were watched by the French, who were always jealous of their assembling. Among them was a lady, Nympha by name, the wife of one Rogero Mastrangelo, whose beauty made an impression on one of the ministers of justice, Droghet. Under the pretext of ascertaining whether she had arms (which the Sicilians had been for-

1281.

Gestis Manfredi Caroli Andegevensis et Conradini (apud eundem, viii. 520, &c.) Bartholomæus de Neocastro, Historia Sicula à Morte Frederici Imp. p. 1005, &c. (apud eundem, tom. xiii.). Monachus Rivipullensis, Gesta Comitum Barcionensium, cap. 26. (ad calcem Marcæ, Limes Hispanicus). Chronicon Barcionense (apud eundem, col. 756.). Chronicon Vilanense. (apud eundem, col. 759.) Lucius Marineus Siculus, De Rebus Hispaniæ, lib. xi. (apud Schottum, Hispania Illustrata, tom. i.). Blancas, Rerum Aragonensium Commentarii, p 658. (apud eundem, tom. iii.). Zurita, Anales de Aragon, tom. i. lib. iv. Paternio Catinensis, Sicani Reges, p. 87, &c.

bidden to carry) concealed under her garments, he approached her, and was guilty of such disgusting rudeness, that the lady swooned away in the arms of her husband. The insult fired all who were present at the procession; but none had courage to avenge it, until a young man, whose name history has concealed, but whose memory will ever be dear to his patriotic countrymen, seized the sword of Droghet and plunged it into the owner's heart. A shout of exultation was immediately raised by the multitude; who, in the excitement of the moment, swore to exterminate the odious strangers. As they had no arms at hand, they seized stones and other missiles, which they hurled with such effect at the heads of the Frenchmen, that the ground was soon covered with dead bodies. The citizens of Palermo rose as one man, and destroyed every Frenchman on whom they could lay hands. Their example was followed by other towns,—by none more heartily than Messina; so that scarcely a Frenchman was left alive from one extremity of the island to another. This indiscriminate butchery — a butchery it must be called, because indiscriminate — occupied a full month. The church was no asylum for the proscribed victims; nor, we are told, though on authority somewhat apocryphal, was much mercy shown to the Sicilian women who had married them. Such is the famous massacre which posterity has called the Sicilian vespers; which was the result, not of a preconcerted design, but of sudden indignation acting on a hatred smothered indeed, but deep and deadly. That this massacre was deliberately planned by the whole Sicilian people, who religiously kept the secret; that the signal for the general rising was the tolling of the vesper bell, and that the Frenchmen were cut off simultaneously in every part of the island, are statements which, however generally received, are as much at variance with reason as with facts. Whatever be the guilt of the natives, impartial history cannot justly charge them with that of premeditated murder.[*]

[*] Some of the French historians are ignorant enough to ascribe this massacre to the express command of Pedro

While the inhabitants of Messina were negotiating 1282. with the pope and Charles of Aragon for pardon and a redress of grievances, and while the latter was preparing to inflict a terrific vengeance on both them and all their countrymen, Pedro, at the head of his formidable armament, left the ports of Catalonia, and steered towards the African coast. He wished to await the issue of the insurrection previous to disembarking on the island. But when he learned that the Messenians were courageously repelling the assaults of Charles, who had passed over from Naples to reduce them, and when a deputation from Palermo arrived, beseeching him to accept the crown, he laid aside his extreme caution, and proceeded towards the western coast of the island. In August he landed at Trapani, where his reception was enthusiastic: he hastened to Palermo, where he was joyfully proclaimed king of Sicily. The inhabitants of Messina, still invested by Charles, besought the new monarch to relieve them, and to receive their homage. Indignant at the proposal of the French prince, who insisted on the fall of 800 obnoxious heads as the price of forgiveness, they had defended themselves with a valour almost superhuman: even the women and children had joined in the resistance, and from the walls had harassed the besiegers. Pedro now hastened to their aid; his fleet proceeding along the coast, while he rapidly marched by land; and, to raise their courage, he sent before him 500 ballasteros *, and a few companies of Almogaveres.† Elated by the arrival of these formidable allies, and by the vicinity of their new king, they redoubled their hostilities against the French. Charles now raised the siege, and conducted his powerful armament towards the ports of Calabria: it was pursued by that of Aragon, headed by don Jayme, a son of Pedro, who took twenty vessels, with 4000 prisoners. But the young prince, listening only to his ardour, instead of returning to Messina, pursued

* See Vol. II. page 208.
† For a description of these troops see the last chapter of the present book.

Charles to a fort in Calabria, which he attempted to take; where, being repulsed with some loss, he reimbarked his troops. His father, indignant at his failure, deprived him of the naval command, which was intrusted to a more experienced chief, Roger de Lauria.

1283. No sooner did pope Martin hear of Pedro's proclamation at Palermo and Messina, of the enthusiasm shown towards the monarch by the Sicilians, and of the flight of Charles, than he excommunicated the Aragonese. A defiance next followed between the two rivals; who agreed to decide their quarrel by combat, 100 knights on each side, in the city of Bourdeaux, in June the following year. Until the appointed day arrived, Pedro employed himself in causing his queen, who had arrived from Aragon to be acknowledged by the Sicilians, and in reducing some of the forts on the Neapolitan coast. Leaving Constanza and his son don Jayme in the government of the island, he returned into his states, for the purpose, as was believed, of preparing for the combat. But that combat never happened, nor, amidst the conflicting statements of historians, can we easily decide, to which of the royal rivals the disgrace of its failure must be imputed. It is certain that Pedro caused 100 knights to be selected for the occasion, and that he appeared secretly at Bourdeaux, attended by three horsemen only, and returned to his dominions before the lists were opened. For this extraordinary proceeding he appears to have had sufficient reason. He found that a considerable number of troops were silently moving towards the south of France, with the view, as he feared, of seizing his person. If the Aragonese writers are to be credited, the seneschal of Bourdeaux, whom he consulted on the subject, informed him that the field was not a safe one, and advised him not to risk his person. This account is the more probable, from the fact that pope Martin had previously condemned the combat, and had required our Edward I., to whom Bourdeaux belonged, and who was to be present on the occasion, not to guarantee a fair field, nor to be present, either in person or by his seneschals. What confirms the suspicion that some treachery was meditated is, that though the English monarch was thus enjoined not to visit the field, in other words, was given to understand that the battle would not take place, no such intimation was made to the king of Aragon.

While Pedro remained in Aragon, his admiral, Roger de Lauria, reduced the greater part of Malta. He afterwards defeated a French fleet within sight of Naples, taking the prince of Salerno, the son of Charles, prisoner. The vindictive pope now proclaimed a crusade against the excommunicated king of Aragon: his legate zealously preached it in France, declaring Pedro deprived of the crown, which he conferred on Charles de Valois, who was thus to possess both it and that of the two Sicilies. Fortunately for Pedro both Sicily and Aragon required other weapons than a furious churchman could wield before they could be drawn from his sway. Though the same indulgences as were awarded to all who warred for the holy sepulchre were promised to such as engaged in this Spanish crusade; though vast numbers, among whom was Jayme, king of Majorca, brother and vassal of the Aragonese king, flocked to the standard of Philip; though that monarch lost no time in penetrating, by way of Roussillon, into Catalonia, at the head of 100,000 men, these formidable preparations ended in nothing. If Gerona, after a long and bloody siege, capitulated, the French fleet was almost annihilated near Rosas by the famous Roger de Lauria. Even this advantage was so dearly bought,—the ranks of the invaders were so thinned by pestilence and the sword,—that Philip, leaving a garrison in Gerona, immediately returned to Perpignan, where he died. The rear of his army in this retreat was dreadfully harassed by don Pedro, who recovered Gerona with facility.

Pedro had just despatched his eldest son Alfonso with a small armament to dethrone his brother don Jayme, as a punishment for the aid which that prince had lent to the invaders, when death surprised him at Villa Franca de Panades. In his will he left Aragon and Catalonia to Alfonso, and Sicily to his second son, don Jayme.*

1285. Though ALFONSO III. heard of his father's death immediately after his disembarkation, he refused to return until he had dethroned his uncle. As Jayme was not much beloved by the inhabitants of these islands, whom he had offended by his exactions, the enterprise was successful. The dethroned king had still Montpellier, Conflans, and other possessions in France: to these he retired, but they appear the same year to have been laid waste by Roger de Lauria, the able and intrepid admiral of Aragon.

1286. During Alfonso's absence, the nobles of Aragon had assembled in Saragossa, to provide for the due administration of justice. Some of them were not a little scandalised that he should have assumed in the Balearic Isles the title of king, since, by ancient custom, it could be assumed only after he had sworn before the assembly of the states to observe the customs, privileges, immunities, and laws of the realm. No sooner did they hear of his return to Valencia, than they despatched several of their body to wait upon him, and to express their surprise at his thus arrogating to himself the supreme power without their formal sanction. He justified himself by replying that the crown was his by right of succession, and that there would be time enough to guarantee the constitutions of the realm at the ceremony of his coronation. Accordingly, when that ceremony took place in the cathedral of Saragossa, he fulfilled the conditions of the compact. But, in the states which

* Monachus Rivipullensis, Gesta Comitum Barcionensium, cap. 28. (ad calcem Marcæ, Limes Hispanicus). Chronicon Barcionense, col. 756., necnon Chronicon Vlianense, col. 759. (apud eundem). Anonymus, et Saba Malaspina, Historia Sicula (apud Carusium Biblioth. Hist. Regni Siciliæ, tom. ii. p. 814, &c.). Nicolas Specialis, Rerum Sicularum, lib. i. (apud Marcam, Limes Hispanicus), necnon apud Muratorium, Rerum Italicarum Scriptores, tom. x. Anonymus, Chronicon Siciliæ, p. 800, &c. (apud eundem eodemque tomo). Bartholomæus de Neocastro, Historia Sicula, p. 1130, &c. (apud eundem, tom. xiii.). Paternio Catinensis, Sicani Reges, p. 957, &c. Lucius Marineus Siculus, De Rebus Hispaniæ, lib. xi. (apud Schottum, Hispania Illustrata, tom. i.). Blancas, Rerum Aragonensium Commentarii, p. 660. (apud eundem, tom. iii.). Zurita, Anales de Aragon, tom. i. lib. iv.; cum multis aliis.

were held on that occasion, the same turbulent nobles, whose object was to transfer the royal authority into the hands of their own order, demanded the appointment not only of the ministers, but of the domestic servants of the king. So monstrous a proposal filled the royal party with indignation: it was denounced as an odious innovation, — as a direct attack on the regal office. Though Alfonso transferred the states from Saragossa, — where the aristocratic and democratic spirit was too fierce to be resisted, — to Huesca, he gained little by the change: he was threatened with open rebellion, unless he agreed not only to satisfy their demands, but to sanction the supreme judicial authority of the grand justiciary of the kingdom.* The loyal portion of the aristocratic body, indeed, were averse to this dangerous innovation; but the minority, by increased activity, by the boldness of their tone, and their threats of violence, silenced the calm voice of the rest, and attained their end. Alfonso, indeed, was placed in a situation of some difficulty: though he knew that three fourths of the deliberative body, and a still greater portion of the people, were in favour of his prerogatives, he saw that the discontented would not draw the sword in the impending war with France and the pope, unless he consented to sacrifice them: indeed, during the late wars, even when Catalonia was invaded by the French, several cities of Aragon had shown no disposition to defend the country. Knowing well how necessary union was at such a crisis, he acquiesced in their demands; and in so doing he transformed the monarchy into a republic. Some of these concessions he afterwards revoked when the confederates invaded Valencia, which refused to join their cause: but he was a second time compelled to grant them.

The short reign of Alfonso was not, however, much harassed by foreign war. Through our Edward I., who

1286 to 1291.

---

* See the last chapter of the present book.

had agreed to a matrimonial connection between him and a princess of England, conferences were frequently held by the ambassadors of the powers concerned, for the restoration of peace. He was no less eager for the liberation of the prince of Salerno, his kinsman, who had been transferred from Sicily to Spain. But as one of the conditions was, that Charles should surrender his rights over that island to the actual king, don Jayme, brother of Alfonso, the pope annulled the proceedings. In 1288, however, after the death of the pontiff, in an interview between Alfonso and Edward, at Conflans, and in presence of the papal legate, Charles consented, as the price of his liberty, not only to renounce the Sicilian throne, but to procure the sanction of the new pope and France to the step; or, if such sanction could not be obtained, to return voluntarily to his imprisonment. Having given two of his sons as hostages for his due performance of the covenant, he was enlarged. To this treaty don Jayme, the dethroned king of Majorca, now lord of Roussillon and Montpellier, was averse, since it contained no stipulations in his favour. Resolved to obtain by his own arms what his allies had neglected to demand for him, he invaded Catalonia; but, on the approach of Alfonso, he precipitately returned to France: his frontiers, however, were laid waste by the Aragonese. Instead of approving, the pope, with characteristic obstinacy, condemned every article of the treaty; the excommunication was renewed against Alfonso; Philip of France was invited to invade Aragon; and the investiture of the kingdom of Sicily was conferred on the prince of Salerno. As Charles was bound by his knightly faith to return to his captivity, yet was naturally averse to it, he is said to have entered into a compromise with his conscience, by actually visiting the Pyrenees, as if to surrender himself into the hands of the Aragonese; but finding no one ready to receive him,—doubtless because he chose to appear on some solitary part of the frontier,—he considered himself absolved from the obligation, and hastened from so dangerous a neighbourhood. Perceiving that his thunders had little effect on the hardy Alfonso, and anxious to unite all Christian princes in the holy war, Nicolas, at the persuasion of our Edward, consented to a congress, which was held at Tarascon in 1291. It was there agreed that all ecclesiastical censures should be revoked; that Charles de Valois should renounce the title of king of Aragon; that Alfonso should be recognised as king of Majorca; but that, so far from aiding his brother, don Jayme, king of Sicily, to retain that kingdom from the pope's vassal, he should, if need were, assist in its conquest; and, lastly, that, on the ratification, king Edward should restore the children of prince Charles. These conditions are humiliating to the character of Alfonso, who was bound to support his brother; especially as that brother was the choice of the Sicilians, and as he himself was, in some measure, the guarantee of his father's will. The brave islanders seeing themselves deserted by one to whom they had looked for protection, after loudly expressing their indignation at his want of generosity, returned to animate their sovereign against all his enemies.

Alfonso scarcely survived the conclusion of this peace: he suddenly died at Barcelona, in June 1291, in the midst of his negotiations for the hand of the princess Eleanor, daughter of his ally the English king. As he left no issue, the crown devolved to his brother, the king of Sicily, who hastened to claim the rich inheritance.*

JAYME II. was no sooner in possession of the throne of Aragon, than, to retain it without opposition from

1291 to 1295.

---

* Monachus Rivipullensis, Gesta Comitum Barcionensium, cap 29. (ad calcem Marcæ, Limes Hispanicus.) Chronicon Barcionense, necnon Chronicon Vlianense, col. 756, 757. 765. (apud eundem.) Nicolas Specialis, Rerum Sicularum, lib. li. (apud eundem, et apud Muratorium, Rerum Italicarum Scriptores, tom. x.). Anonymus, Chronicon Siculæ, p. 860, &c. (apud eundem, eodemque tomo). Bartholomæus de Neocastro, Historia Sicula, p. 1140, &c. (apud eundem, tom. xiii.). Paternio Catinensis, Sicani Reges, p. 99, &c. Lucius Marineus Siculus, De Rebus Hispaniæ, lib. xl. (apud Schottum, Hispania Illustrata, tom. i.). Blancas, Rerum Aragonensium Commentarii, p. 661. (apud eundem, tom. iii.). Zurita, Anales de Aragon, tom. i. lib. iv.; cum aliis.

the pope, the French king, and Charles, now king of Naples, he showed a disposition to make peace with those powers. Alarmed at the intelligence, his Sicilian subjects conjured him not to become a party to any project which did not unite the two crowns; and he promised to regard their prayer. In 1295, however, through the care of Boniface VIII., a new congress was held, to procure the same conditions as had been sanctioned by Alfonso. To cement the alliance between Jayme and the Neapolitan king, the former agreed to marry the princess Blanche, daughter of the latter. Thus were the Sicilians a second time betrayed: on receiving the hand of the princess, Jayme made a formal cession of the island in favour of his father-in-law. For some time previous to the actual ratification of the treaty, they were unwilling to believe that loyalty so devoted, and courage so unbending, would be thus rewarded*; and by the counsel of Constanza, the king's mother, they sent another deputation, beseeching him not to desert them. But seeing that their remonstrances were of no effect, the deputies, after upbraiding him in fierce terms, put on mourning and returned to the island.

1295 to 1300. To the conduct of the Sicilians in this age it is impossible to refuse the tribute of admiration. Rather than submit to the enemies of their national independence and of their individual liberty, — though their resources were few, and they were then abandoned by one whose duty to protect them was most solemn, — they resolved to brave their numerous and formidable antagonists. Nay, even when assured that the ranks of their enemies were to be swelled by the troops of their king, they did not despair; their courage rising with the occasion, they proclaimed Frederic, brother of Jayme, and prepared for a vigorous defence. To the exhortations of the king of Aragon that they

---

* Cum primum pervulgata per universam insulam fama fuit, Jacobum Bonifacio VIII. opera ad reddendum Carolo II. Siciliam proclivem esse, nemo fuit inter Siculos qui eam haud mendacem esse sibi persuaderet.— *Paternio Catinensis, Sicani Reges*, cum notis Abbatis Casinensis, p. 100.

would submit to the holy see, they listened with indignant contempt. In an interview with the pope, who gave him the investiture of Sardinia and Corsica, he was so strongly pressed to fulfil his conditions of the treaty, that, though he was averse to contend with a brother, he could no longer delay assisting his ally the Neapolitan king. Having recalled his Aragonese and Catalonian subjects in the service of Frederic, in 1298 he passed over to Italy with a considerable armament. There having conferred with the pope and the king of Naples on the plan of hostilities, he sailed for Sicily. In this unnatural, and, on the part of king Jayme, unjust war, it is some consolation to perceive that he was not entirely deaf to the voice of blood. Hearing that his brother was advancing with a fleet to oppose him, he besought that prince to return to the island, and thereby avoid the danger no less than the disgrace of a battle. The latter, believing that he was an unwilling, and would prove no very destructive, enemy, obeyed the intimation. But at first he showed no want of zeal in the cause of the church: he took several fortresses and laid siege to Syracuse. The vigorous resistance, however, of the inhabitants, and the capture of a part of his fleet by the vassals of his brother, compelled him to return to Spain for reinforcements. His absence was diligently improved by Frederic, who immediately recovered the places which he had gained. With a powerful fleet, he a second time appeared off the coast: he was encountered by the Sicilian king; who, after a gallant action, was defeated, eighteen of the Sicilian vessels, and numerous prisoners, remaining in the power of the victors. There is every reason to believe that Jayme could have taken his brother's galley on this memorable occasion, but that nature urged him to connive at its escape. Nor would he improve his advantage: instead of proceeding to the Sicilian coast, he returned to Naples, declared that he had fulfilled his share of the treaty, that Charles must now prosecute the war with the French and Neapolitans alone, and that he should return to his dominions, the affairs of which demanded his presence. And return he did, notwithstanding the remonstrances of his father-in-law and the pope; nor would he, at any subsequent period, renew the unnatural strife.*

1300 to 1319. The part which Jayme took in the troubles of Castile, especially his protection of the infantes de la Cerda, has been noticed on a former occasion.† In fomenting those troubles he had no regard for the princess, but purely for his own advantage. Murcia was to be the reward of his assistance; but in 1306, in a treaty with Fernando IV., he resigned all claim to that important province, and, in 1309, in an interview with Alfonso XI., he not only confirmed the renunciation, but strengthened the good understanding by the prospect of a matrimonial alliance between his eldest son, don Jayme, and a princess of Castile. As the destined bride was yet a child, she was sent, in conformity with the manner of the times, to be educated at the court of Aragon. On the approach of the period appointed for the solemnisation of the nuptials, the infante, whose disobedience to the paternal commands had before caused much mortification to the king, loudly declared that he would not marry any one; that he was resolved to resign his right to the crown, and enter the cloister. His father remonstrated with him on the madness as well as guilt of a resolution which evidently rested on no religious foundation, and exhorted him to receive the hand of the princess as the means of averting a war with Castile. With extreme difficulty he allowed him-

---

* Chronicon Barcionense, necnon Chronicon Vlianense (ad calcem Marcæ, Limes Hispanicus, col. 757—759) Nicolas Specialis, Rerum Sicularum, lib. iii et iv. (apud eundem, et apud Muratorium, Rerum Italicarum Scriptores, tom x.). Anonymus, Chronicon Siciliæ, p. 872. &c. (apud eundem, eodemque tomo.). Anonymus, Diaria Neapolitana, p. 1050, &c (apud eundem, tom. xxi.). Ludovicus de Raimo, Annales de Raimo, sive Brevis Historia Rerum in Regno Neapolitano Gestarum, p. 225, &c. (apud eundem tom. xxiii.). Lucius Marineus Siculus, De Rebus Hispaniæ, lib. xi. (apud Schottum, Hispania Illustrata, tom. i.). Blancas, Rerum Aragonensium Commentarii, p. 663. (apud eundem, tom. iii.). Zurita, Anales de Aragon, tom. i. lib. 5. cum aliis.

† See the History of Castile and Leon, reigns of Enrique IV. and Alfonso XI.

self to be conducted to the altar,—went through the ceremony with indifference,—and, on its conclusion, refused to greet his bride with the customary kiss of peace: he had previously protested against the union, which he declared he contracted only to please his father. Instead of accompanying the princess to the palace, he silently withdrew to one of his usual haunts. His conduct, unexpected as it was unaccountable, filled the bridal company with surprise, the princess herself with the deepest mortification, and king Jayme with indignation. Being warned of the consequences which might result from conduct so indecent, he replied that he knew them well; that he was firm in the resolution he had expressed of renouncing his rights of primogeniture, and that he would have neither bride nor crown. The king now insisted that the renunciation should be public. The states were accordingly convoked at Tarragona, where the infante deliberately signed the act of his own exclusion, and where the necessary oaths were taken to prince Alfonso, his brother.

History presents us with other instances in which princes have voluntarily resigned the royal dignity; but some adequate motive has been always assigned for so extraordinary a step. With some it has been love of ease, or apprehensions of danger; with others an ardent spirit of devotion; with a few impaired health, or a contempt for human distinctions. With don Jayme none of these considerations prevailed. He resigned his dignity and entered into a religious order, for no other end than that, being freed from the moral restraints inseparable from a high station, he might abandon himself, without shame, to the lowest debauchery. Knowing that if he chose one of the regular monastic orders, and consequently subjected himself to ecclesiastical jurisdiction, he should have little opportunity of gratifying his brutish inclinations, he selected the military order of Montesa, the members of which were guilty of some vices. Of these fornication and drunkenness are known to have been practised in more isolated commanderies, and to an extent that called down the frequent reprimands of popes. We do not hear that the royal debauchee ever regretted his choice: he appears to have persisted through life in his licentious course, without casting one repining look at the splendid scene he had abandoned.*

1309 to 1312. In the reign of Jayme the Templars sustained the persecution to which allusion has before been made.† Being accused of heresy,—a senseless and malicious accusation, as applied to the whole body,—the knights, to escape the fury of the multitude, threw themselves into their fortresses. This act, which self-preservation rendered necessary, was represented to the king as an open rebellion. He speedily collected troops, and marched to reduce them to obedience; but, on his approach, the places submitted without a blow, the knights informing him that what they had done had been only in self-defence; that they were too loyal to oppose their liege lord; and that as to the charge of heresy, they wished for nothing so much as an open trial. The justice of their plea was acknowledged by the king; who, not content with restoring their possessions, published an edict, in which he rigorously forbade every species of insult to the knights. And when, in 1312, the order was abolished by the council of Vienna, he, in conjunction with the kings of Castile and Portugal, procured an honourable exemption for those of Spain, who were allowed by the fathers of the council to retain their possessions during life.

1321 to 1326. Mention has been already made that the sovereignty of Sardinia and Corsica was conferred by the pope on the king of Aragon; but though the investiture was his, the national government of Sardinia was in the hands of the Pisans, whose exactions are said to have oppressed, and their tyranny to have exasperated, the natives. In 1321, some of the nobles confederated, and sent a depu-

* This prince would have been a better subject for Lord Byron's pen than Sardanapalus.
† See Vol. II. p. 201.

tation to Jayme, requesting him to wrest the island from the tyrannical governors, who despised alike his authority and their privileges. To deliberate on the enterprise, he convoked his states at Lerida, where the project was approved, and the necessary supplies granted, and where don Sancho, king of Majorca, as the vassal of the Aragonese crown, engaged to furnish twenty galleys at his own expense. The preparations being completed, Jayme applied to the pope for a subsidy: the latter, in the fear that if he became absolute master of Sardinia, he would probably take part in the war which still so furiously raged respecting Sicily, not only refused him the slightest aid, but endeavoured to turn him from his design. But he was resolute in his purpose, though prudence caused him to suspend the execution until the following spring. In the mean time he sent a small reinforcement, under his son Alfonso, to aid his partisans, who were already in arms. Cagliari was invested, but was instantly relieved by the Pisans: the infante, however, continued the siege, and obtained a considerable advantage in the open field over the troops of the republic. In 1324 the city capitulated, the Pisans being still left in the government, as vassals of Aragon, on the condition of their surrendering the other fortresses and towns of the island. The following year, however, witnessed many commotions, produced by the agents of the republic, who laboured to regain their lost domination; so that the king was compelled to send a second armament to reduce Cagliari, and thereby establish his authority. In 1326 that important place surrendered, and the Pisans abandoned the island.

King Jayme died in 1327, and was succeeded by his second son, Alfonso.*

1327.

* Chronicon Barcionense, necnon Chronicon Vlianense (ubi supra). Nicolas Specialis, Historia Sicula, lib v. (apud Muratorium, Rerum Italicarum Scriptores, tom. x.). Stella, Annales Genuenses, p. 1000, &c. (apud eundem, tom. xvii.). Anonymus, Monumenta Pisana, p. 996, &c. (apud eundem, tom. xv.). Anonymus, Diaria Neapolitana, p. 1060, &c. (apud eundem, tom. xxi.). Ludovicus de Raimo, Annales de Raimo, sive Historia Brevis Rerum in Regno Neapolitano Gestarum, &c. (apud eundem, tom. xxiii.). Paternio Catinensis, Sicani Reges, p. 164, &c. Also Lucius Marineus Siculus, Zurita, Blancas, &c. nearly ubi supra.

For the Italian events of this and the following periods the less learned

1327 to 1336.
Alfonso IV. was doomed to much annoyance from the new conquest of Sardinia. In 1330 the Genoese, incensed that the Catalonians, their rivals in commerce, should have obtained a settlement in seas which they considered as exclusively their right, not only fomented a spirit of disaffection among the islanders, but sent a fleet to invest the capital. A bloody war ensued, the details of which would afford little interest to the reader. Though the troops of Alfonso were usually successful, his loss was severe; especially as his enterprising enemies, not satisfied with opposing him in Sardinia, made some descents on the coasts of Catalonia and Valencia, which they ravaged with perfect impunity during the absence of his fleet. To stay these hostilities the pope frequently interfered, but without effect: the Genoese insisted on an ample indemnification for the expenses of their armaments; the Aragonese would consent to none. Thus the warfare raged during the whole of this prince's reign.

Alfonso, like his predecessors, was not averse to encourage the rebellions which at this period almost continually afflicted Castile; but without deriving any ultimate advantage from his ungenerous policy. If the internal state of his own kingdom was tranquil, it was not so in his own house. His eldest son and destined successor, don Pedro, offended that he had bestowed on Alfonso — another son, by a second wife — some domains of the crown, complained loudly of his prodigality. The queen, Leonora of Castile, at whose instigation the alienation had been made, cherished a deep resentment against her step-son. Pedro despised her anger; and, to incense her the more, seized on Xativa, which had been assigned to her on her marriage with his father, and loudly proclaimed his intention of revoking every grant

---

reader may consult the comprehensive work of Sismondi, "Histoire des Républiques Italiennes du Moyen Age," in 16 vols. 8vo. If we do not refer to this valuable work oftener, it is from no want of respect to the author, but from our wish to adhere as much as convenient to writers nearly contemporary.

made by the king, whenever he should succeed to the sovereignty. It was not in Alfonso's power to stifle these dissensions, which not only embittered his peace, but aggravated the hydropsical disease under which he had long suffered. He died at Barcelona, in 1336.*

No sooner had PEDRO IV. ascended the throne, than queen Leonora, apprehensive of the consequences of her late quarrel with him, fled to Fraga, whence she implored the protection of her brother Alfonso, king of Castile. At the same time, she wrote to don Pedro, reminding him that she was his father's widow,—that her children were his brothers; and beseeching him to bury past remembrances in oblivion. He replied that she need be under no apprehensions from him; that his object was to procure a good understanding with her and his brothers: yet such was his duplicity, that, at this very moment, his troops were reducing the fortresses which belonged to her. Finding that Fraga was not sufficiently secure for her, she fled to Albarracin, on the confines of Castile. Alfonso naturally espoused his sister's cause: by his ambassadors he requested Pedro to fulfil the clauses in her favour contained in the will of the late king; to confirm her in the possession of the fortresses, revenues, appanages, &c. to which she was so justly entitled. As the Aragonese king was in no disposition, however he might promise, to see justice done the widowed queen and her offspring, and as he knew that something more than remonstrances might be expected from the Castilian, he leagued himself with that curse of the neighbouring state, don Juan Manuel †, put his frontiers in a state of defence, and col-

1336 to 1349.

---

* Chronicon Barcionense, necnon Chronicon Vlianense, col. 756—759. (ad calcem Marcæ, Limes Hispanicus) Nicoles Specialis, Rerum Sicularum, lib. v.—viii. (apud Muratorium, Rerum Italicarum Scriptores, tom. x.) Stella, Annales Genuenses, necnon Anonymus, Monumenta Pisana, ubi suprà. Ludovicus de Raimo, Annales de Raimo, sive brevis Historia Rerum in Regno Neapolitano Gestarum, &c. p. 235. (apud eundem, tom. xxiii.). Paternio Catinensis, Sicani Reges, p. 104. &c. Lucius Marineus Siculus, De Rebus Hispania, lib. xl. (apud Schottum, Hispanica Illustrata, tom. l.). Blancas, Rerum Aragonensium Commentarii, p. 666. (apud eundem, tom. iii.). Zurita, Anales de Aragon, tom. ii. lib. 7.; cum multis aliis.

† See Vol. II. p. 204.

lected troops. His foresight was justified by the event: a strong body of Castilian cavalry now hastened to Requeña. His first step was to reduce Exerica, the patrimony of a baron who had espoused the queen's cause, and whom the late king had constituted one of the executors; but his nobles refused to invest it, on the plea that the proceeding was unjust, and an infraction on the privileges of their body. However, he laid waste the surrounding territory. To punish this wanton violence, that baron, don Pedro Exerica, advanced with the Castilian troops into Valencia, where he collected abundant spoil. To re-establish tranquillity in this kingdom, and restore peace between it and Castile, was now the anxious endeavour of the pope, who despatched a legate to exhort the two kings to settle their dispute by negotiations, and to insist on justice being done to queen Leonora. The interests of the three parties were confided to three commissioners, one chosen by each; but, owing to the demands of king Pedro their deliberations ended in nothing, beyond a suspension of actual hostilities. Some years having elapsed, in 1345 the king, so far from wishing to do his step-mother justice, endeavoured to seize the domains belonging to his two brothers, Fernando and Juan, on the pretext that the revenues of the crown were materially injured by the prodigality of their common father. On the representations of the Castilian king, he again suspended, though he was far from abandoning, his purpose. The troubles which agitated his kingdom, and to which we must now advert, will account for this temporary forbearance.

1336 to 1347. The dissatisfaction of some of Pedro's barons commenced with his reign. Before their coronation his predecessors had always passed into Catalonia, to confirm the privileges and to receive the homage of the three states, the prelates, barons, and deputies. The Aragonese could not behold, without some jealousy, this precedence of a minor state; and, on the present occasion, they insisted that Pedro should be crowned at

Saragossa before his visit to Barcelona. The Catalonian lords and deputies, in great discontent, withdrew from the capital and returned home. Another innovation gave offence to the clergy. Considering the pretensions of the holy see over the kingdom, Pedro was advised not to receive the crown from the archbishop of Saragossa,—as the act might be construed into one of dependence on the pope,—but to place it on his own head. Accordingly, after mass had been celebrated by that prelate, just as he had confirmed the national laws and privileges, he crowned himself, amidst the acclamations of the populace. The Valencians now petitioned him to pass into their capital, and confirm *their* privileges, before visiting Catalonia; and on his refusal, his preference, as they considered it, of a province so much less important, was highly resented by them. A fourth party he offended, in 1347, by purposing to set aside the order of succession, as established by don Jayme el Conquistador, which, on the failure of direct heirs male, called in the collateral male branches,—or, in other words, which enforced the Salic law. As Pedro, by his queen Maria of Navarre, had only a daughter—the infanta Constanza—his brother don Jayme was the presumptive heir to the crown. To secure the succession to his daughter, he assembled twenty-two theologians and civil jurists, nineteen of whom readily sanctioned her right. They knew that doña Petronilla had not been excluded by the accident of sex; that in Navarre and Castile women were called to the succession; and they could not approve the arbitrary regulation of Jayme I., nor recognise it as binding on his successors. But however weighty these reasons, they had no effect on the prince whom they tended to exclude, and who resolved to vindicate his supposed claims by force. Amid the elements of discontent which lay scattered on every side, he had no difficulty in collecting means of resistance. Several of the great towns, and a large proportion of the barons, declared for him: in revenge, he was deprived by the king of the government of Valencia. It was the imprudence, no less than the fortune, of Pedro, to multiply his personal enemies. Hearing that his brother Fernando was in treaty for the hand of Leonora, infanta of Portugal, he demanded and obtained (his queen was no more) that princess for himself.*

1347. From the causes just detailed, and from the restless ambition of his barons, who constantly aimed at diminishing the royal authority, a formidable confederacy was soon formed against the king. It consisted of prelates, barons, magistrates, and a majority of the great towns; of which four only, Huesca, Calatayud, Daroca, and Teruel, adhered to the royal interests. They formed themselves into a political union, and bound themselves by oath never to cease their opposition to the king until their privileges rested on some surer guarantee than the royal engagement, and until the Salic law became fundamental in the state. At the head of this league was don Jayme. A similar one was soon formed in Valencia, under the guidance of the infante Fernando. Both diligently raised troops to take the field against the king; the latter obtained leave from Alfonso to raise 800 horse in Castile. To render their force resistless, both combined in the pursuit of the same object—the annihilation of the royal power—and engaged to assist each other whenever assailed by the troops of Pedro. Conscious of their united strength, they now loudly demanded the convocation of the states, which accordingly met at Saragossa, and which were, as usual, opened by the monarch. Seeing that some of the members were armed, he left the assembly; but the leaguers, who were surrounded by partisans, could well afford to dispense with their weapons; and he was persuaded to return. In the fermentation which prevailed, however, he saw that he must yield to violence; and he made a secret

---

* Authorities, the Chronicon Barcionense and Vlianense, Lucius Marineus Siculus, Zurita, Blancas, and others.

protest against any concessions that might be wrung from him injurious to his royal authority. Among the demands made by the union, not the least obnoxious was the nomination of his public officers by themselves, —a concession which, as before related, Jayme II. had been constrained to grant, and which they insisted should thenceforward be held as a fundamental law of the realm. Pedro showed great reluctance to sanction it; but on being told that, if he refused to do so, the states would immediately proceed to a new election, he no longer withstood the torrent. From that moment, however, he resolved to effect the destruction of the union, if not by force, by corruption. So well did he labour, so efficaciously were his gold and promises distributed, that in a few days he gained over a few of the most influential members. As he knew that their example would constrain others, he no longer feared to meet the faction. One day, shortly after the concession just mentioned, when others as exorbitant were demanded by don Jayme and the leaguers, he rose in great fury, taxed the infante with treason and rebellion, as one who, without honour or faith, aimed at subverting the royal power, by working on the untutored minds of the people. The confederates, in consternation at his unexpected boldness, and convinced of the bitter truths contained in his invectives, stared at each other in astonishment, until one of them hastened to the door, and invited the populace to draw the sword in defence of their rights. A furious multitude, with arms in readiness, immediately entered, with the resolution of sacrificing the king and his partisans. Now his adherents drew their weapons, and placed themselves in a corner of the apartment (a hall in the monastery of the preaching friars at Saragossa), while all the nobles present, scandalised at this disgraceful outrage, arrested the popular violence. The king soon closed the states, without yielding any further to the demands of the union, and hastened into Catalonia, with the avowed purpose of collecting troops, to reduce the whole body to obedience. That the leaguers did not prevent his departure, was owing to the suspicions irresistibly forced on their minds, that there was treachery in their camp and that he had more secret adherents than they had expected. He was followed to Barcelona by the infante don Jayme, who sickened and died in that city, not without suspicions of poison.*

1347. The union of Valencia, nowise discouraged by the ill success of that of Aragon, immediately invested the fortresses which held for the king, whose troops they defeated before Xativa. The infante Fernando, who was now proclaimed lieutenant-general of that province, and head of the confederacy, with a force estimated at 30,000, obtained a second victory over the royalists. Pedro now hastened from Barcelona, to crush in person this formidable rebellion. Hearing of his march, the union of Aragon sent to that of Valencia a large reinforcement, of which though a portion, through a recent attachment to the crown, separated from their companions, near 20,000 joined Fernando. That infante was now at the head of near 60,000 men, with whom he purposed to invest Pedro in Murviedro. In vain did the king endeavour to detach him by bribes and promises from the union, by investing him with the lieutenancy of the monarchy, and by recognising him as heir to the crown, in the event of a failure of male issue by the new queen. While this fruitless negotiation was pending, the inhabitants of Murviedro rose, seized both king and queen, and transferred them to Valencia, as a place of greater security. The popular disposition in that city was not more favourable than in the other: though he was received with much outward respect, a mob collected to sacrifice two of his ministers, the reputed advisers of all his measures. That their

* The poisoning, and that by command of the king, is expressly affirmed by Père Tomich. The royal historian himself — for Pedro has left a history of his own actions and times — assigns that event to natural causes.

purpose would have been perpetrated, that he himself would have run great risk, is certain, had he not, through the advice of a faithful servant, adopted an extraordinary expedient, but one well calculated to overawe them. He mounted his horse, brandished a club in his hand, rode fearlessly among them, and upbraided them for their violence. The result showed that the adviser had no mean knowledge of the people of that day, of their fear of royal authority, of their levity, and liability to captivation by whatever was unusual. Shouts of *" The king* for ever!" succeeded the deep-breathed curses and savage yells which the moment before arose; and the monarch was triumphantly accompanied to one of the suburbs. Thither the disconcerted chiefs of the league, Fernando among the rest, repaired, to yield him his accustomed honours. With well-dissembled courtesy, he received the arch-rebel; published an amnesty for all who had taken up arms; and, on leaving the city, conceded to the Valencians the privileges which the union had demanded. In the mean time his partisans were not inactive in Catalonia: he had soon an army on foot with which two of his generals attacked, defeated, and took Fernando. The infante, however, from fear of the king's vengeance, was conducted into Castile. Pedro himself advanced against Saragossa, the very strong-hold of faction. One instance of ill fortune had damped, as much as success had encouraged, the rebels: they received him with great humility, renounced the privileges of the union, and threw themselves wholly on his mercy. Thirteen of the most obnoxious ringleaders were put to death; the rest he pardoned. In an assembly of the states, which he was no longer afraid of convoking, the ricos homes and deputies solemnly renewed the renunciation of the absurd privileges claimed by the union: in presence of them all, the king tore in pieces the registered act of that body, but at the same time he confirmed his subjects in the possession of all their ancient rights. Aragon was now pacified; its union was no more: but Valencia remained in rebellion. Having assembled a formidable army, Jayme marched into that province, and, in a general battle near the capital, triumphed over the leaguers. Valencia immediately surrendered at discretion. In the first transport of his fury, he intended to level the walls with the ground, to raze every house, and to convert the site into pasture land; but his barbarian ferocity yielded to the remonstrances of his advisers, who could not consent to the sacrifice of that ancient and noble city. Thus in a few short months was this vast confederacy dissipated, and by none other than the most ordinary means.*

1348 to 1374.
On the termination of these troubled scenes, Leonora and one of her sons took refuge in Castile. But misfortunes assailed them there, superior, perhaps, to any which would have befallen them in Aragon. How the infante Juan was murdered at Bilbao, and Leonora herself in the castle of Castro Xeres, by order of Pedro the Cruel, has been related in the reign of that monarch.† Fernando, indeed, escaped the vengeance of the tyrant; but, as we shall soon see, a fate no less tragical awaited him. The misunderstanding between the two Pedros commenced in 1356, on the refusal of the Castilian to restore a prize made at sea by one of his Biscayan pirates. The second offence was committed by an admiral of Catalonia, who, under the eyes of the Castilian, captured two Pisan vessels — a power with which the Aragonese were at war — in the port of Santa Maria. With some justice, the Castilian remonstrated against the violation of a neutral port; and

* Lucius Marineus Siculus, De Rebus Hispaniæ, lib. xI. (apud Schottum, Hispania Illustrata, tom. i.). Zurita, Anales de Aragon, tom. ii. lib. 7. Blancas, Rerum Aragonensium Commentarii, p. 668. (apud Schottum, tom. iii.). Ferreras, Histoire Générale d'Espagne, by Hermilly, tom. v. The chronicles of Pedro Lopez de Ayala and Rodrigo Sanchez, and the Navarrese history of Moret, also throw incidental light on these troubled transactions.
† See Vol. II. p. 216, 217.

on the refusal of his brother sovereign to make satisfaction for it, he levied a heavy contribution on the Catalan inhabitants of Seville, and declared war against Aragon. Hostilities now commenced, with various success and many suspensions. It was the policy of the Aragonese to engage in his service the discontented barons of Castile, especially of Enrique, count of Trastamara, who in the sequel succeeded Pedro the Cruel. In this warfare the count was a useful auxiliary to the Aragonese king; but whenever a truce was made, he had reason to complain that his services were no longer remembered; since one of the conditions invariably was, that he should be expelled from Aragon. On the other hand, the infante Fernando was sometimes leagued with the Castilian. In 1357, Pedro took Tarragona and some other fortresses; but he lost Alicante and Orihuela. In 1359, his fleet infested the coast of Valencia, insulted Barcelona and Iviça. The same year, however, his generals were defeated by land, and the following witnessed the recovery of Tarragona. Such were invariably the indecisive results of this desultory warfare — results which it would be useless to particularise. In general, the success of the war rested with the Castilian. In 1363, through the interference of the papal legate, the first peace was made, the secret conditions of which were of an atrocious character. Pedro of Aragon engaged not only to remove by death the obnoxious brothers of the Castilian, but his own, the infante Fernando. The latter, by some means, arrived at the knowledge of the fate intended him; but, his confidence being restored by the artful hypocrisy of his brother, he did not either arm in his own defence, or consult his safety by flight. Having one day dined with the Aragonese king, and left the table to enter into another apartment, an officer of the household desired him to surrender himself prisoner: he refused, and, on soldiers advancing to seize him, drew his sword for a vigorous defence. But the contest was unequal, though he and two or three of his friends who were with him made a desperate defence, and killed some of their assailants; he and they at length fell before the eyes, and by the encouragement, of count Enrique of Castile, his vindictive enemy.* A servant of that count was the first who dealt the victim a fatal blow. Enrique himself was spared — doubtless because Pedro foresaw that his new ally of Castile would not fulfil his engagements; perhaps, also, because he himself had no disposition to do so. His anticipations were right: war was renewed by the Castilian. His operations were as indecisive as those of the former. If Valencia was invested by the Castilians, the siege was raised on the approach of the Aragonese; and if two or three important fortresses were gained by the former, they were shortly after recovered by the latter. Seeing that the war did not and could not lead to any result, in 1365 Pedro concerted with the count of Trastamara the invasion of Castile, and the dethronement of the Castilian king. The aid which Enrique obtained from France, the fate of his first and second invasions, we have already related.† But the Aragonese king — so true it is that no honour can long subsist among the wicked — was never on good terms with the new king of Castile. He insisted on Murcia, which Enrique, while count of Trastamara, had agreed to resign, in the event of his obtaining the Castilian throne; and on the refusal of that prince to dismember so important a province from the crown, not only coolness, but actual hostilities, between the two kingdoms were preparing. But those hostilities were soon averted by the papal legates; and the truce was, from time to time, prolonged, until 1374, when peace was finally arranged between the two monarchs.‡

---

* Enrique's enmity is sufficiently explained by the fact that Fernando was the next heir to the Castilian crown; his mother, Leonora, being the sister of king Alfonso of Castile. By his murder the right devolved on the king of Portugal. See Vol. II. p. 232.
† Vol. II., reign of Pedro the Cruel.
‡ Pedro Lopez de Ayala, Cronicas de los Reyes de Castilla (in regno don Pedro). Rodericus Santius, Historia Hispanica, pars iv. cap. 14. (apud

The foreign transactions of Pedro were of some importance. In 1338 began his misintelligence with don Jayme, king of Majorca, whose dethronement he appears to have meditated from the commencement of his reign. Though, in 1339, Jayme did homage for his kingdom, his destruction was no less resolved; his unpopular rule — unpopular, because tyrannical and rapacious — afforded Pedro well-founded hopes of success. The islanders complained to the Aragonese king of the sufferings they endured; praying that their kingdom might be incorporated with his, and promising to join him whenever he should send an armament to effect that end. His promise was confirmed by an embassy from the king of France, who informed him that Jayme had long aimed at independence, and was even then preparing to erect the standard of revolt. The following year he artfully drew up a list of grievances, more imaginary than real; and cited his vassal to appear, within twenty-six days, at Barcelona, to answer them. As the latter disregarded the summons, he was declared contumacious and rebellious, and deprived of the fiefs he held from the Aragonese crown. Through the interference of the pope, however, Clement VI., who was anxious to restore peace between them, Pedro was persuaded to have an interview with Jayme in Barcelona. But the conduct of the former, on this occasion, was marked by equal violence and duplicity. Having invented a plot by which he pretended that his liberty was in danger, — that his person was to be seized, and conveyed to Majorca, — he used it as a pretext for forcibly detaining his sister, the wife of don Jayme. In vain did the latter demand his queen, and complain of the violation of the safe-conduct which had been granted him: loudly

---

Schottum, Hispania Illustrata, tom. i.). Lucius Marineus Siculus, De Rebus Hispaniæ, lib. xi. (apud eundem, tom. i.). Franciscus Tarapha, De Regibus Hispaniæ, p. 563. (apud eundem, in eodemque tomo). Alfonsus à Carthagena, Anacephalæosis, cap. 88. (in eodem tomo). Zurita, Anales de Aragon, tom. ii. lib. 7. Hieronymus Blancas, Rerum Aragonensium Commentarii, p. 672, &c. (apud Schottum, tom. iii.).

disclaiming all allegiance to his brother-in-law, he sought his ships, returned to Majorca, and, in the impotence of his passion, declared war against Aragon, thereby sealing his own ruin. In 1343, don Pedro sailed with a formidable armament, landed in Majorca, and was immediately joined by the islanders. Thus universally deserted, Jayme fled, leaving the three islands in the power of his brother-in-law. In opposition to the remonstrances of the pope, who compassionated the misfortunes of the fugitive king, his possessions in France were threatened, and several places in Roussillon speedily reduced. This war beyond the Pyrenees appears to have been as disagreeable to the Catalans and to the Aragonese as it was to the pope; and only by force could the king obtain supplies for conducting it. The following year (1344) he declared by a solemn decree that the Balearic isles should for ever form an integral portion of the Aragonese crown; and again penetrated into Roussillon, the whole of which, except the capital, Perpignan, he speedily reduced. The unfortunate Jayme now solicited a safe-conduct; and, throwing himself at the victor's feet, acknowledged his errors, and pathetically implored forgiveness, in consideration both of his kindness and of the family ties which united them. As well might he have knelt to a rock. He was told, indeed, that, if he would give directions for the surrender of Perpignan, he should experience the clemency of his brother; and, with his usual weakness, he complied with the demand: but no sooner was Pedro in possession of that capital, than another decree declared the whole of Roussillon for ever united with Aragon. With still greater infatuation did he believe the protestations of his betrayer, that, though necessity at present demanded this rigour, he should be speedily indemnified by the states. But when these states were held at Barcelona, no other indemnification was proposed than a miserable pension of 10,000 French louis, and that on the condition of his resigning the royal title.

His French possessions, indeed, were declared his rightful inheritance; but half of them had been already seized by Philip de Valois, his liege superior, with whom he had characteristically quarrelled; and the rest were in danger. He indignantly rejected the proffered pittance, and loudly exclaimed against the treachery which had been practised towards him. His invectives were too late; a detachment of Aragonese advanced to expel him from Catalonia; and, with his few remaining adherents, he was compelled precipitately to cross the Pyrenees, in a severe winter, and exposed to the keenest blasts. Though Clement, his unfailing friend, assisted him with money, and made earnest appeals to the king of Aragon in his favour, nothing was to be obtained; nor was it without extreme difficulty that he could procure the restoration of his wife Constanza, and Jayme his eldest son; his other children were denied him. Unable to bear adversity with common patience,— though the state which could still afford him many of life's comforts could scarcely be called adversity,—in 1349 he sold his lordship of Montpelier for 120,000 crowns in gold to the French king, and with the money raised 3000 foot and 300 horse, in the wild resolution of re-conquering his kingdom. With this small force he embarked, made a descent on the chief island, and marched against the viceroy Gilbert. But every action of this prince was doomed to be as unfortunate as his designs were imprudent. At the very commencement of the engagement he was deserted by his mercenaries; he fought desperately with the handful who remained, refused to surrender, and was killed on the spot: his eldest son remained in the power of the victors. The young prince subsequently escaped from prison, procured allies, and more than once harassed the frontiers of Catalonia; but he was never restored to his natural inheritance. He died without issue; but though his sister Isabel, now heiress to the throne, ceded her rights to the duke of Anjou, and though the French prince arrived to enforce them, the Balearic Isles remained united with the Aragonese crown.*

1340 to 1386. To this monarch, as to his two predecessors, Sardinia proved a sharp thorn in the crown. In 1340, some of the chief inhabitants concerted with the Pisans and Genoese on the project of subverting the Aragonese sway; but, from his efficacious measures, and the vigilance of his viceroy, they were compelled to defer the execution. In 1347, hearing that his attention was wholly occupied by the opposition of the union, they broke out into an open insurrection, defeated the Aragonese troops, and slew the viceroy. Another was sent, who in 1349 defeated them; and the following year many of the discontented chiefs were gained over to the royal cause. But this temporary tranquillity was owing rather to the weakness than to the attachment of the natives, and to the wars between Genoa and Venice, which compelled the former to suspend its intrigues in the island. In this war he entered into an alliance with the latter republic to punish his enemies; but in 1352 the combined fleet was defeated by the Genoese in the Thracian Bosphorus, whither it had repaired to effect a junction with that of the Greek empire. The same year the civil war again desolated Sardinia: one party, as usual, in the interests of the republic; the other of Aragon. The Genoese sent troops to support their adherents, Pedro to oppose them. A naval engagement followed, in which the combined fleets of Venice and Catalonia triumphed: a second was soon obtained on land, but indecisive; since the discontented, with their Genoese allies, remained under arms, and held several strong fortresses. To finish the war, in 1354 Pedro himself passed over to that island, and convoked the states at Cagliari; but he found it impossible to assuage the animosities which burned between certain nobles, who were always disposed to take opposite sides: if one declared

* Lucius Marineus Siculus, De Rebus Hispaniæ, p. 396. (apud Schottum, Hispania Illustrata, tom. i.). Zurita, Anales de Aragon, tom. ii. lib. 7. Blancas, Rerum Aragonensium Commentarii, p. 672, &c. (apud Schottum, tom. iii.). Ferreras, Histoire Générale d'Espagne (by Hermilly), tom. v.

for Aragon, the other was sure to league with the republic. Seeing that the entire extinction of the strife was hopeless,—that hostilities might be protracted for years,—he returned in a few months to his dominions. Thus the war continued; subject, indeed, to many suspensions, through the good offices of the popes, who were solicitous for peace, and who often prevailed on the parties interested to send plenipotentiaries for the purpose. In 1368 the judge of Arborea, who had for years, in defiance of Pedro, exercised sovereign sway over a considerable portion of the island, attempted to gain the whole, defeated the Aragonese, and circumscribed their dominion to the capital and the few fortresses on the coast. To oppose this formidable baron, Pedro raised up another native of great hereditary influence, who checked the victor in his career, and even recovered several fortresses. But though, from the peace which had been made between Pedro and the Genoese, he could procure no assistance from the republic, he was not discouraged; nor, when a powerful reinforcement arrived in aid of his viceroy, did he show any signs of submission: he threw himself into one of his fortresses, where he defied the royal forces. In 1373 the republic again armed, and joined him. He besieged Cagliari, while his allies invested Algeri; and though both held out, it was only in the hope of ultimate succour from Spain. Had not his death intervened, this enterprising man would have assuredly attained the sovereignty of the island; but his son and successor, unequal to the task of continuing his great work, was unable to expel the Aragonese. On the tragical death of this son, whose tyranny roused the people to arm, and put him to death, the war was conducted with vigour by his sister Leonora until 1386, when a kind of compromise was effected between the Genoese and the king of Aragon. Each power agreed to abandon to the other certain ports and dock-yards for the construction of ships. Leonora was confirmed in the extensive dominions left her by her father and brother; and a full amnesty was granted to all political offenders. But this divided sovereignty was but a poor compensation for the blood and treasure which had been expended. The obstinacy of Pedro, in retaining possession of an island which experience had shown would never willingly own his sway, which had already cost him so many successive campaigns, drew on him the frequent remonstrances of his states, and the refusal of supplies.

1377 to 1384. As if one ruinous war for an unattainable object were not sufficient, on the death of Frederick king of Sicily, in 1377, who had married his daughter Constanza, he claimed that crown, and showed a disposition to arm in defence of his claim. Frederic II. left no male issue; and as, by the will of Frederic I., females were excluded from the succession, he applied to the pope for its ratification. But Maria, daughter of Frederic, in conformity with the last will of that prince, had ascended the throne; and her right was sanctioned by Gregory. If the new queen, as the pontiff justly observed, was incapacitated by her sex, what became of Pedro's right, who could claim only as the descendant of the princess Constanza, daughter of Manfred? However convincing this reply, it had no effect on the king, who, in 1379, equipped a fleet, for the purpose of taking forcible possession of the crown; but, when on the eve of embarkation, he was persuaded to relinquish his purposes by his advisers, who represented to him, that one so fruitful in policy as he was, could not fail to attain his end by milder and surer means. He soon proved that he was fully deserving their confidence in his political manœuvring. Hearing that the regent of the island had agreed to marry the princess with a baron of Milan, he caused the destined bridegroom to be intercepted at sea. At the same time, one of his partisans scaled by night the walls of the castle of Catania, where the princess resided under the care of her guardian, and bore her away to another fortress. Maria was subsequently brought into Aragon, and married by her grandfather to the infante don Martin, another of his grand-children. He thus hoped, that, if he himself could not be recognised as king, the crown would at least remain in his family, and perhaps, at no distant day, be incorporated with that of Aragon. But for the obstinacy of his eldest son and heir, don Juan, who, in 1384, became a widower, whom he wished to marry with the young princess, but who secretly formed the indissoluble connection with a French princess, the effect of his policy would have been an immediate union of the two crowns. It may, however, be doubted whether such a union was desirable; since, from the distance of the two kingdoms, and the contiguity of the island to Naples, it could not long have been perpetuated.

The ambition of Pedro was insatiable; but it was also senseless, as it grasped at impossibilities. Hearing that some people of Athens and Patras, who were of Aragonese extraction, — the descendants of the crusaders, who had conquered this duchy, — had risen to establish his domination, he sent an armament to their aid, and was ultimately acknowledged. It need, however, be scarcely observed, that possessions so far removed from the seat of power would yield but a nominal allegiance, and would soon be lost. But there was no advantage, however small in magnitude or transient in duration, which he was not at all times ready to grasp, — generally without much regard to the rights or feelings of others. The avidity with which, in 1386, he seized on the city of Tarragona, the government and sovereignty of which had long rested with the archbishops of that see, is affirmed by some historians to have been the cause of his death.* He died early in the month of January, 1387, after an agitated reign of fifty-one years.

1382 to 1387.

The duplicity of this monarch was only equalled by his violence: of sincerity and justice he was wholly des-

* St. Thecla, patroness of the church of Tarragona, appeared to him, upbraided him with impiety, and gave him so good a box on the ear, or smack in the face, that he never recovered from it. "Está muy recibido que fue contigado de la mano de Dios, y se le aparecio en vision Santa Tecla, la qual le hirio de una palmada en el rostro, y que este fue la ocasion de su dolencia."—*Zurita*, ii. 388. Who would expect Ferreras, a writer of the eighteenth century, to believe such a relation?

titute; and in savage barbarity he was scarcely exceeded by his namesake of Castile. His behaviour to a papal legate, who enforced in the apostolic court certain ecclesiastical dues, is too characteristic to be unnoticed. Some of the persons on whom this tax fell, (which was doubtless an unpopular one,) and who had been excommunicated for refusing to pay it, complained to Pedro. He sent for the legate, whom he required to stay the proceedings, and remove the ban. The churchman refused, even when confined to a close prison, to forego the rights of his order. Further severities were now devised: he was dragged from his prison, stripped of his canonicals, and hung by the feet from the top of a high tower, with an intimation that he would be suffered to fall from his elevated position, and consequently be dashed to pieces, if he any longer refused to yield the point in dispute. The terrified canon, now half dead, consented to whatever was demanded. Not so his master the pope, who compelled Pedro not only to allow the levying the tax, but, fierce as he was by nature and habit, to submit to a suitable penance for the sacrilege. With many of the vices and none of the virtues of humanity, he was neither loved nor respected; but, in return, he was feared. It is impossible not to admire his constancy in reverses: he deviated not from his purposes, nor suffered his mind to be depressed, in the most critical periods of his reign,— and few princes were ever placed in circumstances more critical;—yet he almost uniformly gained his end. Justice must also allow that, whatever were his personal vices, he was no enemy to the lowest class of his people.

During the reign of this prince, the era of Cæsar was abolished, and the Christian adopted for the two chief kingdoms of Spain; in 1350 at Saragossa, and in 1383 at Segovia.*

* Stella, Annales Genuenses (apud Muratorium, Rerum Italicarum Scriptores, tom. xvii.). Anonymus, Diaria Neapolitana (apud eundem, tom. xxi.). Annales de Raimo, sive brevis Historia Rerum in Regno Neapolitano gestarum, &c. p. 230, &c. (apud eundem, tom. xxiii.). Lucius Marineus Siculus, De Rebus Hispaniæ, lib. xi. (apud Schottum, Hispania Illustrata, tom. i.). Zurita, Anales de Aragon, tom. ii. lib. 8—17. Blancas, Rerum Aragonensium Commentarii, p. 672, &c. (apud Schottum, tom. iii.

In 1387, JUAN I. was peaceably acknowledged. His accession was regarded with great apprehension by his stepmother, Sibilla (the late king led four ladies to the altar), who, since 1384, had been his open enemy. The reason of this animosity was here, as in former cases, the eagerness of the king to alienate the crown domains in favour of his new queen and her family, and the indignant opposition of the heir apparent. At one time, so vindictive was the queen, that she had expelled the infante from the palace, and had probably instigated her uxorious husband to try him, and exclude him from the succession; but the protection of the grand justiciary of Aragon had screened him from her malice: now, it was her turn to dread his displeasure. Just before the death of Pedro, she fled from Barcelona, accompanied by her brother: they were pursued by the Catalonians; were brought back, and imprisoned until the pleasure of the new monarch, who then lay ill at Gerona, could be learned. On his recovery, he hastened to that city; caused the queen to be tried as a witch, who had enchanted the late king, and several of her kindred and servants as accomplices. Some of the latter were executed; and she herself would probably have shared the same fate, but for the interference of the papal legate, and more still for the facility with which she restored the fortresses conferred on her by her royal husband. These possessions were immediately transferred to the new queen.

The eagerness which the new king showed to gratify his queen Violante, surprised and offended the Aragonese. As her disposition was gay, she insisted on converting the palace into a theatre: balls, concerts, theatrical representations, and the exhibitions of the gaya ciencia, succeeded each other without intermission. As the Aragonese themselves were too sober or too dull

---

Paternio Catinensis, Sicani Reges, p. 125, &c. Ferreras, Histoire Générale d'Espagne, by Hermilly, tom. v. See also Appendix E.

For the Italian events of this period we again refer to Sismondi's comprehensive work, Histoire des Républiques Italiennes du Moyen Age, in 16 vols. 8vo. Paris, 1826.

to excel in such diversions, professors were brought from France, and even schools established for instruction in the idle art. It became not merely the relaxation, but the business of life; the duties of government were neglected or despised, until remonstrances both frequent and loud fell on the royal ear. Apparently, however, they produced little effect, beyond the convocation of the states at Monzon, to deliberate on this pernicious novelty. There the prelates, nobles, and deputies insisted that he should expel from his palace his singers and dancers, his buffoons and his poets—above all, doña Carraza Villaragut, one of the queen's ladies, and the chief promoter of such fooleries. At first he resisted this interference with his royal recreations; but when he perceived that his barons were in earnest, that they were even preparing to arm for his moral reformation, he yielded: the fiddlers were dismissed, and with them the obnoxious lady.

1389 to 1395. The short reign of this prince was not without its troubles. Having repelled an invasion of the licentious disbanded troops of the south of France, headed by the count d'Armagnac, he was harassed by the insurrection of those most restless and faithless of subjects, the Sardinians. As usual, the efforts of his generals to repress it were but partially successful. The affairs of Sicily were not more promising. There was a party there in the interests of France, which, during the continued absence of the young queen, Maria, the wife of the infante don Martin, broke out into open rebellion, and seized on several strong places. Nor when the queen and her husband returned to the island (in 1392), accompanied by a strong body of Aragonese cavalry, did the rebels submit: in 1393 they were strong and audacious enough to besiege their queen in Catania; and the place would certainly have been compelled to capitulate, but for the arrival of another reinforcement from Spain. None of these commotions appear to have occasioned king Juan the least anxiety: he resumed his diversions, that of hunting especially, with as much eagerness as before, leaving the cares of government to his queen. One day, while occupied in this favourite occupation in the forest of Foja, he fell from his horse, and was killed on the spot.*

On receiving intelligence of this catastrophe Aragon, 1395. Catalonia, and Valencia proclaimed DON MARTIN, brother of the late king, who was then in Sicily, supporting the rights of his son and daughter-in-law, sovereigns of that island. This choice gave great umbrage to Matthieu count de Foix, who had married the eldest daughter of Juan, and who contended that the crown belonged to him in her right. He collected troops and penetrated into Catalonia; but he found the inhabitants averse to his pretensions, and indignant at his proceedings. As the states were sitting at Saragossa, he now adopted the wiser mode of deputing ambassadors to that assembly, with instructions to espouse his rights, which, according to the laws of legitimate succession, were well founded. But Aragon had seen only one female sovereign, doña Petronilla, and had for some time been inclined to consider the Salique law as tacitly in force. The count met with a repulse both there and at Barcelona; but he hoped that arms would be more effectual than arguments; and, with a second and more numerous army, he invaded Aragon. There he and his countess solemnly assumed the royal title and arms, and reduced several towns, among which was Balbastro; but his rear was so harassed, and such was the scarcity of provisions, that he was soon compelled to retire into Navarre by way of Huesca, Bolea, and Ayerba.

Having pacified Sicily, in appearance at least, and 1396. caused his son and daughter-in-law to be acknowledged by the rebels, Martin, who seems to have been in no anxiety about the security of his kingdom, proceeded to Sardinia and Corsica, with the view of restoring tranquillity also in those islands. As, during his presence, hostilities were suspended, he indulged the hope that his sway would thenceforth be established. On landing at Barcelona, in 1397, he declared the count and countess

* Authorities,— the Chronicles in Muratori, Lucius Marineus Siculus, Paternio Catinensis, Zurita, Ferreras, and many others.

de Foix traitors to the state, and their ample domain in Catalonia confiscated. The following year he convoked his prelates, barons, and deputies at Saragossa, and caused his son, the Sicilian king, to be acknowledged his successor; it was also decreed that Sicily and Aragon should for ever be united under the same sceptre. The count de Foix was soon afterwards forced to recross the Pyrenees; and his death, without issue, freed the king, if not from a formidable, from a troublesome rival.

1397 to 1409. No sooner had Martin arrived in Spain, than Sardinia again became the theatre of civil war. It was fomented by pope Boniface, who, incensed that the Aragonese had acknowledged the rival pontiff, Benedict, conferred the fiefs of Sardinia and Sicily on the count de Molineto. Fortunately for the king, a papal investiture was not all-powerful: to give it effect an armament was required, and he could raise a greater one than his rival. He speedily caused reinforcements to be sent to both islands: in the former they could do no more than restrain the open hostilities of the rebels; in the latter they restored tranquillity. And, though this tranquillity was disturbed on the death of the queen, Maria, in 1401, who, as she left no issue, bequeathed the crown to her husband, yet, as the Sicilian king was heir to such extended states, his alliance was sought by the greatest princes, and he easily triumphed over internal agitation and external intrigue. (The following year he received the hand of the princess Blanche of Navarre.) But Sardinia continued torn by the two parties,—one in favour of the native family of Arborea, the other of the lawful monarch. In 1408, the Sicilian king, indignant at seeing a portion of his future inheritance thus wasted, sent a body of troops to oppose the chief rebel; and, the following year, accompanied by a greater, he himself passed into that island. Having also received a powerful aid from his father, he marched against the head of the rebels, Brancaleon Doria, who, with 18,000 infantry, did not refuse the battle. It ended in a complete triumph for the king, and was followed by the surrender of an important fortress. As the heat of the weather began to be intensely felt, the victor returned to Cagliari. That heat and the festivities consequent on his success threw him into a fever, which, though not in itself fatal, he is said to have rendered so by incontinence.* He died on the 24th of July, 1409.†

On the death of this prince, Martin and the Aragonese were anxious to name a successor to the crown. Of the princes who could show any pretensions to the dignity, the chief were, first, the count of Urgel, who descended in the male line from the royal house, and whom the king made vicar-general of the realm; secondly, the duke d'Anjou, who had married the infanta Violante, daughter of the late king Juan I.; thirdly, the infante Fernando, regent of Castile, whose mother was the princess Leonora, sister of the reigning king, don Martin; and, fourthly, don Alfonso of Aragon. The fierce rivalry of these candidates, and the factions which began to agitate the kingdom, so disgusted Martin, that to disappoint them all, though advanced in years, he married Margarita, daughter of the count de Prades, and a princess of the royal house of Aragon. He next sent troops to pacify Sardinia and Sicily, which were again torn by rival dissensions. In the former, his generals were suc-

1410.

---

* According to Père Tomich, he died of the plague; but Laurentius Valla disproves this statement by the fact that none besides the king died on that occasion. Zurita gives the true cause:—" Martin de Apartal añade otra causa, por donde le sobrevino la muerte, que creyendo que avia convalecido le devaron por complazerle una donzella, que era hermosissima y siendo muy rendido a aquel vicio le acabo la vida." Tom. ii. fol. 453. Ferreras (supposing Hermilly to have correctly interpreted him) is very incorrect in this place:—" La il s'amouracha extrêmement d'une jeune fille, et, ayant passé une nuit avec elle, il porta si loin son incontinence, qu'il fut attaqué d'une fièvre maligne, qui le précipita au tombeau." Tom. vi. p. 129.

† Laurentius Valla, De Rebus à Ferdinando Aragoniæ Rege Gestis, lib. ii. (apud Schottum, Hispania Illustrata, tom. l.). Lucius Marineus Siculus, De Rebus Hispania, lib. ix. p. 398. (apud eundem, eodemque tomo). Blancas, Rerum Aragonensium Commentarii (apud eundem, p. 677, &c.). Zurita, Anales de Aragon, tom. ii. lib. 10. Stella, Annales Genuenses (apud Muratorium, Rerum Italicarum Scriptores, tom. xvii.). Anonymous, Diaria Neapolitana (apud eundem, tom. xxi.) Ludovicus de Raimo, Annales de Raimo, sive Brevis Historia Rerum in Regno Neapolitano Gestarum (apud eundem, tom. xxiii.) Paternio Catinensis, Sicani Reges, p. 129, &c. Ferreras, Histoire Générale d'Espagne, by Hermilly, tom. vi.

cessful in two decisive engagements; in the latter, he caused the regency to be confirmed in the widowed queen, Blanche. In 1410 he died without issue, and before the settlement of the disputes concerning the succession. This prince had not vigour to rule spirits so turbulent as the Aragonese; he could not enforce the administration of justice. Several families, mutually and hereditarily hostile, took up arms, and pursued each other with the most vindictive feelings. Tranquillity was at length restored, through the armed exertions of the grand justiciary.

1410, 1411. The death of Martin was followed by troubles greater than any which had yet afflicted the kingdom. In Aragon, three or four of the most powerful enemies, whose dissensions had for some time disturbed the public tranquillity, openly paraded their armed partisans, declared for different candidates, and made war on each other. In Valencia, two factions sharpened their weapons, and ultimately came to blows; the one in favour of the infante Enrique, the other of the count of Urgel. In Sardinia, the viscount de Narbonne, who on the maternal side was related to the rebellious family of Arborea, and who aspired to the power formerly held by that family, had a numerous party, and was enabled to make some important conquests. In Sicily, the regent, the widowed queen Blanche, had to sustain a siege by a faction which aimed at the supreme authority, and from the persecution of which she was not rescued for some months. In short, every where were the laws disregarded — every where were violence and blood triumphant. Though Catalonia was at first tranquil, that province was soon harassed by the irruptions of the count de Foix, who, in the fear that his pretensions would not stand the test of deliberation, endeavoured to overawe the states. To restrain the angry passions of the nobles, Benedict, the rival pope, passed into Aragon: his voice could not hush the storm, which seemed to acquire fury in proportion to its duration. The indiscretion of the count de Foix soon alienated the parliament of Catalonia, with whose order to disband his troops he neglected to comply. In Aragon, the archbishop of Saragossa was no less hostile to his pretensions. To remove this prelate was now the resolve of Antonio de Luna, head of the Aragonese faction in favour of the count de Urgel. As a truce had just been concluded between the hostile parties, don Antonio solicited an interview with the archbishop, each to be accompanied by a certain number of horsemen: it was to take place in the highway from Almunia to Almonazid. As the churchman proceeded, he was met by the count de Luna with twenty lancers—two hundred had been hid behind a hill—and the conference began. The object of Antonio was to quarrel with the prelate, and thereby have something like a pretext for the deed he meditated. Finding that the latter would strenuously support the infante of Castile, he at length demanded in a furious tone, "Shall the count de Urgel be king or not?"—"Not while I live!" replied the other. "He shall, whether you live or die," rejoined the count, who at the same time struck him with his mailed hand on the face. Seeing that mischief was intended, the archbishop pushed his mule to escape, and his domestics endeavoured to save him; but, as most of them were unarmed, and as the lancers whom don Antonio had laid in ambush now rode up, the strife was soon ended. The sword of the count descending on the head of the victim, caused him to stagger in his seat, and almost instantly to fall on the ground, where he was speedily despatched and beheaded.* This dark deed, brought the count de Urgel into detestation throughout Aragon and Catalonia, and powerfully tended to his exclusion. In Valencia, in-

---

* Another account says that his hand was amputated, but makes no mention of the head. The real murderer of the prelate was believed to be the count of Urgel; but Antonio did not escape. The states of the kingdom pronounced him a traitor and rebel, and confiscated his possessions: by the church he was excommunicated. His remaining days were few, and passed in misery.

deed, the deputies assembled in the capital were in his favour; but, in the same kingdom, another parliament was held directly opposed to him. The partisans of don Fernando solicited and obtained troops from Castile, not only to oppose the count de Luna, but to encourage his own party. This armed demonstration of the two parties—for though there were other candidates, none of the rest had the slightest chance of success—the states in vain endeavoured to repress. By both, many excesses were committed; by both were the territories of their personal enemies laid waste, and those enemies themselves put to the sword with perfect impunity. The case was still worse, when the count de Urgel and his fit support, don Antonio, poured Gascon troops into Catalonia and Valencia. In the latter kingdom the two parties came to a general engagement, in which victory declared for that of Fernando, several thousands of the other being left dead on the field.

1412. To end these violent scenes had long been the aim of the wise and good among all parties; but the number of such is always small, and, during the tempest of civil strife, their voice is seldom heard. In the present case, the difficulty was to unite the three states,—Aragon, Catalonia, and Valencia—in one deliberative assembly or general congress of deputies, assisted by the respective local parliaments; and when deputies from the two first were named, it was found impossible to procure any from Valencia, which was perhaps about equally divided between the two factions,—each having its parliament, and each refusing to concur in any proposed measure. When those nominated by the parliaments of Aragon and Catalonia assembled at Alcañiz, finding that no union was to be expected from their southern fellow-subjects, and that unless some extraordinary expedient were adopted, anarchy might be for ever perpetuated, they resolved to proceed to the election without the Valencians, if the latter still persisted in their division. The expedient proposed was, that the right of choosing the monarch should be intrusted to nine arbitrators—three from each of the kingdoms. Had each nominated its judges, the expedient might have been lawful, as it certainly was convenient; since, in a promiscuous assembly, nothing could have been expected beyond confusion, uproar, and bloodshed. But it was opposed by the party of the candidate count, who well knew, that, as the election was to be determined by a majority of votes, and as Aragon and Catalonia were united to exclude him, he could expect nothing from such a congress. His only chance of success lay in introducing new bodies of troops, and carrying his point by force. At first he had endeavoured to prevent the meeting of the deputies at Alcañiz; but the advance of the Castilians compelled him to take refuge in Valencia, the viceroy of which was his partisan.

The choice of the arbitrators was one which would have been attended with interminable difficulties, had it been left to the deputies of the three states. But confiding in their power, the assembly of Alcañiz, which consisted chiefly of Aragonese, and the parliament of Tortosa, which was formed of Catalonians, agreed that these arbitrators should be nominated by the viceroy, and the grand justiciary of Aragon. Accordingly, these two functionaries named three for each of the states, all eminent legalists, all men of unblameable lives, and of whom all would have been unexceptionable had they been less illegitimately chosen. As two thirds of the number were known to be friendly to the claims of the infante Fernando, the result might easily have been anticipated. Having assembled at Caspe, whither the advocates of the candidates appeared also — thus confirming the legality of a tribunal which they had so much opposed — the nine arbitrators commenced their deliberations, or rather the registering of their suffrages. In the end, six of the number decided for Fernando; viz. the three Aragonese, two Valencians, and one Catalonian: two only voted for the count de Urgel, and one refused

1412.

to give his suffrage.* Their opinions, however, must not be received as strictly representing the states for which they had been nominated: if those of Aragon were faithful interpreters of the popular voice, the case was not so with regard to Valencia, which was mostly for the count of Urgel; nor with respect to Catalonia, where the people were generally in favour of Fernando. These judges were the nominees, not of the three states, but of the viceroy and justiciary; who, provided the aggregate were favourable to the great object, were little solicitous about a nice adjustment of the relative proportions. They were, indeed, approved by the parliaments of Aragon and Catalonia; and were not very much disapproved by those of Valencia; both because their personal characters were entitled to respect, and because, in the two first instances, their bias was known. Thus, when, on the 28th day of June, the important decision was made known to the public in the church of Caspe, the partial murmurs which were raised by the partisans of the count were drowned in the loud applause of the multitude.

However illegal the construction of this celebrated and novel tribunal, no fault can be found with the deci-

* The following will show the respective claims of the chief candidates:—

Fernando's.
Pedro IV., king, who had no issue.
|
Leonora, his eldest daughter.
|
Juan II., king of Castile.   FERNANDO.

The Duke d'Anjou's.
Juan I., who left no male issue.
|
Violante.
|
LOUIS D'ANJOU.

The Count of Urgel's.
Alfonso IV., father of Pedro IV.
|
Jayme, second son, count of Urgel.
|
Pedro, also count.
|
JAYME, present count.

sion. Fernando was beyond all comparison the best fitted of the candidates for the vacant dignity. If that decision had been regulated by the strict principles of succession alone, the crown would have devolved on the brows of Juan II. king of Castile, whose father, Enrique, elder brother of Fernando, was the eldest son of Leonora, daughter of Pedro IV. king of Aragon. However much it is to be regretted that the opportunity was now lost of uniting the two crowns, nothing is more certain than that neither Castile nor Aragon showed the slightest wish for such a union: probably both would have opposed it. To promote the views of the infante, the queen mother of Castile and the council of the kingdom placed at his disposal a considerable sum which had been voted for the war with Granada; another, and not very creditable illustration of his eagerness to grasp the tempting sceptre.*

The arrival of FERNANDO I.—of a prince whose administration had been distinguished alike for its internal wisdom and its triumph over the Mohammedans—increased the number of his adherents, or rather disarmed all his opponents, except a small band, which still adhered to the count de Urgel, until that chief, perceiving the danger of resistance, reluctantly submitted. He was acknowledged, not only by the three Spanish states, but by Sicily, in the regency of which he confirmed queen Blanche, and by that portion of Sardinia which still owned the supremacy of Aragon. The following year, the viscount de Narbonne surrendered his rights over the latter island for a certain sum,—a sum very ill applied.

1411.

But the count de Urgel had no intention of acknowledging the new sovereign, though that sovereign pro-

1413.

---

* Laurentius Valla, De Rebus à Ferdinando Aragoniæ Rege Gestis, lib. ii. (apud Schottum, tom i.) Lucius Marineus Siculus, De Rebus Hispaniæ, lib. xi. (apud eundem, eodemque tomo). Blancas, Rerum Aragonensium Commentarii, p. 682, &c. (apud eundem, tom. iii.) Zurita, Anales de Aragon, tom. iii. lib. ii. Paternio Catinensis, Sicani Reges, p. 129—133. Rodericus Santius, Historia Hispania, pars ii. cap 23. (apud Schottum, tom. i.). Franciscus Tarapha, De Regibus Hispaniæ, p. 565. (in eodem tomo). Alfonsus à Carthagena, Anacephalæosis, cap. 92. (in eodem tomo). Ferreras, Histoire Général d'Espagne, by Hermilly, tom. vi.

posed to indemnify him in his recent losses, and even to marry the infante Enrique, son of Fernando, with his daughter. He temporised until he had formed an alliance with the English duke of Clarence, to whom he proposed, as the condition of aid, both the hand of that daughter and his domains in France. But this alliance proved of no avail: though Antonio de Luna invaded Aragon with seven hundred lances, the want of pay, the formidable preparations of the king, and the necessity of the duke's return to England, soon caused them to retire. The count, however, who had received a reinforcement from his hereditary domains, marched on Lerida; but some of his troops were defeated, others fell from him, and he was invested in Balaguer. The place was so vigorously pressed, that, in the end, he left it, and surrendered himself to the king's mercy. He was consigned to the castle of Lerida, whence he was afterwards transferred to a fortress in Castile. By the assembled states he was declared a traitor and a rebel, deprived of his domains, and sentenced to perpetual imprisonment. He never recovered his liberty. By the son and successor of Fernando, he was forcibly removed from Castile, which was then at war with Aragon, to the fortress of Xativa, where he died. The following year, his mother, the princess Margaret, was placed in confinement, on the charge of her having corresponded with some French princes to procure the liberation of her son and the death of the king.

1414 to 1416. Fernando, like his predecessors, cast a longing eye on Naples as well as Sicily. Knowing that Jane, who had succeeded to that throne on the death of her brother Ladislas, was inclined to a union with his family, he made overtures to her in favour of his second son, Juan; they were accepted, the marriage conditions arranged, and the infante embarked for Sicily, where he expected to meet his intended bride. On his arrival, however, he found, to his mortification, that the queen,—an extraordinary instance of mutability even in *her* sex,—

had precipitately married with the count de la Marche, a prince of the house of Bourbon. That the infante bore the disappointment with indifference is probable, as he soon directed his attentions to another quarter, the widowed Blanche, and through her to the crown of Sicily. This object he would soon have gained, had not his father, apprehensive of his designs, recalled him. His subsequent marriage, however, with that princess, and his accession, through her, to the throne of Navarre, have been related in the history of that kingdom. In 1416, death surprised Fernando at Igualada.*

ALFONSO V., the eldest son of the deceased king, 1416 gave a signal proof of magnanimity or of prudence to immediately after his accession. Hearing that Antonio 1429. de Luna, then in Guienne, had bribed several nobles of Catalonia and Aragon to espouse the cause of the imprisoned count de Urgel, whom they proposed to place on the throne, and being presented with a list of the traitors' names, he not only refused to read it, but tore it into pieces. Nor was his firmness less remarkable. Though he knew that, by investing Castilians with posts in his household, he had offended the jealousy or avarice of his subjects, he disdained to notice the senseless clamour: and to the deputies of Saragossa and Valencia, who, insisted in his presence, that all employments in the palace should not only be bestowed on natives alone, but with the concurrence of the states assembled, he sharply replied, that he saw no reason why a king should not have the same privilege of appointing his domestics as a private individual, and that future remonstrances of this description would subject such as dared to make them to imprisonment, if not something worse. The frightened deputies were glad to escape from his pre-

---

* Laurentius Valla, De Rebus à Ferdinando Aragoniæ Rege Gestis, lib. iii. (apud Schottum, Hispania Illustrata, tom. i.). Lucius Marineus Siculus, De Rebus Hispaniæ, lib. xi. (in eodem tomo). Zurita, Anales de Aragon, tom. ii. lib. 12. Blancas, Rerum Aragonensium Commentarii, p. 698, &c. (apud Schottum, tom. iii.). Paternio Catinensis, Sicanl Reges, p. 134, &c. Ferreras, Histoire Général d'Espagne, by Hermilly, tom. vi.

sence. But the greatest qualities of our nature require control: if he was thus fitted, by the vigorous exercise of his prerogative, to preserve internal peace, that vigour on some occasions degenerated into undue severity — in one into the most odious of crimes. The mysterious disappearance, in 1429, of the archbishop of Saragossa, filled the people with consternation. That the prelate had incensed the king, by opening a secret correspondence with Juan II. of Castile, then at war with Aragon*, is certain; but some deeper crime than even treason must surely have given rise to his untimely fate. Had he, as one contemporary writer intimates, made dishonourable proposals to the queen? — The subject is wrapt in hopeless darkness, and so is the mode of the victim's death: whether he was strangled in prison, or thrown from a Carmelite monastery into the Ebro, need not be enquired. What is certain is, that no steps were taken to punish the sacrilege; a circumstance that may be attributed either to the absence of papal vigour during the famous schism, or to some grievous crime on the part of the prelate which rendered enquiry inexpedient.

The transactions of Alfonso in the islands and on the continent of Italy occupied the greater part of his reign: though, from their number, a volume would be required to detail them; and though they belong rather to the history of the Two Sicilies than to that of Spain; they must not altogether be passed over in silence, since a general notice of them is necessary towards a right understanding of the position, not of Aragon only, but of the Spanish monarchy, during the sixteenth and seventeenth centuries.

1417 to 1420. Though the investiture of Corsica had been conferred at the same time as that of Sardinia on a preceding king of Aragon, and though some places on the island had at various periods been held by the Aragonese, the conquest of the whole had never been seriously at-

---

* See Vol. II. p. 250.

tempted—doubtless, because, from the contiguity of the Genoese, who considered themselves its lawful sovereigns, and from the never-ceasing rebellions of the Sardinians, that attempt would have appeared hopeless. In 1417, however, some Catalans having come into collision with the forces of the republic, don Alfonso meditated the conquest. But though he reduced Calvi, after some fruitless assaults on Bonifaccio, which the Genoese relieved, he was forced to abandon the siege under the pretext of more pressing interests. The pretext, indeed, was not without foundation. As usual, the troubles of Sardinia were renewed, occasioned by the Genoese and by the partisans of the viscount de Narbonne, who complained that neither Alfonso nor Fernando had fulfilled the conditions of the sale. While here, occupied, as his predecessors had vainly been, in striving to restore tranquillity, he was surprised by the solicitations for aid from Joanna queen of Naples, who, as related in the previous reign, had deceived his brother Juan by marrying the count de la Marche. That fickle princess, disgusted alike with her husband and his nation, had expelled the French from her dominions, and the count himself, apprehensive that his life was in danger, had fled. The constable Sforza, jealous of the influence possessed by the minister, Caraccioli, had offered the kingdom to the duke d'Anjou, provided the latter would appear with a sufficient French force. The alarmed queen proposed to Alfonso to adopt him as her heir (she was without issue), on the condition of his preserving her on the throne. Though the members of his council dissuaded him from interfering in the affairs of such a kingdom and such a queen, he disregarded their prudent advice; the instrument of adoption was prepared and signed at the same time with the treaty which bound him to aid her [*]

---

[*] Lucius Marineus Siculus, De Rebus Hispaniæ, lib xl (apud Schottum, Hispania Illustrata, tom. i.). Rodericus Santius, Historia Hispanica, cap. 27, &c (in eodem tomo) Alfonsus a Carthagena, Anacephalæosis, cap. 92. (in eodem tomo). Zurita, Anales de Aragon, tom. iii. lib. 13. Blancas, Rerum Aragonensium Commentarii, p. 701. (apud Schottum,

1420 to 1423.

In the mean time the duke d'Anjou had sailed from Genoa with an armament, invested Naples, and ordered his fleet to defend the entrance into the port against the expected measures of the Aragonese. But, on the approach of Alfonso's admiral, the duke raised the siege, and retired into the mountains. The king himself now hastened to that capital, and was received by the queen with extraordinary honours: his adoption was celebrated by the Neapolitan nobility, and he was put in immediate possession of the duchy of Calabria. But his opponent had retired only to raise reinforcements. Aided by the republic of Genoa and the pope, the French prince soon resumed hostilities. The Genoese fleet was defeated; the duke's general shared the same fate on land; a truce was mediated by the pope, who aimed at uniting the Italian princes in expelling the Aragonese: it was followed by renewed attempts, on the part of Alfonso, to gain possession of the Neapolitan fortresses, still held by his rival. But however successful his arms, he had soon reason to find how just had been the representations of his advisers. The fickle queen began to regard his authority with jealousy, and even to show a disposition to renew her alliance with France: perhaps she also distrusted his ulterior intentions; at least she made them the pretext for her subsequent conduct.* Though there appears little or no foundation for her suspicion that he

---

* tom. iii.). Stella, Annales Genuenses, (apud Muratorium, Rerum Italicarum Scriptores, tom. xvii.). Anonymus, Diaria Neapolitana (apud eundem, tom. xxi.). Ludovicus de Raimo, Annales de Raimo, sive Brevis Historia Rerum in Regno Neapolitano Gestarum (apud eundem, tom. xxiii.). Bartholomæus Facius, De Rebus Gestis ab Alphonso I. Neapolitano Rege, lib. i.—vi. Anonymus, Storia di Napoli, tom. ii. p. 220, &c. Giannone, Istoria Civile del Regno de Napoli, tom. lii. Paternio Catinensis, Sicani Reges, p. 143. Anonymous, Histoire du Royaume de Naples, tom. ii. p. 207, &c.

* The hatred of the queen was in no small degree owing to the jealousy of her minister and *favourite* Caraccioli. Finding that the graceful person of the king was likely to destroy his influence, the latter invented the most ingenious reports to rouse her apprehensions. "Hic (Caraccioli) cum à regina Alphonsum salutaturus venisset, atque regis venustatem agnovisset crescit statim ζηλοτυπία angi, ne si ad Joannæ conspectum venerit, hæc quæ non admodum casta erat, ejus amore caperetur, seque rejecto omnem confidentiam in Alphonso collocaret."—*Paternio Catinensis*, Sicani Reges, p. 144.

had resolved to dethrone her, she zealously plotted against his authority, and even his life. Having failed to remove him by poison, she next planned his assassination, and sent one of the conspirators to request an interview with him. The messenger was arrested by the seasonably apprised king; who, however, with the view of continuing the course of duplicity that had lately characterised both him and the queen, proceeded towards the castle of Naples, where the interview was to take place. As he approached the walls he was saluted by a shower of arrows; in a transport of fury he assailed the gates; his forces were at the same time attacked by some French and Neapolitans, under Sforza: he was defeated, and compelled to seek refuge in his quarters, where he was immediately invested. He stood out, however, until reinforcements reached him from Sicily and Spain: now he assumed the offensive, took Naples by storm, and used the advantage with very little moderation. The queen retired to Nola, revoked the adoption, and applied for aid to the French, the pope, the Genoese, and the duke of Milan, who promised to raise forces in her behalf. Alfonso now returned to Spain, to procure the liberation of his brother Enrique, who had long been detained prisoner by Juan II. of Castile.* Another brother, the infante Pedro, he left in the command of the city and fleet; yet he sailed with a force sufficient to take and pillage Marseilles, a portion of which he consumed by fire.

Having procured his brother's liberation, made peace with the Castilian king, and seen another brother, Juan the husband of Blanche, raised to the throne of Navarre †, Alfonso again turned his attention to the affairs of Naples. It was almost too late, as that city, and many other places held by the Aragonese in the Neapolitan kingdom, were recovered immediately after his departure by the allies of the queen. Incensed at one of these, the pope, he rigorously forbade his subjects all

1423 to 1435.

* See the reign of that prince in Vol. II.
† See the History of Navarre.

manner of intercourse with the see of Rome; nor was he in the least degree troubled by the excommunication which the pontiff Martin V. hurled at his head. But new dissensions with Castile, and, perhaps, the refusal of his states to furnish him with the supplies he demanded, prevented him from seriously attempting to regain his lost dominion. In 1430, however, hearing that the Neapolitan queen, with something more than the characteristic fickleness of her sex, had quarrelled with and expelled the duke d'Anjou,—who in revenge was committing hostilities in Apulia and the Calabrias,— and being solicited by some Neapolitans to appear personally in the kingdom, he again prepared for the expedition. This purpose was strengthened by the encouragement of Martin, whom policy induced to assist him at the expense of the French. But the death of that pope a second time suspended the execution of his design. In 1432 he set sail, leaving the regency of Catalonia to his queen; that of Aragon and Valencia to his brother, the king of Navarre. After a successful attack on the isle of Gerbes, where he defeated the king of Tunis, the piracies of whose subjects had long afflicted his coasts, he proceeded to Sicily. There he received deputies from Joanna (Caraccioli had been removed by assassination), who proposed, that if she would not land his troops in Naples, she would revoke her adoption of the duke d'Anjou, and confirm his own. But though the queen actually fulfilled the proposal, he could place no dependence upon her; and his embarrassment as to what he should do was increased by the hostility of the new pope, Eugenius III., of the emperor Sigismund, of the duke of Milan, of the Venetians, Genoese, and Florentines, of whom all were at this time in the interests of France. He resolved to wait in his kingdom of Sicily the course of events. In 1434 the duke d'Anjou died; but this event availed him little with the faithless queen, who adopted René, brother of the duke, as her successor to the throne. The following year, when she also paid the debt of nature, Alfonso passed over to the Italian continent, with the determination of seizing the kingdom. On the other hand, the pope claimed it as a fief of the Roman see, and promised the investiture to René, now duke d'Anjou. Disembarking at Gaeta, which was garrisoned by the troops of the Genoese republic and of the duke of Milan, Alfonso pressed the siege with great vigour. A fleet approached to relieve the place; and a maritime engagement followed, in which he was not only signally defeated, but he, his brother Juan of Navarre, and his brother Enrique, so famous in the Castilian troubles, were taken prisoners. All three, and a considerable number of barons, were conducted to the city of Milan. The generosity with which he was treated by that prince, who considered him not as a captive, but as a guest, is deserving of high admiration.*

No sooner was the captivity of Alfonso known, than the queen convoked the states, to deliberate on the means of procuring his enlargement. But the arrival of his brother, the king of Navarre; the intelligence which followed of his own liberation, and that of his nobles, without ransom, and of the league, offensive and defensive, between the two princes, dispelled the anxiety of the queen and nation. Instead of relinquishing his designs on Naples, this new alliance furnished him with means for their execution. The infante don Pedro, who remained in Sicily, in compliance with the royal orders, besieged, and, partly by surprise, gained possession of Gaeta. The states of Aragon, Valencia, and Catalonia voted large supplies for the war: with these Alfonso resumed hostilities, and soon made several conquests. The thunders of the church passed harmless over his head, and he prosecuted his successes to the

1435 to 1443.

---

* See the history of Navarre. Stella, Annales Genuenses (apud Muratorium, Rerum Italicarum Scriptores, tom. xvii.). Anonymus, Diaria Neapolitana (apud eundem, tom. xxi.). Annales de Raimo, sive Brevis Historia Rerum In Regno Neapolitano Gestarum (apud eundem, tom. xxiii.). Also Lucius Marineus Siculus, De Rebus Hispaniæ, lib. xi. (apud Schottum, Hispania Illust., tom. iii.). Alfonsus a Carthagena, Anacephalæosis, cap. 92. (in eodem tomo). Blancas, Rerum Aragonensium Commentarii, p. 702. (apud eundem, tom. iii.). Zurita, Anales de Aragon, tom. iii. lib. 13, 14. Paternio Catinensis, Sicani Reges, p. 144, &c. Ferreras, Histoire Générale d'Espagne, by Hermilly, tom. vi.

gates of the capital. In 1438, the duke d'Anjou arrived from France, to support his pretensions in person; but his efforts could not arrest the career of his rival: his fleet was defeated, and the capital invested; and though the Aragonese were compelled to raise the siege, the victories of the latter at length compelled him to quit the city, in search of reinforcements. With these he sought the enemy, and was again defeated: he had now few possessions in the kingdom beyond the capital and another fortified town. In vain did pope Eugenius IV. propose an accommodation: Alfonso would listen to no terms, not even when the papal troops joined those of Genoa, and marched against him. Near Ursaria he triumphed over Sforza, general of the combined forces, and again invested Naples. The operations of the siege were frequently rendered inefficient, not by the valour of the besieged so much as by the diversions of the French prince; but, in the end, a party of Aragonese, being introduced by night into the city, seized one of the towers; and the following day the place was carried by storm, the duke escaping on board a Genoese frigate. A victory over the generals of the republic and of the pope followed; and this constrained the submission of all Calabria and Apulia. Both popes, Eugenius IV. and Felix V.[*], were now willing to grant him the investiture of the two Sicilies, on the condition of his recognising each exclusive of the other. He accepted the offer of the former, consented to hold the kingdom, not by right of conquest, but as a fief of the holy see; and engaged to serve his liege lord in the recovery of the march of Ancona. In return, Eugenius promised to declare legitimate his bastard son Fernando, whom he designed as his successor on the throne of Naples.

1443 to 1458. As a return for the papal favour,—for the investiture of the kingdom, and declaration of the legitimacy of his son,—Alfonso, during the following years, served the

---

[*] For the ecclesiastical transactions during the famous schism, the reader is referred to some work expressly on the subject.

holy see in the various wars which that power waged with its neighbours, but the details of which are wholly foreign to this compendium. During his long absence, his states were governed by his brother of Navarre and his queen, — by the former, whose constant aim was to humble the king of Castile, with little benefit to the realm. His subjects had many reasons for complaining of his preferring Naples as a residence to his hereditary states. The wars in which he was engaged, however glorious to his military enterprise, were of no avail to them. His conquests, which their blood and treasure had assisted him to procure, were not to be united with his Spanish dominions, but to be held as a separate kingdom by the bastard Fernando, whom he had made duke of Calabria: if these conquests were brilliant, they conferred no solid advantage either on him or his people; nor was it difficult to foresee that they would form a perpetual subject of dispute between his successors on the one part, and the pope, the Italian princes, and France, on the other.

In 1458, Alfonso was seized at Naples with his mortal sickness. In his last will he left his Spanish dominions, with the Balearic isles, Sardinia and Sicily, to his brother Juan of Navarre; and Naples to his son Fernando. That he posssesed qualities of a high order, — unbending courage, perseverance, capacity of mind, and some virtues, — is admitted by all his biographers; but his neglect of a virtuous queen for an Italian mistress, his boundless ambition, and his tortuous policy, greatly detract from the admiration with which posterity must regard him.[*]

1458.

Of JUAN II. so much has been related in the histories of Castile and Navarre, that little remains to be said here. The greater part of his reign was occupied in wars with his Catalonian subjects or Louis XI.

1458 to 1473.

---

[*] Anonymus, Diaria Neapolitana (apud Muratorium, Rerum Italicarum Scriptores, tom. xxi.). Annales de Raimo, (apud eundem, tom. xxiii.). Anonymus, Storia de Napoli, tom. ii. p. 260—285. Giannone, Dell' Istoria Civile del Regno di Napoli, tom. iii. Bartholemæus Facius, De Rebus Gestis ab Alphonso I. lib. xii. x. Lucius Marineus Siculus, De Rebus Hispaniæ, lib. xi. (apud Schotrum, Hispania Illustrata, tom. i.). Blancas, Rerum Aragonensium Commentarii, p. 702. (apud eundem, tom. iii.). Zurita, Anales de Aragon, tom. ii. lib. 14—15. Paternio Catinensis, Sicani Reges. p. 145. &c.

of France, who encouraged them in their rebellion. Knowing how much they resented the fate of Don Carlos *, and how great a progress the love of republican institutions had made amomg them, in 1460, the latter, who had an eye on Roussillon and Narbonne, began to urge them to revolt, promising them his constant support. But though this novel sentiment, which had been transplanted from the Italian republics, was thus cherished by the reckless spirits who aimed at power, the bulk of the people, however hostile to the person of Juan, were satisfied with their ancient institutions. The former durst not, therefore, immediately proclaim a republic: besides, they had need of aid in the struggle in which they were about to enter. Distrusting the perfidious character of Louis, they sent a deputation to Enrique IV. of Castile †, offering to become his liegemen, on the condition of his joining them in breaking the chain of their vassalage. Enrique accepted the offer, was proclaimed at Barcelona, and sent a strong body of troops towards the frontiers. The whole principality now flew to arms, and besieged the obnoxious queen in Gerona. At this period the Aragonese king was assisted by a strong body of French troops, and by money advanced by Louis, who was put in temporary possession of the lordships of Roussillon and Cerdaña. Though repulsed in the attempt, and soon afterwards defeated by Juan in person, who invested Barcelona, they were but the more confirmed in their resolution of resistance. Not satisfied with heroically defending that city, another division, having effected a junction with the Castilians, again invested Gerona, though without effect. They soon appear to have been dissatisfied with the aid of Enrique; for, in 1463, they invited don Pedro, infante of Portugal, and descended on the maternal side from the counts de Urgel, to receive the crown of Aragon and Sicily. He accepted the invitation, and placed himself at their head;

* See the History of Navarre, reign of Juan I.
† See the reign of Enrique IV. in Vol. II.

but, as the king was well supported by the Aragonese and Valencians, victory generally declared for the rightful cause. The war, however, was desultory enough to continue for some years, even after the natural death of Pedro in 1466. Their next chief was the duke de Lorraine, son of the duke d'Anjou, to whom they also offered the crown. Juan was not daunted at the menacing preparations of the duke; and in the obscure hostilities perpetually recurring, he was greatly aided by his Amazonian queen, who had been nursed in civil dissensions, and whose delight was in the field.* The infante Fernando too, soon to become the husband of Isabel of Castile, here passed his apprenticeship in arms. In 1468, that prince was declared king of Sicily, and associated with his father in the government of Aragon. In 1470 the duke died, while soliciting reinforcements from France, and thus rid Juan of a formidable and active enemy. Though the Catalans in general were induced to return to their duty, a desperate faction at Barcelona preferred submitting to the king of France. But Juan profited so well by the event, that, in a short time, he reduced most of the Catalan fortresses. At the siege of Paralada, however, he ran imminent risk of his life. While asleep, a detachment of 500 lancers forced his camp, and made towards his tent. In the confusion inevitably caused by the darkness and sudden onset, he would certainly have been taken or slain, but for the devotion of a few attendants, who withstood the assault long enough to enable him to mount a horse, and flee almost naked to Figueras, where the main body of his forces lay. Perpignan, which had so long suffered from the rapacity of the French governors, and which found that Louis had no intention of surrendering it to the Aragonese king, took advantage of his proximity to request a Spanish garrison; but the castle, which was too strong to be forced, still held for Louis.

---

* She was the daughter of the constable of Castile, the second wife of Juan, and the mother of the infante Fernando.

Paralada having submitted, Barcelona alone remained in rebellion: it was invested by the king. The following year (1472), while this city persisted in its defence, the province of Ampourdan, which the duke of Lorraine had reduced, was recovered by the Aragonese. At length, through the clemency of Juan, who promised to pass an act of oblivion for all offences, and to confirm the inhabitants in the enjoyment of their ancient privileges, the place capitulated, and rebellion was at an end. The year afterwards, the people of Perpignan rose against the French garrisons, which they put to the sword; and their example was followed by those of Elne, who were no less disgusted with the troops of Louis.*

1473 to 1476.
It was not to be expected that the French king would quietly suffer the loss of these places. His army marched against Perpignan, into which Juan threw himself. The siege was prosecuted with spirit; but the approach from Castile of the infante Fernando caused the French to retire. Though the place was invested a second time, the attempt was equally unsuccessful; and Louis, who had other enemies, was compelled to suspend his designs on this province, and consent to peace. No sooner were his arms at liberty, than he prepared for a renewal of hostilities, and at a time, too, when his agents were treating with the ambassadors of Juan on a permanent pacification. The perfidy of his character was more than ever manifest in his detaining as prisoners the ambassadors, until his preparations were completed. To meet the coming storm, Juan applied for aid to his nephew Fernando, king of Naples; to whom, in consequence of such aid being readily afforded, he gave

---

* Rodericus Santius, Historia Hispanica, pars iv. cap. 34—37. (apud Schottum, Hispania Illustrata, tom. i.). Alfonsus à Carthagena, Anacephalæosis, cap. 93. (apud eundem, eodemque tomo). Franciscus Tarapha, De Regibus Hispanica, p. 566. (In eodem tomo.). Lucius Marineus Siculus, De Rebus Hispaniæ, lib. xii.—xvii. (in eodem tomo.). This writer contains by far the best and fullest account of the wars of Catalonia. Blancas, Rerum Aragonensium Commentarii, p. 703. (apud eundem, tom. iii.). Zurita, Anales de Aragon, tom. iv. lib. 16—18. Paternio Catinensis, Sicani Reges, p. 151., &c.

the hand of his daughter Joanna. Elne, however, was soon reduced by the overwhelming forces of Louis; Perpignan shared the same fate; and Juan, whose son Fernando was too much occupied in the troubles of Castile to assist him, was compelled to consent to a truce; nor could he, during his short remaining reign, recover those places from the enemy.

By this peace Sardinia and Sicily were declared for ever united to the crown of Aragon; the latter island was internally tranquil under the administration of his viceroys; the former, on one occasion at least, vindicated its prescriptive right to rebel; but the disaffected were crushed, and the estates of their leaders confiscated to the crown. While Juan was thus harassed by the French, by his disputes with Aragon, and the rebellion in Catalonia, we need not be surprised that his kingdom was frequently in commotion. The turbulent nobles of Aragon and Valencia required a firm hand to restrain them; and whenever that restraint was removed by the absence of the king, they broke out into their party feuds, or into open plunder, and set at defiance the authority of the ordinary tribunals. Some of these nobles maintained organised bands of robbers. A citizen of Saragossa, a man of low extraction, but who had credit enough to fill the office of the magistracy with his kindred and creatures, and who, at length, obtained a greater power in the city than had ever been exercised by its kings, followed the alluring example, and filled the highways with his dependants. His destruction was effected by treachery, for open force at such a period would have been vain. Don Jayme of Aragon, a prince of the royal house, collected several bands of these outlaws, raised the standard of revolt, and seized on some important fortresses: he was invested in Muela by the viceroy of Valencia, was taken prisoner, conducted to Barcelona, and beheaded.*

1476 to 1479.

* Lucius Marineus Siculus, De Rebus Hispaniæ, lib. xvii. et xviii. (apud Schottum, Hispania Illustrata, tom. i.). Rodericus Santius, Historia His-

On the death of Juan in 1479, FERNANDO II. was immediately acknowledged by the three Spanish states. As his transactions with the Mohammedans, the Castilians, Portuguese, and Navarrese, have already been related, nothing remains but to advert to such as could not be classed among the events of those kingdoms.

1479 to 1483. Soon after his accession, Fernando was naturally anxious to procure the restitution of Roussillon and Cerdaña. But to his pressing embassies on this subject, Louis XI. returned evasive answers. His successor, Charles VIII., though eager to preserve a good understanding with the monarch who united all Spain under his sceptre, was loth to restore a province, the possession of which, in the event of future wars, would be invaluable. But when Fernando, indignant at the evasions of Charles, began to arm for the recovery of this frontier, the latter, who meditated the conquest of Naples, and who wished to have no enemies to harass France during his absence, commanded Perpignan and the fortresses of the province to be evacuated by the French troops: they were immediately occupied by those of Aragon.

1492, 1495. The severity of Fernando king of Naples had long been borne with dissatisfaction by the people. Their discontent appeared to the French king an excellent opportunity for vindicating the claims of his family on that country, and for gratifying an ambition which was seldom restrained by considerations of justice. He was the more confirmed in his purpose, when several Neapolitan nobles, through disgust with their ruler, sought his protection, and offered to aid him in gaining possession of so fair a kingdom. There was another party

---

panica, pars iv. in ultimis capitulis (apud eundem, in eodemque tomo). Alfonsus à Carthagena, Anacephalæosis, cap. 93. (in eodem tomo). Franciscus Tarapha, De Regibus Hispanica, p. 567. (in eodem tomo). Ælius Antonius Nebrissensis, Hispanarum Rerum Decades, dec. 1. lib. i. (in eodem tomo). Blancas, Rerum Aragonensium Commentarii, p. 704. (apud eundem, tom. lii.). Zurita, Anales de Aragon, tom. iv. lib. 18—20. Paternio Catinensis, Sicani Reges, p. 151—154.

equally dissatisfied with the tyrant, but not at the outset equally favourable to Charles. These applied to the king of Aragon with the same view as their countrymen had applied to the Gallic monarch; and it was only when the former received their message with some displeasure, that they joined his rival. The death of the Neapolitan king, and the accession of his son Alfonso, in 1494, produced no change, either on the intentions of Charles, or the disaffection of the people: Alfonso was as unpopular as Fernando. In alarm at the preparations of the Frenchmen, and the suspected hostility of the pope, the new king implored the aid of his Spanish brother and received the assurance he solicited. In the mean time Charles invaded Italy by way of Grenoble, and passed through Pavia and Florence direct on Rome. Having forced the pope into his interests, he continued his march towards Naples. Alfonso, terrified at the approaching danger, and convinced how much his subjects wished for his overthrow, abdicated in favour of his son Fernando, who, he hoped, would be able to rally them round the national standard; and retired to a monastery in Sicily. The hope was vain: the Neapolitans fled—perhaps as much through cowardice as disaffection — the moment they came in contact with the French; and the capital, with the fortified places, submitted to the invader: Frederic took refuge in the isle of Ischia.

But Fernando of Spain was not idle: by his ambassadors at Venice he formed a league with the pope, the republic, the duke of Milan, and the fugitive Frederic, for the expulsion of the French from Italy. Fortunately for the common cause, the rapacity and insolence of the invaders had turned the eyes of the Neapolitans towards their dethroned king, whom they invited to resume his dignity, and at whose approach they opened the gates not only of the capital, but of several important fortresses. At this time, don Gonsalo de Cordova, the captain of Fernando, who had acquired distinction in the wars of Granada, commenced his

1495 to 1498.

brilliant career. The rapidity with which he reduced many of the fortified places, and triumphed over the French generals on the field, drew the attention of Europe towards this part of Italy. His exploits at the very first campaign procured him the appellation of the Great Captain. The Calabrias were soon entirely forced from the invaders, who were glad to take refuge in the states of the church, until the arrival of the expected succours from France. The restored king did not long survive his success: the fatigues of the campaign consigned him, in 1496, to the grave. He was succeeded by his uncle, Frederic, son of the first Aragonese king of Naples. To the new monarch Gonsalo continued the same eminent services; and not unfrequently the pope made use of his valour in humbling the temporal enemies of the church. The king of France in vain attempted, by way of diversion, to withdraw the attention of Fernando from the affairs of Italy, by the powerful armaments which he frequently moved on Roussillon: he found the Spanish king, as usual, prepared both to defend the frontiers, and to secure the crown on the head of Frederic.*

1498 to 1500. But in that relative's behalf Fernando soon ceased to be interested. For his progressive coolness towards that prince, various reasons have been assigned: the chief one has been omitted,—the king's all-grasping ambition, which sometimes took no counsel from justice. On hearing that Louis XII., the successor of Charles, was preparing to arm for the recovery of Naples, he besought that monarch to desist from the undertaking; and when

* Marini Sanuti, De Bello Gallico (apud Muratorium, Rerum Italicarum Scriptores, tom. xxiv. p. 1—74.). Senaregar, De Rebus Genuensibus (apud eundem, p. 509, &c). Camillo Portio, Congiura de Baroni del Regno di Napoli contra Ferdinando I. dopo l'anno 1480, &c. passim. Giannone, Dell' Istoria Civile del Regno di Napoli, lib. viii. Paternio Catinensis, Sicani Reges, p. 151, &c. The Spanish authorities are,— Lucius Marineus Siculus, De Rebus Hispanica, lib. xx.—xxi. (apud Schottum, Hispania Illustrata, tom. i.); Franciscus Tarapha, De Regibus Hispanica, p. 567. (apud eundem, eodemque tomo); Ælius Antonius Nebrissensis, Hispanarum Rerum Decades, dec. 1—3. (in eodem tomo); Gomecius, De Rebus Gestis Francisci Ximenii, lib. i.—iii. (in eodem tomo); Blancas, Rerum Aragonensium Commentarii, p. 705. (apud eundem, tom. iii.); Zurita, Historia del Rey Hernando el Catolico, tom. i. lib. i.—iii.; Mariana, De Rebus Hispanicis, lib. xxiv.—xxvi. (apud Schottum, tom. iv.).

he found that solicitations were useless, he was unprincipled enough to propose a division of the whole kingdom. Louis eagerly seized the proposal, and the royal robbers immediately entered into negotiations for adjusting their respective share of the spoils. At first the city and kingdom of Naples were adjudged to Louis; the two Calabrias and the Abruzzo to Fernando: the revenue arising from the pasturage of Apulia was to be divided between them. But a dispute arising, a new division was effected: the latter assigned the two Calabrias and Apulia to the Spanish king; Naples and the Abruzzo to the Frenchman. To preserve harmony in other quarters, Louis agreed, at the same time, to relinquish his claims over Roussillon and Cerdaña, and Fernando over Montpellier. Both sovereigns sent powerful armaments to execute this iniquitous compact. No sooner did it reach the ears of the unfortunate Frederic, than he complained to the Spanish monarch of the monstrous injustice. Fernando replied,— no doubt with truth,— that he had done his utmost to prevent the French king from the enterprise; that when entreaties failed, he had even offered a considerable sum to the same effect; and that it was only when he found Louis bent on the undertaking, and leagued with the Italian powers to ensure its success, that he had consented to the division; he added, that as such a division was inevitable, it was better that France should have a part than the whole. In private life such reasoning would be characterised as it ought; but kings have too often pleaded their sovereign exception from obligations which they have been ready enough to enforce on the rest of mankind.

While the French troops on one side, and the great captain on the other, were seizing his provinces, it was impossible for Frederic, with a people so disaffected and cowardly as the Neapolitans, to make head against them. As Louis promised to allow him a pension suitable to his rank, he sought an asylum in France. Scarcely were the armies in possession of the country, when their lead-

1501 to 1504.

ers began to quarrel about the precise extent of their respective territories. As each longed to seize the portion held by the other, an appeal to arms only could decide their pretensions. A bloody war followed; the details of which may be found in the Italian histories of the period, and the more recent work of Sismondi. It exhibits little beyond a continued succession of victories for the great captain, who triumphed over the veteran general and armies of France: it ended, in 1504, in the entire subjugation of the kingdom by the Spaniards.

1504 to 1508. The brilliant success of the Spanish general now roused the envy of a few brother officers, who represented him to the sovereign as meditating designs inconsistent with the preservation of the new conquest to the Castilian crown. In the frequent orders he received, he but too plainly saw the distrust of Fernando, whom, however, he continued to serve with the same ability and with unshaken fidelity. In 1506, Fernando arrived at Naples, and his distrust was greatly diminished by his frequent intercourse with the general. But, as his own heart taught him that human virtue is often weak, he brought Gonsalo with him to Spain, leaving the viceregal authority in the hands of don Ramon de Cardona.

1508. Into the interminable affairs of Italy, from this time to the death of Fernando, the ever varying alliances between the pope, the emperor, the Venetians, and the kings of France and Spain, and their results, as they had not any influence over Spain — scarcely, indeed, any connection with it — we forbear to enter. We need only observe, that Spain retained uninterrupted possession of her conquest; the investiture of which, in 1510, was conferred by the pope, as a fief of the church, on Fernando.

1485. During the reign of this prince, the inquisition, as before observed*, was introduced into Aragon. This introduction was strongly but effectually opposed, by both the Valencians and the Aragonese — by none more bitterly than the inhabitants of Saragossa. Having vainly so-

---

* See Vol. II. p. 271.

licited the grand justiciary to interfere, a few of its more desperate *converts*—such were those whose immediate forefathers had been reclaimed from the Jewish or Mohammedan faith — resolved to assassinate Pedro d'Arbues, canon of the cathedral and head of the tribunal in Saragossa, together with the assessor, and another minister of the holy office. Their first design, was to enter the churchman's apartments, which lay within the cloisters of the cathedral, and murder him in bed. For this purpose they removed one of the iron bars of the window which looked towards the door; but, being interrupted, they repaired to the choir, where early matins were singing, in the hope that their victim would be present. That night, however, he did not appear; so that they deferred their purpose until the following midnight. At the time apppointed, viz. between the hours of twelve and one, they entered the cathedral in two bands, and at two doors, the better to escape detection, and took their stations, standing in the opposite cloisters, with the choir between them. The canon soon appeared, carrying in one hand a small lantern, in the other a spear; a precaution which he had adopted in consequence of a rumour that his life would some time or other be attempted. The weapon he leaned against a pillar, while he knelt before the high altar. Some of the conspirators stole silently towards the place to secure the spear, while three of their number made softly towards the victim, whose back was turned to the choir. One of them struck him on the neck, and fled; another pierced him twice with a sword, and was preparing to cut off his head, when, seeing him fall with an expression of thankfulness that he was deemed worthy to suffer for the faith, and finding that the noise was heard by the ecclesiastics in the choir, the conspirators precipitately fled, before measures could be taken for their apprehension. He was found weltering in his blood, and was conveyed to his bed, where he lingered till the following night.[*]

---

[*] He now ranks among the saints, as well as martyrs, of the Spanish church.

The following day the indignation of the populace was boundless: nothing less than the blood of all the converts would have satisfied it, had not the archbishop, though with great difficulty, allayed the tumult. This horrid sacrilege had no other effect than that of more securely establishing the authority of the holy office.*

CHAP. V.

PORTUGAL.†

1095—1516.

DURING the ninth, tenth, and eleventh centuries, most of northern Portugal was subject to local governors, dependent on the counts of Galicia. But though the chief fortresses in the provinces Entre Minho e Douro, and Tras os Montes, and generally those of Beira, were frequently in possession of the Christians, the Mohammedans sometimes seized and occupied such as lay contiguous to their own, until expelled by a superior force. Thus Coimbra, Viseu and Lamego, which had been reduced by Alfonso I. and his immediate successors, were recovered in 997 by the great Almansor: in 1027, king Alfonso V. of Leon fell before the

---

* Marini Sanuti, Commentarius de Bello Gallico, p. 70—154. (apud Muratorium, Rerum Italicarum Scriptores, tom. xxiv. Anonymus, Storia de Napoli, tom. ii. p. 306, &c. Idem, Histoire du Royaume de Naples, ii. 369, &c. Lucius Marineus Siculus, De Rebus Hispaniæ, lib. xxi. (apud Schottum, Hispania Illustrata, tom. i.). Gomecius, De Rebus Gestis Francisci Ximenii, lib. lii.—v. (in eodem tomo). Franciscus Tarapha, De Regibus Hispaniæ, p. 568. (in eodem tomo). Blancas, Rerum Aragonensium Commentarii, p. 706. (apud eodem, tom. iii.). Mariana, De Rebus Hispanicis, lib. xxvi. &c. (apud eundem, tom. iv.). Zurita, Historia del Rey Hernando el Catolico, tom. i. lib. iii. p. 3. et tom. ii. lib. vi. Paternio Catinensis, Sicani Reges, p. 160, &c.

† For this chapter, our authorities are, we are sorry to say, very few. Of those few, however, we have endeavoured to make a proper use.

second of these places*, the siege of which was in consequence abandoned; but in 1057, both it and Lamego were recovered by his son-in-law, Fernando I.; and the following year Coimbra shared the same fate.† In 1093, Santarem, Lisbon, and Cintra were reduced by Alfonso VI., the famous conqueror of Toledo, whose arms were generally so successful against the misbelievers‡. As these conquests were continually exposed to the irruptions of the Almoravides, in 1095 that monarch conferred the government of Portugal from the Minho to the Tagus, and the right of conquering as far as the Guadiana, on *Henri* of Besançon, who in 1072, had married his illegitimate daughter Teresa, and to whose arms he had been so much indebted for many of his recent successes.§

The nature of the authority conferred on the new count 1095. has been a matter of much controversy between the Castilian and Portuguese writers. While the latter maintain that the concession of Alfonso was full and entire,—a surrender of all feudal claims over the country, which the count was to govern in full sovereignty,—the former no less zealously contend that the government was to be held as a fief, hereditary indeed, but no less dependent on the crown of Leon. In the absence of documentary evidence, probability only can guide us. It is unreasonable to suppose either that the king was willing, or, if willing, that his nobles would allow him, to dismember at once and for ever, so fair a territory from his crown, and that too in favour of a stranger and an illegitimate daughter—for illegitimate she was, notwithstanding the allegations to the contrary by some Portuguese writers, who seldom regard truth if unpalatable to their national

* See Vol. II. p. 148.
† Ibid. p. 153.
‡ According to the Chronicon Lusitanum (apud Florez, España Sagrada, tom. xiv. p. 406.), the Chronicon Complutense (apud eundem, xxiii. 316.), and other authorities, Lisbon and Cintra were taken by Alfonso. They must, however, have been soon recovered by the Moors.
§ See Vol. II. p. 159. That Henri, whose extraction has given rise to much disputation, was of the family of the first duke of Burgundy, and of the royal blood of France, is indisputable from a MS. discovered in the monastery of Fleury. La Clède, Histoire Générale de Portugal, ii. 23.

vanity. That Portugal was conferred as a dependent fief, is also confirmed by the disputes between its early sovereigns, and those of Leon;—the former striving to maintain their avowed independence, the latter to reduce them to their reputed original vassalage.

1095 to 1112. The administration of Henri was vigorous, and his military conduct glorious. His triumphs over the Mohammedans were frequent, whether achieved in concert with his father-in-law, Alfonso, or by his own unaided arm; several of the *reguli* in the fortresses south and east of the Tagus he reduced to the condition of tributaries. In 1107, he constrained Ali ben Yussef, son of the first emperor of the Almoravides, to raise the siege of Coimbra. Nor were his efforts to crush rebellion, whether of his local Christian governors, or of his Mohammedan vassals, less successful. One of his last acts was to assist his natural sovereign, Urraca, against her husband the king of Aragon. He died in 1112, leaving many ecclesiastic structures enriched by his liberality. Braga, Oporto, Coimbra, Lamego, and Viseu, were the places most indebted to his piety. Unfortunately for his memory, many of the great deeds recorded of him by his partial people rest on authority too disputable to be received. Probably some of them have been confounded with those of his more famous son.[*]

1112 to 1128. During the minority of Alfonso, the son of Henri, who, at his father's death, was only in his second year, the administration of the kingdom was assumed by the widowed *Teresa*. The character of this princess is represented as little superior to that of her sister Urraca: the same violence, the same unbridled passions, and the same unnatural jealousy of her son, appear, though in a

[*] See Vol. II. p. 163. Pelagius Ovetensis, Chronicon Regum Legionensium, p 473. (apud Florez, España Sagrada, tom. xiv.). Rodericus Toletanus, Rerum in Hispania Gestarum lib. vii. cap. 5. (apud Schottum, Hispania Illustrata, tom. ii.). Lucas Tudensis, Chronicon Mundi, p. 94, &c. (apud eundem, tom. iv). Chronicon Lusitanum, p. 406. (apud Florez, tom. xiv.). Annales Complutenses, p. 314. (apud eundem, tom. xxiii.). Chronicon Complutense, p. 316. (in eodem tomo). Chronicon Conimbricense, p. 330. (in eodem tomo). Brandaon, Monarchia Lusitana, part ii. Lemos, tom. iii. lib. 8. Vasconcellos, Anacephalæoses; id est, summa Capita Actorum Regum Lusitaniæ, p. 1—9. La Clède, Histoire Générale de Portugal, tom. ii. liv. 5.

degree undoubtedly less criminal, to have distinguished her conduct. Yet on that sister and her nephew, the successor of Urraca, she sometimes made war, in the hope of profiting by the dissensions of the period: on every occasion she was repulsed, and was forced to sue for peace. Her intimacy with dom Fernando Perez, whom she is supposed to have secretly married, and through whom all favours were to be solicited, roused the jealousy of the courtiers. By their persuasion Alfonso, whom she had rigorously endeavoured to exclude from all participation in public affairs, undertook to wrest the sovereignty from her hands. He had little difficulty in collecting troops; for no sooner did he erect the standard of resistance, than the discontented nobles flocked round it. His preparations reached the ears of his mother, who wrathfully armed to defend her authority. The two armies met near the fortress of Vimaraens, where the princess was utterly routed, and forced to seek refuge in the castle of Leganoso. There she was speedily invested, and compelled to surrender the reins of government into the hands of her son, while her favourite or husband fled into Galicia. She survived her fall about two years.*

The new count was destined to prove a more formidable enemy to the Mohammedans than even his able father. During the first years of his administration, he was at variance with his cousin, Alfonso VIII., whose Galician territories he invaded, and with whose enemy,

1128 to 1137.

---

* Lemos (tom. iii. lib. 8.) endeavours to vindicate the character of Teresa from the charges imputed to her: the same vain effort, as the reader will remember (see Vol. II. p. 164. of this history) has been made by the Castilian writers in favour of Urraca. What proves the justice of the charges, no less than the national prejudice of the disputants, is the fact, that, while each party stoutly defends its idol, it allows that of the other to be assailed without mercy: neither scruples in the least to violate historic truth. Perhaps, however, the actions of the two princesses have, to a certain extent, been confounded.

La Clede (ii. 68.) certainly exaggerates the crimes and frailties of Teresa. "Oubliant ce qu'elle devoit à son rang, à sa conscience, et au sang illustre dont elle sortoit, elle se livroit à la plus honteuse débauche, épousa en secret Ferdinand Peres, comte de Trastamare, et se deshonora par ce mariage, d'autant plus criminel qu'elle avait eu un commerce de galanterie avec Bermond frère de son mari. Non content de cet inceste, elle en occasionna un second, en faisant épouser à ce même Bermond la princesse Urraque sa fille." Much of this is improbable, and, we believe, at variance with history; at least, there is no *contemporary* authority for it.

(the king of Navarre) he entered into an alliance. But though, in 1137, he obtained a considerable advantage over a detachment of Alfonso's army, he was little able to contend with that prince. Through the persuasion of his subjects, who dreaded the threatened invasion of Portugal by the Castilian, and the good offices of the papal legate, whose master he had acknowledged as lord paramount over Portugal,—doubtless with a view of escaping vassalage to Alfonso,—he solicited and obtained peace from the other. He was accordingly at liberty to prosecute his long meditated designs against the natural enemies of his country and faith.

1139. In 1139, the count assembled his army at Coimbra, resolved to reduce the fortresses west of the Guadiana, which had before acknowledged the kings of Badajoz, and which were now dependent on the Almoravides. The Mohammedan governor of that important place not only summoned all his brethren of the neighbouring provinces to arms, but procured a powerful—we are told a vast—reinforcement from Africa, and advanced towards the plains of Ourique*, where the Christians had penetrated, and where they lay encamped. On perceiving the hills and valleys literally covered with the misbelievers, the Lusitanians are said, and not without reason, to have trembled for the result. Though their prudent count placed them on an eminence overlooking the plain, and fortified a position naturally strong, by the aid of art, they conjured him to save them from the impending danger; in other words, to fall back on their fortresses in the vicinity of the Tagus. But Alfonso, who knew the advantages of his position, and who, perhaps, perceived that retreat would be impracticable or fatal, resolved to await the approaching assault. So effectually did he banish the despondency of his followers, so well did he infuse his own spirit into them, that the inequality of the contest no longer dismayed them: their courage

---

* In the province of Alemtejo, about two hours' brisk ride from the frontiers of Algarve, and the same distance west of the Guadiana.

became elevated by faith, and they looked forward with certainty either to the victor's or the martyr's crown. But though the count was thus prepared for the strife, he could not regard its issue without emotion. On the eve preceding the battle, he is said to have opened a bible; that the first passage which struck his eyes was one that related the triumph of Gideon over the Midianites, and that he regarded the accident as ominous of success. Unfortunately, however, all the important events of these times are so blended with the marvellous, that such even as in themselves have no great improbability must be regarded with doubt. When we read that the count fell asleep over the sacred volume; that a venerable old man appeared to him in a vision, and bade him be of good cheer, as became one who was destined to obtain an immortal triumph over the infidels; that he was awakened by one of his chamberlains, who announced that an aged hermit earnestly besought admission to his presence on matters of the deepest moment; that the stranger was the identical person he had just seen in his heavenly dream, who confirmed the joyful hope of victory; that on issuing from his tent he perceived a celestial light in the heavens, in the centre of which appeared the Saviour of men nailed to a cross; that he was commanded by the divine personage to assume the regal title, and was promised prosperity to the sixteenth generation[*], we should be inclined to reject even the battle itself, were it not too well attested by Mohammedan as well as Christian writers, to render doubt possible. That in this battle he obtained an imperishable victory over the countless Africans, an incredible number of whom were left dead on the field or destroyed in the pursuit[†], is indubitable. Whether his assumption of the royal dignity preceded or followed this glorious success, has been

---

[*] This messenger was a hermit, who had passed sixty years in a neighbouring cave. The ruins of a hermitage near the spot were still subsisting in the time of king Sebastian, who raised a parish church on the site.
[†] The number is estimated by the Portuguese at two hundred thousand!

matter of dispute: it is more reasonable to suppose that, while exulting over the destruction of the enemy, his grateful and enthusiastic people proclaimed him on the field. Notwithstanding the fabulous circumstances with which superstition and imposture have disfigured the relation, the plains of Ourique will be venerated so long as patriotism and valour are held in esteem among men.*

1140 to 1147. ALFONSO I., after his elevation to the dignity which he had long sought, and of which he had shown himself so deserving, was not likely to relax in his hostilities against the Moors. Though Santarem had, with other places, been reduced by Alfonso VI., it must, in the sequel, have been recovered by the Almoravides, as, in 1146, we find the Portuguese king intent on regaining it. As the fortifications were strong, and the defenders numerous, he caused a small but resolute band to scale the walls by night: scarcely had twenty-five reached the summit of the wall, when the Moorish inhabitants took the alarm, and flew to arms. In vain one of the gates was opened by the Christians, and the rest of the assailants rushed in. The struggle which ensued, amidst the darkness of night, the clash of weapons, the groans of dying warriors, the shrieks of women and infants who were indiscriminately butchered, constituted a scene which none but a demon would have delighted to witness, which none but a demon would have commanded.† In an hour this important fortress, one of the great bulwarks of Christian Lusitania, was in possession of the victor.‡ His success,

---

* Rodericus Toletanus, lib. vii. cap. 6. (apud Schottum, tom. ii.). Lucas Tudensis, lib. liv. p 103, &c. (apud eundem, tom. iv.). Chronicon Lusitanum, p. 409, &c. (apud Florez, tom. xiv.). Chronicon Conimbricense, p. 330. (apud eundem, tom. xxiii.). Brandaon, part ii. 1. Antonius Vasconcellius, p. 13—16. Lemos, tom. iii. liv. 9. La Clede, tom. ii. liv. 5. To these Christian authorities may be added Abu Abdalla, Vestis Acu Picta (apud Casiri, Bibliotheca Arab. Hisp. tom. ii.), and Condé by Mariés, &c. tom. ii

† "Mas o rei mandando fazer as mortes indistintas, sem differenca de sexo, e idade; o horror dos gemidos, o tropel da gente, o clamor das mulheres, a meninos, o escuro da noite causan hum espanto tao geral."—*Lemos*, iii. 84. Well done the *holy* king Alfonso Henriques!

‡ Of course, there must be a miracle in every great feat of the Portuuese. Santarem was recovered by the prayers of St. Bernard, then in

and the embarrassment of the Mohammedan princes of Spain, both on account of the rising power of the Almohades in Africa, and of the hostilities of the kings of Leon and Castile, emboldened him to attempt the recovery of Lisbon. That city was invested; but the valour of the defenders, and the strength of the walls would doubtless have compelled him to raise the siege, had not a succour arrived which no man could have expected. This was a fleet of crusaders, chiefly of English, under the command of William Longsword, who was hastening to the Holy Land. The Portuguese king had little difficulty in persuading them that the cross had no greater enemies than the Mohammedans of Spain, and that the recovery of Lisbon would be no less acceptable to Heaven than that of the Syrian towns: the hope of plunder did the rest; the crusaders disembarked, and joined in the assaults which were daily made on the place. After a gallant defence of five months, the besieged showing no disposition to surrender, the Christians appointed October the 25th for a general assault on the city. It was carried by storm; a prodigious number of the Moors were put to the sword; the crusaders were too much enriched to dream of continuing their voyage; so that, with the exception of a few who received lands in Portugal, the rest returned to their own country. [1147.]

But the Mohammedans had still possession of one half of Portugal, and of several strong fortresses. Having reduced Cintra, Alfonso passed the Tagus, and seized on several fortified places in Estremadura, and even in Alemtejo. It was not, however, until 1158, that he seriously attempted the reduction of Alcaçar do Sal, [1152 to 1166.]

France, in honour of whose rule the king had vowed to found, and royally to endow, the monastery of Alcobaça. The saint arose the very night Santarem was taken, called some of his disciples, and bade them speed away for Portugal, to receive the donation which king don Alfonso was ready to make his order. After the fall of Lisbon, the vow was right royally fulfilled: a monastery was built, and endowed with the seigniory over thirty-one towns and villages: it was enlarged and beautified by succeeding kings; so that in time it was able to contain 1000 monks.

which fell, after a vigorous resistance of two months. In 1165 Cesimbra and Palmela were invested: the former place was speedily taken; while, before the latter, he had to encounter a strong force sent to relieve it by the Moorish governor of Badajoz.* The misbelievers were defeated, and many places made to surrender. Among these was Beja, the most important fortress of Alemtejo; but we have no particulars of a conquest which seems to have been the frequent subject of contention between the rival powers. The way in which Evora was recovered is more minutely recorded. One Giraldo, surnamed from his valour Sem Pavor, or the Dauntless, having incurred for some violence the indignation of king Alfonso, fled from justice, assembled some determined companions, and commenced a freebooting life amidst the wilds of Alemtejo. He was long the terror alike of Christians and Moors; but, in the end, being visited by remorse, he resolved to achieve some feat which should procure his pardon from the king. Passing one day by the walls of Evora, and perceiving that the place was negligently guarded, he concerted with his companions, all eager like himself to obtain their pardon, on the means of surprising it. On a gentle eminence before the city was a redoubt, guarded by an alcalde. One night, as the Moor slept, and his daughter, who was left to watch the gate, yielded also to the drowsy power, Giraldo, with the assistance of his companions, quietly ascended, and cut off the heads of father and daughter, which he showed to his comrades below. The communication between the redoubt and the city, and consequently the means of giving the alarm, being thus intercepted, one party of the adventurers, in obedience to a concerted plan, appeared before the gates of the city, as if to brave the garrison, while another lay in ambush, to take advantage of the manœuvre. The

* On this occasion Alfonso, with no more than 60 horsemen, is said to have encountered 500 horsemen of the Almoravides, and 40,000 foot; and, what is more, to have defeated them! (See Chronicon Lusitanum, p. 414.) These prodigious relations are admitted without scruple by all the historians of Portugal.

sentinels on the walls, hearing that a small band thus defied them, acquainted the garrison with their audacity; to punish it, a strong body issued at one of the gates, and pursued the now fugitive robbers. This was the signal for the party in ambush, with their chief, to seize the gate. They spread along the streets, forced the houses, and inflicted a truly horrible carnage on the inhabitants, until the place consented to own Alfonso. When the Moors who had been engaged in the pursuit returned to the gate, they were not a little surprised to find the city in the power of the Christians: some of them attempted to recover the place, but were overpowered and slain; the rest fled. The king was immediately acquainted with this almost incredible feat; and, in the fulness of his admiration, he not only pardoned the banditti, but appointed their chief to the government of the city.

The martial character of the Portuguese king, as well as the almost uninterrupted success of his arms, inclined him to perpetual war,—whether with Moors or Christians appears to have given him little concern. In 1167 he seized on Limia, a territory of Gallicia, which he claimed on the ground of its having formed part of his mother's dowry. The following year he advanced against Badajoz, the Moorish governor of which was a vassal of the king of Leon. Fernando II. hastened to its relief; but before his arrival the Portuguese standard floated on the towers.* The forces of Fernando were greatly superior in number, and the Portuguese king prepared to issue from the gates,—whether, as the national writers assert, to contend for his new conquest on the open field, or, as the Castilians say, to escape from the incensed monarch of Leon, is uncertain. What is indubitable is, that as he was passing through the gate with precipitation, his thigh came into contact with the wall or bars, and was shattered. He was taken prisoner by the Leonnese, and conducted to their king, who treated him

---

* See Vol. II. p. 170.

with courtesy, and consented to his liberation on the condition of his surrendering the places which he had usurped in Galicia. From this accident, however, he never recovered so as to be able to mount a horse; but it had a much worse effect than his own personal decrepitude: it encouraged the restless Mohammedans to resume their incursions into his territories. Though these incursions were repressed by the valour of his son, dom Sancho, who, not content with defending Portugal, penetrated into the Moorish territory, to the very outskirts of Seville, his people could not fail to suffer from the ravages of the misbelievers. This irruption, too, had its ill effect; it so much incensed Yussef abu Yacub, the emperor of the Almohades, that he despatched a considerable force into the kingdom. The discomfiture of this army under the walls of Abrantes, and the exploits of dom Fuas Roupinho, one of Sancho's captains, preserved the country indeed from the yoke of the stranger, but not from the devastation: Alemtejo, above all, suffered in this vindictive warfare.*

1180 to 1181. This dom Fuas is too celebrated in Portuguese history to be dismissed without a passing notice. Being intrusted with the defence of Porto de Mos, a fortress which was furiously assailed by a numerous body of the Andalusians and Almohades, he left a sufficient garrison in the place, while with the rest he proceeded to the neighbouring forts to demand succours. On his return, he halted on the sierra which overlooked the fortress, and exulted greatly to see with what valour his soldiers were repelling an assault of the enemy. Those who were with him, in the fear that their comrades might in the end give way, thought this a favourable opportunity for attacking the misbelievers in flank; but he

---

* Rodericus Tol. lib. vii. (apud Schottum, tom. ii.). Lucas Tud. p. 106, &c. (apud eundem, tom. iv.). Chronicon Lusitanum, p. 412—418. (apud Florez, tom. xiv.). Chronicon Conimbricense, p. 330—333. (apud eundem, tom. xxiii.). Brandaon, part ii. 1. Vasconcellos, p. 19, &c. Lemos, tom. ii. liv. 9. et 10. La Clede, tom. ii. liv. 6.

To these Christian authorities must be added Abu Abdalla (apud Casiri, Bibliotheca, &c. tom. ii. p. 220.). D'Herbelot, Bibliothèque Orientale, art. Moahedoun, Yacoub, &c. Condé, by Marlés, ii. 400, &c.

restrained their ardour, in the certainty that the place would continue to hold out. At nightfall, however, when the fatigued Moors had retired to their tents, he told his Christian companions that now was the time to discomfit an enemy whom God had put into their hands. They descended the hill, fell on the sleeping Moors, whom they slaughtered with impunity; a few only are said to have escaped. His valour rendered him so agreeable to king Alfonso, that he was placed over a squadron destined to avenge the piratical descents of the misbelievers on the western coast of the kingdom, especially in the neighbourhood of Setubal and Lisbon. With equal success did he triumph on this new element; for, not satisfied with destroying the hostile fleet, he even insulted the Barbary coast. But for none of his deeds, which are doubtless greatly exaggerated, is he so much celebrated as for the special aid of our Lady at a time when human aid would have been invoked in vain.*

The successive defeat of his best troops, made Yussef resolve to pass over into Spain, and take the field in person. His death, before Santarem, has been related in the history of the Mohammedan peninsula.† This was the last occasion on which the Lusitanian king put on his armour. He died at the close of the year 1185.‡ His memory is held by the Portuguese in the highest veneration; and hints are not obscurely given that he merited canonisation. He, who had been favoured by the celestial vision at Ourique, whose holy intentions had been so miraculously communicated to St. Bernard, and, after death, whose mantle, preserved with religious reverence, could cure the diseased, was surely worthy of ecclesiastical deification. That, in after-times, when Joam I. gained Ceuta, he appeared in white armour in the choir of Santa Cruz at Coimbra, and informed the holy bro-

1184 to 1186.

---

* See Appendix F.
† See Vol. II. p. 40. Both the date and circumstances of this invasion are very differently given by the Mohammedan and Christian writers.
‡ The Anales Toledanos give 1187.

therhood that he and his son dom Sancho were proceeding to Ceuta to assist their vassals, no true Portuguese ever yet disbelieved: hence the peculiar office, which the monks of that magnificent house solemnised in his honour. To a less catholic reader, " this always adorable king," (*sempre o rei adoravel*) may, from his indiscriminate slaughter of the innocent and guilty, and from his amours, appear to have been imbued with the imperfections of our nature.

It was in the reign of this prince that the celebrated laws of Lamego, to which the reader's attention will hereafter be directed, were promulgated.*

1186. SANCHO I., the eldest surviving son of Alfonso, had soon to sustain the persecutions of the pope, for marrying his daughter Teresa to her cousin, Alfonso IX., king of Leon.† As the royal pair, notwithstanding the bigoted opposition of the pontiff, continued to live together, the latter laid an interdict on both the kingdoms of Leon and Portugal. The complaints of both people, not against the vindictive pope, the real author of their privation, but their monarchs, for contracting a marriage within the forbidden degrees, were loud and general. How this matrimonial alliance ended, has been seen in the history of Leon.

1188 to 1202. The transactions of Sancho with the Moors were not destined to be so glorious as those of his father. Though, by the aid of some crusaders, whom a tempest forced to take refuge in the port of Lisbon, he took Silves in Algarve; and though, in 1190, he defended that fortress with success against the power of the African emperor; yet when that emperor arrived in person (possibly the expedition into Portugal might be

---

* See the last section of the present book.
Rodericus Tol. lib. vii. Lucas Tud. p. 106, &c. (apud Schottum, tom. ii. et iv.). Chronicon Lusitanum, p. 418. (apud Florez, tom. xiv.). Chronicon Conimbricense, p. 333. (apud eundem, tom. xxiii.). Anales Toledanos i. (in eodem tomo, p. 392.). Brandaon, part iv. Vasconcellos, p. 16—26. Lemos, tom. iii. liv. 10. La Clede, tom. ii. liv. 6.
To these Christian authorities add Abu Abdalla, Vestis, &c. (apud Casiri, tom. ii.). D'Herbelot, art. Joussouf, Yacoub, &c.; and Condé, by Marlès, &c. tom. ii.
† See Vol. II. p. 172.

headed by the son of Yacub ben Yussef), the tide of Lusitanian conquest began to ebb. Silva, Almeida, Palmela, and Alcaçar do Sal, Coimbra, Cesimbra, and many other towns, were taken; many more were levelled with the ground; nowhere durst the Portuguese attempt to arrest the destructive torrent; and though the Mohammedans at length retired, to humble the Christians on the plains of Alarcos[*], a generation was scarcely sufficient to repair the mischiefs they had done. Famine and pestilence next visited the people, who, in their deplorable blindness, attributed their misfortunes to the incestuous marriage of their infanta with the Leonnese king. Their complaints effected what the pope had attempted in vain — the separation of the royal pair. It was followed by a misunderstanding between Sancho and Alfonso, which the common danger of Christian Spain, and the earnest remonstrances of the church, could scarcely prevent from exploding. On the restoration of outward harmony, the Portuguese monarch recovered most of the places which the Africans had reduced; an enterprise in which he was again fortunately assisted by a crusading armament. His next care was to rebuild and repeople the towns which had been destroyed; a labour of many years. As during the remainder of his reign he was no more troubled by the Mohammedans, he made a few, but apparently unimportant, conquests in Algarve.

The tranquillity which the kingdom continued to enjoy, greatly assisted Sancho in his beneficent designs of encouraging population, and of alleviating the distresses of his people. Towards the close of his reign he appears to have again incurred the censure of the church, by encouraging certain marriages within the forbidden degrees, — among others, that of a son with one of his nieces, — and to have shown some violence towards the ecclesiastics who condemned them. His subsequent repentance doubtless occasioned his re-

1203 to 1211.

---

[*] See Vol. II. p. 45—47.

conciliation with the offended pontiff. He died in 1211. In his last will he bequeathed great riches to his children, and made his successor, Alfonso, swear to observe his dispositions. Of his children, two had the honour to be canonised, — Teresa, the divorced wife of Alfonso IX., and Sancha, who professed in the convent of Lorvam: a third, Mafalda, who after his death married Enrique of Castile, and was left a widow in 1217, and who passed her remaining days in another convent, is said to have been no less entitled to the enviable distinction.*

1211 to 1216.
Alfonso II. had no sooner ascended the throne than he showed a disposition to evade the execution of his father's will. Not only did he refuse to allow his brothers the money which had been bequeathed them, but he insisted on the restitution of the fortresses which belonged to his two sisters, the saints Teresa and Sancha; and on their refusal to surrender them, he seized them by force. The infantas complained to the pope and the king of Leon: the former ordered his legate to see justice done to them; the latter, who still bore an affection towards his divorced wife Teresa, interfered more effectually by way of arms. The Leonnese entered Portugal by way of Badajos, reduced several fortresses, and spread devastations around them. As the Lusitanian still persisted in retaining his usurped possessions, the king of Leon next assembled an army in Galicia, passed the Minho, and with equal success laid waste the towns and open places. To arrest his progress, the Portuguese king hastened to his northern frontier; the latter was signally defeated; but the victor, after having garrisoned the conquered places, retired to repel the probable hostilities of the Castilians. In the sequel, Alfonso of Portugal, at the command of the pope, and doubtless through fear of the Leonnese, consented to treat with his sisters. By the papal commissioners it

* Same authorities, nearly in the places last quoted. To these may be added the Annales Compostellani, p. 823. (apud Florez, España Sagrada, tom. xxiii.).

was agreed that the fortresses in dispute should be held for the princesses by the templars, but subject to the royal jurisdiction; and that, on the demise of the two feudatories, they should revert to the crown.

The transactions of Alfonso with the Mahommedans were not so remarkable as those of his predecessors — a circumstance that must be attributed not to his want of military spirit, but to his excessive corpulency, which rendered the fatigues of the field intolerable. Though he sent a handful of troops to aid in the triumphs of the Navas de Tolosa*, he did not take the field in person against the enemies of his faith, until 1217 when the arrival in his ports of another crusading armament, which promised to co-operate in his designs, roused him to attempt the reduction of Alcaçar do Sal, a place that still remained in the power of the misbelievers. It held out till the end of September, when a strong Mohammedan army arrived to relieve it. Notwithstanding the disproportion in numbers, the Christains resolved to hazard a general action, especially on receiving a reinforcement from Alfonso of Leon. As usual when any great event was impending, Heaven miraculously encouraged the faithful by assured hopes of success. First a luminous cross appeared in the sky conspicuous to the whole army; next, during the heat of the battle, a legion of angels was seen in the clouds, not as spectators, but as aiding in the good cause, by throwing darts with terrific effect among the infidels. If the Moors could contend with mortals, they quailed and fled at the sight of their celestial enemies; but they could not avoid the angelic weapons, nor those of their fleet pursuers; so that most of them were destroyed in the retreat. Alcaçar was again recovered; and the Mohammedans who had remained in Alemtejo, and were pressing the siege of several fortresses, were compelled to retire. And if we are to believe ancient chronicles, the important town of Moura, on the eastern bank of the

---

* Vol. II. p. 45—47.

Guadiana, was also recovered, in a manner too singular to be passed over in silence. One Saluquia, daughter of a powerful man in Alemtejo, had been promised to a countryman, the Moor Brafama, and with her, as a dowry, the town just mentioned. Knowing that the wedding was to be celebrated on a given day within the walls of that fortress, two hidalgos, dom Pedro and dom Alvaro Rodriguez, assumed, and caused their people to assume, the Moorish dress, and placed themselves in ambush near the way by which the bridegroom would be constrained to pass. On his appearance they arose, massacred him and his attendants, and rode towards the fortress, on the tower of which Saluquia was awaiting his arrival. As they approached they shouted in Arabic that they escorted the happy Brafama. The maiden ordered the gates to be opened; but no sooner did she perceive the carnage which followed, than, suspecting the truth, and disdaining to become the captive of her lover's murderers, she threw herself headlong from the tower. From that day the town, which had hitherto been called *Arouche*, was known by the name of *Moura*, or the female Moor.

1220 to 1223. During the last three years of his reign, Alfonso had new disputes with the church. He appears to have borne little respect for the ecclesiastical immunities, some of which were, indeed, inconsistent with the interests of the community. That the clergy should be exempted from *personal* military service, is too obvious to be denied; and, whatever may be the customs of the times, it might well be doubted whether men whose mission was peace, were justified in sending even their armed retainers to the field. Alfonso insisted on churchmen heading their own vassals in the wars he undertook, and such as refused were compelled to go. For such violence there was no excuse; but in subjecting the ecclesiastical possessions to the same contributions as were levied on the property of the laymen, and churchmen themselves to the secular tribunals, he attempted a salutary innovation on the established system of the clerical exemptions. The archbishop of Braga, like our Becket of the preceding century, remonstrated with the king; and when remonstrances were ineffectual, hurled at the head of his abettors the thunders of the church. In return he was deprived of his revenues, and compelled to consult his present safety by flight. He complained to the pope: Honorius III. ordered three Castilian bishops to insist on ample reparation to the injured prelate; and, if their instances were disregarded, to excommunicate the king, and impose an interdict on the nation. The afflicted people now endeavoured to effect a reconciliation between the king and the archbishop: the former promised to make satisfaction, and in future to respect the privileges of the church; he was accordingly absolved, and the interdict removed, but before he could fulfil his share of the compact he was surprised by death.*

SANCHO II., having reluctantly promised to respect the immunities of the church, prepared to extend the boundary of his dominions at the expense of the Mohammedans. He recovered the important town of Elvas, which had been regained by the Moors: next Jarumeñha and Serpa yielded to his arms. He now carried the war into Algarve; in which, though his conquests are not specified, we know that some must have been made, as, by contemporary writers, encomiums are passed on his valour and success. He appears to have left the enemy no fortified places in Alemtejo: the frontier fortresses of that province, thus rescued from the infidels, he intrusted to the defence of the order of Santiago, who made successful irruptions into Algarve, and triumphed in several partial engagements. Tavira, Faro, and Loule were reduced by these knights; and when the

1223 to 1240.

---

* Rodericus Tol., lib. viii. (apud Schottum, tom. ii.). Lucas Tud., Chronicon Mundi (apud eundem, iv. 111). Chronicon Conimbricense (apud Florez, tom. xxiii. p. 334.). Anales Toledanos I. (apud eundem). Rodericus Santius, Historia Hispanica, pars ii. (apud Schottum, tom. i.). Alfonso el Sabio, Cronica de España, parte iv. Brandaon, part iv. Vasconcellos, p. 51—57. Lemos, tom. iii. liv. 12. La Clède, tom. ii. liv. 6.

Moorish governor of Silves attempted to aid his co-religionists, he lost his capital, and immediately afterwards his life, as he attempted to swim over a little river in that hilly region to escape from his resistless enemies. These successes of the Christians will be readily admitted, when we remember that while the fortresses of Algarve were thus won, Fernando of Leon and Castile was prosecuting his glorious career in Andalusia, and thereby precluding all hope of aid from the rest of Mohammedan Spain, which was soon to be confined within the narrow limits of Granada. Yet it must not be forgotten that some of these fortresses were subsequently occupied for a short period by the Mohammedans. In fact, the frontier places continued for some years to change masters, according as either of the hostile powers prevailed.

1226 to 1245.
In his domestic administration, dom Sancho was doomed to be far less fortunate. From his infancy he appears to have been of a weak constitution, and of a still weaker mind; but if he was weak, we have no proof that he was vicious, though great disasters afflicted his kingdom, and the historians of his country have stigmatised his memory. His hostility to the immunities of the clergy appears to have been the first and chief cause of his unpopularity. This, however, would not have led to the events which followed, had he not overstepped the line of prudent reform, and claimed for the crown, prerogatives which the church could not allow to any monarch. He not only, we are told, seized the revenues of vacant cures, but nominated ecclesiastics, whose only merit was their favour with him. His ministers are charged with heavier offences,— with seizing the property of the church without scruple, under the pretext that it was required for the service of the state, but in reality to waste it on their own creatures and connections. It is possible, perhaps probable, that these charges are somewhat exaggerated, and that the king's zeal to subject churchmen to the ordinary tribunals may have given rise to the invectives of malig-

nity; yet if his own character has been to a certain extent unjustly darkened, there seems to be little justification for the acts of his creatures, who are known to have possessed unbounded influence over him, and to have conducted themselves with equal violence and rapacity. It is certain that the infante Fernando was guilty of so much violence at Santarem, that he was excommunicated, unable to obtain absolution without going to Rome, and submitting to a rigorous penance. The same censures were passed on the monarch for his persecution of the dean of Lisbon, whom the chapter had raised to the see of that capital in opposition to his menaces. His subsequent repentance disarmed the pontiff; and, notwithstanding the complaints of the people that the laws were silent, and brute force only triumphed, he would doubtless have ended his reign in peace, had he not resumed or permitted the spoliation of the church. At length, both clergy and people united their murmurs: they perceived that the king was too feeble to repress the daily feuds of his barons, who broke out into open war, and committed the greatest excesses The contempt with which their remonstrances were treated passed the bounds of human endurance; and they applied to Innocent IV., then presiding over a general council at Lyons, to provide a remedy for such evils. The application was readily received by the pontiff; who, in concert with the fathers of the council, issued a decree by which, though the royal title was left to Sancho, the administration was declared to be vested in the infante Alfonso, brother of the king.

No sooner did Alfonso hear of this extraordinary proceeding of the pope and council, than he prepared to vindicate the title which it had conferred upon him. He was then at Boulogne-sur-Mer, the lordship of which belonged to him in right of his wife Matilda Having sworn before the papal commissioners to administer Portugal with justice, and leaving the government of Boulogne in the hands of his countess, he embarked at that port, and safely landed at Lisbon. At first the king

1245 to 1248.

intended to oppose the infante; but seeing how generally the deputies owned him, — how all classes, nobles and citizens, prelates and peasants, joined his brother,— he retreated into Spain, to solicit the support of his cousin, Fernando III. As that saintly monarch was too busy in the Andalusian wars to assist the fugitive king in person, he recommended the interests of his guest to his son Alfonso. The Castilian infante showed no want of zeal in behalf of his relative. He first applied to the pope for the restoration of the royal exile; and when he found the application useless, he collected a considerable army, and invaded Portugal. Arriving before Leyria without much opposition, he was preparing to storm that fortress, when he was visited by a deputation from the archbishop of Braga, which represented to him the crimes of Alfonso, and the necessity of the papal interference; and conjured him, as a true son of the church, not to incur excommunication by opposing the execution of the pontifical bulls. The Castilian infante listened, and obeyed: he led back his army; and the deposed monarch, now bereft of all hope, retired to Toledo, where, early in 1248, he ended his days. So long as the latter lived, some of the fortified places in Portugal refused to acknowledge the regent; but on his death without issue, — there is no evidence that he was ever married, — his brother was peaceably acknowledged as his successor.*

1248 to 1254. ALFONSO III., on arriving at a height which, a few years before, his ambition could scarcely have reached, was not without apprehensions that the Castilian king or infante might trouble him in his usurpation, and assembled the three estates of his realm to deliberate on the means of defence. Fortunately for his ambition, both father and son were absorbed by their Andalusian conquests. To secure, if possible, the good-will of the

* Rodericus Tol. (apud Schottum, tom. ii. et iv.). Chronicon Conimbricense, passim (apud Florez, tom. xxiii.). Annales Compostellani, p. 323, &c. (in eodem tomo). Anales Toledanos II. p. 412 (in eodem tomo). Brandaon, part iv. Vasconcellos, p. 61, &c. Rodericus Santius (apud Schottum, tom. I.). Lemos, tom. ii. liv. 13. To these must be added Abu Abdalla (Vestis, tom ii.); and Condé, tom. iii.

former, he sent a considerable aid to the Christian camp, which was readily received by the hero. In the mean time he himself resolved to profit by the reverses of the misbelievers, and finish the conquest of Algarve. At the head of a sufficient force, he accordingly penetrated into that province, and speedily recovered the places which the Mohammedans had again surprised. In his next campaign he recovered Serpa, Moura, and other places on the eastern bank of the Guadiana—places which his predecessors had reduced, but which the active enemy had contrived to regain. In a subsequent expedition, his ardour or avarice led him to encroach on the possessions of Alfonso el Sabio, Fernando's successor. The wali or regulus of Niebla, perceiving that hostilities were directed against him, implored the aid of his liege superior, the king of Leon and Castile. The latter enjoined the Lusitanian not to molest Mohammed. The instruction appears to have been disregarded; for the Castilian army immediately marched against the Portuguese, who were compelled to retreat. The Castilian king did not stop here. On the pretext that Algarve, as chiefly conquered by his subjects, the knights of Santiago, belonged to him, he invaded that province, and quickly reduced its chief fortresses. The Portuguese was glad to sue for an accommodation; and it was at length agreed that he should marry doña Beatrix de Guzman, a natural daughter of the Castilian, and with her receive the sovereignty of Algarve. As the province had been conquered by the subjects of both crowns, equity would have indicated its division by the two monarchs; but as such a division would probably have led to future wars, the present arrangement might be a politic one. The Castilian appears to have reserved to himself the sovereignty of Algarve; his feudatory being required both to pay tribute, and to furnish a certain number of forces whenever he should be at war. The cession, with whatever conditions it was accompanied, was disagreeable to the Castilians, who thought that their monarch had sacrificed the interests of the state in favour of his daughter.* The marriage was solemnised in the following year (in 1254), and a few years afterwards Portugal was declared for ever free from homage to the Castilian kings.

1255 to 1262.
From the facility with which this matrimonial connection was formed, it would be inferred that the Lusitanian was become a widower. But the countess Matilda still lived, and was anxious to return to her lord. He pleaded that the former marriage remained null, *ob impotentiam naturæ*, in that lady; but that such an impediment existed, may well be doubted. No complaint of it was made by her former husband, a prince of the royal house of France; nor by her second husband, until some time after his accession to the Portuguese throne. Her only defects were her barrenness and her age, — two which, though no canonist would recognise, were sufficient in the mind of so unscrupulous a prince as Alfonso. The lady applied for the restoration of her rights; he refused to recognise them: she sailed for Portugal to plead them in person; but he refused to see her: and when at length she forced her way into his presence, he heard, unmoved, her entreaties, her expostulations, and threats; and witnessed, unmoved, a grief which would have softened the heart of any other man. The queen (for such history must call her) retired to Boulogne, and laid her complaints before the pope and her liege superior, St. Louis. After a patient examination of the case, Alexander IV. expedited a bull, by which he declared Matilda the lawful wife of Alfonso, and annulled the recent marriage with doña Beatrix. The king persevered in his lust, as he had already done in his usurpation, even when excommunicated by the pope; and he and his household were interdicted from the offices of the church. A second time is she said to have visited Portugal, but with as little success. In his conduct towards this devoted lady,

---

* See Vol. II. p. 186.

there is something that must strike every reader with indignation. She had married him when poor — when almost an exile from his native court — and had thereby raised him to power and riches *: and her unshaken attachment — unshaken even by his sickening ingratitude — proves that though the empire of the passions had ceased, she possessed an uncommon share of woman's best feeling. Her last act, by which she bequeathed a considerable sum to this faithless deserter, was characteristic enough of her ruling misfortune. On her death, in 1262, his prelates readily obtained from the pope a bull to render legitimate the present marriage, and the issue arising from it.†

The rest of this prince's reign was passed in ignoble disputes, either with his prelates, in relation to the ecclesiastical immunities, which he had the wish but not the power to limit; or with his military orders, whose possessions he justly considered too ample. In the latter case, a compromise procured him what he coveted: in the former, the papal thunders were too much for him; and he was forced not only to express contrition for his past sacrilegious attempts, but to exact from his son and successor a promise that in future no attempts should be made by the crown, either to levy a tax on ecclesiastical property, to nominate to bishoprics or other dignities, or to subject churchmen to the secular tribunals. In these conditions, the peasantry, and even the citizens, had reason to complain of the excesses to which the royal officers resorted; but they had no advocate beyond the justice of their cause, — an advocate not likely to be regarded in times of violence. Like all usurpers, Alfonso in the beginning of his reign was lavish of gifts, and still more of promises: when his throne was established by his brother's death, he ap-

1263 to 1279.

---

* "Cum enim gratiam reponere debuit uxori, quæ pauperem opimâ domo exceperat, effœtam et sexagenariam pertæsus, veritusque ne inopia heredum Lusitana domus ad reges Legionenses, in quibus fluxerat, iterum dilibaretur, scelestas nuptias contraxit," &c.—*Vasconcellos*, p 72.
† "Ergo Beatrice *justis fuscibus in thorum admissâ*, et duobus ex ea liberis regni successione firmatâ," &c.—*Idem*. This author's style is much superior to his matter.

peared in his true colours — a rapacious and unprincipled tyrant. His opposition to the injurious privileges of the church a rose not from any regard to the interests of his people, but from avarice, or the lust of power. He died in 1279.*

1279, &c. DINIS, like his deceased father and most of his predecessors, was embroiled with the church. He showed little disposition to observe the concessions of the late king; and, as usual, his punishment was excommunication, and the imposition of an interdict. Finding by the experience of preceding kings, that the church, however protracted his resistance, must eventually triumph, he wisely endeavoured to obtain conditions as the price of his voluntary submission. With a convocation of his prelates, he arranged the articles of his reconciliation with the church: these, which chiefly related to the grievance before mentioned, were submitted to the pope, who modified and approved them. On one point, to which no strenuous opposition was made by his holiness, he insisted with becoming and successful earnestness, — that no order of ecclesiastics should be allowed to purchase land. In another demand, that Portuguese youths should not be allowed to take money from the country under the pretence of studying in foreign universities, he was less successful, though he partially reduced the evil. If he could not effect all that he desired, he had the consolation at least of effecting something, and of setting a salutary example to his successors. In these ages papal encroachments were systematic and uniform, and statutes similar to that of mortmain were found necessary in most European states.

1286 to 1298. In the troubles which afflicted Castile during the reigns of Sancho IV. and Fernando IV., dom Dinis took a part, — sometimes by granting asylum to the rebels, sometimes by arming in their cause, and making hostile

---

* Chron. Conim. p. 338, &c. (ap Florez, tom. xxiii.). Rod. Sant. iv. 3. (ap. Schott. i.). Francisous Tarapha, De Regibus Hispaniæ. Brandaon, v. Vasconcellos, 71, &c. Lemos, iii. liv. 14. La Clède, ii. liv. 7.

irruptions into the neighbouring kingdom. But as these troubles were obscure and indecisive, and as allusion has been made to them on a former occasion *, they need not be repeated here. At length, through the marriage of his daughter Constanza with the youthful Fernando, he became the friend of the Castilian government.

As if Heaven had decreed that the guilty conduct of Dinis, in fomenting rebellion among his neighbours, should be visited on his own head, in 1299 one of his brothers openly rebelled. Though this ill-planned disturbance was soon quelled, and was followed by some years of internal tranquillity, new troubles arose in his son and heir Alfonso. The king had a natural son, Alfonso Henriques, who appears to have possessed an undue share of his affections, and on whom he lavished the chief favours of the crown. The heir loudly exclaimed against this evident partiality, as unjust towards himself; and even asserted that it was the design of the king to procure the legitimacy of the bastard, and exclude him from the throne. That such a design was ever formed, is exceedingly improbable: it was indignantly disavowed by the father; who solicited the pope to interfere, and deter the partisans of the prince from resorting to arms. But though the pontiff called on the Portuguese to set aside Alfonso from the succession if he persisted in his undutiful course, the menace had no effect on the latter. On the contrary, he collected all the idle and dissolute youths of the kingdom, with all who had rendered themselves obnoxious to justice by their crimes, and took the field. His first design was to surprise Lisbon, and he left Coimbra for that purpose: he was pursued by his incensed father, who overtook and defeated him. In vain did the saintly Isabel, his mother, endeavour to effect a reconciliation between them, by persuading the one to compassion, the other to obedience: Alfonso retreated, seized on Leyria, plun-

---

* See Vol. II. pp. 193—199.

dered Alcobaça, marched on Santarem, which soon submitted, and was acknowledged by Oporto, and other places in the vicinity. Before Vimaraens, however, he was vigorously repulsed by the loyal governor, whom neither promises nor threats could draw into the prevailing stream of rebellion. The king, who had recovered Leyria, now threatened Coimbra. To defend this important place, Alfonso raised the siege of Vimaraens, and advanced with his whole force. The two armies soon came in sight, and were preparing for a general action, when Isabel again appeared and renewed her attempts at reconciliation. Finding her husband inaccessible to her prayers and remonstrances, she visited the prince, who, influenced by her assurances that no intention had ever existed of excluding him from the throne, showed signs of repentance. The king was, in the end, persuaded to grant a truce of four days, while commissioners appointed by each party endeavoured to arrange their unhappy differences. Their attempts were vain; the period expired, and the two armies engaged: the action, however, though somewhat bloody, was indecisive,—a circumstance that more inclined the two combatants to peace than all the considerations of nature or decency, or all the exhortations of pope or prelate. It was now agreed that the king should return with his troops to Leyria, the prince to Pombal, while the negotiations were renewed. The commissioners reassembled; and, after a long deliberation, proposed that Alfonso should retain possession of all the places which then acknowledged him, but that he should govern them as a vassal of his father; that he should disband his lawless followers, some of whom had committed the most heinous crimes, and were daily inflicting the heaviest calamities on the people; that his partisans should be forgiven, and his natural brother, Pedro, the chief fomenter of the recent disturbances, should be restored to the royal favour; and that the obnoxious Alfonso Henriques should be exiled from the court and kingdom. The conditions were accepted by father and son, who swore to fulfil them faithfully.*

But this reconciliation was of short continuance. One cause of its rupture is said to have been the return of the bastard Alfonso Henriques; another, that the prince, on finding that his revenues, however ample, were insufficient for his prodigality, applied to his father for their augmentation, and met with a refusal. In the soreness of mind consequent on the recent disputes, few incentives were required to renew the mutual animosity. To prevent the repetition of the scenes which had so much disgraced the kingdom, Dinis convoked the states; in which the demands of the son were discussed, and rejected as both unreasonable and prejudicial to the royal authority. Alfonso indignantly retired to Santarem; where, through the persuasion of his unprincipled advisers, he again armed, and proceeded towards Lisbon. As many inhabitants of that capital complained of the severity with which the king enforced the administration of justice, he hoped that they would embrace the party of one who advocated and permitted every possible licence,—the consistent friend of disobedience and anarchy. As he approached, he was met by a royal messenger, who in the king's name commanded him to retire; but he disregarded the summons, and with banners displayed pursued his audacious march. The outraged father left the city to chastise him; and a battle would immediately have ensued, but for the timely interference of Isabel, who was again fortunate enough to persuade both to suspend their differences. Alfonso retired to Santarem, where he passed some months in his usual manner, without regard to the sufferings of the people, caused by the rapacity and violence of his creatures. That place had always been a favourite residence of the king. In 1324, he paid it a visit, after acquainting his son with his intentions, and protesting that he did not mean to incommode any one

---

* Authorities same as before.

during his short stay. But he was accompanied by his illegitimate son, whom he had not only recalled to court, but restored to a high office in the household. As usual, the jealousy of the prince vented itself in murmurs; the king retorted; and a quarrel ensued, in which the attendants of both took a part, and in which blood was shed. As the party of Alfonso increased, the king was at length constrained again to dismiss the obnoxious bastard; to depose the justiciary of the kingdom — a person peculiarly hateful to the prince; and to accord the latter a considerable addition to his revenues.

1325. Dom Dinis did not long survive this reconciliation with his undutiful son. On his return to Lisbon he sickened, and remained in that state till his death. It is some consolation to find that, before his departure, he solicited and obtained a visit from Alfonso; and that both met with sentiments not merely of mutual forgiveness, but of affection.—Dinis was a superior prince: with great zeal in the administration of justice, he combined a liberality truly royal, and a capacity of mind truly comprehensive. In 1284, he laid in Lisbon the foundation of a university; but in 1308, finding that the students were more addicted to the pleasures of a capital than to the fatigues of science, he obtained the pope's permission to transfer it to Coimbra. With the confiscated possessions of the Templars, he founded and endowed a new military order — that of Christ; the knights of which, by the bull of that institution, were bound to interminable war with the Moors. Most of the deprived Templars were readily admitted into the new community; a proof that, whatever might be their conduct in France, in Portugal (and the same is equally true of the rest of the peninsula) they had done nothing to forfeit the esteem of their countrymen. The queen of dom Dinis, as before observed, doña Isabel, a princess of Aragon, has been canonised for her piety. But, with all her virtues, she could not escape persecution. She was accused of aiding her son in his rebellions; and by her incensed husband was both exiled from the court, and deprived of her appanage, until the affection of the people, who readily espoused her cause, procured her restitution to the royal favour and the rights of her station. On another occasion she was accused of a much more heinous offence, — of adultery with one of her domestics, who was thrown into a furnace; but who, like the three witnesses of old, miraculously escaped unhurt. The miracles adduced in evidence of her deification may be found in the Jesuit Vasconcellos.*

ALFONSO IV., surnamed the *Brave*[†], had scarcely grasped the reins of sovereignty, when he exhibited, in a manner little becoming royalty, his vindictive feelings towards his illegitimate brother, Alfonso Henriques, who, to escape his wrath, had just fled into Castile. That brother, by a sentence of the new king, was deprived of his honours and lordship of Albuquerque, which he had held through his marriage with an heiress of that house, and was in addition condemned to perpetual exile. His first step was to write a supplicatory letter to Alfonso, whose anger, by ardent and probably sincere protestations of allegiance and duty, he hoped to disarm; but when he found that these were despised, he resorted to arms. Having collected some troops in Castile, and been joined by a prince of that kingdom, he entered Portugal, laid waste the frontiers, put to the sword every living being that fell in his way, and defeated the grand master of Avis, who attempted to arrest his progress. The king now took the field in person, demolished Albuquerque, and laid waste the neighbouring territories of Castile. These harassing though indecisive hostilities might have continued for

1325, 1326.

---

* Brand. v. Chron. Conimb. (Flor. xxiii. p. 340, &c.). Rod. Sant. iv. (ap. Schott. i.). Vasc. p. 79, &c. La Clède, tom. ii. Ferreras, tom. iv. Lemos, iv. liv. 15.

† The reign of this prince is more remarkable than most other periods for the disagreement between the Castilian and Portuguese historians, not merely as to motives, but facts. Both write with all the heat of partisans, and both endeavour to give such a colouring to events as to favour their peculiar views. In these disputes, honesty or candour has little share. To seek the truth from either party alone would be vain; it can only be discovered from a careful and unbiassed examination of both. On such a subject a foreigner should have no prejudices, yet La Clède proves that they are not confined to the peninsula.

years, had not Santa Isabel left her retreat in the convent of St. Clair, which she had founded, and prevailed on her son to permit the return of the exile.

1325, 1326. Another defect of the new king gave great offence to the people,—his neglect of public business, and his addiction to the chase. The first months of his reign were almost wholly passed in the royal forests in the vicinity of Cintra; and when he visited his seat of government, it was to converse with his ministers, not on the affairs of the kingdom, but on the sport he had witnessed. As they had been taught by the late king, whose attention to the duties of government is represented as constant, how salutary the vigilance of the chief ruler must prove, where power is ever prone to oppress, they first disapproved by their silence, and next condemned by their remonstrances, the favourite pursuits and uniform topic of Alfonso. They reminded him that the cares of justice, not the love of pastime, were incumbent on royalty; and that the account which he must one day give to the King of all would regard not the number of beasts he had killed, but the good he had procured for his people. Their freedom displeased their new master, who reproached them for it in terms at once of indignation and surprise. We are told that they listened to his torrent of abuse with perfect composure; that when he had finished they replied, he must either change his habits, or resign his dignity in favour of a worthier ruler; that his first impulse was to punish them for their audacity; but that, in the end, he applauded their honest zeal, restored them to his confidence, and became as attentive as he had before been indifferent to the duties of his station.*

1327 to 1329. The first twelve years of Alfonso's reign were distracted by hostilities with his namesake of Castile, who, as before related, was the husband of his daughter.† Though these hostilities were chiefly owing to the per-

---

* Though this in substance is the uniform relation of all the historians of Portugal, native or foreign, we do not vouch for its accuracy; at least, not for the latter portion of it.

† See Vol. II. pp. 203—205.

versity of the infante don Juan Manuel, it cannot be denied that the Portuguese king had abundant reason for dissatisfaction with his son-in-law. The usage experienced by the Castilian queen at the hands of her husband; her mortification at seeing a mistress, Leonora de Guzman, not only preferred to herself, but the sole depository of the royal favour; the studied insults to which she was daily exposed both from her husband and his minion; at length exhausted her patience, and drew forth some complaints to her father. The influence, too, which don Juan Manuel obtained in the Portuguese court through the marriage of his repudiated daughter Constanza with Pedro, son and heir of the Lusitanian king[*], was uniformly exerted to embroil the two crowns. The most unjustifiable and least politic act of the Castilian was his detaining the princess Constanza in his kingdom, and consequently preventing her from joining her husband. To the indignant remonstrances of the Lusitanian, he returned answers studiously evasive,— anxious to avert hostilities, yet no less resolved to persevere in detaining the princess. Another subject of complaint was now added to the rest. In a storm at sea, the Portuguese admiral, who was cruising in search of the Mohammedan pirates, put into the port of Seville, and was treated as an open enemy: both he and his ships were detained. Alfonso not only refused to restore them, but behaved to his queen with greater contempt than before; so much so, that she left the court, and fled to Burgos. For such repeated acts of violence there must have been some cause, and that cause was probably the readiness of the Portuguese king to assist the rebels of Castile: even now, don Juan de Lara, whom the Castilian was besieging in Lerma, was in alliance with the former. Alfonso of Portugal now sent a herald at arms to defy his son-in-law, on the ground, both of the unjust treatment of the queen, whom her husband was suspected of seeking to repudiate, and of

---

[*] See Vol. II. p. 203.

the continued detention of Constanza. His next step was to enter Castile, to invest Badajoz, and ravage the country as far as the vicinity of Seville. But on that almost impregnable fortress he could make little impression, and he reluctantly raised the siege. The war was now as destructive as it was indecisive and even inglorious: it was one of mutual ravage, of shameless rapine, and unblushing cruelty. Instead of meeting each other on a fair field, they seemed intent on nothing but laying waste each other's territory, and collecting as much booty as they could carry away: sometimes, however, the contest was decided on the deep, but with little success to either party. Of the provinces which suffered by these devastating irruptions, Estremadura and Entre Minho e Douro, had most reason to complain; though the two extremes of Galicia and Algarve were not without their share of evil. Though Maria, the Castilian queen, had sought refuge with her father, she was so far from listening to her personal wrongs by encouraging hostilities, that she was the unfailing advocate for their cessation. At length, through the efforts of the common father of Christendom,—when neither the prerogatives nor the immunities of the church have been concerned, the popes have always discouraged war between Christians,—the two princes agreed to a truce, and to the opening of negotiations for peace. But one of the conditions was the removal of Leonora de Guzman; a condition which Alfonso of Castile, who was entirely governed by that lady, was in no disposition to execute. Hostilities would probably have continued during the whole of his reign, had not the preparations of the Mohammedans, which he knew were chiefly directed against himself, and the loud complaints of his own subjects, forced him to *promise* at least that it should be conceded. Negotiations were re-opened, and with a much fairer prospect of success. To the departure of Constanza, the restitution of some insignificant fortresses which had been reduced, and even to the return of his queen, the Castilian felt no repugnance;

but though he consented for Leonora to leave the court, he recalled her immediately after the conclusion of peace. To his queen, however, he no longer exhibited a marked neglect: on the contrary, he treated her with all the outward respect due to her character and station; and the good understanding was confirmed by her admirable moderation.*

In the wars which the Castilians had to sustain against the Mohammedans, the Portuguese — so nobly did he forget his wrongs when the interests of Christendom were at stake — was no inefficient ally. Finding that his first aid of 300 lances was inadequate to the formidable preparations of the African and Spanish Moors, he himself hastened to the head-quarters of his son-in-law. As he approached Seville, the joy caused by his arrival was such, that the clergy met him in procession, singing, " Beatus qui venit in nomine Domini!"† He was present at the great battle on the banks of the Salado, in which the barbaric power was so signally humbled.‡ Though he had nobly borne his part in the triumphs of the day, he refused to have any other share in the immense plunder won on that occasion, than the standard, and some trifling personal effects of Abul Hassan. And if after this splendid victory he returned to his own dominions, he did not cease to send reinforcements to his ally. That he was no less interested in the destruction of the Mohammedan power than the other princes of the Peninsula, is evident from the position of his kingdom, and from his procuring a grant of the tithes during two years, and the publication of the crusade, from the reigning pope. This aid he continued readily to supply, until the death of Alfonso, by the plague, before Gibraltar, in 1350.§

1340 to 1350

---

* Chron. Conim. p. 340, &c. (apud Florez, xxiii.). Roder. Sant. iv. (apud Schottum, i.). Alf. à Carthag., &c. necnon Franciscus Tarapha, De Reg. Hisp. Vasc. p. 113. La Clède, ii. Lem. iv. 17. Arabian fragments in Casiri, and Condé by Marlès. Villasan Cronica del May Esclarecido Principe y Rey Alfonso el Onzeno; Chronica Domini Joannis Emmanuelis (apud Florez, tom. ii.).
† "Blessed is he who cometh in the name of the Lord!"
‡ Vol. II. p. 84.   § Vol. II. p. 206.

1340 to 1355.

The tragedies represented in Castile by Pedro the Cruel, successor of Alfonso XI., were fully equalled by one in Portugal. Soon after his marriage with Constanza, daughter of don Juan Manuel, Pedro, the infante of Portugal, had become passionately smitten with one of her attendants, doña Iñes de Castro, a lady of surpassing beauty, and frail as beautiful. That he made love to her, and that his criminal suit was favourably received, is indubitable, both from the deep grief which preyed on the spirits of Constanza, and from the anxiety of the king, lest this new favourite should be the cause of the same disturbance in Portugal, as Leonora de Guzman had occasioned in Castile. To prevent the possibility of a marriage between the two lovers, Alfonso caused Iñes to hold over the baptismal font a child of Pedro's,—in other words, to contract a near spiritual affinity. But the man whom the sacred bond of wedlock could not restrain, was not likely to be deterred from his purpose by an imaginary bar. After Constanza's death, which was doubtless hastened by sorrow, he privately married the seductive favourite. How soon after the death of the first wife this second union was contracted, whether immediately, or after Iñes had borne him three children, has been matter of much dispute. But the documents recording it have long since been produced; and from these it appears that the marriage was celebrated on the 1st day of January, 1354, when Iñes must have borne him four children, of which three survived. It also appears that a papal dispensation was obtained for it, and that it took place at Braganza, in presence of a Portuguese prelate and his own chamberlain. However secret this step, it was suspected by some courtiers, who, partly through envy at the rising favour of the Castros, and partly through dread of the consequences which might ensue, endeavoured to prevail on the king to interfere in behalf of young Fernando, the son of Pedro and Constanza, and the lawful heir to the monarchy. With the view of ascertaining whether a marriage had really been effected, the prince was urged to take a second wife from one of the royal families of Europe; and the manner in which he rejected the proposal confirmed the suspicion. But mere suspicion was not enough. The prince was summoned to court, compelled to a private interview with his father, and urged, in the most pressing terms, to declare whether his connection with doña Iñes was one of matrimony or gallantry. He solemnly and repeatedly replied, that she was not his wife, but his mistress; yet, when the entreaty was renewed, that he would abandon so guilty an intercourse, he firmly refused. The king now secretly consulted with his confidential advisers, as to the precautions he ought to adopt in regard to young Fernando, since, from the boundless influence possessed over the mind of Pedro by doña Iñes, it was feared that the true heir would be set aside from the succession in favour of her offspring. Unfortunately, both for his own fame, and for the interests of the kingdom, Alfonso consulted with such only as were personally hostile to the lady: they did not scruple to assure him, that unless she were forcibly removed, the state after his death would become a prey to all the horrors of a disputed succession. We are told that his soul revolted at the deed; but that, in the end, they wrung from him, a reluctant consent to her death. The time, however, which elapsed from the formation to the execution of this murderous purpose, proves that pity was a sentiment strange to his breast. That purpose was not so secret as to escape two friends of Pedro, — his mother, the queen Beatrix, and the archbishop of Braga. Both, in the design of averting the catastrophe, warned him of the plot; but he disregarded the intimation — doubtless, because he could not believe that the royal mind of his father could be contaminated by the guilt of murder, and because he considered the warning as a feint to procure his separation from Iñes. After the lapse of some months, the king hearing that his son had departed on a hunting excursion for a few days, hastily left Monte Mór, and proceeded to the convent of St. Clair, at Coimbra, where she then was. On learning his approach, she at once apprehended his object. Her only resource was an appeal to his pity. Taking her three children by the hand, she issued from the convent to meet him, prostrated herself at his feet, and in the most pathetic terms begged for mercy. Her beauty, her youth, her deep emotion, and the sight of her offspring,— his own grand-children,— so affected him, that after a struggle between policy and nature, the latter triumphed, and he retired. No sooner, however, was he in private with his confidents, than they censured his compassion, though natural in itself, as ruinous in its consequences to his family and kingdom. By their artful representations, they not only confirmed him in his original purpose, but obtained his consent that they should be entrusted with its immediate execution. Accordingly they hastened to the convent, and the unfortunate, guilty Iñes, fell beneath their daggers.

1355. The fate of this lady has called forth the deepest commiseration of novelists and poets, and has given rise to some vigorous effusions of the tragic muse. But her crimes have been carefully thrown into the shade. The woman who could consent to a criminal connexion with a married man— the object of an amiable wife's love;— who, by her guilt, broke the heart of that excellent princess; who, before the remains of that princess were cold, renewed the criminal intercourse; and who, during so many successive years, was the ready, nay eager creature of his lust, must, by unbiased posterity, be regarded with any thing but respect. Her tragical end must indeed command our sympathy, and cover her assassins with abhorrence; but let not these natural sentiments blind us to her crimes.

When Pedro returned from the chase, and found his wife so barbarously murdered, his grief was surpassed, if possible, by his thirst for revenge. He leagued himself with the kindred of Iñes; and though he coueld not fall on the murderers, who were protected by the king, he laid waste the provinces of Entre Douro e Minho, and Tras os Montes, where their possessions chiefly lay. He next marched on Oporto, but the archbishop of Braga threw himself into the place, with the resolution of defending it to the last extremity, and the enterprise was abandoned. King Alfonso was in consternation at the unexpected fury of his son. It was probably at his suggestion that the queen, accompanied by several prelates, hastened into Tras os Montes. They represented, but without effect, to the prince, the madness of desolating an inheritance which must soon be his: he threatened to continue his hostilities until the murderers were delivered up to him. To such a demand Alfonso could not consent; but in the end he proposed, as the price of reconciliation, that the obnoxious nobles should be banished from the court,—perhaps also from the kingdom, —and his son admitted to the chief share of the administration. Pedro accepted it, laid down his arms, and proceeded to court, where he was received with an affection truly paternal, and where he engaged, though with a fixed resolution of breaking the engagement, never to seek revenge on the assassins of doña Iñes.

Alfonso did not long survive this forced reconciliation with his son. His death, which happened at the beginning of 1357, is said to have been hastened by remorse for the tragical deed of which he had been the occasion. That he exhibited great—let us hope availing—repentance, is certain; but his character was unamiable. He had been a disobedient son, an unjust brother, and a harsh father. The rebellion of *his* son was but fit retribution for his own conduct to the royal Dinis. His justice too often degenerated into blind vengeance. During his reign (in 1348) Portugal was afflicted with the plague which spread throughout most of Europe, but which raged with more violence in that kingdom than any where else. Whole towns are said to have been left desolate, and some priests to have abandoned their flocks to the care of the monks.[*]

1356, 1357.

---

[*] Chron. Conim. p. 344. &c. (ap. Flor., xxiii.). Roder. Sant. iv. (ap. Schott. i.). Vasc. p. 116. &c. Ferr. par Hermilly, v. La Clède, ii. Lem. iv. 17.

1357 to 1360

PEDRO I. was scarcely established on the throne, before he gave way to his uncontrollable desire for vengeance on the murderers of doña Iñes. Knowing that they had sought protection in Castile, and how eager his namesake of that country was for the surrender of several Castilians, who, in like manner, had obtained an asylum in Portugal, he seems from the very beginning of his reign, to have indulged the expectation that a surrender of the individuals obnoxious to each other might be negotiated. He therefore paid court to that monarch, with whom he entered into a close alliance, and to whom he dispatched ten of his galleys to serve in the war against Aragon. Having declared the fugitive nobles, who were three in number, Pedro Coelho, Alvaro Gonsalves, and Diego Lopes Pacheco, traitors to their country, and confiscated all their possessions, he either proposed or received the proposal — there is some doubt from which of the two monarchs it originally came, or whether it may not be equally attributed to both — for the arrest of their personal enemies. By whichever of the tyrants it was first suggested, it was speedily and eagerly embraced by the other: on a given day the obnoxious Castilians were arrested in Portugal, the Portuguese in Castile, and were surrendered to their respective executioners. Of the three Portuguese, however, Pacheco escaped, and in a manner singular enough to be detailed. Early on the morning of the day destined for the arrest of himself and his countrymen, he left the city in which he abode to join in the chase. That no one might apprise him of the fate intended him, and that he might be secured immediately on his return, the gates were closed, and egress forbidden to the inhabitants. A poor mendicant, however, whom Pacheco had often relieved, and who became acquainted with the design, resolved to save his benefactor. The meanness of his habit, and his squalid appearance lulled the suspicions of the guards, who allowed him to pass through the wicket. In the neighbouring forest he found the Lusitanian, whom he exhorted to flee from the imminent peril. The better to escape detection, he clad the noble in his own mean attire, and advised him to flee into Aragon with the first body of muleteers he should happen to overtake. Pacheco followed the directions of the generous beggar, safely arrived in Aragon, and afterwards joined count Enrique in France, to whose fortunes he adhered until he was allowed to revisit his native country. History, however, would be more anxious to know what became of the poor mendicant than of Pacheco; but of the former no further record remains on earth.—The escape of even one victim was gall to the Portuguese king; but he resolved to satiate his rage on the two who were placed in his reach. Both were thrown into a deep dungeon in the city of Santarem, where the tyrant was then abiding, and were speedily put to the torture, with the view of eliciting whether others were implicated in the same crime, and whether certain secrets had been communicated to them by the late king. They withstood the acute torments they were made to endure with a firmness truly admirable;—a circumstance that increased beyond measure the rage of Pedro, who was present at the hellish scene. With Coelho, in particular, whom not a word, not a groan had escaped, he was so exasperated that he seized a whip and struck him on the face. This indignity affected the high-spirited knight far more than his present sufferings. Regarding the king with eyes full of fury, he loaded him not merely with the keenest reproaches, with the most violent invectives, but with a torrent of abuse. The latter foamed at the mouth, and ordered his victims to be transferred from the dungeon to a scaffold erected in front of his palace. There he appeared at the window, expressing a savage delight at the new torments they sustained. At length the living hearts of both were plucked from their bodies; hearts and bodies were next consigned to the flames; and when consumed, the ashes were scattered by the winds. —Was this a man or an incarnation of the demon?

The next proceeding of Pedro was to honour alike the remains and memory of the unfortunate Iñes. He

1361.

convoked the states of his kingdom at Castanedo, and, in their presence, made oath on the holy gospels, that, in the year 1354, he had married that lady. The witnesses of the fact, the bishop of Guarda and his own chamberlain, were likewise publicly sworn, and the bull of dispensation produced which pope John XXII. had granted for the celebration of the ceremony. No doubt was entertained by the assembled nobles and clergy that Iñes had been the lawful wife of their prince; and she was unanimously declared entitled to the honours usually paid to the Portuguese queens. That the legitimacy of her offspring might never be disputed, copies of the papal dispensation, and of the oaths taken on this occasion, were multiplied and dispersed throughout the kingdom. The validity of the marriage being thus established, Pedro now proceeded to show due honour to her remains. He ordered two magnificent tombs, both of white marble, to be constructed, one for himself, the other for that lady, and placed them in the monastery of Alcobaça. He then proceeded to the church of St. Clair at Coimbra, caused her corpse to be brought from the sepulchre, to be arrayed in royal ornaments, to be placed on a throne with a crown on the head and a sceptre in the hand, and there to receive the homage of his assembled courtiers. From that church it was conveyed on a magnificent car, accompanied by nobles and high-born dames, all clad in mourning, to the monastery of Alcobaça.

1362 to 1367. As the subsequent transactions of the Portuguese king with his namesake of Castile have been already related*, nothing now remains but briefly to notice his internal administration. It is allowed to have been as rigorous as it was whimsical. With the view of correcting the extravagance which had long seized on the higher orders of his people, he made a law that whoever bought or sold on credit should be punished — if the first offence, by stripes; if the second, by death. In

* Vol. II. pp. 220, 221.

his own household he set the example of paying for every thing in money the instant it was purchased. If he was thus severe against thoughtless imprudence, he could not be expected to be more lenient towards guilt. Of the vices which he visited with unpitying vengeance, fornication and adultery were the most obnoxious to him. That the lover of Iñez de Castro should thus hold in abhorrence those which he had so long practised might create surprise, were it not proved by general experience, not only that we are most forward to condemn in others imperfections to which ourselves are prone, but that kings are too often eager to plead an exemption from obligations binding on the rest of mankind. Hearing that the bishop of Oporto lived in a state of concubinage, the royal moralist hastened to that city, entered the episcopal palace, and, after fiercely reproaching the guilty prelate, laid on him so unmercifully with a whip, that had not some of his attendants interfered, the chastisement would have been efficacious enough—for the possibility of future sin would have been removed. As he was one day proceeding along a street, he heard a woman call another by an opprobrious name. He speedily enquired into the affair; and, finding that the latter had been violated previous to marriage by her husband, he consigned the offender to the executioner. Suspecting that the wife of a certain merchant was unfaithful to her conjugal duty, he caused her to be watched until he detected her in the actual crime; both lady and paramour were immediately committed to the flames. The husband, who had been walking for a short time in the environs of the city, heard on his return both of the sin and its punishment, and, in the impulse of his gratitude, he hastened to thank the king for his summary justice. An old woman prostituted her daughter to a Portuguese admiral; the woman was burnt, the admiral sentenced to lose his head; a sentence, however, which he escaped by flight. Other offences against the laws were punished, sometimes in proportion to their magnitude, but generally to his caprice. One countryman lent another a few silver cups, which the borrower refused to return: he was sentenced to pay nine times the value to the lender. An inferior officer of the law one day complained that a gentleman on whom he had served a process, had struck him and plucked him by the beard; Pedro turned to the presiding judge, and said, " I have been struck, and my beard has been plucked, by one of my subjects!" The judge, who understood the appeal, caused the culprit to be arrested and beheaded. Perceiving that causes were frequent, tedious, and expensive, and shrewdly divining the reason, he purged his courts of all advocates and proctors, —of all who had a manifest inerest in litigation, and reduced all processes to a simple statement of the case by the parties concerned, and of the sentence by the judges, reserving, however, to himself the privilege of deciding appeals. We are told that the result was similar to that which took place in ancient Rome after the expulsion of the physicians—that as in the latter case diseases, so in the former law-suits, incredibly diminished. These details will exhibit the character of Pedro in a truer light than the most laboured description. If we add that he was liberal of rewards, and fond of music and dancing, the character of the royal barbarian will be completed.*

1367. FERNANDO I., son of Pedro and the princess Constanza, was ill fitted to succeed monarchs so vigorous as his immediate predecessors. Fickle, irresolute, inconstant, without discernment, directed by no rule of conduct, obedient only to momentary impulse, addicted to idleness, or to recreations still more censurable, the very benevolence of his nature was a calamity, since it exposed him to the designs of men whose uniform aim was solely their own advantage.

1369 to 1382.
After the death of the Castilian Pedro, Fernando, as

* Chron. Conim., p. 320. &c. ap. Flor. xxiii. Vasc. 128, &c. Lem. iv. La Clède, ii. Ferr., par Herm. v.

before related * considering himself the true heir to the crown, assumed the regal title and arms of Castile. His ambition was lamentably inadequate to an enterprise so important as that of encountering and attempting to dethrone the bastard usurper Enrique. After his inglorious flight from Galicia †, he seldom took a personal share in the contest; and, from the recesses of his palace, he appeared to witness the invasion of his kingdom and the defeat of his armies with indifference. His frivolous occupations, his worse than frivolous amusements, absorbed his whole time: according as the stream of war approached his retirement, he removed from Lisbon to Santarem, and from Santarem to Lisbon, as intent on his own personal gratification as if Castile, not Portugal, were the theatre of a destructive war. When, in 1373, Lisbon itself was invested by the Castilian king, the defence of the place was abandoned to the valour of the inhabitants, and to their deep-rooted hatred of the Spanish sway. The same year, indeed, peace was made through the mediation of the pope; but it was often broken by Fernando during the reign both of Enrique and Juan I., the son and successor of that prince. The marriage of Beatrix, daughter of Fernando, with Juan, in 1362, and the treaty for uniting the two crowns, have been related in the history of Castile, and to that history the reader is referred for an account of the obscure and indecisive, however destructive, wars between the two kingdoms.‡

During these transactions proposals were frequently made for restoring permanent harmony by matrimonial alliances. At first Fernando cast his eyes on the infante Leonora of Aragon, whom he engaged to marry; but, with his usual fickleness, he escaped from the obligation. As the condition of one of his frequent acts of pacification with Castile, he next promised to raise a daughter of Enrique, also named Leonora, to the

1370 to 1372.

---

* See Vol. II. p. 232.   † Ibid.
‡ Vol. II. p 232. 236. Roder. Sa., Alf. à Carth., Franc. Tar., De Reg. Hisp., Lop. de Ay., Chron.

Portuguese throne. When the time approached for the celebration of this marriage, Fernando fell passionately in love with one of his own subjects — a Leonora like the rest.* He first saw this lady on a visit to her sister, doña Maria, who was one of the attendants on his own sister, the infanta Beatrix. To beauty of the finest order, Leonora added a sprightliness which charmed and a wit which captivated him; but these were far inferior to her ambition, and were unsupported by one single principle of honour or virtue. The king first mentioned his passion to doña Maria, whose good offices he solicited. Whether to enhance the value of the prize by the difficulty of its attainment, or from more worthy motives, — though common charity, as well as the general mildness of her manners must incline us to the more favourable hypothesis — she first objected his engagement with the royal family of Castile; and when he replied that he would set it aside without a rupture with that family, she reminded him that her sister was already the wife of don Joam Lourenzo da Cunha, lord of Pombeiro. "Of that we are well aware," replied Fernando; "but they are related by blood, and they married without a dispensation: the engagement may easily be annulled." The proposal was made to Leonora, who readily accepted it; proceedings for the cassation of the marriage were instituted in the ecclesiastical courts; and as the husband offered no opposition to them, — doubtless because he had no wish to contend with a plaintiff whose cause was backed by legions of soldiers, — it was declared null. Not considering himself safe in Portugal, dom Lourenzo fled into Castile, evidently little afflicted at the loss of an unprincipled woman.† There is reason to believe that it was Fernando's original intention to make her his mistress; but

---

* "Nome para este rei terrivel," says Lemos. This name, indeed, in all the three cases, is a most singular coincidence: it did not prove *terrible*, however it might be pernicious to the interests of the kingdom.

† To disarm ridicule by braving it, and to prove how little the affair had affected him, the exiled husband attached to each side of his cap a golden horn.

she had too much policy to become the tool of one whom she had resolved to rule; and she assumed the appearance of so much modesty, that to gain his object he was forced to marry her. But this marriage was strictly private; a precaution adopted as well to stifle the murmurs of his subjects, as to prevent the indignant remonstrances of Enrique. It was, however, suspected, and the very suspicion produced great dissatisfaction throughout the kingdom — no where so great as in the capital. A mob, formidable from its numbers, assembled in the streets, and, headed by a tailor, proceeded to the palace to reproach the king for his imprudence. The popular orator, with more vehemence than eloquence, declaimed against the monarch's base inclinations, and against the insult offered to both throne and people by the preference of a humble Portuguese lady to the infantas of Aragon and Castile. Fernando listened with forced tranquillity to the rude discourse; and, fearful that the 3000 mechanics and artisans before him might proceed to some greater outrage, he had the meanness to add a deliberate lie to his glaring imprudence. He said that he had neither married nor intended to marry Leonora. This declaration satisfied the mob; who, however, insisted that he should take an oath the following day to the same effect in the church of San Domingo; a promise which he readily made. At the time appointed, they proceeded to the church, but found to their mortification that, during the night, the king and Leonora had fled to Santarem. In the height of their fury they apostrophised both in no measured terms. Their insulting conduct so incensed the queen, that she procured a royal order for the arrest and execution of the tailor and his chief associates. The fear which this act of severity struck into the people, emboldened the king to publish his marriage. The nobles and prelates now hastened to court, to recognise their new queen. All readily kissed her hand with the exception of dom Dinis, son of Pedro, and Iñez de Castro, who accompanied his refusal in open court with expressions of contempt.

Fernando drew his poignard, and would doubtless have laid his obnoxious brother at his feet, but for the interference of two nobles who arrested his arm. Even Joam, the grand master of Avis, a natural son of the late king, who is about to perform so memorable a part in the national history, bowed before the triumphant Leonora. To render her power more secure, she began to act with great policy. For the people she procured an exemption from certain onerous contributions, and the enjoyment of certain privileges; for many of the most powerful nobles honours and posts; for her own immediate connections the best things which the crown could bestow. By these measures she certainly disarmed hostility, and secured to herself an undisturbed possession of her new dignity.*

1372 to 1378.
The insult to the royal family of Castile involved in this imprudent marriage, was one of the causes which led to the hostilities that followed — hostilities in which the country was laid waste, from Badajoz to Lisbon, and that capital invested.† On the conclusion of peace, in 1373, which was cemented by the marriage of a natural daughter of Fernando with a natural son of Enrique ‡, tranquillity visited the kingdom for some years; but the Portuguese court, through the ambition and wickedness of the queen, was often distracted and disgraced. As Fernando had only a daughter,— the princess Beatrix,— by Leonora, and as no hopes of future issue appears to have been entertained, the infante Joam, brother of the king,— not the bastard of that name who was the grand master of Avis, but the eldest surviving son of Pedro and Iñes de Castro, — was regarded as the presumptive heir to the crown. To set him aside from the succession was now the object of the queen. Fortunately for her purpose, the imprudence of the prince presented her with the means. Struck with the personal charms of dona Maria, sister of the queen, he privately married her.

* Chron. Conim. xxiii. Vasc p. 133. &c. Lem. v. 18. La Clède, li. Ferr. par Herm. v.
† Vol. II. p. 234. ‡ Ibid, note.

The step was not hidden from Leonora; who, so far from betraying her knowledge of it, and to lull her intended victim into profound security, proposed to the infante the hand of her own child, and with it the throne of Portugal. As she expected, her offer was declined; but she was resolved to move heaven and earth rather than see her sister and brother-in-law in the possession of supreme power. The former she appears to have hated: her destruction was certainly planned with demoniacal coolness. Sending one day for the infante, she assumed the appearance of intense affliction; assured him that she knew of his marriage with her sister; but that regard for him and his honour, as well as for the honour of the royal family, would not permit her to conceal that sister's depravity. "You are betrayed, prince!" was the substance of her address. "Maria loves another, to whom she grants her favours!" Unfortunately, Joam, who was unacquainted with her real character, and who could not suppose her capable of deliberately destroying a sister, implicitly believed her; and, in the madness of his rage, hastened to Coimbra, where the princess then abode. She met him with her usual smiles; and, on being repulsed, falteringly demanded the cause. "Because," replied the infuriated husband, "you have divulged our marriage, and sacrificed my honour!"—"Bid your attendants retire, and I will satisfy you!"—"I come not to hear your excuses," he furiously returned, "but to punish your guilt!" and at the same time his dagger found a way to her heart! She fell into the arms of her weeping attendants, while he mounted his horse and fled. The detestable cause of all this wickedness affected inconsolable grief, threw herself at the royal feet, and cried for vengeance on the murderer. But whether she found the king averse to justice, or whether she feared the indignation of the infante, who, sooner or later, would become acquainted with the innocence of Maria, she suddenly changed her proceedings, and obtained permission for him to return to court. But there every one shunned him — no one more eagerly than Leonora; so that, seeing his hopes of Beatrix at an end, he retired into the province of Entre Douro e Minho, where he was soon acquainted with the bloody perfidy of the queen. Having reason to distrust his safety, he fled into Castile, his heart torn by remorse for the fate of one whom he had passionately loved, and whose bleeding image was incessantly before him.*

1379 to 1382. Though on the accession of Juan I. of Castile Fernando readily renewed the peace between the two crowns, and consented to marry his daughter Beatrix to the heir of the Castilian†, his characteristic fickleness was such that he soon resolved to resume hostilities. To engage the duke of Lancaster in his cause, he sent a trusty messenger to England, dom Joam Fernando Andeiro, who concluded a league with the Plantagenet. To conceal this negotiation from the world, especially from the Castilian, he pretended great anger with Andeiro, whom he arrested, and confined to the fortress of Estremos. During his agreeable captivity in this place, he was frequently visited by the disguised king, who was sometimes accompanied by the queen, and was made to unfold the conditions he had contracted, and solicited for his advice. Sometimes, too, the queen, at her husband's command, or her own suggestion, repaired alone to the fortress for the same purpose. Perceiving her vanity, as well of her person as of her talents, and how gratified she was by adulation, Andeiro offered her the accustomed incense. As his person was unexceptionable, his address elegant, and his manners prepossessing, he soon won so far on the credulous Leonora, that she became the willing partner of his lust, and still more of his ambition. In the hostilities which followed the arrival of the earl of Cambridge‡, he was released, and, by her influence, was invested with the lordship of Ourem. His wife and children were brought to court; but his intimacy with Leonora so incensed the countess,

* Same authorities.
† The transactions to which this relation refers, will be found in Vol. II., reign of Juan I.
‡ Vol. II. p. 236.

that though she did not reveal — perhaps because she had not witnessed — the actual guilt of the parties, she did not scruple to assert that there was more than an ordinary attachment between them. Whether these reports reached the ears of Fernando, or, if they did, whether he believed them, is unknown; but so complete was the ascendancy of Leonora over his feeble mind, that, had he been acquainted with the whole extent of her amour, he would probably have trembled to punish her. But guilt is subject to alarms, which in themselves, to say nothing of the sting of conscience, or the anticipated justice of Heaven, more than counterbalances the pleasure or advantage it is intended to procure. Here was a proud queen doomed to be the slave of her minion, and in daily apprehension of being betrayed by the most common accident. Her own imprudence increased the danger of her situation. One day, when Andeiro and another noble entered her apartments, both, through the heat of the weather, covered with dust and perspiration, she asked them if they had no handkerchief. As this was a luxury in that age possessed by few, both replied in the negative. She divided a veil into two halves, one of which she gave to each. The conde Gonsales received his part with respect, and retired into a corner to remove the nuisance; while Andeiro approached the queen, and addressed to her what he intended to be a compliment, but licentious enough to show the terms on which they lived with each other. Neither the words, nor the smile which rewarded them, escaped the ears of a lady of honour, the wife of the baron de Azevedo. This lady was thoughtless enough to disclose the circumstance to her husband, who, with still greater imprudence, one day hinted to the queen his knowledge of her connection with Andeiro. Leonora now trembled for her safety, especially as Azevedo was the friend of don Joam, grand master of Avis, who had lately declared himself her enemy, and who might at any time reveal the amour to the king. She vowed the ruin of both. Having forged some letters, which compromised the loyalty of both,—which made both the secret agents of the Castilian king,—she went to Fernando, laid them before him, procured an order for their arrest, and saw them securely confined. This was not enough. Grown desperate by her sense of danger, she fabricated a royal order for the immediate execution of the two prisoners, addressed to the governor of the fortress. But the governor knew her character, suspected her purpose, and replied, that he could not obey it until the following morning. A second mandate was sent, in terms much more peremptory; but, instead of complying, the governor took both orders to the king. Nothing can so clearly show the wretched dependence of Fernando on his queen, than the fact that, though these audacious instruments completely opened his eyes as to her real character, he dared not attempt to punish her. He merely enjoined the officer to preserve a deep silence on this extraordinary transaction, and to respect the lives of the two prisoners.

1382 to 1383. Any other than Leonora would have been utterly confounded at this signal exposure of her deeds; but her wickedness was distinguished by a boldness which would have done honour to the most celebrated female adventurer of an Italian court. To a conviction expressed by the king that the grand master was innocent, she listened with much apparent pleasure, and even solicited the release of him and his companion. With an effrontery which has no parallel in history, the very day of their enlargement she invited both to her palace; expressed great commiseration for their late danger; and imputed the whole blame to one of the knights of Avis. That she had resolved to poison both in an entertainment given on the occasion, is the opinion of all the national historians; but the destined victims were on their guard, and escaped. Though the grand master complained of his arrest to Fernando himself, he could obtain no clue to the cause. But the latter was now evidently unhappy; he saw that the affections of his queen were estranged from him, and transferred to Andeiro.

Yet — such was his deplorable weakness! — he met both with constrained smiles, and deputed both to be present at the marriage of his daughter Beatrix with Juan of Castile.* On this occasion the favourite appeared with a splendour which might have become a sovereign prince; but which filled the beholders with indignation or envy. The perpetual sight of a faithless wife and her insolent paramour, was at length too much even for the feeble Fernando. In the agony of his feelings he one day opened his heart to the grand master, who he knew hated Andeiro, and with whom he planned that minion's assassination. But his own death, the result alike of constitutional weakness of frame and mental suffering, saved him from the guilt of murder.

The reign of this sovereign was one of the most deplorable that ever afflicted Portugal. The wars with Castile, — wars lightly undertaken and ingloriously conducted — and the consequent invasions of his territory by his more powerful neighbours, impoverished his people. Yet there were moments when he was not inattentive to the duties of his station. In some of his edicts he provided compulsory employment for the dissolute and idle; restrained the licentiousness of the vagabonds whose depredations were severely felt in the provinces; placed bounds to the avarice of the monastic orders, by rendering it illegal for them to succeed by testamentary bequest to landed property; improved the police of the towns, and the discipline of his fleet; he also rebuilt the walls of Coimbra and Lisbon which had been levelled in the recent wars. But these regulations were but the impulse of the moment, and were succeeded by some mischievous freak. Among these was the fatal one of raising by an arbitrary enactment the value of the current coin far beyond its intrinsic worth.†

* Vol. II. page 236.
† Chron. Conim., 307, &c. Froissart's Chron., by Johnes, iv. Lopez de Ayala, Cron. de Cast. Zurita, An. de Arag. Roder. Sant. iv. Alf. a Carth., cap. 89. Francis. Tar., p. 564, &c. Brand., iv. Vasc., p. 139, &c. Lem. v. 18. La Clede, ii.

1383. INTERREGNUM. By the death of Fernando, his daughter Beatrix, queen of Castile, was the true heir to the throne of Portugal. But the kingdom, far from expecting a foreign yoke, had, on the marriage of the infanta, expressly stipulated that, in case of Fernando's death, the government should be vested in a regent, until she had a son capable of assuming the sovereignty; that son, too, to be educated not in Castile but in Portugal. When that event happened, she had no child, — a circumstance that induced her husband to claim the crown in her right, and that filled the Portuguese with vexation. They were satisfied neither with their intended sovereign, Juan, nor with the regent, Leonora, the queen-mother, whom the will of the late king appointed to that dignity. And when, in conformity with the demands of the Castilian, Beatrix was proclaimed in Lisbon, the people either exhibited a mournful silence, or cried out that they would have no other king than their infante Joam, son of Pedro and Iñes de Castro, and the unfortunate husband of Maria, sister of Leonora, whose tragical fate has been recorded. But Joam and his brother Dinis now languished in the dungeons of Castile*, whither they had been consigned by the king, who knew that, if suffered to enter Portugal, they would speedily thwart his views of dominion. Until these princes could be restored to their country, and until Beatrix should have an heir, the Portuguese resolved to deprive the queen-mother of the regency, in favour of the grand master of Avis, who alone seemed able to defend their national independence.

Don Joam, as before observed, was an illegitimate son of king Pedro, by a lady of Galicia, and born in 1357. At seven years of age he had been invested with the high dignity of grand master, and his education intrusted to one of the ablest commanders of the order. No man could be better adapted for the conjuncture in which circumstances placed him. Cool, yet prompt;

---

* A bastard daughter of Fernando and her husband were about the same time placed in confinement.

prudent, yet in the highest degree courageous; unrestrained by conscience, and ready to act either with cunning or violence, according as either appeared necessary to his purpose, he would indeed have been a formidable opponent to any sovereign, much more to one so weak as the Castilian. Seeing the favourable disposition of the people, and confiding in his own mental resources, he commenced a policy which, if at first cautious, was sure to prove efficacious. To have a pretext for the design he meditated, he first solicited the regency from Juan; and having sustained a refusal, he employed his creatures, and all whom hatred to the Castilian yoke rallied round him, to secure its execution. Though Leonora pretended great sorrow for her husband's death, and endeavoured, by affected mildness, as well as by an administration truly liberal, to win the popular favour, her object was penetrated and despised. But a stronger sentiment was felt for Andeiro, who directed her at his pleasure, and whose death was now decreed by the grand master. To remove the latter under some honourable pretext from court, he was charged by Leonora with the government of Alemtejo: a province that, in the war inevitably impending with the Castilians, would be most exposed to their fury. He accepted the trust with apparent satisfaction; but scarcely had he travelled two leagues on his journey, when, accompanied by twenty-five resolute followers. he returned to Lisbon, and hastened to the royal apartments, where he knew he should find Andeiro. The guilty pair were as usual together. To the demand of the queen as to the motive of his unexpected return, he replied, that, having received certain information of the formidable armament preparing by Juan of Castile, he came to request the permission for raising a larger force. This reply appeared to satisfy her, and all animosity seemed so far banished, that the favourite invited the grand master to dinner. The latter, who offered some excuse, solicited a few moments' private conversation with the count, and both passed into another apartment. While engaged in this way, Joam struck the count with a dagger, at the same time a knight of his suite advanced, and by a second blow deprived the victim of life. The noise alarmed his domestics, who, instead of avenging his death, escaped along the roof of the palace: it more sensibly affected the queen, who was not only inconsolable for his loss, but apprehensive that the same fate was designed for herself. The tragical deed was hailed with characteristic acclamations by the populace, who, profiting by the example, massacred every one suspected to be hostile to the pretensions of their new idol, and plundered on every side. Among these was the bishop of Lisbon, a man of great merit and virtue, who, eager to put a stop to the horrid scenes which were perpetrating, and accompanied by two others, ascended the tower of the cathedral, and sounded the tocsin. His desire to spare the effusion of blood was considered as an unanswerable proof that he was in favour of Andeiro, or at least opposed to the grand master: a licentious band instantly rushed up the tower, and threw him and his companions from the summit. Their mangled corpses remained long without sepulture; a prey to dogs and beings more savage than dogs.* Leonora now fled from the city to Alenquer. On the way, she turned her eyes for a moment back on the towers of that capital, and, in the bitterness of her heart, prayed that she might live to see it wrapt in flames. After her departure, the grand master seemed pensive and melancholy; deplored the calamities of his country; complained that he was unequal to oppose his powerful enemies; and pretended that he would retire into England, to pass his remaining days in tranquillity. This hypocritical policy had its effect: it alarmed the mob, who dreaded being aban-

---

* The fate of this prelate has excited little pity among the orthodox Portuguese, because — he favoured the anti-pope: — " Queda mysteriosa, que permitio Deos para mostrar castigo as mãos dos Portuguezes, anida que com indignidade (it is a wonder this saving clause is added) o unico prelado que entre elles sustenton o escandaloso scisma."— *Lemos*, v. 153. The orthodoxy was carried still farther by the plunder and murder of the Jews.

doned to the justice their recent crimes so well merited, and who tumultuously flocked around him, insisting that he should assume the regency until Beatrice should become the mother of a son destined to rule over them. With much apparent reluctance, he accepted the proffered dignity, in the resolution of securing one much higher.*

The first measures of the new regent were characteristic of the man. Having selected as the members of his council men as distinguished for knowledge as they were for a courage tempered by prudence, he published an edict in which entire pardon was promised to all criminals, whatever their offences, who within a short period should rally round his standard, and assist him in opposing the queen and the Spaniards. At this unexpected call, great numbers—amounting, we are told, to thousands—hastened from their prisons or their haunts to swell his army. At first the nobles and prelates, suspicious of his character, and disgusted with his crimes, stood aloof; but, by bribes, by honours, and by the magnitude of his promises, he weaned many of them, gradually yet surely, from the cause of Leonora. Through the active exertions of his emissaries, many of the great towns were persuaded to follow the example of Lisbon. The impunity with which his followers perpetrated every possible crime, was too alluring not to increase the number. Murder, plunder, rape, and sacrilege were the constant attendants of this lawless party.† The abbess of the convent of Castres was dragged from her cloister, was poniarded before the high altar, and her body subjected to brutalities of which not even the mention would be tolerated by the reader. In the end it was dragged to a public square, and there

1383 to 1385.

---

* Roder. Sant. iv. Lopez de Ayala. Froissart, by Johnes, vol. vii. Vasc. p. 143, &c. Alf. a Carth. cap. 90. Franc. Tar. p. 584. La Clede, iii. liv. 10. Lemos, v. liv. 20. et 21. Ferr. par Herm. v.

† The modern historians of Portugal pass gently over the horrors of this period. Their want of candour on such occasions, and their general dishonesty on all where the national character is involved, are deserving of the severest reprehension.

left: there too it might have remained, had not the darkness of night emboldened some pious hands to remove it, and honour it with the rites of sepulture. The nuns were fortunate enough to effect their escape. This is but one instance, among numbers which have been preserved, and among thousands of which the memory has perished, of the monstrous crimes of this interregnum; yet no attempt was made to punish them by the regent, who felt that the licence thus allowed was his only tenure on the attachment of his adherents. Strange that these very men, who thus abandoned not merely the obligations of religion, but every human feeling, should still be the slaves of superstition! Amidst these scenes, a hermit who had passed many years of his life on a neighbouring mountain, and who had been gained by Joam, appeared in Lisbon. His studied simplicity of manner, his sonorous declamation, his apparent zeal, and still more the nature of his subject — obedience to " the powers that be "—procured him a willing audience. He was soon regarded as a prophet, and was persuaded to exercise his imaginary vocation in favour of the regent, to whom he accordingly predicted every success with which Heaven could reward its favourites. Undaunted by these predictions, the king of Castile invaded the kingdom, received the submission of several places, and penetrated to Santarem, to concert with his mother-in-law, Leonora, the means of annihilating the resources of Joam. But that ambitious woman, who perceived that with the arrival of the king her authority had ceased, soon regarded his cause with indifference, ultimately with dislike. Her intrigues were planned more frequently to thwart than to aid his measures; so that, aware of her faithless character, he at length surrounded her with spies, and reduced her nearly to the condition of a prisoner in her own palace. This was not the way to remove her growing disinclination to his cause; nor was it long before she openly expressed her wishes for the success of the grand master. To show her that she was in his power,— to prevent her meditated flight and probable junction with Joam, and to be thenceforth free from her restless intrigues, he caused her to be arrested, to be conducted into Spain, and to be confined in the convent of Tordesillas, near Valladolid.*

As allusion has already been made to the chief events of the present war†, and as those events are not in themselves of much interest, little more remains to be said of them. Though Lisbon was invested both by sea and land, and in a few months reduced to the greatest distress, it was defended with equal ability and valour by the grand master and his captains, still more by the unconquerable spirit of the inhabitants. In the end, however, the provisions being exhausted, and the ranks of the defenders thinned as well by famine as the sword, the place must inevitably have surrendered, had not the king, who loss had been much more severe, and who had now to encounter pestilence no less than the armed enemy, precipitately raised the siege. He at first retired to Torres Vedras, where, having issued directions for the preservation of the fortified places which still acknowledged him, he returned into Castile. His absence was well improved by the grand master, who, with great celerity, obtained possession of several important towns,—some by assault, but more through voluntary submission. But, amidst these successes, he was near falling a victim to a conspiracy, fomented by the partisans of the Castilian king, and encouraged by that monarch. Two of the conspirators, however, influenced either by remorse or the hope of gain, revealed the plot to Joam. To end the distractions of the country, the states, early in 1385, were convoked at Coimbra. There the creatures of the regent proposed his proclamation as king, as the only measure capable of restoring internal tranquillity, and of enabling the nation to withstand the arms of Castile. They even endeavoured to show that he was the nearest heir to the

1384, 1385.

* Vasc. Lemos. La Clede. Ferreras by Hermilly.
† See Vol. II. p. 237, &c.

crown. The issue of Iñes de Castro they set aside, as sprung from an adulterous connection; and the same objection they urged against Beatrix*, whose mother they considered as the lawful wife, not of the late king, but of the lord de Pombeiro. In extolling the personal qualities of the regent,—his military capacity, his talents for administration, his diligence, prudence, and firmness,—they were more successful. Had Joam, the eldest son of Iñes, or even his brother Dinis, who were prisoners in Castile, been present, there would have been little need of such a display; but the possibility of their return seemed so remote, and the present danger so pressing, that, in the end, those who had most loudly advocated their rights, joined the party of the regent; and, on the 6th day of April, 1385, he was unanimously proclaimed king.

1385 to 1403. Joam I. having, through the eloquence of his advocates, and the no less effectual martial attitude of his friends, attained the great object of his ambition, vigorously prepared for the war with his rival of Castile. Through the promises as well as the menaces of his barons, many of the most considerable fortified places in the interest of the Castilian king were recovered. The events which followed; the decisive victory gained by Joam at Aljubarota; the alternations of success and failure that succeeded; the arrival of the duke of Lancaster to obtain the Castilian crown in right of his wife Constanza, daughter of Pedro the Cruel; the alliance between the two princes, Joam marrying Philippa, a daughter of the duke; the subsequent reconciliation between the latter and the king of Castile, cemented by the marriage of the princess Catherine, daughter of the

---

* Might not a still stronger one have been urged against her marriage with a *foreign* prince, and her consequent inability to wear the crown? " Se a filha do rei desposar principe ou senhor de huma nacaõ estrangeira, ella naõ sera reconhecida rainha, porque nos naõ queremos que os nossos povos sejaõ obrigados a obedecer a rei que naõ nascer Portuguez," is certainly a fundamental law of the monarchy. It is somewhat strange that Regras the famous jurisconsult, and the eloquent advocate of Joam at these cortes, did not appeal to this law. But if the law excluded Beatrix, did it also exclude her issue, especially as that issue had been recognised both by king Fernando and the cortes which approved the conditions of the marriage?

Plantagenet, with Enrique, son of Juan, and other transactions of these troubled times, have already been noticed so far as the limits of this compendium can allow.* Nor, though, long after this reconciliation of the duke and the Castilian king, a desultory warfare raged between Portugal and that power, are the details sufficiently interesting to be laid before the reader. It must be sufficient to observe, that peace was made and broken more than once; that the success lay with the Lusitanian king,—a success, however, attributable as much to the internal troubles of Castile after the death of Juan I., as to the valour of Joam; and that, when a more durable peace was concluded in 1403, the Portuguese had recovered their fortresses, and were in possession of Badajoz.†

The next few years were passed in tranquillity, interrupted, indeed, by one or two misunderstandings with Castile, which led to no result. This time appears to have been passed by the king in improving the administration of the realm, which had been so fatally relaxed since the death of Fernando, and which had not been in much vigour since the time of Pedro. His salutary severity was above all directed against murderers and robbers by profession, and also against such as took justice into their own hands. By these means he became a popular monarch with all but some of his nobles, whose discontent he had powerfully excited during the late wars. To his valiant constable, don Nunho Alvares Perciro, he was more indebted than to any other cause, both for his crown, and for the successful issue of the Castilian war; and he had thought no rewards,—not even the revenues of whole towns, nor vast estates,—too great for such services. But if he had thus showered his royal bounty on that able and faithful man, he had rewarded with a pitiful spirit the attachment of others. To stifle the complaints which were

1404 to 1411.

* See Vol. II. pp. 238—240.
† Ibid. 241—243. Roder. iv. Alf. a Carth. Franc. Tar. Lopez de Ayala. Froissart, vii. Vasc. p. 144. &c. La Clede, iii. liv. 10. et 11. Lemos, v. liv. 21. et tom vi. liv. 22. Ferreras, par Her., v. et vi.

breathed against his parsimony, and doubtless to allay the envy which was entertained towards himself, the constable, with a generosity wholly unequalled, voluntarily abandoned a considerable portion of his vast possessions in favour of these unrequited knights; of such, especially, as had been the faithful companions of his own fortunes. His liberality, however, gave great offence to the king, who regarded it as an assumption of the highest and most valuable prerogative of royalty. His dissatisfaction was increased by the enemies — and no favourite was ever without them — of dom Nunho, who represented him as already too powerful for a subject, and as aiming at a popularity which might become injurious to the state. Joam no longer hesitated to commit an act unworthy of his station, — to revoke the grants which he had made to the constable, and which had been employed by the latter in the manner just related. Both the knights who had received, and the nobles who had granted, these just rewards of the most splendid services, were deeply affronted at this indignity, and both prepared to bid a final adieu to their country. With some difficulty *he*, who sincerely loved his sovereign, was persuaded at that sovereign's earnest request to remain, but *they* passed into Castile. This was not the only injustice which this celebrated man sustained from his master. He had only a daughter: to deprive her of the ample possessions which still remained to him, a law was promulgated, that no female should thenceforward succeed to such as had been conferred by the crown, and that on the demise of the male feoffees, they should revert to their original source. But nothing could shake the fidelity of the constable, who continued to serve the king with equal zeal and equal success. Nor can it be denied that, however individuals might suffer, the community benefited by these resources; by them the royal revenues were increased, and in the same degree the people were relieved.

1411 to 1415. By his queen Philippa, daughter of the duke of Lancaster, Joam had several children, of whom five were sons. As these princes grew in years, they displayed great martial ardour, and promised to become the bulwarks of the country and throne. He had resolved to confer on them the honour of knighthood, and to celebrate the occasion by a magnificent tournament. But they despised the peaceful lists, and besought his permission to win their spurs in a nobler manner, by an expedition against the Moors. The fortress of Ceuta*, on the African side of the straits of Gibraltar, seemed to them the most inviting of conquests; it promised also to be the most useful, as it was inhabited by pirates, who were daily disturbing the commerce of the kingdom, and who had accumulated riches sufficient to satisfy even avarice. Though eager to gratify a propensity which he loved, the king was at first startled by the magnitude of the proposed enterprise. The fortifications of Ceuta were strong, and defended by the bravest portion of the Mohammedan population: to reduce them, a considerable armament must be prepared, and at an expense which he was loth to incur. In the end, however, he yielded to their urgent entreaties; the expedition was resolved, two confidential officers were sent to reconnoitre the place, and the royal council gave a reluctant consent to the project. But, as secrecy alone could insure its success, as a premature disclosure of the design would have enabled the pirates to increase the number of their defenders, and the strength of their works, the whole peninsula was in suspense, and not without alarm at the preparations of the king. Having tranquillised the Castilians, the Aragonese, and the Moors of Granada, as to his intentions, and fearful of rousing the suspicions of the Africans, he intimated that his armament was to be led against the count of Holland. Not even the death of his queen, who was carried off by the plague†, nor his advanced years, could suspend

---

* Is this a corruption of *Civitas*, or of *Septem*, the number of hills on which the town and fortress are built?

† The memory of this English princess is held in high respect in Portugal " Tantæ enim opinionis apud populum erat, quod solùm illud rectè factum videbatur, quod ipsa comprobásset."—*Matthæus de Pisano, De*

his preparations. At length, having collected a considerable number of vessels from most parts, and been joined by adventurers from most nations of Europe, accompanied by his sons and his chief nobles, Joam embarked, proceeded towards the straits, and, the middle of August, 1415, arrived before Ceuta. The Moorish governor, Sala ben Sala, a man advanced in years, but of undaunted courage, prepared for a vigorous defence. In spite, however, of his opposition, the disembarkation was effected without loss; the Moors who lined the coast were dispersed, and forced to seek shelter in the fortress. The ardour of the two infantes caused them to pursue the fugitives so closely, that both entered into the place at the same moment. Perceiving that they were accompanied by no more than 500 Christians, the former sent messengers for assistance, and were soon joined by a few hundred more. By this time, another of the princes, Pedro, had disembarked, and hastened to rejoin his elder brothers, Duarte and Henrique. Before reaching them, however, he found that the Moors had rallied, and were fiercely contending in various parts of the city for their domestic hearths. One party of Portuguese was giving way before the desperate valour of the besieged: he arrested their motion, led them to the attack, and dispersed the misbelievers. But he, too, pursued with as little foresight as his brothers; and, with no more than four companions, was soon enveloped by a host. The *five* heroes turned a desperate front to their assailants, and, though every moment in danger of being cut down, maintained their ground until a party of their countrymen hastened to relieve them. Seeing the impossibility of continuing the struggle, so long as they remained in scattered bands, they fought their way to a mosque, where they found dom Duarte. If such valour was exhibited before the

---

Bello Septensi, p. 21. From the bed of death this queen, who had all the martial spirit of her high race, delivered each of her sons a sword, with a charge to wield the weapon in defence of widows, orphans, and the country, and especially against the misbelievers.

disembarkation of the king, it was not likely to decrease when he himself advanced with the main body of the forces. Sala ben Sala, who had retired to the fortress, mounted his horse and fled; and his example was imitated by a great portion of the inhabitants. On the towers of that fortress the royal standard of Portugal was soon hoisted; resistance was every where quelled, and immense spoils rewarded the victors. At first the king knew not what to do with his new conquest. The difficulty of retaining it seemed a sufficient reason for razing it to the ground, and this would probably have been the best policy; but, after some deliberation, the preservation was resolved " for the glory of God and our Lady." The grand mosque was immediately purified, Te Deum sung, and mass pontifically performed in it. At the same time the infantes, who had nobly won their spurs, were solemnly knighted. The loss of the two hostile parties on this eventful day cannot be ascertained. With their usual exaggeration, the Portuguese estimate that of the enemy at 5000, or even 10,000, and their own at eight individuals only! It was probably about equal. The government of the place was at first offered to a valiant knight, Martin Alfonso de Mello; and when he declined the dangerous honour, it was solicited and obtained by one of greater prowess still, dom Pedro de Menezes, founder of the illustrious house of Villa Real. Having left a small but select garrison in Ceuta, and provided for the defence of the place against the inevitable assaults of the Moors, Joam reimbarked, and with the remainder of the armament returned to Lisbon.*

* Matthæus de Pisano, De Bello Septensi (apud José Correa de Serra, Colleccaõ de Livros Ineditos de Historia Portugueza, dos Reinados de D. Joaõ I., D. Duarte, D. Alfonso V., e D. Joaõ II.; publicados de Ordem da Academia Real das Sciencias de Lisboa, tom. i. p. 7, &c. Gomes Eannes de Zurara, Cronica do Conde dom Pedro de Menezes, p. 213. &c. (apud eundem, tom ii.) Vasc. p. 151, &c. La Clede, liv. ii. (xi). Lemos, vi. liv. 23.

This collection by Da Serra is of great value to the historian. Matthæus de Pisano, the preceptor of Alfonso V. and Gomes de Zurara, historiographer of Portugal, were both contemporary with the princes whose deeds they relate.

1416. The heroism of the governor, dom Pedro, and of the horsemen he commanded, is the constant and enthusiastic theme of praise by the national writers. The number of skirmishes which he was compelled to sustain during the three years immediately following the reduction of Ceuta, is said, no doubt hyperbolically, to have exceeded the number of days. It is certain that during his government, the place was frequently assailed by the whole power of the African Moors, aided by the fleet of their brethren of Granada, and that he triumphed over them all. That the Moors should lament the loss of so fair a city, — a loss for which, considering the strength of the fortifications, they were unable to account on natural grounds *; and that they should burn with the desire of recovering it, was to be expected. Their grief is poetically described by the contemporary biographer of the governor. During the night some retired into the forest, to mourn in silence over the death of kindred and friends; some made the neighbouring valleys echo with their sighs; many, who had lost their kindred, startled at the sound of the wind which passed through the trees; others sought consolation by a mutual relation of what they had seen and heard — of the dreams in which the shades of their departed brethren had appeared to them; while the more resolute foamed with rage, as they beheld from an eminence the Christian banners floating on the towers of their lost city.† After this tribute to sor-

---

* " Ha no mundo, deziaõ, intendimento humanal em que podera caber, que huma taõ nobre e taõ real cidade, em hum soo dia, se podessa perder, e naõ ainda em hum dia, mas em huma ora: por certo nao furam estes homens viventes, mas foram os poderios do inferno que chegaraõ sober nos."—*Cronica do Conde dom Pedro*, p. 248.

† " Depois que foi noite andando per aquelles bosques era piandosa cousa de ouvir os gemidos delles, puestoque fossem infieis."... " E assy comecaraõ de se sahir daquelles matos, cada hum per sua parte, e chamarse, hum aos outros, per seus propios nomes,—as madres chamaraõ os filhos, os maidos as mulheres."... " E assim contavaõ, hums aos outros, quantas abusões sonharaõ, e onvisiaõ de cent' anos até aquelle dia, aas quaes naquella ora todos davam o entendemento da perda presente."... " Muitos hy ouve que dissevaõ que virom assy dormindo muitas almas daquelles que foraõ mortos no dia passado."... " Caa assim vinham amedrentados da grande mortindade que virom fazer em seus padres, filhos, e parentes, e naturaes que o soom que o vento fazia nas arvores lhes gerava temor."—*Ibid.*

row, all joined in cursing the authors of their calamity, and in devising means for repairing it. No sooner did they see the fleet of Joam depart, than hope cheered them. They resolved to invest the place, and if unable to reduce it by open force, they were sure to obtain it by famine — unless, as some of the more superstitious or more timid seemed to fear, the defenders neither ate nor drank.* The king had ordered the governor not to leave the walls, but to be ready to repel assaults, which he foresaw would soon be made; and this inactivity aided their rising courage. They advanced to the fortifications, and burnt a few vessels which still lay in the harbour: to chastise their presumption, some knights, without their governor's consent, issued from the gates, and a skirmish commenced, which ended in the repulse of the assailants. The prudent count now hastened to the scene of strife, and recalled his troops, whom he reprimanded for their unauthorised sortie. Such bravadoes could only weaken by slow, but sure degrees, the feeble garrison; while the number of Moors in so populous a country, could suffer no sensible diminution. Thenceforward, in the hope of alluring them from the place, and, if possible, of drawing them into an ambuscade at some distance from it, the Africans resolved, almost daily, to appear at the foot of the ramparts and insult them. For some days this was borne, but with great indignation, by the Christian soldiers and hidalgos; when their murmurs became so loud, that dom Pedro was compelled to permit a few of them to combat with the enemy, but on the express condition that they would not remove far from the walls. The skirmishes which followed this concession were perpetual, and always honourable to the Portuguese. In one of these irruptions they cut down the trees, and razed the walls of the spacious and magnificent gardens in the vicinity,— a measure, per-

---

* Como, diziam elles, gente avera no mundo que nos defenda nossa cidade per continuaçom de tempo, por certo seria estranha cousa, *salvo se elles nunca comerem nem beberem e ouverim as causas necessarias do ceo.* — Cronica do Conde dom Pedro, p. 248.

haps, rendered necessary from the facility with which the Moors intrenched themselves; but the havoc so incensed the latter, that they plucked their beards, and swore to be avenged on the dogs who had done it. To omit no opportunity of fulfilling their vow, they took up their abode in the neighbouring hills; and, for fear of surprise, fortified their position. To dislodge those who dwelt in the valley of Larenjo, the governor one night despatched a select band, which made great carnage among them. But as the Christians, with more ardour than prudence, persevered in their vocation, morning dawned upon them, and showed their small force to the enemy. The latter now rallied, and closed round the devoted band, who fought with desperation, until a detachment from the city arrived, freed them from their perilous situation, and aided them in clearing the whole valley of misbelievers. In other sorties they were more successful, as they went in sufficient numbers to defy resistance; and by removing the enemy's line of habitation to a greater distance, they were in less danger of surprise. Sometimes they obtained considerable booty, especially in flocks and herds. This warfare was as horrid as it was picturesque. When the Christian hidalgos and Almagaveres arrived at the village which they had been ordered to destroy, and the inhabitants of which were sure to be sunk in sleep, they generally divided into two or three bands, forced the doors of the houses, which they set on fire, and either massacred such as attempted to escape, or forced them back into the flames. The sudden conflagration, the shrieks of the women and children, rendered still more dismal by the silence of night, and the bloody figures of the assailants, gazing with ferocious joy on the scene before them, bore a character too demoniacal for this world. When all was finished; when the flames were expiring, and the last groan had pierced the sky, the orthodox warriors returned to the city, "praising God and our Lady for their success."*

* Gomes Eannes de Zurara, Cronica do Conde dom Pedro de Menezes

To avenge these atrocities, the Moors now gathered in formidable numbers, not merely from the neighbourhood, but from wherever the fame of their wrongs had penetrated; but they were always repulsed by the valiant count, whose exploits are represented as not much inferior to those of the cid Ruy Dias, in Valencia. The very exaggerations, however, proves that dom Pedro was the most valiant knight of a valiant nation. In one of these sorties against some thousands of the misbelievers he was wounded, and the intelligence brought another body of Moors to the city, but with no better success; for so valiantly were they received by his captains, that they were glad to escape with their lives. But during three years no formal siege was laid to the place; a circumstance sufficiently explicable by the perpetual struggles for empire among the Mohammedan princes of western Africa. In 1419 the fortress was first invested, and by an army formidable enough to inspire the assailants with the hope of success. In the combats which ensued, the Christians, notwithstanding the loss of some brave captains, were, as usual, victorious; and "a pleasant thing it was," says the chronicler, "to see our men, like the waters which flowed on the beach, sprinkled with infidel blood." After some days the siege was raised, with the loss of some thousands on the part of the Africans. But scarcely had the governor time to congratulate himself on this event, before he received news which filled him with apprehension,—that a more formidable army, and a fleet from Granada, were preparing to move against him. He lost no time in soliciting succour from king

---

(apud Serra, Colleccaõ de Livros Ineditos de Historia Portugueza, tom. ii.). Lemos, Historia Geral de Portugal, tom vi.

The first of these chroniclers, though a Portuguese, shows some pity for the poor infidel wretches: he first curses Cain for setting the exampel of mortal enmity; and still more the "abominable Mahomet" for separating so many souls from the true faith, and by subjecting his followers both to temporal death by Christian swords, and to everlasting torments by the devils. When a Christian soldier dies, intimates the orthodox sage, he has the prospect of eternal bliss; but for the cursed Moors, what remains for them but brimstone and fire, with Dathan and Abiram?

Joam, who as readily granted it. Again was the place invested,—this time by sea and land; and, as before, the valour of the besieged was almost superhuman. Fearing, however, that it must ultimately surrender, if not more effectually succoured, the king ordered two of his sons—the infantes Henrique and Joam—to sail with a considerable armament. As they approached the place, they perceived that the Mohammedans had landed, and furiously assailed dom Pedro, who, with his handful of brave companions, was making terrific carnage among them. This formidable host was totally routed; while the infantes took or dispersed the Moorish vessels, commanded by a prince of the royal house of Granada. This splendid success drew the eyes of all Europe towards this extremity of Africa. That a Christian noble, with so few companions in arms, should not only retain possession of a distant fortress against the frequent attacks of great armies, but should triumph over those armies in the open field, would appear incredible, had not equal wonders been exhibited by the knights of some religious orders. The exploits which have been already recorded were frequently equalled in the sequel by this renowned baron; but the limits of a compendium will not permit us to detail them. It must be sufficient to observe, that from this period to the close of king Joam's reign, hostilities never ceased; and that victory, in all cases, declared for dom Pedro. In the subsequent wars, he was greatly aided by his son, a youth of the same dauntless courage as himself, who made frequent incursions into the Moorish territory, and never failed to return with abundance of spoil.*

1430 to 1433. During these years, the king was constantly employed in the duties of administration. In 1422 he ceased to be assisted by the advice of his constable, who left the court for the cloister, and passed the last nine years of his life in penitence and prayer. In 1433 he followed

* Gomes Eannes de Zurara, Cronica do Conde dom Pedro de Menezes, liv. i. et ii. (apud Serra, Colleccaõ de Livros, tom. ii.) Lemos, Historia Geral de Portugal, tom. vi. liv. 23.

that celebrated man to the grave. His actions will best bespeak his character. We may add, that his generosity was truly royal; that he rewarded his servants with a prodigal hand; that he founded some religious edifices, and made some addition to the legislative code of his country. As he advanced in years, his sense of justice appears to have greatly improved; at least we hear no more of the violent acts which disgraced his early days, and which will for ever tarnish his memory. Of this violence he gave a signal proof soon after his accession. The jealousy of the Portuguese monarchs was such, that the man who ventured into the private apartments of even the ladies of honour subjected himself to the capital penalty. Joam had a chamberlain, by name Fernando Alfonses, to whom he bore great attachment. This man fell violently in love with dona Beatrix de Castro, a young attendant on the queen, and was successful in his suit. But the lady, who had more passion than virtue, allowed him to pay her stolen visits within the forbidden precincts; and though they escaped for some days the notice of the king, accident or jealousy at length betrayed them. The king sent for the culprit, reminded him of the penalty he had incurred, and ordered him to see his mistress no more. His clemency, — the effect of his attachment for the chamberlain, and perhaps of a natural reluctance to shed blood for such an offence, — was lost on the other: the crime was repeated, the offender arrested, and consigned to the charge of the corregidor. He found means, however, to escape, and took sanctuary in a church; but he was dragged from thence by the incensed monarch, was condemned, and publicly burned. The partner of his guilt was permitted to live; a punishment which, if she had any sense of shame left, Joam rightly considered as superior to that of the chamberlain. But this barbarous execution filled the court with horror; and for this reason, perhaps, was never repeated.

In the reign of this prince the Portuguese began their famous career of maritime discovery. His son, the in-

1419 to 1430.

fante Henrique, who had made the mathematical sciences and navigation a continual study, was the first to enter on this course. To facilitate his long-meditated enterprise, he fixed his abode in the kingdom of Algarve, on the most elevated point of Cape St. Vincent; a spot which he also considered as favourable to his astronomical observations, and where he founded the town of Sagres. The first voyage, with two frail barks, was undertaken in 1419, and extended only about five degrees of latitude, and was consequently unsuccessful. The following year, however, three vessels being equipped for a much longer adventure, arrived at the Madeiras, which had been previously discovered by our countryman, Machin, and of which they took possession. A subsequent expedition penetrated as far south as Sierra Leone, within three degrees of the line. But this enterprise was considered too hardy to be immediately improved: from this time half a century elapsed before any Portuguese vessel ventured beyond these latitudes, though the Canaries were, in the interim, discovered by some Biscayan mariners. Martin V. granted to the nation of the royal Henrique the dominion of the regions which might thenceforward be discovered from Cape Bojador to the Indies. If this prince was thus given to voyages, his brother Pedro was no less addicted to travelling. In 1424, accompanied by twelve of his most faithful servants, he first repaired to the court of the Greek emperor, where he was received in a manner becoming his birth. The soldan of Babylon afforded him a no less magnificent reception. Having worshipped in the holy places of Palestine, he sailed for Rome, where the pope presented him with a bull permitting the kings of Portugal, like those of France, to be anointed and crowned. While in Germany, he aided the emperor Sigismund in the wars against Hungary and Venice. By our Henry VI. he was received with even greater distinction, and admitted among the knights of the garter. He returned to his own country, after an absence of about four years, and was regarded as a living prodigy; and a prodigy he really was, at a time when long journeys were unknown, and when no man travelled from one kingdom to another without making his will.*

By Joam I. the era of Cæsar was abolished in Portugal†, and the Christian mode of computation adopted.‡

The reign of DUARTE, though short, was doomed to be more disastrous than that of any preceding monarch of Lusitania. The first great calamity was the plague which raged during the whole of his reign, and which lamentably thinned the population. But a greater was an expedition against Tangier, the preparations for which oppressed his people, and the result of which filled the kingdom with murmurs. 1433.

The restless ambition of the king's brother, Fernando, hurried him into this disastrous enterprise. This infante had been too young to share in the glorious conquests of Ceuta: and had not, like Pedro or Henrique, obtained celebrity either by travelling or science. But he burned for distinction as much as either: and he now solicited the royal permission to leave the kingdom and to enter the service of some European power. Duarte, who regarded this request as the offspring of discontent, promised to increase his revenues, but forbade him to depart. Henrique next proposed an African expedition, at first with no better success; but both infantes having gained the queen to their views, whose influence over the mind of the king was all-powerful, a reluctant consent was at length wrung from him. He seems, however, to have entertained very honourable scruples as to the justice of the warfare in which he was about to engage. The Moors had not lately injured his people except in their natural endeavour to recover Ceuta; and he could no more reconcile to his 1435 to 1437.

* Gomes Eannes de Zurara, Cronica do Conde dom Pedro de Menezes, liv. ii. (apud Serra, Colleccaõ de Livros, &c., tom. ii). Vasc. p. 145, &c. La Clede, &c. iii. liv. 2. Lemos, &c. vi. liv. 24. Ferreras, &c. vi. Ruy de Pina, Cronica do Senhor Rey dom Duarte, cap. i. (apud Serra, tom. i.).
† Of these princes mention will frequently be made in the ensuing reign.
‡ See also Appendix E to the present Volume.

conscience the forcibly depriving them of their possessions than if he entered the house and despoiled the substance of a neighbour. He proposed the subject to his theologians and the pope. The chief of the Christian world, with more reason than has dictated some papal decisions, replied that there were only two cases in which war against misbelievers could be lawfully undertaken: 1st, when they were in possesion of territories which had belonged to Christians, and which the latter sought to recover: 2d, when by piracy or war, or any other means, they injured or insulted the true believers. In other cases, proceeded his holiness, hostilities are unjust: the elements, earth, air, fire, and water, were created for all; and to deprive any creature without just cause of those necessary things, was a violation of natural right. There was, however, one point which the pontiff omitted to notice,—the obligations contracted by every catholic sovereign, and still more solemnly by every military order, to advance the glory of God—in other words to convert or to destroy the heathen. This consideration removed the scruples of Duarte, and the expedition was resolved.*

1437. The inexperience which governed the preparations, and the accidental hindrances which impeded their completion, were regarded as melancholy omens by the people. The armament sailed on the 22d day of August, and on the 26th, arrived before Ceuta, a place which the heroic governor, and his no less heroic son had continued to defend with the same success. From the gates they had made frequent excursions to a considerable distance,—twice as far as Tetuan; the first inroad had been without success, but the second time the terrified inhabitants had abandoned the city to the Christians, who had wrapt it in flames. The two infantes Henrique and Fernando, who commanded the present expedition, were inflamed by the desire of equal glory; but their ardour was for a moment damped

---

* Authorities, Gomes Eannes de Zurara, Ruy de Pina, Vasconcellos, La Cléde, Lemos, Ferreras, &c. nearly in the places last quoted.

when they perceived that instead of 14,000 men, the number ordered by the king, they had no more than 6000. Whether this deplorable proof of mismanagement was their work, or that of the ministers at home, was now vain to enquire. They were advised to solicit and wait for a considerable reinforcement, but with their usual impatience they resolved to proceed to Tangier, — Henrique by land, and Fernando by sea, so as to co-operate with each other. The former, who proposed to march by way of Alcacer, despatched Joam de Pereira, one of his captains, with a thousand men, to reconnoitre the country. Pereira soon fell in with a great body of Moors whom he attacked and dispersed. On his representation that the route from Ceuta to Alcacer was impracticable, Henrique proceeded by way of Tetuan. He reached Tangier without accident on the 23d day of September, and found that his brother had arrived before him. The Portuguese immediately encamped before the place, which was defended by Salà ben Salà, former governor of Ceuta, with 7000 Moors. Scarcely were the operations commenced when a report was artfully spread by the Africans that they were preparing to abandon the fortress, the gates of which were opened as if for the purpose. The credulous Christians hastened to take possession, but as they approached the gates the Moors spitefully shut them, and increased their rage by an insulting laugh. After a siege of thirty-eight days, when some parts of the walls were shaken, a general assault was decreed. While the infante, Fernando, and the Count de Arroyalos attacked on the side of Fez, the martial bishop of Ceuta and dom Fernando Continho advanced on another: the infante Henrique assaulted the fortress as being best defended. But as if every measure of this ill-concerted expedition were doomed to be at once imbecile and unsccessful, after sustaining a heavy loss, the besiegers finding that their scaling ladders were too short, were compelled to retreat with shame from the foot of the ramparts. Before others could be procured from Ceuta, the Moors of Fez and Morocco, amounting, we are gravely told, in number to 10,000 horse, and 80,000 infantry, advanced to raise the siege.* Instead, however, of being alarmed at this prodigious force, Henrique with 4000 of his valiant troops hastened to give them battle; but so great was the dread which this heroic little band had struck into that immense host, that none of the misbelievers daring to wait for the onset, all escaped with precipitation over the neighbouring hills! But as their numbers soon increased by new accessions to 130,000 men†, they returned, and this time fought with courage. After a struggle of some hours this vast force yielded to the impetuosity of the infante Fernando and fled, leaving some thousands dead on the field! These wondrous fables are not enough. Indignant at their repeated losses of their brethren, the kings of North-western Africa combined the whole of the respective forces, and marched towards the place. The surprise of Henrique was great on seeing the neighbouring hills moving with life; the number of enemies on this occasion, we are veraciously assured, being 60,000 cavalry, and 700,000 foot!‡ But if surprised, he was not despairing: he intrusted the command of the artillery to one officer, of the infantry to another, and with the cavalry posted himself on an eminence. On contemplating, however, the dense and widely extended ranks of the Moslems, even he acknowledged, that to withstand such a host, would be temerity. He accordingly gave directions for his little army to fall back and to regain the ships. Before this could be effected, the Africans, like tigers of their own deserts, sprang upon them, eager to drink their blood. Like a wall of adamant the infante and his devoted band received the shock and repelled it! His horse falling under him, he mounted

* In Portuguese computation of the number of their enemies, the reader will do well to drop one cipher; hence he will have 1000 horse and 8000 foot; as many no doubt as were present.
† Read 13,000.
‡ The rule before recommended of subtracting a cipher will not do in this case. The aggregate of horse and infantry must be divided by about 50 to come near the truth.

that of a page, turned round on the enemy, and made dreadful havoc among them. But what could even a Portuguese do against myriads? his guards were killed by his side, and he was compelled to retreat, fighting, however, at every step, until he reached the intrenchments, where the contest became more bloody and desperate than it had yet been. Some of the defenders now fled,—for the chroniclers reluctantly allow that even a Portuguese may flee,—but the seamen on board the vessels landed, forced the fugitives to return, and the conflict was sustained during some hours with miraculous valour! Towards night it was suspended; and the infante agreed with his remaining captains that at midnight the Christians should silently leave their intrenchments, pass to the beach, and be received on board. As the invaders were now without provisions and water, this expedient was the only hope of safety which remained to them. But even of this they were soon deprived by the treachery of Martin Vieyra, Henrique's chaplain, who passed over to the misbelievers, and acquainted them with the project. At this very day the Portuguese are seized with indignant wonder at this almost incredible instance of apostasy and treason; and however great their confidence in the powers of the visible head of the church, or even of the Glorious Mother, they doubt whether either or both could, even in the event of repentance, procure for such a wretch the commutation of everlasting to purgatorial fire.* In consequence of this information, the Moors stationed a formidable guard along the passages to the sea and on the beach. The following morning they advanced to the trenches; the battle was renewed, and, we are told, sustained, for eight hours with unshaken firmness, though with greatly diminished numbers. On this occasion no one exhibited more valour than the bishop of Ceuta; who, as he strode from rank to rank to distri-

---

* Even the mild Lemos (vi. 327.) can curse this man: " Hum malvado monstro horror de sacerdocio, indigno da humanidade, Judas de seu Senhor, o inferne clerigo Martim Vieira."

bute indulgences with one hand, with the other hewed down the misbelievers in a style that called forth the enthusiastic admiration of the faithful. His armour was so shattered by the blows he received that his pontifical robes underneath were partially visible: sometimes he turned for a moment to bless or absolve; but no sooner had the words of peace left his lips, than another stroke of his sword sent a pagan soul to its dark account. Now he exhibited the consecrated host, and with tears of devotion besought his dear children in Christ to defend the holy body; while, at the same time, he gave a practical illustration of his meaning, by aiming another deadly blow at some rash son of perdition.* In the end the enemy, unable to force the intrenchments, set them on fire, and on the approach of night retired. The hours which should have been given to rest were occupied in extinguishing the conflagration, a labour not less fatiguing than the conflict of the day. To allay the hunger of his followers, the infante ordered the horses to be killed; but as there was no water, and as every one raged with a burning thirst, the boon was scarcely acceptable, until heaven sent a copious shower of rain. But however seasonable this relief, it could only be momentary. Famine, or death by the sword, or what was still worse, perpetual captivity, stared the unhappy Christians in the face, when they received a proposal which they could not have expected. They were promised both life and liberty, as the condition of their surrendering the artillery, arms, and baggage, and restoring the fortress of Ceuta. To men in their desperate condition this proposal was too liberal not to be joyfully accepted. For their performance of the covenant the infante Fernando offered himself as hostage; and was accompanied by four other knights. The Moors delivered into the hands of Henrique a son of Salà ben Salà. The chiefs, and a great part of the African army now left Tangier; while the Portuguese,

* This is no exaggerated description; it is taken from a contemporary chronicler.

reduced to 3000, prepared to re-embark. But with characteristic duplicity, the barbarians attempted to prevent the departure of the Christians, who were constrained to fight their way to the ships.*

While this once proud armament was slowly returning to Lisbon, Henrique ashamed to appear at court, proceeded to Ceuta, where fatigue of body and anxiety of mind, threw him into a serious illness. No sooner did prince Joam, who was then in Algarve, hear of the illness of one brother and the captivity of another, than he repaired to Ceuta. The two infantes there agreed, that as the royal consent to the restoration of the fortress could not reasonably be expected, Joam should propose the exchange of their brother for the son of the African. The proposal was scornfully rejected by the Moors, who threatened, if the place were not immediately restored, to take signal revenge on the person of the infante. Joam now returned to Portugal to acquaint the king with the melancholy position of affairs. Henrique also repaired to court from his observatory on Cape St. Vincent, to consult on the means of enlarging the royal captive. The states were convoked and the subject proposed. Some deputies voted for the restoration of the fortress and the delivery of the infante; but others considered that the recovery of the prince would be too dearly purchased by the surrender of a place which had cost so much, and which might serve as a point of departure for future conquests. The archbishop of Braga contended that Ceuta, which was now a Christian town, could not be restored without the express permission of the pope; and foreign sovereigns, who were consulted on the subject, advised Duarte to try every means of ransom, before relinquishing so important a possession. It was accordingly resolved that the prince should remain in captivity until the efficacy of money should be proved vain. His sufferings are represented,—probably,

1437 to 1443.

* Gomes Eannes de Zurara, Cronica do Conde dom Pedro de Menezes, liv. ii. (apud Serra, Colleccaõ de Livros, &c., tom ii.). Ruy de Pina, Cronica do Senhor Rei dom Duarte (apud eundem, tom. i.). Vasconcellos, Anacephalæoses, p. 161. &c. Lemos, vi. liv. 25. La Clede, tom. iii. liv. 2.

with truth,—for the African Moors are destitute of any virtue, as at once cruel and humiliating. No sooner was he delivered into the hands of Salà ben Salà, than he began to experience the most savage barbarity. He was, at first, paraded to a dungeon at Tangier, exposed to the insults of assembled thousands, of whom some spit in his face, others covered him with filth; and, on reaching his temporary abode, his food consisted of the vilest aliments, and his bed was the hard ground. From Tangier he was transferred to Arsilla; but two hours before his departure he was placed on a platform, and again subjected to the insults of the populace. All this he bore with unshaken constancy. So long as there was hope that Ceuta would be restored, this treatment was sometimes suspended; but when no answer arrived to the letters written by the Moor to the Portuguese court, it was aggravated in severity. No ransom would be received by Salà, whose only object was the recovery of his lost seat of government. But when the king of Castile, Juan II., began to remonstrate against the detention of the infante, and even to threaten hostilities unless a ransom were received for him, the Moor, unwilling to incur the responsibility of his charge, delivered it into the hands of his superior, the king of Fez. By that tyrant Fernando was consigned to a subterraneous dungeon, excluded alike from air and light. After some months, however, he was drawn from his prison,—doubtless, because his persecutors knew that a longer confinement would soon place him beyond their reach—and made to work, like the vilest slave, in the royal stables and gardens. In this situation he heard of dom Duarte's death [*]; but the intelligence, which was confirmed by events, was accompanied by a report, which, unfortunately for him, proved to be untrue,—that, in his last testament, his brother had directed Ceuta to be restored. It was for a time believed by the Moorish king, who ordered him

[*] Not to interrupt the narrative we anticipate a few years by here following the sufferings of the infante to their termination.

to be treated with less severity, but who, at the same time, resolved that not even the surrender of the fortress, without a large of sum of money, should set him free. No sooner was the intelligence found to be erroneous*, than, in revenge, the victim was subjected to new indignities. Not only was he deprived of all food, except a crust of bread once in twenty-four hours, but he was ironed, put to harder labour, and allowed no apparel beyond a rag, for the modesty of nature. The relation of his sufferings at length moved the pity of his brother, Pedro, regent of the kingdom, who, in the name of the royal Alfonso, despatched commissioners to Ceuta, to receive the infante, and to remit the keys of that fortress into the hands of the king of Fez. But they soon found that the barbarian had further views; that he insisted on the restoration of the place prior to the delivery of his captive; that his object was to gain possession of their persons, and be thereby enabled to dictate whatever terms he pleased. The negotiations were abruptly ended, and the ill-fated prince transferred to his dungeon, where he languished until 1443, when death put a period to his sufferings. The constancy with which he bore them; his resignation to the divine will; his sweetness of disposition, are said to have endeared him to his gaolers; and his decease to have called forth the tardy compassion of the royal Moor, who exclaimed, that so good a man deserved to know the true faith. His memory accordingly is, as it ought to be, revered in Portugal; but that superstitious nation, not satisfied with the rational sentiment, represents him as a martyr and saint,— as one fully entitled to the honours of semi-deification. Miracles† are recorded of him with unblushing effrontery, and with the full con-

---

* It is true, however, that in his last will Duarte commanded his queen and brothers to procure the liberation of Fernando: a recommendation which, owing to the troubles that ensued, was of no avail.
† These miracles are alluded to by Ruy de Pina (Cronica do Senhor Rey dom Alfonso, v. p. 945.), by Vasconcellos (Anacephalæoses, p. 162.), and are more boldly detailed by Lemos (tom. vi. liv. 25.).

viction, that by his countrymen, at least, they will be received with a proper faith.

1438. The unfortunate issue of the African war, and the complaints of his captive brother, most sensibly affected the heart of Duarte, over whom, had his life been spared, fraternal affection would, doubtless, have triumphed. That he meditated another expedition, and that he commenced preparations on a formidable scale, is honourable to his heart; but his subjects were thinned by the plague; commerce was suspended; the fields remained uncultivated; the public revenues were exhausted, and the people unwilling to make further sacrifices. He was consequently compelled to desist from the undertaking; but he might naturally indulge the hope that when the scourge of pestilence forsook his shores, when the national industry revived, and happiness revisited the countenances and hearts of his subjects, he might resume it with greater prospect of success. In the mean time he devoted himself, with a persevering zeal, to the administration of justice, — to the improvement of the tribunals, to defining the powers of the judges, and to simplifying as well as abridging the forms of legal processes; nor were his efforts less successfully applied to the encouragement of trade and industry. Unfortunately for his people, his life was too short for the benefits he meditated. In 1438 he was seized by the plague at Tomar, whither he had retired to escape its fury, and in a few days he breathed his last. This prince was worthy of a better fate. He had qualities of a high order;—he was enlightened, just, and patriotic; and if virtue or talent would have controlled the course of human events his kingdom would have been happy.*

1438, Alfonso V., the eldest son of Duarte, being only six
1439. years of age on his father's death, the regency devolved

* Ruy de Pina, Cronica do Senhor Rey dom Duarte (apud Serra, Colleccaõ de Livros, &c. tom. i.), necnon Cronica do Senhor Rey dom Alfonso V. (in eodem tomo). Vasconcellos, Anacephalæoses, p. 162 &c. La Clede, Histoire Générale de Portugal, tom. ii. liv. 2. Lemos, Historia Geral, tom. v. liv. 25.

in conformity with the last will of her husband, on the queen-mother, a princess of excellent disposition, but not exempted from the fickleness of her sex, and ill qualified to rule a fierce people. To such a people, the sway even of a native woman could scarcely have been agreeable; as a foreigner (a princess of Aragon), she was peculiarly obnoxious. Seeing this general discontent, some of the nobles, with three uncles of the king, resolved to profit by it. By their intrigues, by their artful reports and injurious surmises, they contrived to embarrass her from the beginning of her administration. Of the three infantes, the hostility of Joam was the most bitter; of Henrique the most disinterested; of Pedro the most politic, the most ambitious, and consequently the most to be dreaded. Though possessed of no great sagacity, the queen perceived where the danger lay, and endeavoured to avert it. By her winning measures, by present favours and promises of greater, and through the medium of her women who had relatives or lovers among the nobility, she gained over a considerable number to her party. Her next step was to transform a powerful rival into a friend: she offered to dom Pedro to affiance his daughter Isabel with the young king,—an offer which he readily accepted, but which in no manner interrupted his career of ambition. Other nobles were as anxious as he to attain the same object, the regency, but they had neither his ability nor his address. He perceived that the populace were for him: by his liberalities, and by the artful discourses of his creatures, he so confirmed the feeling, that in the states of the kingdom he procured, not only the sanction of the deputies to the proposed marriage, but his recognition as joint regent, or at least as entitled to exercise a degree of authority fully equal to her own. But this regulation was of no long continuance: the nobles in the interest of the queen, and of the count de Barcelos, a natural brother of the infante's, and the more numerous party who envied the success of Pedro, organised an opposition which threatened to displace him from his eminence. At this crisis, Henrique proposed in the states assembled at Lisbon that the executive should be divided,—that the education of the king and the care of the finances should rest with the queen, that the administration of justice should be intrusted to the count de Barcelos, and that Pedro should be nominated protector of the kingdom. At first, Leonora opposed this extraordinary expedient to satisfy the ambition of the princes; but, finding that the populace were arming in great multitudes to espouse the cause of their favourite, she was terrified into submission. Where, however, so many conflicting interests and rival passions were at work, harmony could not be established. Pedro was dissatisfied with the division of power; the count de Barcelos with the proposed marriage of the princess Isabel with the king, for whom he intended his own daughter; and the queen with them both. She joined the count in forcing Pedro to surrender the written engagement as to the marriage; but the latter had soon his revenge. It was apparent to every one that the finances were inadequately, in some cases improperly, administered; the people complained, and began to exclaim that there would be no prosperity for them until their idol was invested with the undivided power of the executive. As he had sagacity enough to perceive that violence would injure his cause more deeply than all the schemes of his enemies, he lent no ear to those who counselled him to assume the reins of government; he saw that the natural course of events would soon afford him the opportunity of obtaining his object without odium. The imprudence of Leonora powerfully aided his views. Some of her partisans she mortally offended, by dismissing their relatives, ladies of her palace, on a charge without foundation. The citizens she exasperated, by sending the revenue officers to visit the shops, for the purpose of ascertaining whether the royal duties were not evaded. The populace assembled, proceeded to the infante's palace, and insisted on his assuming the regency. Hearing of this commotion, the queen sent one of her nobles to allay it. He was assailed by the people, who, in no measured terms, upbraided him for his attachment to the queen. Apprehensive that they might proceed further, he ordered a dominican friar, a creature of the court, to address them the following day, and to justify his conduct. The foolish churchman, instead of endeavouring to soothe the excitement, added to its fury by the intemperate tone of his discourse. He called them traitors, rebels, rascals, and denounced on them the same punishment as had lately been inflicted on the citizens of Bruges by duke Philip. A tailor at length interrupted the discourse, by exclaiming, "What does this friar mean by comparing us to the Flemings? Are *we* traitors, or do *we* seek, like them, to murder our sovereign lord the king?" The audience rose at these words, with indignation in their looks, and mischief in their hearts. Perceiving the storm he had raised, he hoped to avert it by escaping to a neighbouring monastery; but he was pursued by the mob, who threatened, unless he were immediately surrendered, to reduce the pile to ashes,—a threat which would doubtless have been executed, had not Pedro arrived, and persuaded them to disperse. With the queen's consent, the states were again convoked at Lisbon, to decide finally on the form of government. In the view of repressing both him and his party, she wrote to her own adherents, enjoining them to appear well armed, for the purpose of overawing the mob. As protector, and in virtue of his office at the head of the military force, Pedro took effectual measures to secure impunity for his adherents: he did more; he published the orders which Leonora had secretly transmitted to the nobles, and thereby rendered her so odious to the populace that, apprehensive for her safety, she retired to Alemquer. The archbishop of Lisbon, being imprudent enough to arm in her behalf, or perhaps for the purpose of repressing the lawless violence of the mob, was compelled to escape from the kingdom: he went to Rome, and was immediately followed by an exposure—

no doubt an exaggerated one — of his life and morals. To bring the great question to issue, the mob, the only authority then subsisting, assembled in the church of St. Dominic, and swore, that until Alfonso reached his majority, the government should rest in dom Pedro. Their violence knew no bounds. Knowing that the fortress of Lisbon held for the queen, they invested it in form, and forced the governor to surrender. In vain did she endeavour to sow dissension among the leading partisans of her rival: her arts were detected; the states assembled, and by a great majority confirmed the decision of the populace. Fidelity was sworn to the new regent in the cathedral of Lisbon; and, to exclude Leonora from the hope of any share in the administration, it was at the same time ordained, that if Pedro died he should be succeeded in the office by his brother Henrique, and the latter by the infante Joam, and that thenceforward no woman should be allowed to rule the Portuguese. This was not all: the princess was to be wounded in her affection, as well as her ambition. Under the pretext that the education of the young king, if left to her, must necessarily be effeminate, and unfit him for his station, he was removed by a sudden decree of the same cortes, from her care, and placed under that of the regent.*

1440 to

Though compelled to obey the popular voice, which, on this occasion, was that of the kingdom, Leonora was eager to regain her authority. Among the nobility she had still some partisans, who were ready to undertake any thing at her command; and her brothers, the infantes of Aragon, were easily persuaded to advocate her rights. But the ambassadors of those princes effected nothing. In fact, the wisdom of dom Pedro's administration daily reconciled to it some of his former enemies: he restored tranquillity, encouraged the national

---

* Ruy de Pina, Cronica do Senhor Rey dom Alfonso V. cap. 3—50. (apud Serra, Colleccaõ de Livros, &c. tom. i.). Vasconcellos, Anacephalæoses, p. 199. &c. La Clede, Hist. Gén. de Portugal, tom. vii. liv. 12. Ferreras Hist. Gén. tom. vi. Lemos, Hist. Geral, tom. vii. liv. 26.

In these transactions, La Clede sometimes strangely confounds persons and dates.

industry, was indefatigable in his labours, and impartial in his judgments. Grateful for the benefits he procured them, the people of Lisbon would have erected a statue in his honour, had he not rigorously forbidden them. He was too well acquainted with both history and human nature not to know that popular favour is fleeting as the wind. He observed, that if such a statue were erected, it would be one day disfigured by the very hands which had made it. We are assured, indeed, by a contemporary chronicler, that he had some anticipation of the melancholy fate which awaited him. But his *present* authority was secure; a fact of which the queen attained so full a conviction, that she demanded permission to leave the kingdom. To such a step he was averse, but he would not attempt to control her movements. He was satisfied with sending his brother Henrique to remonstrate with her on its impropriety, and to assure her that, so long as she chose to remain, the honours and revenues due to her character and station would willingly be paid her. She replied, that her determination was irrevocable; yet, with her usual fickleness, when the time arrived for her departure, she expressed her resolution to remain. This would doubtless have been the wiser course, had she been capable of profiting by the lessons of experience; but, in the vain hope of displacing her rival, or from an unjust fear of his designs, she threw herself into Crato, the prince of which was her steady adherent, and by her letters exhorted the local authorities of the country to arm in her defence. This step embarrassed the regent, who vainly endeavoured to draw her to Lisbon, where he knew her intrigues would be harmless: the ambassador of her brother, the king of Aragon, gave her the same advice, but to as little effect. Had her imprudence ended here, the mischief might have been repaired; but, yielding to the representations of her pretended friends, she openly erected the standard of rebellion, and at the same time published a manifesto, insulting alike to the power and government of the regent. Pedro now sent troops to quell the insurrection, and a civil war commenced: its horrors were increased by a body of Castilians, who, at the instance of Leonora, penetrated into the kingdom, and committed many ravages. To pluck up the evil by the roots, the regent himself prepared to invest her in Crato; but not until he had vainly endeavoured to procure a reconciliation with her. At his approach she fled into Castile; while the count de Barcelos armed in her behalf in Entre Douro e Minho. The infante marched against the count, who submitted, on the condition that his relative, the expelled archbishop of Lisbon, should be recalled. From Castile the queen, supported by the representations, and even threats, of Juan II., laboured to regain her lost influence; but in vain. Those representations and threats were treated with open contempt; yet the states agreed to pay her an annual pension corresponding to her rank, on the condition that she remained out of the kingdom, — a condition which she rejected. In 1445, she formally requested permission to return, to end her days with her children; and her wish would doubtless have been gratified, had not death surprised her at Toledo.*

1446 to 1449. In 1446, king Alfonso reached his fourteenth year, — the period of his majority. His first acts were regarded by the people as favourable omens of his future administration, and, above all, of his disposition to cultivate a good understanding with the regent. When, in the cortes convoked for the occasion at Lisbon, Pedro resigned the delegated authority into his hands, he desired the latter to retain it till he was better able to bear the load; and he soon afterwards married Isabel, to whom he had been affianced in his tenth year. But these buds of hope were soon blighted. The regent was powerful; he therefore had enemies, — and enemies the

---

* Ruy de Pina, cap. 50—84. Vasconcellos, p. 200, &c. La Clede, tom. iii. liv. 12. Lemos, tom. vii. liv. 26. Ferreras, par Hermilly, tom. vi.

By the Portuguese historians, the death of Leonora is suspected to have been violent, and the guilt is thrown on the constable of Castile, the famous Alvaro de Luna. But what interest could he have in her destruction? And when did he commit a *useless* crime?

more bitter, that there was now a master who could destroy him with ease. Of these none were more vindictive or base than his natural brother, the count de Barcelos: we may add, that none could be more ungrateful; for on this very brother he had just conferred the lordship of Braganza, with the title of duke. This duke, — for such we must hereafter call him, — whose soul was as base as his birth*, endeavoured by the most abject flattery, and by the meanest attentions, to win the favour of the young sovereign: he succeeded too well: his society became a necessary not to be dispensed with. That it should prove more acceptable to Alfonso than that of Pedro, who knew not how to flatter, and who sometimes admonished him for inattention to business, need not surprise us. No sooner did the duke of Braganza perceive the secure place which he held in the king's affections, than he began to inveigh against the character and actions of Pedro, whose zeal he stigmatised as selfish ambition, and whose popularity he represented not merely as injurious, but as dangerous to the stability of the throne. These discourses, often repeated, and always with increased venom, and the mention of his mother's wrongs, which were artfully distorted, made a deep impression on the king, who at length regarded his father-in-law with abhorrence. The regent perceived the change, and was at no loss to divine the cause; but he had continued in power with reluctance, and he felt that he could resign it with pleasure. Believing that his enemies were such, not from personal but from ambitious motives, and hoping that in a private life they would cease to persecute him, he requested permission to retire to Coimbra, of which he was duke. His request was granted; and so also was another, — an act, under the royal signature and seal, approving the whole of his administration. He had yet to learn of what wickedness

---

* It is somewhat singular that persons of base birth should generally be as base in principle. That such is the fact, is abundantly proved both by history and the common experience of life. The lives of celebrated bastards would form a curious, and, perhaps, not an uninstructive addition to our literature.

human nature — that portion of it, at least, which breathes the infected atmosphere of a court *— is capable. No sooner had he departed than a hundred reptiles darted their stings. Among the new charges brought against him was one of incredible boldness, — that which fastened on him the guilt of poisoning the late king and queen. In vain did the sage Henrique hasten from his aërial residence above Cape St. Vincent, to vindicate the character of his brother; in vain did dom Alfonso de Almado, a nobleman of unsullied honour, join in the chivalrous act, — for chivalrous it was, when the lives of both were threatened as their reward, if they did not immediately retire from the court †; in vain did the latter enter the royal council, inveigh against the atrocious designs of some courtiers, and challenge all who dared to dispute dom Pedro's virtues to a mortal combat; in vain did the royal Isabel plead her father's innocence; — the victim's doom appeared to be sealed. Alfonso published an edict debarring all his subjects from communication with the prince, and ordering him to remain on his estates. Fearful of his repelling injustice by force, and with the view of his falling an easy victim, his arms were next demanded: these he naturally, though perhaps unfortunately, refused to surrender; and the refusal increased the wrath of the king. One of the courtiers then proposed that he should be summoned to court; yet, in a characteristic spirit, that very courtier, — a nephew, too, of Pedro ‡! — secretly warned him

---

* " 'Tis now the raven's bleak abode;
'Tis now the apartment of the toad:
There the *Fox* securely feeds,
And there the poisonous adder breeds."
Gronger Hill.
To no " ruined tower " in existence can the lines be so appropriately applied as to a court.

† The address of this count to the king and council, as it appears in Ruy de Pina (cap. 91.), is a noble instance of magnanimity and courage. He appealed to his services — and they had been splendid — as a Portuguese noble; to his honour as a knight of England's proud order — *then* at least a proud one — the Garter; to his unimpeachable integrity; and to his intimacy with dom Pedro — that he knew and spoke the truth. Neither his zeal nor the challenge with which he concluded, affected Alfonso.

‡ This was the count de Ourem, eldest son of the duke de Braganza. Both father and son may be ranked among the most detestable members of a detested house.

not to come. The duke of Braganza now assembled his troops, and marched towards Coimbra: he was met by dom Pedro, before whose handful of brave friends he fled with ignominy, and returned to court, to incense the king still more. Finally, by manœuvres which no stranger to a court could suppose possible, he and his murderous faction obtained a royal decree, declaring the duke of Coimbra a traitor and rebel. Seeing that his destruction was resolved, the latter no longer hesitated as to what course he should pursue. In self-defence, he laid in provisions for a siege in Coimbra. Hearing, however, that the king in person was coming to besiege him, he hastily prepared to meet his enemies,—not, he said, to oppose his king, but to vindicate his own cause, and to defy his calumniators. Again did his daughter affectionately labour to avert his fate. In an agony of tears she cast herself at her husband's feet, and besought his pardon; if not for his own sake, for hers. Alfonso was affected: he raised his queen, whom he tenderly loved, and promised that if her father would acknowledge his crime, it should be forgiven. The joyful Isabel wrote to the count; and immediately received a reply,—but a reply which for ever sealed his doom. More jealous of his honour than fond of life, the high-spirited prince would acknowledge no crime, simply because he had none to acknowledge; and asserted that the only reason of his replying to the letter was to please his daughter. The incensed monarch tore the reply into pieces, and said,— "Your father wishes his destruction; he shall have his wish!" But the duke's personal enemies were not satisfied with his ruin: they endeavoured to effect hers. Under the pretext of hunting, they drew him a few hours from her society, and accused her of adultery with a nobleman of her household; but however credulous Alfonso might be, this diabolical calumny made no impression on his mind.[*]

[*] Authorities, Ruy de Pina, Vasconcellos, La Clede, Lemos, and Ferreras.

1449. Before the duke left Coimbra, he retired into his chapel with his friend dom Alvaro, who had so courageously defended him before the royal council. To the count he unbosomed his heart, asserted; that he was tired of life; that, unless his justification were received by the king, he could not and would not support it; and concluded by hoping that in this last extremity he should not be forsaken by his friend. Dom Alvaro fell at his feet, kissed his hands, and expressed an unalterable resolution of living and dying with him. A confessor was called, who shrived and communicated both: and who, over the consecrated elements, received their oath to share the same fortune. They next embraced each other, and set out, persuaded that they were marching to certain death. Their troops were composed of 1000 horse and 5000 foot, all resolved to perish rather than permit a beloved leader to be oppressed; and on their banners were engraven, *Fidelity! Justice! Vengeance!* The duke first repaired to the monastery of Alcobaça, where he was received by the monks in procession, and where *Te Deum* was sung in much solemnity. There lay the bones of his ancestors, whose tombs he visited. Gazing on that which had been prepared for himself, he sighed, — " I shall soon be laid here!" and left the monastery. Advancing towards Santarem in the way to Lisbon, he soon encountered a detachment of the royal cavalry, which, though it did not dare to attack him, watched his motions, and loaded him with the most opprobrious epithets. For some time he bore insult with even temper, and charged his followers to refrain from revenge: but in the end the infirmity of nature prevailed; the detachment was charged, and thirty of the horsemen were made prisoners, and put to death. This act of vengeance did his cause no good: it was blamed by some of his own adherents. His enemies took care to represent his march towards the capital as the consequence of his resolution to dethrone Alfonso. To arrest it, the king hastened to meet him, with about

30,000 veteran troops; they approached each other on the banks of the Alfarrobeira, above which was an eminence where Pedro entrenched himself. Just before the assault was given, a royal edict was proclaimed, ordering his followers to forsake the infante, unless they wished to be involved in his destruction. Some abandoned him, but the majority remained faithful. At the commencement of the struggle, however, a ball from the artillery of the infante struck the royal tent,— whether by chance or design has never been determined,— but it roused the wrath of many who had before pitied the fate of the victim, and gave new fury to the attack. For some hours, notwithstanding the alarming disproportion of numbers, that attack was repelled with heroic valour; but the prince, who desperately sought the most dangerous post, and who evidently resolved to sacrifice his life, fell through a wound in the throat. No sooner was the surviving friend, dom Alvaro, acquainted with this catastrophe, than, having retired to his tent for a moment, as well to bemoan it, as to prepare his own mind for his last remaining duty, he seized his lance, mounted his horse, and plunged into the midst of the hostile squadrons. Though he laid many low, he was not long in receiving the death he sought: a shower of arrows and darts brought him to the ground; and as numbers hastened to deprive him at once of a life which was fast ebbing away, he had just strength to exclaim,—" Now, tigers, satiate yourselves!" The carnage which followed was terrific: the troops of the fallen infante, intent on revenging his death and resolved on their own, would neither give nor receive quarter: almost all fell on the field. The vengeance of Alfonso passed beyond the grave: he ordered the corpse of Pedro to remain on the ground, to be for ever deprived of the last rites of humanity; but in a few days some compassionate peasants, whose souls might have put to shame the boasted chivalry of nobles, privately removed it, and interred it in the church of Alverca. This was not the worst: amidst the excitement of the moment, many suspected of sympathy for the ill-fated prince were massacred, and the descendants of all his adherents to the fourth generation declared infamous, — incapable of holding any public charge. The mob of Lisbon testified characteristic joy at his catastrophe, — a remarkable confirmation of his prudence, in forbidding them to erect the projected statue of him.

1450 to 1456. The death of this prince, — the greatest whom Portugal had lately seen, — caused a deep sensation throughout Europe, and from Rome to Britain drew forth nothing but execrations against his murderers. But let us not defend his armed opposition to his sovereign: he might have escaped, lived to vindicate his character, and been recalled with honour. The vengeance of which he was the victim was too furious, too blind, to be lasting. Through the indignant remonstrances of the pope and of his brother-in-law, the duke of Burgundy; through the increasing influence of his daughter, whose virtues were appreciated by her husband, and whose efforts to honour his memory were at length successful; and more still through the king's conviction of his innocence, in the fifth year from this tragedy his bones were removed from their humble sepulchre, and were transferred with great pomp to the mausoleum of the Lusitanian kings. Of his children, who were compelled to flee from the kingdom, and who were in the sequel permitted to return, the eldest, Pedro, was the only one that availed himself of the permission. Another, Jayme, who entered the church, and attained the dignity of cardinal, was invited to take possession of the archiepiscopal see of Lisbon; but he died in Burgundy in 1456. To prevent the return of these princes, and to escape the justice due to its crimes, was the constant aim of the base house of Braganza. That the queen, whose favour with the king was too firm to be shaken, would at length have procured the punishment of her father's murderers, is exceedingly probable; but in 1455, while in the possession of youth and health, she suddenly sickened and died. That her death was the effect of poison administered by her enemies, and those of her father, — among whom were doubtless the detestable princes of Braganza, — is the unshaken opinion of her own times and of posterity.*

The disastrous captivity of the infante Fernando had sunk deep into the heart of Alfonso, as into that of most princes of his family; and the desire of revenge had been suspended, not abandoned. A circumstance which was calculated to suspend it some time longer, hastened its execution. The reduction of Constantinople by the Turks had filled Christian Europe with consternation, and had led to the formation of a general league, the object of which was to drive back the misbelievers into their Asiatic wilds. But the death of the pope, who had so zealously espoused the holy warfare, and the dissensions of the Christian princes, occasioned the dissolution of the confederacy. Of these none had exhibited more zeal than Alfonso, whose preparations in the ports of Lisbon, Setubal, and Oporto, were now disposable against the African Moors.† His original intention was to reduce the fortress of Tangier, the siege of which had proved so unfortunate to the princes Henrique and Fernando; but the advice of a Portuguese noble, then at Ceuta, who probably dreaded the issue of an attempt on that strong fortress, determined him to invest Alcaçar Seguer. In September, 1457, the armament, consisting of above 200 vessels, and carrying 20,000 men, sailed from the three ports, effected a junction at sea, and steered towards the Moorish coast. On the 17th of the following month it arrived before the place, where, notwithstanding the opposition of the enemy, the disembarkation was effected without much loss. The batteries

1457 to 1459.

---

* Ruy de Pina, Cron. Alfonso V., cap. 100—138, Cronica do Conde dom Duarte de Menezes, passim (apud Serra, Colleccaõ de Livros, &c. tom. i. et iii.). Vasconcellos, p. 200, &c. La Clede, tom. ii. liv. 12. Lemos, tom. vii. liv. 28. Ferreras, tom. vi. et vii.

† To pay the expenses of this armament, Alfonso caused a new golden coin to be struck, named the cruzado from the *cross* impressed on one side.

were now erected; towards sunset a general assault was ordered; scaling-ladders were placed against the walls, and a resolute body of the besiegers mounted. The reception, however, which they experienced, was so warm, that a suspension of the combat followed. It was now dark, yet the Portuguese soldiers remained under arms, and about midnight the artillery began to play upon the city. The terrified inhabitants, who were hitherto but imperfectly acquainted with the effects of gunpowder, soon proposed an accommodation. The king would consent to no other than that they should immediately leave the place. After ineffectual attempts to procure terms less rigorous, they gave hostages for their performance of this condition; and at daybreak the following morning, with their families and moveable property, they evacuated the town, which was instantly entered by the Christians, and the government of which was confided to dom Duerte de Menezes, son of the deceased hero of Ceuta. That trust could not have been placed in better hands, as it soon proved by the sequel. No sooner did the king of Fez hear that the Portuguese were preparing to invest Alcaçar Seguer, than he collected troops and marched to relieve it. On the way he heard of its fall, but he resolved to recover it. Having halted to receive reinforcements, on the 13th of November, the following year, the king appeared before the place, at the head, we are told, of 30,000 horse and a prodigious number of foot. In vain did Alfonso, who advanced from Ceuta, endeavour to throw supplies into the fortress. Disappointed in his hope, and afraid, with forces so greatly inferior, to run the risk of an action, he caused a letter to be thrown over the walls, and exhorted the governor to hold out until his return from Portugal, whither he found it necessary to repair for reinforcements. His departure animated the courage of the Moors, but did not deject that of the defenders. After a siege of many days, the Mohammedan king ordered a general assault, which was repulsed with heavy loss; so heavy, indeed, that he was compelled to retire in search of reinforcements. Duarte took advantage of his absence to construct a wall, extending from the town to the beach, by means of which supplies coming by sea could easily be received into the place. In July the following year, the Moorish king appeared a second time before it, accompanied, we are told, by the most numerous army ever collected in this part of Africa.* But on the present, as on the former occasion, success refused to shine on his banners, and, after some desperate efforts, which were signally repulsed, he resolved to raise the siege. Duarte hearing of the intention, added insult to defeat: he representing to him, by letter, how ignominious the step would prove to his fame, and beseeching him not to take it until he had repeated his assaults. The enraged Moor cursed the presumption of " the Christian dog;" reminded him of the disastrous defeat before Tangier, and how a prince of Portugal, the hapless Fernando, had recently adorned his stables at Fez. This boast was but a poor return for the loss of two great armies, and for two inglorious retreats from an obscure fortress.*

The success which had attended the defence of Alcaçar Seguer animated Alfonso to renew the attempt on Tangier. Accordingly, in 1464, he sailed with another armament; but, on his reaching the African coast, he returned to Ceuta, confiding the attack on that formidable fortress to his brother Fernando. The infante, declining the aid of Duarte de Menezes, lest the latter should reap the whole glory of the conquest, hastened to claim it for himself. But though the assault was vigorously made, it was repulsed with deplorable loss; the flower of the Portuguese chivalry either perished on the spot, or were compelled to sur-

1464

---

* The chronicler seems afraid to assign a given number, lest it should be found inadequate. " Aparaceo el rey de Fez sobre a ryla *com ynfindo poder de jente nacoones muy desvairedas* et com coniagens d' allimerias, espantosas, que cobriam toda a terra."—*Cronica do Senhor Rey dom Alfonso,* cap. 142.

† Ruy de Pina, Cronica do Senhor Rey dom Alfonso V., necnon Cronica do Conde dom Duarte de Menezes, passim. Vasconcellos, La Clede, Lemos, Ferreras, omnes ubi supra.

render. The victorious Moors eagerly examined the bodies of the slain, in the hope of discovering that of Menezes. "You need not look for it," said a Portuguese prisoner; "dom Duarte is not here,— for we are vanquished!" This disastrous issue filled the king with dismay, and he resolved to return home. Before he embarked, however, four Moors, with characteristic perfidy, intimated, that if he made an excursion to a neighbouring mountain, he might take abundant spoil. He credulously believed them, and, with 800 horse and a small body of infantry, proceeded towards the place. Being artfully drawn into the passes, he was assailed by the Moors in ambush, most of his knights, among whom was the heroic dom Duarte, were cut off on this excursion, and he himself had considerable difficulty in effecting his escape. For some years the result of this inglorious expedition seems to have inspired him with too much dread to renew the attempt; but, in 1471, he embarked 30,000 men on board 308 transports, and proceeded to invest Arsilla, a fortress on the Atlantic, about seventeen leagues from the straits of Gibraltar. This place, the foundation of which is ancient, was colonised by the Romans in the reign of Claudius. It was subsequently possessed by the Goths, the Arabs, and the Moors; and, under every change of domination, had been celebrated for its commerce, its wealth, its public edifices, and its civilisation. It was furiously assailed by the Portuguese; was as furiously defended by the inhabitants, who scorned to submit, until most of them had perished with arms in their hands. The king himself, and his son the infante Joam, were among the foremost in the assault, the former loudly invoking the aid of Our Lady. On this occasion, the remembrance of their late reverses steeled the Portuguese against humanity, and they massacred all—as well those who resisted as those who threw down their arms in token of submission—with diabolical fury. In this work of destruction Joam was behind none of his countrymen.

1471. In the mean time Muley, king of Fez, advanced to

raise the siege. His consternation, on finding that the place had been carried, and the defenders exterminated, was so great, that he sued for peace. But his mortifications did not end here. Terrified by the fate of Arsilla, and convinced that the victorious army would next march against them, the inhabitants of Tangier abandoned the city with all their moveable substance. It was immediately occupied by the Christians, and it was formed into an episcopal see. Of this city, anciently called Tingis, and capital of the province of Tingitana, the foundation is lost in the depths of antiquity: Pomponius Mela, Strabo, and Plutarch assign it to the giant Antæus. From the time of Augustus it was subject to the Romans; under the Gothic, and even Saracenic domination, down to the destruction of the Mohammedan kingdom of Cordova, it followed the fate of the southern provinces of the peninsula. From these successors, the Lusitanian courtiers surnamed their king Africanus—an epithet which, with any other people, would have been considered a bitter satire. Throughout his operations in Africa he had shown great incapacity, and had met with unparalleled reverses; nor were the successes recently obtained in any way attributable to his valour or abilities, but to those of his generals and his son. The latter, who had attained his sixteenth year, was knighted on this occasion.[*]

The transactions of Alfonso with Castile, through his meditated union with Juana, reputed daughter of Enrique IV., more usually termed the Beltraneja, his wars with the catholic sovereigns, and the peace of 1479, have been already related.[†] There are, however, some circumstances attending his assiduous court to the French king, that must not be passed over in silence. Not satisfied with sending an embassy to Louis XI.[‡],

1474 to 1479.

---

[*] Ruy de Pina, Cronica do Senhor Rey Dom Alfonso V. (down to cap. 165.), necnon Cronica de Conde Dom Duarte de Menezes (ad finem, ambo apud Serra, Colleccaõ, &c. tom. i. et iii.). Vasconcellos, p. 204—208. La Clède, tom. iii. liv. 12. Lemos, tom. vii. liv. 28. Ferreras, par Hermilly, tom vii.
[†] See Vol. II. page 268—270.
[‡] In the same volume, page 269., we have mentioned Charles VIII. Instead of Louis XI.; yet Charles did not ascend the throne until seven years after Alfonso's visit. We know not how the mistake was committed.

who promised to aid him to the extent of his wishes, in 1476 he resolved to visit that prince in person — a mark of confidence which he hoped would operate more powerfully in his favour than any embassy. How little he knew the perfidy of that pretended ally, appeared from the result of this extraordinary voyage. He landed at Perpignan, traversed Languedoc, and proceeded by way of Lyons to Bourges, where he was received with great ceremony by the local authorities, and was complimented, on the part of the Gallic sovereign, by the celebrated historian Philip de Comines. At Paris, where he was met by Louis in person, his reception was such that he no longer doubted he should be enabled to triumph over the Aragonese king. That his ally, who was then at war with the duke of Burgundy, might be at liberty to assist him, he waited on the latter prince. Duke Charles endeavoured to open his eyes as to the true character of Louis, in whom was neither faith nor honour, justice nor generosity, and who made sport of the most sacred obligations. The Lusitanian was staggered — still more when he found that Louis showed no disposition to fulfil any one of the promises that had been made, and had reason to suspect that his negotiations at Rome for a dispensation to marry the hapless Juana, were traversed by this ally. Nay, if there be any truth in a report of the time — a report too well confirmed by the character of Louis — his arrest and delivery into the hands of king Fernando were seriously intended. It appears certain that he himself suspected the perfidy, and that, in the first impulse of his disappointment, he resolved to visit Palestine, and afterwards to end his days in some monastery. It is no less certain that he sent a confidential messenger to his son Joam, whom he acquainted with the resolution, and whom he ordered to be proclaimed king; that he secretly repaired into Normandy, for the purpose of effecting his escape; that he was pursued and arrested by order of Louis, who, however, soon repented of the violence, set him free, and provided vessels for his return into Portugal. The resolution to pass his days in religious exercises he abandoned with the same levity he had formed it. On landing in his kingdom, he found that his son had been proclaimed; and by his attendants apprehensions were entertained lest Joam should refuse to descend from the dignity. It is said that when the intelligence first reached the prince, that Alfonso, whom he thought on the voyage to Syria, had landed in Portugal, he was walking on the banks of the Tagus, accompanied by the duke of Braganza and the archbishop of Lisbon; that he asked the two nobles in what manner he ought to receive his father; that they advised him to hasten and welcome Alfonso, not merely as his father, but as his king; that he returned no answer, but taking up a stone with a peculiar expression, he threw it violently into the river; that the action was noticed by the archbishop, who whispered to the duke, "You see with what force the infante has just thrown that stone into the water; it shall not fall on *my* head!" and that the prelate, seeing how disagreeable the advice that had been given, and knowing how soon the infante would be called to the throne, hastened to Rome, where he ended his days. However this be,—yet it is probable enough,—Joam met his father, to whom he resigned the dignity, and was, in appearance at least, contented to remain a subject so long as Alfonso lived. The king's return caused great joy in Portugal; he was loved, while his son was feared; the one was clement and indulgent, the other was severe in his disposition, and of inflexible justice; the one pardoned real guilt, the other spared not even the suspicion of crime.

Alfonso did not long survive the conclusion of peace with Castile.* Like his father, he died of the plague, and like him, too, in the prime of life; the former at the age of 37, himself at 49, of which he had passed 43 on the throne. With the exception of the accidental success in Africa, his reign was almost uniformly dis-

1479 to 1481.

* Vol. II. page 269.

astrous,—a misfortune, more owing to the deplorable weakness of his character, than to any other cause. He founded the order of the Tower and Sword, under the invocation of Santiago*, and was a great patron of literature; he was the first of the Portuguese kings to collect a library, and to order the national history to be treated by competent writers. His reign is, however, somewhat redeemed by the discoveries of the infante Henrique, who, from his residence at Tagus, continued to fix his eyes intently on the maritime regions of Western Africa. Through this enlightened prince, the Azores, with the Madeiras, the Canaries, Cape de Verd, and other islands west of that great continent, were discovered or colonised. The discovery of the Cape de Verd, the last which illustrated the life of Henrique, was owing to the enterprise of a Genoese, Antonio Nolle, who had derived a confused knowledge of their existence from the ancient geographers, and who, from some dissatisfaction with his own country, offered his services to the prince. Having coasted from Morocco to Cape de Verd, he deviated westwards and soon fell in with the islands, which he called after the cape of that name. Whether these are not the Gorgon Isles of Pomponius Mela, Pliny, and the poets, or the Hesperides so celebrated in Grecian lore, has been matter of much vain dispute.†

1481. When JOAM II. ascended the throne, he found the royal revenues so much diminished by the profusion of

---

* The institution of the order related to a sword, reputed to be carefully guarded in a tower of the city of Fez: respecting it there was a prophecy, that it must one day come into the possession of a Christian king; in other words, that the Mohammedan empire of north-western Africa would be subverted by the Christians. Alfonso seemed to believe that he was the destined conqueror, and the same belief has been entertained by some of his successors.

† Philippe de Comines, Mémoires, lib. iv. Ruy de Pina, Cronica do Senhor Rey Dom Alfonso V. (down to cap. 203, in the collection of Serra, tom. i.); also, Cronica do Senhor Rey Dom João II. cap. i. (in the same collection, vol. ii.). To these may be added some of the Castilian chroniclers, Ælius Antonius Nebrissensis, Decades, dec. l. lib. 1—7; Lucius Marineus Siculus, De Rebus Hispaniæ, lib. xviii. et ix. Franciscus Tarapha, De Regibus Hispaniæ (apud Schottum, Hispania Illustrata, tom. i.). Salazar de Mendoza, Cronica Gran Cardenal de España, lib. ii. Hernando del Pulgar, Cronica de los Señores Reyes Catolicos, parte segunda. Vasconcellos, Anacephalæoses, p. 208., &c. La Clède, Histoire Générale, &c. tom. iii. liv. 13. Lemos, Historia Geral, &c., tom. vii. liv. 29. Ferreras, Histoire Général, &c. tom. vii.

his father, that he was at a loss how to conduct the administration of the kingdom, much more, if the necessity should arise of defending it against foreign ambition. The avarice no less than the haughtiness of the aristocracy — haughty alike to the monarch and peasant — had long sunk deep into his mind; and he was now resolved to commence a series of reforms, rendered imperative alike by his own necessities and the interests of his people. In virtue of their feudal jurisdiction within their respective possessions, they were not only the natural chiefs of the army, but judges even in criminal prosecutions, and, as such, exercising the power of life and death. Their armed retainers, their insolent menials and favourites, were the perpetual source of disorders, and consequently of complaints on the part of their vassals. It is true, that the privilege of appeal lay from the local tribunals, in each of the six governments into which the country is divided, to the three tribunals established at Lisbon — in other words, from the feudal to the royal judges; but it was a privilege which the ignorant could not, and the the timid dared not, exercise. Joam soon discovered where the real grievances lay. His first object was to introduce a new oath, to be taken by the governors of all towns, fortresses, and castles, and by all holders of fiefs, limiting and defining their dependence on the royal authority, and on that alone. He next ordered all who had received grants, whether of possessions or dignities, from his predecessors, to produce the necessary instruments, for the purpose of showing the tenure by which they were held. Where the title was defective, the claim was at once dismissed; where the secession was extravagant, it was greatly modified. He next abolished the worst evil of feudal institutions, — the power of life and death by the lord over the vassal; and reserved to himself alone, or his own judges, the prerogative of deciding in capital cases. By another ordinance, he subjected the feudal to the royal tribunals, and provided for the gradual extinction of the former:

thus transferring his people from the jurisdiction of local tyrants, to magistrates nominated by and dependent on the crown. Nor were these nominations henceforth to be made from the nobility alone, but from all classes of the people, the only qualifications to be, learning and merit.

1481, 1482. Reasonable as these regulations must appear to every modern reader, they were exceedingly disagreeable, nay odious, to the nobles, whom they deprived of irresponsible power, and reduced to the class of subjects. They murmured at such an innovation; contended that their possessions, and with these their jurisdiction, were but rewards justly conferred on their ancestors for signal services; and had the effrontery to insinuate that the king, by reducing them to the condition of slaves, intended only to throw down a salutary barrier, which had hitherto prevented the heads of the state from trampling on the people themselves. From murmurs they proceeded to remonstrances, which they confided for presentation to the duke of Braganza, as chief of their order. This prince, who possessed immense estates, and who, both by blood and alliances, was related to the royal family and most of the Portuguese nobility, willingly undertook to be their organ. Relying on his influence in the state, this lord of thirty towns and villages represented to the king the injustice visited in the recent ordinances, and requested their revocation. The reply he received was truly regal; and one, as it was publicly delivered, that deeply mortified his pride. He was sternly told, that he had no right to judge the actions, much less to censure the motives, of kings; that the only duty and only glory of subjects was submission; and that, if such submission were not voluntarily and freely paid, it would not fail to be enforced. He had the additional pain to perceive, that not only himself but his family were become obnoxious, chiefly through the rashness of this remonstrance, but partly, no doubt, from the extent of its possessions and the number of its dignities; both which were thought, perhaps with justice, too much for subjects. His brother, the marquis Montemor, was exiled for some trivial offence — though the exile was intended to be merely temporary — from that place to Castel Branco. Another brother, the count of Olivença, was deposed from the dignity of chancellor. These nobles, all staunch advocates for the privileges of their order, and among the proudest of men, were mortified beyond measure to find that they had a master. Two of them bore the humiliation with outward resignation; but the marquis, not satisfied with denouncing in violent terms what he called the insulting injustice done to the nobles, exclaimed with vehemence against the character alike of king and government. His libels were not merely verbal, but written: some of the latter he forwarded to Fernando of Aragon and Castile, with whom he maintained an imprudent, even a treasonable, communication.*

Though the duke of Braganza condemned the violence of his brother, that his own hostility was equal, and his conduct no less treasonable, appeared from an incident which now took place. He had deferred producing the tenure by which he held his possessions until the issue of his remonstrances with the king; but finding that obedience was compulsory, he directed his steward to visit Villa Viciosa, to search for them among the archives of his house. The steward being indisposed devolved the duty on his son, a youth of little industry and less reflection; who, to lessen the burthen of the task, took with him one Lope Figueiredo. While examining the mass of papers, Lope discovered the copies of several letters from the duke to the Castilian king, with the answers; and to him the correspondence seemed suspicious enough to be laid before Joam. The latter had the letters secretly transcribed, and the originals returned to their place. To be convinced that the duke really held such a correspondence with his enemy, he sought

1482, 1483.

---

* Ruy de Pina, Cronica do Senhor Rey Dom Joaõ II, cap. i—xii. Vasconcellos, p. 215. La Clède, iii. 13. Lemos, tom. viii. liv. 13. Ferreras, par Hermilly, tom. vii.

the society of that nobleman, treated him with great confidence, and intrusted him with the knowledge of several affairs known only to himself. This knowledge was soon communicated to the Castilian king; and so, indeed, were generally the affairs of his council. He now resolved to destroy the duke; but his first object was to procure the exchange of the hostages, among whom was his own son, dom Manuel, that had been mutually given on the last peace. Knowing that those held by Castile were his only security, that nobleman endeavoured by his intrigues with king Fernando to prevent the exchange, but in vain. The infante, Manuel, soon arrived in Portugal; was met by him with courtier duplicity, and escorted to Evora, where the king joined the party. On this occasion, Joam resolved to arrest and bring him to trial; a resolution of which he seems to have been ignorant, though he knew his safety was precarious. It was, however, known or suspected by his brother, who advised him to escape from the court. Unwilling, however, to increase the suspicion under which he lay, he would not leave it without permission, and he one day entered the royal cabinet for the purpose. On his entrance, the king, who was transacting business with his ministers, made him sit down, and conversed with him with apparent cordiality. When the ministers had retired, he endeavoured to dissipate the suspicions of Joam by professions of dutiful attachment; and observed, that with respect to his dispute with his monarch, he wished for nothing more than for justice to be done him by the tribunals of the country. It was probably the observations which showed his obstinacy in resisting the royal reforms that sealed his fate. He was that moment arrested, and consigned to a neighbouring tower. His trial was immediately instituted, and pushed by the king with indecent haste. The charges were easily proved, he was sentenced to death, and his effects to be confiscated. He received the sentence with unshaken firmness; applied his few remaining hours to the exercises of devotion; and in a last letter to the king, recommended to the royal mercy his innocent wife and children. The following day (July 23. 1463), a scaffold was erected in the great square of Evora, and at the hour appointed he was conducted to it. He was accompanied by several ecclesiastics, bearing crosses, and thereby showing honourable respect towards a disgraced man. He suffered his punishment without a sigh or a groan; observing that, however humiliating his death, his Saviour had undergone a worse. The moment his head was separated from the body, the city bell tolled; and the king, who was listening for the signal, exclaimed, " The duke's soul is just departed: let us recommend it to God!" He and his attendants instantly knelt; while, with a loud voice, his countenance bathed in tears, he hypocritically performed this catholic duty. The canons of the Dominicans bore away the corpse to their church, whence it was transferred to the mausoleum of the Braganzas, — a pious duty, which subjected them to no degree of disapprobation on the part of Joam. The three sons of the duke immediately fled into Castile: and their example was followed by the marquis of Montemor, whose estates were confiscated, and by his brother the count: a third brother, the deposed chancellor, who had been charged with no crime, at first proposed to remain, but a royal mandate compelled him to leave the kingdom. By the historians of Portugal this justice of dom Joam has been severely blamed: it is however certain that the duke deserved his fate, and that their affected pity arises only from the fear of displeasing his descendants, who have so long occupied the Portuguese throne.*

* The following scheme will show the relationship in which the deceased duke stood towards the royal house of Portugal: —

```
            JOAM I.
              |
   Duarte ———————— Alfonso, bastard and count of Barcelos.
     |                |
  Alfonso V.     Fernando, first duke of Braganza.
     |                |
  Joam II.       Fernando, second duke, beheaded.
```

Authorities: — Ruy de Pina, Vasconcellos, La Clède, Lemos, Ferreras, &c., nearly in the places last quoted.

This tragedy was soon to be followed by another. The fall of the house of Braganza, and the consequent failure of their schemes to retain possession of their tyrannical privileges, so incensed the nobles, that a conspiracy was formed by some of them to assassinate both the king and his son don Alfonso, and to place the duke of Viseo on the vacant throne. This prince, named Diego, was son of the infante Fernando, brother of Alfonso V., and consequently cousin to the king; and his connection with the throne had been strengthened by the marriage of his sister Leonora with his sovereign.* He readily entered into the views of the conspirators; he was ambitious of reigning; he regretted the deceased duke; he was generous, and therefore popular with the nation; and he was the friend of Fernando of Castile;—advantages which he regarded as sufficient to aid him in bringing about the meditated revolution. The details of the conspiracy were finally arranged at Santarem. Of the guilty individuals concerned in it, one of the most restless was the bishop of Evora, dom Garcia de Menezes. The conduct of this turbulent prelate was on a par with his principles. He had a mistress, Margarita by name, of whom he was passionately fond, and from whom he had nothing hidden: he not only acquainted her with the approaching change of government, but with the names of the nobles by whom that change was to be effected. The mistress had a brother, to whom she communicated all that she had heard; the latter, eager to obtain a better livelihood than he enjoyed through his sister's prostitution, revealed the whole to one of the ministers. The minister secretly introduced him to the king, to whom he repeated the details and actors of the plot, and from whom he received promises of a magnificent recompence.

---

* DUARTE.

Alfonso V.————Fernando, first duke de Viseo,
Joam II.   Leonora————Diego, second duke.

But though Joam was thus in possession of this momentous information, his sense of justice would not permit him to act on the declaration of such a man; and he merely charged his body guards not to lose sight of his person. It was soon confirmed by one of the actual conspirators, dom Vasco Coutinho, who had been admitted into the number by his own brother. This man, who had feigned great zeal for the success of the plot, had been introduced to the duke de Viseo, and by that prince had been acquainted with every detail. The information which he hastened to lay before the king caused the latter to redouble his precautions of defence, until he could collect and arrest the conspirators at the same time. The brother of dom Vasco and dom Pedro de Ataide, who were charged with the assassination, now closely watched the movements of their intended victim. One day as Joam, almost unaccompanied, was ascending the great staircase of his palace, he met the assassins; and from the motions instantly made by Pedro, he divined that now was the crisis of his fate. With a presence of mind and a commanding manner almost peculiar to himself, he demanded what was the matter. "Nothing," replied Pedro, "but that I was near falling."—"Beware of falling!" rejoined the other, with his usual coolness, and walked on before the opportunity could be regained. A few days afterwards, however, being so imprudent as to venture with a few attendants to a church outside the walls of the city, he perceived that he was enveloped by most of the conspirators. Again was he saved by his presence of mind. He entered into conversation with them, in a manner so polite and so tranquil, and kept his eye so constantly on them, that they forbore to strike him: perhaps there was something in the royal carriage which imposed on their imaginations, and by which their principle of concert was dissipated. But they soon repented of their involuntary weakness, and resolved to perpetrate the deed on his return. Acquainted with his peril through Coutinho, he sent for his guards, by whom he was escorted to the city. These repeated disappointments terrified the head of the conspiracy, who by letter reproached the actors with their cowardly delay: he exhorted them to be instant in executing their object, or prepare to fall the victims of their design; and assured them that in the present circumstances despatch was the truest wisdom. They felt the force of his remonstrance, and swore to obey him without delay. Joam, who was informed of this, as he had been of every other measure, now perceived that he could temporise no longer. Under the pretext of communicating some confidential affairs, he sent for the duke to court; and the latter with some reluctance obeyed the summons. Being ushered into the room of audience, near which three men were concealed as witnesses, and, if necessary, as actors, in the impending tragedy, dom Diego appeared with a cheerful and loyal countenance, and Joam with one of equal benignity. After a few moments' conversation, the latter asked, in a manner of studied carelessness, "Cousin, suppose you knew a man who had sworn to take away your life; what would you do?"—"I would hasten to take his!"—"Die, then!" rejoined the king; "thou hast pronounced thine own doom!" and a dagger, wielded by the royal hand, entered the traitor's heart.

1484. This deed, so unworthy of royalty, which transposed a king into a vile executioner, happened in Setubal: the inhabitants, filled alike with horror and dismay, remained in their houses until the cause was generally known, when Joam had then the gratification of seeing that he was popular. They hastened to his palace, as well to perform the duty of guards, as to call for revenge on the heads of the conspirators. The nobles not implicated in the guilt also flocked to the same place, but not with the same feelings: though all execrated the memory of the duke, many had to tremble for their kindred and friends. Vasco Coutinho and Tinoco, brother of Margarita, deposed their evidence before the superior tribunal of justice; and such of the accomplices as could be arrested acknowledged the crime. Three nobles were executed in the public square of Setubal; two contrived to escape, but one was overtaken and slain; the brother of Coutinho was confined in a fortress, where he soon died, — doubtless through poison; the bishop of Evora, who was in the palace, tranquilly conversing with the queen, was called out, arrested, and conveyed to a dungeon, to end his days like Coutinho; two others (brothers) threw themselves into a fortress, where they were defended by the wife of one — the Amazonian countess of Peña Maçor, — who disdained to submit until she, her husband, and brother-in-law, were allowed to retire into Castile. The two delators were magnificently rewarded: — Coutinho with the lordship of Borba; the other, whose birth was mean, with a considerable pension, and in addition a rich benefice. Thus ended this formidable conspiracy. The king was generally condemned for so savagely performing the functions of executioner; but many, in a true Turkish spirit, defended him, on the ground that, as punishment was justly done, the manner — whether by the royal hand or by the headsman — was immaterial. Dom Manuel, brother of the duke, was subsequently brought to court, created constable of the kingdom, duke of Beja, and invested with many of the fiefs possessed by that nobleman. After Alfonso, son of Joam, he was the next heir to the throne.[*]

In the reign of this prince, the Portuguese spirit of maritime enterprise was carried to a high pitch; a spirit which, except in one instance[†], he was always anxious to foster. His first care was to found a fort on the coast of Guinea, which had been discovered during the preceding reign, for the purpose of maintaining a permanent commercial intercourse with the natives. The barbarian king, who had entered into an alliance with

1482 to 1486.

---

[*] Ruy de Pina, Cronica do Senhor Rey Dom João II., cap. xi. 18. Vasconcellos, p. 228. &c. La Clède, iii. 13. Lem. vii. 30. Ferreras, par Hermilly, tom. vii., sub propriis annis.
[†] That of Christopher Columbus, whose proposals he himself was ready enough to receive, but was over-ruled by his council. See Vol. II. pp. 279, 280

the strangers, consented to the erection of the fortress. From this moment Portugal, or rather her monarchs, derived a great revenue in ivory and gold from this unknown coast; so great, indeed, that he feared lest the vessels of other European nations should be attracted to it. To damp their avidity, he took care that the voyage should be represented not merely as difficult, but as in the highest degree dangerous; and as impossible to be undertaken in regular ships; in any other than the flat-bottomed round smacks at that time peculiar to Portugal. A pilot, too dull to perceive the royal design in such reports, one day ventured to assert, in Joam's presence, that the voyage was practicable in any vessel. The king fiercely upbraided him for his presumption, in calling that practicable which experience had shown to be the reverse. He took the hint, and was silent; an act of prudence which procured him, a few days afterwards, substantial marks of the royal approbation. The secret, however, was near coming to the knowledge of the vigilant monarch of Castile, who suspected the truth, and who longed to obtain a settlement on the same coast. In the hope of a princely reward, a Portuguese captain and two pilots proceeded to Castile. They were pursued into the neighbouring territory by the agents of Joam; and, as they refused to obey the summons of recall, two were killed on the spot, and the third brought back to Evora, where he was quartered. The severity of this punishment sunk deep into the minds of the other pilots, and retained them in the service of their own sovereign. And when Joam heard that vessels were constructing in the English ports, unknown to our Edward IV., and at the cost of the duke de Medina-Sidonia, for an expedition to Ethiopia, — so the Portuguese termed all central Africa from the Nile to the western coast, — he sent an embassy to the English monarch, whom he reminded of the ancient alliance between the two crowns, and whom he easily induced to prohibit the preparations. In a short time, the fortress of St. George of the Mine became a considerable city, and afterwards infamous from the traffic in slaves.

But this was only the beginning of Portuguese enterprise. The king had been taught to suspect that by coasting the African continent a passage to the East Indies might be discovered; and he not ony equipped two small squadrons expressly for this object, but despatched two of his subjects into India and Abyssinia, to discover the route to and between these vast regions, and what advantages Portuguese commerce might derive from the knowledge thus acquired. The two travellers, Pedro da Covilhan and Alfonso de Payva, passed first to Naples, and thence to Rhodes, by the knights of which they were well received, and enabled to reach Alexandria. There they separated,— Covilhan for India, and Payva for Abysinnia; but agreeing to rejoin each other, in a given period, in Cairo. The former embarked on the Red Sea, visited the most famous cities of India, as far as the Ganges; coasted, on his return, the shores of Persia, Arabia, and Africa as far as Mozambique, where he learnt that the continent terminated in a great cape, much farther to the south. He now returned to Cairo, where he heard of his companion's death. He then visited Abyssinia, where he ultimately settled; but he wrote to the king, to whom he communicated the observations he had made, and a chart of the maritime places he had visited.

The discoveries of this enterprising man encouraged Joam to attempt the passage to India. One of the squadrons,— that under Joam Alfonso de Aveiro— discovered the kingdom of Benin. Aveiro was to open a commercial treaty with the savage chief of this country, when death surprised him before he could accomplish the end of his expedition. The other, under Jayme Cam, was more fortunate. Crossing the equinox, he arrived at the mouth of a large river, the Sahira, on the coast of Congo. Persuaded that the banks of that river were navigable, he proceeded to explore them, and soon fell on various groups of the natives, whose countenances were less ugly and lips less thick than those of Guinea. They were soon induced to approach the vessels, and to make themselves understood by signs; for though Cam was accompanied by a man who spoke several African languages, not a word of the Congo was intelligible to him. He soon learned from them that the whole country was subject to a king, who lived some days' journey distant from the coast. Four of the crew, under the guidance of some negroes, who left five of their countrymen as hostages, proceeded to visit his sable majesty; but as they did not return within the stipulated time, the Portuguese captain weighed anchor, bringing the hostages to Europe. On the voyage, these natives were taught sufficient of the Portuguese language to make themselves understood when introduced to Joam, who took great delight in their conversation, and who treated them with great kindness. After some time, fearful that, unless they were restored to their country, his four subjects in Congo might be ill-treated, he ordered Cam to revisit that country, to form an alliance with the king, and if possible to effect his conversion to Christianity. On reaching the mouth of the Sahira, the captain despatched one of the natives, with suitable presents, soliciting the restoration of the four Portuguese, and an interview. They were instantly freed; but before Cam advanced, he coasted 200 leagues farther to the south; but finding no cape, he returned to Congo, and was honourably received by the barbarian king, whom he disposed to Christianity, and impressed with a favourable idea of European civilisation. His departure affected the half convert, who besought him to return with missionaries, and who at the same time permitted several natives to accompany him, for the purpose of being thoroughly instructed in the new faith. They were accompanied by one of the four negroes who had previously made the voyage to Lisbon. By the Portuguese king and court they were received with great joy, and at their express desire were soon regenerated in the waters of baptism, he, his queen, and many of the nobles standing sponsors at the font. After a residence of two years in Europe, they returned to Congo, accompanied by several monks, some mechanics and agricultural labourers, and an embassy, headed by Ruy de Sousa. On reaching the coast, the missionaries were joyfully received by the uncle of the king, whose government lay in that part of the country. This prince and one of his sons were immediately baptised, the former by the name of Manuel. His zeal was remarkable: he not only punished the slightest disrespect towards the religion of the strangers, but frequently harangued the people; expatiating on the errors of paganism, and exhorting them to follow his example. That example, and the open protection afforded by the king to the strangers and proselytes, produced great effect. Hundreds repaired to the missionaries for instruction; the idols were broken or removed; a church was built, and mass celebrated with the imposing pomp so characteristic of the Romish worship, and so well fitted to captivate the senses of barbarous nations,— Sousa, with some missionaries and a suitable number of attendants, now proceeded into the interior, to effect the conversion of the king. He was provided with an honourable escort of natives; and as he approached the capital, thousands came out to meet him. He was immediately conducted to the palace, where the barbarian king, mounted on a rude throne, naked to the waist, with a chaplet of palm-tree leaves on the head, and bauble ornaments on the wrists, greeted him with a reception intended to be truly royal. Having delivered his presents, and explained the use of the sacred vessels, which were objects sure to strike the attention of a savage, he was lodged in the palace, and his missionaries suffered to preach the gospel in perfect security. Near the palace a church was commenced, intended for the splendid ceremony of the royal baptism; but before its completion, hearing that a tribe of his subjects had

---

* His uncle Gonsalo was first appointed; but death removing that noble on the voyage, he was chosen to succeed.

VOL.

revolted, and his own presence being necessary to reduce them, he insisted on the previous performance of the rite. He received the name of Joam; his queen, that of Leonora; his eldest son, that of Alfonso; and many of his chiefs names corresponding with those of the nobles of the Portuguese court. But Pansa, the second son of the king, persisted in his idolatry; and after the return of Sousa, the father himself apostatised, and even intrigued to exclude Alfonso from the succession. On his death, the two brothers decided the question by force of arms, when victory declared for the Christian and his Portuguese allies. So long as Alfonso lived, Christianity had a firm support in his zeal; but in the same ratio that of his subjects decreased. To renounce worldly pleasures, and to mortify the strongest passions — to forego the privilege of many wives, and the gratification of revenge — were too much for these licentious barbarians. By what degrees the new faith changed, and how it was finally extinguished, would be an enquiry foreign to this compendium. That the Portuguese themselves were obstacles to diffusing the benefits of civilisation, and the blessings of religion, throughout a considerable portion of this vast continent, is a reflection as true as it is melancholy. Congo was not the only kingdom which presented an opening for this great purpose. While these scenes were passing in that region, Bemohi, the Mohammedan king of the Jalofs, a people inhabiting the coast opposite the Cape de Verd Islands, being dethroned by a prince of his family, escaped to Portugal, to implore the succour of Joam. He eagerly demanded baptism; was knighted by the royal hand of his ally; and was promised an aid sufficient to regain his dignity. In the usual terms he sent his submission to the pope, both for himself and his kingdom; and, besides consenting to hold his crown as a vassal of Joam, he proposed to open to the nation of his benefactor the way to Abyssinia and Egypt, and a commerce as extensive as it would be lucrative. Twenty ships laden with soldiers, priests, and architects, under Pedro Vas

rived in the mouth of the Senegal. Here the unfortunate African was murdered by the hands of Da Cunha. The motive of this dark deed is wrapt in some mystery: the most probable supposition is, that he and his troops were unwilling to penetrate into this unknown region; that they dreaded alike the climate, the fatigues of the journey, and the opposition of the inhabitants; and that, in the resolution of evading a grave or captivity, they imbrued their hands in royal blood. The strangest feature of the transaction is, that Da Cunha and his companion, on their return to Portugal, escaped punishment. Whether the guilty were too numerous to be chastised, or whether — a more probable hypothesis — they succeeded in persuading Joam that Bemohi meditated treachery, cannot be known in this world.*

Though no paramount advantage was derived from the alliance with Congo, the discoveries of Cam led to a solid one,— that of the Cape of Good Hope. This memorable discovery was made in 1487, by Bartholomeo Diaz, an officer of equal enterprise and experience. The high winds, and still higher seas, which assailed this vast promontory, induced the captain to call it the Cape of Storms; but Joam, who had more extended views, called it O Cabo de Boa Esperança, or the Cape of Good Hope. On this occasion Diaz ventured little beyond the promontory; nor was it passed by any vessel until the following reign, when the famous Vasco de Gama doubled it on his voyage to India. 1487.

Like his predecessors, Joam was in frequent hostilities with the Moors of Fez. His first expedition was undertaken on the pretext of succouring his royal ally against two rebellious governors; but, in reality, he was incapable of generosity so pure. He triumphed over the two rebels, one of whom he took prisoner, but soon permitted him to be ransomed. The following year (1488), Antonio de Noronha, governor of Ceuta, with a considerable number of Portuguese nobles, was over- 1487 to 1491.

* Ruy de Pina, passim. Vasconcellos, p. 228, &c. Ferreras, tom. viii. La Clède, iii. 13. Lemos, viii. 30.

powered by a multitude of the Africans; but this shock was soon repaired by Francisco Coutinho de Borba, who had been intrusted with the government of Arsilla. This nobleman had a Moorish spy named Albula, who had long served him with fidelity; but who, being at length taken by the governor of Alcaçar-quibir, and condemned to death, promised, in return for life and liberty, to deliver him into the hands of his enemies. Albula being thus permitted to revisit Arsilla, repeated his protestations of attachment, and was, as before, implicitly believed. One day he proposed a profitable expedition, for which he asserted sixty horsemen would be sufficient; and accordingly that number, with Coutinho at their head, repaired to the place assigned. On reaching it, the governor perceived a plain covered with husbandmen, who fled at his approach, and drew him into an ambuscade, where the Moor Talaro lay with near 600 select followers. In no degree daunted at the disproportion, he quickly exhorted his men to imitate his example, and charged the hostile ranks. He and Talaro were opposed hand to hand; and both exhibited the most determined valour: the horse of each being slain in the combat, both continued it on foot. At length Talaro, having received some wounds, and being ready to faint, surrendered, while his companions fled. Seeing by what a handful of men he had been routed, he is said to have observed to Coutinho, " Boast not of thy success: if Allah be a Christian to-day, he will be a Moor to-morrow!" The prediction, however, was not verified; for a reinforcement arriving to the Portuguese, they made profitable excursions into the neighbouring towns and villages. Though an unsuccessful attempt was made to erect a fortress on Graciosa, a small island off the Mauritanian coast, Fernando de Menezes, governor of Ceuta, took Targa, and consumed by fire twenty of the Moorish vessels that lay in the port.

1490 to 1495.
In 1490 Joam married his only legitimate son, Alfonso, to Isabel of Castile * ; but the rejoicings conse-

* See Vol. II. page 281.

quent on this event were almost the last he was permitted to seek. Before their conclusion, the count passed from Evora to Viana, where one day he and two domestics were suddenly taken ill. The cause is wrapt in some mystery; but the general suspicion was, that a fountain from which he and they had drunk was poisoned: their death, and his own tardy recovery, seem to confirm it. Scarcely were a few months elapsed, when a tragical death deprived him of his intended successor. During the summer heats he was accustomed to bathe in the Tagus: one fine evening (July 13. 1491) he invited the young prince to accompany him: the latter, who had just returned from the chase, assigned fatigue as the cause of refusing. While with the princess Isabel, standing at a window of the palace, he perceived the king pass, who gravely saluted him: in the fear that there was displeasure at his remaining behind, and from anxiety to remove it, he ordered a mule to be saddled; but seeing that the order was too slowly obeyed for his impatience, he went into the royal stables, mounted a fine mettled steed that stood ready, and, followed by a knight, hastened to the banks of the river. Perceiving that his father was swimming at some distance, he proposed to his companion to make trial of the swiftness of their horses. As darkness was beginning to fall, the knight attempted to dissuade him from the course, but in vain; he would be obeyed. Both accordingly commenced a rapid gallop; but, in the height of the race, the prince's horse fell on him, and struck him senseless. The afflicted Joam, with half the court, flew to the spot; the son was conveyed into a fisherman's hut, and the proper remedies administered, but without effect: he soon breathed his last in the arms of his parents and his consort. The first shock of the catastrophe prostrated the vigorous mind of the king to the very earth; for some time he refused to be comforted. To the condolence of his people, who gently reproved his grief, and who told him that for them he must live, since in each of them he had still a son, he replied, " The happiness of my subjects is, indeed, my only remaining consolation. I will labour for their good: but let them pardon me; nature is weak, and I am but a man." He soon, however, found another source of consolation, if not so elevated, at least as effectual. He had a natural son, dom Jorge by name, to whom he now transferred his affection, and to remove the disgrace of whose birth he endeavoured to procure from the reigning pope the necessary bull of legitimacy. When, in addition, he caused that son to be invested with the grand mastership of Avis and Santiago, and created him duke of Coimbra, there seemed no doubt that the favourite was designed for the throne, to the exclusion of dom Manuel, whom he had created duke de Beja, brother of the unfortunate duke de Viseo. The mere suspicion of this intention filled the nobility with consternation, since it could not be carried into effect without involving the state in all the horrors of a civil war. His negotiations at Rome for the bull of legitimacy were successfully traversed by others, — by none more zealously than by Fernando of Castile. The last three years of his life were passed in bodily infirmity, but not so severe as to exclude him from public affairs, until a short time before his death. Being persuaded to take the hot baths near Alvor, in Algarve, he became so ill that his life was evidently in danger. In this state he despatched a messenger for the duke de Beja, to whom he doubtless wished to commend his son dom Jorge; but that prince, fearful of assassination, refused to obey the summons. His last moments were devoutly employed. He had an altar erected in his apartment, having the crucifix on one side, and the image of his patron St. John on the other: here he received his confession, asking forgiveness of all whom he had offended. A gentleman present asked him for a boon for the sake of Christ's wounds. "Take it!" was the reply; "I have never refused any thing to such an adjuration!" He refused to be styled *highness* at this awful crisis; yet, such is the inconsistency of man, he reproved a courtier for touching his beard to recover him during a temporary fit of faintness. At length, with difficulty uttering the prayer, " Domine, qui tollis peccata mundi, miserere mihi!" he breathed his last.*

Joam was a great prince; comprehensive in his views, vigorous in the execution of his designs, as he was cautious and politic in their formation; zealous for justice, and for the happiness of his people. That zeal, however, sometimes degenerated into vengeance, and was sometimes disarmed by capricious clemency. But his character will be better conceived from a few striking traits or sayings, and many such are recorded of him, than from any description. A criminal, after fourteen years' imprisonment, was condemned to death — probably because he had not money enough to purchase pardon from his judges, who had, however, accepted of some. The king pardoned the criminal, on account of the long confinement, and the corruption of the judges; and threatened them with the same fate if the offence were repeated. A gaoler persuaded another prisoner to counterfeit death, and thereby to escape the capital punishment: the gaoler was convicted, and condemned; but he experienced the royal mercy in consequence of his ingenuity. A woman one day fell on her knees to obtain pardon for her condemned husband, " Your husband is guilty," replied Joam, " and if I pardon him, he will only commit the more crimes; however, as you are in trouble, he may be enlarged!" Being once struck with the courage of a man in a bullfight, he demanded, " Who are you?"—" I am a criminal, who have fled from justice: I killed a person who insulted me!"—" Corregidor!" said the king, " purge this man of his crime; he shall be employed in my service!" One of his nobles had a sister who suffered herself to be dishonoured by a gallant; the brother slew the gallant, and fled to Arsilla. Joam no sooner knew the circumstance, than he wrote to the governor, whom he ordered to treat the fugitive well,

*The same authorities, together with the contemporary ones of Castile, as quoted in the reign of Fernando and Isabel.

as one who had shown a proper sense of honour. These instances, however, were but exceptions to his general justice, which was characterised by undue severity. In other respects his whimsical disposition exhibited itself in a harmless or even amiable manner. He placed little value on the recommendations of his nobles; and a favour solicited through their medium was almost sure to be denied. But he was fond of honouring and rewarding merit, especially when, as is generally the case, that merit was dumb. To a faithful and valiant knight he one day observed: "You have hands to serve me; have you no tongue to request a recompence?" Being at dinner, he was once served among others by dom Pedro de Melo, a knight of great prowess, who had usefully served him in Africa. The soldier, who was better fitted for handling the sword than a dish in the palace of princes, let fall a large vessel of water, which sprinkled some of the courtiers, and made others laugh. "Why do you laugh?" enquired the king; "dom Pedro has dropped a vessel of water, but he never dropped his lance!" Another brave soldier, Azambuja, who had erected the fortress in Guinea, and received a wound in the foot which made him lame for life, being one day at court, unable to push through the crowd, was ridiculed by some of the worthless audience. Joam perceived the affront; advanced towards the veteran, whom he seated by his side, and to whom he observed, "Let them smile; they shall soon have reason to envy your honourable wound." To a third officer, who on arriving at court could not obtain a hostel, he said, "Be not uneasy that every lodging is occupied; my palace shall suffice you!" He had borrowed money of a rich merchant at Tavira, to whom, at the expiration of the stipulated period, he returned it with legal interest. The merchant — a wonderful instance of disinterestedness in such a capacity — refused to receive more than the principal; Joam sent double interest, with the order to continue doubling it as often as the merchant should persist in the refusal. In one of his public edicts, with the view of recruiting his cavalry, he ordered all his subjects to be in readiness to furnish excellent war horses. The churchmen pleaded their immunities, and some of them went so far as to say that they were not his subjects, but those of the pope. To punish them in the way they deserved, Joam loudly asserted that he had never regarded them as subjects; and by another ordinance he forbade all smiths and farriers to shoe their mules and horses, — a measure which soon compelled them to submit. The monopolists in corn had created an artificial famine by purchasing and piling in their warehouses all the grain in the kingdom, which they refused to sell under an exorbitant price. By a royal ordinance the people were forbidden to purchase from these dealers, and the Castilians were permitted to import in whatever quantities they pleased : the kingdom soon teemed with abundance, and the monopolists were ruined. He was a great enemy to detraction. One day in his hearing a courtier spoke ill of the morals of another, who kept, he said, twenty mistresses. "How many?" enquired Joam. "Twenty!"—"Then," replied the king, "I advise you to keep out of his way: such a man is not to be met with impunity!" Some one praised a recent feat of arms of a Portuguese governor in Africa: another attempted to detract from it by saying that the success was merely owing to chance. "That may be," observed the king : "but how is it that such chance never happens to any one else?" Nor was he less jealous of his dignity with foreign princes than with his own subjects. A Portuguese vessel had been captured by some French pirates: he ordered all the French vessels in his ports to be seized. The owners complained to their king, Charles VIII., who immediately punished the pirates, and caused their prize to be restored. It was found, however, that a parrot had not been restored with the rest, and he insisted that every vessel should be retained until the bird were produced. In short, the success of his administration was unrivalled; he introduced industry and comfort among his people; added largely to the national resources; and was in many respects the greatest monarch that ever swayed the sceptre of Portugal.*

1495 to 1500. Manuel having recalled the exiled princes of Braganza, and received the hand of Isabel of Castile†, resolved to pursue the maritime enterprises of his great predecessor. A squadron of five vessels had been already prepared for the great passage to India: it was intrusted to the celebrated Vasco de Gama; who having received the standard of the cross from the hands of the new king, embarked amidst the acclamations and tears of the spectators, according as fear for the fate of kindred and friends, or hope for the country's greatness, predominated in their breasts.‡ His passage from the Cape de Verds to St. Helena occupied near three months; and before he could reach the Stormy Cape, his crew were so disheartened by the continued winds, and the high seas, that they besought him to return. In vain did he exhort them to dismiss their cowardly fears, assuring them that they would soon arrive in more tranquil seas, and off an abundant coast. Perceiving that he was bent on his purpose, they conspired against his life. This conspiracy was fortunately discovered by his brother, Paulo de Gama; the mutineers were ironed and confined, and the admiral himself took the helm. His courage was crowned with success. On the 20th day of November, 1497, near five months after his departure from Lisbon, he doubled the Cape. Continuing to coast along the African shores, he passed Sofala, and soon cast anchor off the coast of Zanguebar. Finding the natives more humane and civilised than on the western continent, the result of their commercial

---

* Ruy de Pina (in ultimis capitulis) La Clède, tom. iii. liv. 13. et tom. iv. liv. 14 Vasconcellos, p. 224. &c. Lemos, viii. 30—32. Ferreras, tom. viii.

† Vol. II. p. 281.

‡ The adventures of this extraordinary man are detailed with general accuracy, though adorned with poetic rhapsodies, by the immortal Camoëns. A good account of Portuguese discoveries on the coast is also to be found in the Introduction of Mr. Mickle, his able and spirited translator. Our limits will not permit us to do more than glance at the chief circumstances.

intercourse with the Indies, he left two convicts, whom he instructed to learn the language of the country, and await his return. The inhabitants of Mozambique he found to be Mohammedans, who abhorred the Christian name. The pilots, whom he with difficulty obtained to conduct him through these unknown seas, endeavoured to betray him into the hands of the Mohammedan king; but accident thwarted their views, and in revenge he cannonaded the port of Mombaza. At Melinda he met with better hospitality: not only did the Mussulman express a sincere desire to be considered the ally of Portugal, but he furnished a skilful pilot to conduct the stranger to the great Indian peninsula. Having a second time crossed the equinoctial line, he proceeded along the Arabian and Persian shores to Calicut, a rich and populous port on the coast of Malabar. Both he and his crew were not a little surprised to find merchants of Tunis, and other ports of Barbary, in this distant region, — many who trafficked in every great port of India, of Africa, and of the Mediterranean. The favourable reception which the Portuguese admiral received from the zamorin in person, the native sovereign, who readily consented to an alliance with dom Manuel, roused the avaricious fears of the Moorish merchants. These men had long enjoyed a monopoly of the rich traffic of the East and West, and they could not view without alarm the arrival of the adventurous strangers. They hastened to the zamorin, to whom they represented the Portuguese as pirates or spies, as men bound by no ties of honour or principle; and insisted on their destruction. The king entered into their views, a conspiracy was formed to seize and assassinate the strangers, but the plot was discovered. Vasco escaped by night from the city, arrived on board, and sailed with some Malabar natives, whom he had unjustifiably made prisoners, from the perfidious port. Having coasted the Indian peninsula, and finding that his armament was too inconsiderable to command respect, he returned to Melinda, received on board ambassadors from the king to his sovereign, doubled the Cape, April 26th, 1499, and reached Lisbon in September, after an absence of little more than two years.

1500 to 1501. The relation of this renowned seaman inflamed dom Manuel with the prospect of deriving considerable permanent advantage from the rich kingdoms of the East. A fleet of thirteen vessels was now prepared, and confided to the direction of dom Pedro Alvares Cabral. Being forced by a tempest, while passing the Cape de Verd islands, to direct his course somewhat more to the west than had been done by his predecessor, to his astonishment the new admiral discovered land. Having taken possession of the coast, and given it the name of Santa Cruz,—a name, however, which was soon afterwards changed into that of Brazil,—and despatched a vessel to acquaint his monarch with the news, he continued his voyage: but in a second tempest he lost several of his ships. By the king of Quiloa he was greeted with marks of good-will; but the jealousy of the Mohammedan merchants retarded the completion of a commercial intercourse. On anchoring before Calicut, he was not unfavourably received, but the good understanding was of short continuance: at the instigation of the Moors, the Christians were persecuted, and fifty massacred. In revenge, Cabral consumed by fire the Indian and Arabian vessels in the port, of which he secured the cargoes, and committed horrible carnage among the enemy; he then bombarded the city, laying some of the best houses in ashes, and causing great destruction of life. He next proceeded to Cochin, from the governor of which, Trimumpara, he experienced more hospitality. He entered not merely into a commercial treaty, but into a close alliance with the royal Hindoo, who submitted to become the vassal of dom Manuel, and who permitted some Portuguese to form a settlement on the coast. Still greater friendship was shown by the king of Cananor. Having thus laid the foundation of a commercial intercourse, and established factories, the admiral loaded some vessels with the choicest productions of the East, and returned without accident to Europe. Before his arrival, a smaller squadron had left Lisbon for the same destination: its chief success was defeating a fleet belonging to the Moors and the brutal king of Calicut.*

The prospect of advantage, through the factories which had been established on the Indian and African coasts, encouraged Manuel to equip a more formidable expedition. With ten vessels, Vasco de Gama, who had been created admiral of the Indies, again undertook a voyage which was no longer considered dreadful. He was accompanied by his uncle, Vicente Sodre, who, with five vessels more, was ordered to protect the new factories while the admiral caused the Portuguese name to be respected by the zamorin and other enemies. His cousin Estevan de Gama had orders to follow him with four additional vessels; and the following year, six more were despatched into the same seas; three under Alfonso, and three under Francisco de Albuquerque. Having doubled the Cape, the first care of Vasco was to confirm the yet insecure influence of his country on the African coast, especially in Sofala and Mozambique. At Quiloa, he resolved to take vengeance, for the treachery meditated by the inhabitants on the former voyage; and he cannonaded the city so briskly, that the affrighted king hastened on board to appease him. The Mohammedan was then forcibly detained, until he recognised dom Manuel as his superior, and agreed to pay an annual tribute. Off the coast of Malabar, Vasco had the good fortune to fall in with his relative, Estevan. His force now amounting to nineteen ships, (one had been lost on the passage), he prepared to vindicate the authority of his master. His next feat was, to take a large vessel, laden with treasure, belonging to the soldan of Egypt; the second, to punish the zamorin. At first, with characteristic perfidy, the royal Hindoo

1502 to 1054.

* Damian à Goes, Chronica do Senhor Rey Dom Manoel, passim. Barros, Asia, passim. Vasconcellos, p. 263, &c. La Clède, tom. iv. Lemos, tom. ix. et x. See also Raynal, Histoire Philosophique, and Mickle's Introduction to the Lusiad.

tried to inveigle the strangers into a net, spread to destroy them. The admiral detected the perfidy, and commenced a cruel retaliation. Not satisfied with seizing several valuable ships, he cut off the hands, heads, and feet of thirty-two Moors, which he sent in a bark, as a present, to the governor, and furiously cannonaded the city. Leaving his uncle, Sodre, to continue the work of destruction, he proceeded to Cochin, and had the gratification to find the Portuguese factory there in a flourishing state. At Cranganor, about four leagues distant from Cochin, he was surprised to discover a society of Nestorian Christians, who, according to ancient tradition, were the descendants of the converts effected by the preaching of St. Thomas. These, to the number of 30,000, were eager to acknowledge the Portuguese king as their liege lord. While at Cochin, he received an embassy from the zamorin, who entreated him to return to Calicut, that a permanent pacification might be effected between the two people. That he should be so credulous as to rely on the protestation of such a man, is surprising; but he immediately returned, was treated as before with much outward respect, and before he was aware of hostilities being intended, he was surrounded by above a hundred Moorish and Hindoo vessels. Had not Sodre, whom he had ordered to cruise off the coast, unexpectedly appeared in sight, his destruction would have been inevitable; but with his kinsman's aid, he soon triumphed over the enemy. The zamorin now endeavoured, by letter, to prevail on the king of Cochin to assassinate the Portuguese residents; but the latter disdained to imitate the treachery which had been shown to the admiral. As Vasco was on the point of returning to Europe, he left a few Portuguese for the defence of his ally, and ordered Sadre to protect him against the probable vengeance of the zamorin. The governor of Cananor was no less faithful to his engagements, and no less ready to defend them against the zamorin. Scarcely had Vasco left the coast for Africa, and Sadre to cruise in the

Arabian Gulf, than the implacable Hindoo made preparation for war on Trimumpara. This faithful man had soon reason to complain of the ingratitude or cowardice of his allies. Although Sodre returned from a profitable piratical expedition, and was enabled, with his squadron of six vessels, to afford seasonable aid to the king, he refused to fire a shot in his behalf, and quietly resumed his piracies on the Persian shores: off the Arabian coast, however, he met with his reward,— a watery grave. Fortunately for Trimumpara, all the Portuguese were not like the unworthy Sodre: the handful who formed the factory assisted him in sustaining the assaults of the zamorin. But in the end, such was the disproportion in numbers, that this loyal prince must have fallen, had not four small squadrons, under the Albuquerques, seasonably arrived, when the invaders were repelled with heavy loss. The victors now built a fortress on the territory of their ally, with a church, dedicated to St. Bartholomew. The issue of the war compelled the zamorin to sue for peace from his neighbour of Cochin, to whom the conditions were no less favourable than they were to the mediators and guarantees, the Portuguese. After the departure of the two Albuquerques, however, who imprudently left a slender garrison of 150 men in the fortress, and abandoned their ally to the vengeance of the Hindoo, the latter hesitated not a moment to break the peace, and to proclaim that nothing less than the entire conquest of Cochin, the dethronement of Trimumpara, and the destruction of the Portuguese residents, would satisfy him. He little knew the heroism which animated the Christian band, — its leader, above all, Pacheco, whose deeds have been compared by his countrymen to those of the twelve peers of France: they might, with more propriety, have been compared to those of the two Menezes in Africa. This man sailed with Alfonso de Albuquerque, as captain of a vessel; and this was the first occasion in which he had an opportunity of displaying his valour. The forces of the zamorin are stated — no doubt they are monstrously exaggerated — at 50,000; while the king of Cochin had only 5000, exclusive of the 150 Portuguese. The disproportion in no degree terrified Pacheco, who commenced a series of combats for ever memorable in the annals of Portuguese Asia. Though column after column moved on the entrenchments of this heroic little band, — for of their 5000 Hindoos and others the national historians scarcely condescend to speak, — column after column was either wholly destroyed or compelled to fall back on the besieging force, so weakened as to be unfit for immediate service. On four different occasions did the haughty Hindoo assail, by sea and land, the entrenchments of the Portuguese: in all four, if there be any faith in their historians, was he signally and ignominiously defeated. So much was he dispirited by these reverses, — so completely was his proud spirit humiliated, that, fearful of appearing in presence of his own subjects, he resigned the regal dignity in favour of his nephew.*

1505 to 1509. The next considerable armament which the Portuguese king fitted out for these distant regions was confided to dom Lope Suares: it consisted of thirteen vessels, carrying 1200 men. As the soldan of Egypt breathed vengeance against the nation which had taken one of his most valuable ships, and which had annihilated his lucrative traffic in the Indian seas, two vessels were despatched, under Francisco de Almeida, who was nominated viceroy of the Indies. On his side, the soldan constructed a fleet, the materials for which were furnished by the Venetians. When Almeida touched at Quiloa, the king, Ibrahim, who had rendered himself obnoxious to the Portuguese, fled with precipitation from the city. The viceroy offered the throne to

* We omit the details of these exploits, because they are incredible. Enough, however, remains to show that Pacheco was a hero. He soon returned to Portugal, was received with the highest honours by dom Manuel; but on a frivolous charge was soon disgraced. Like Camoens, he died poor and miserable in an hospital, abandoned by his king, his country and his friends.

Authorities, Damian à Goes, Barros, Vasconcellos, La Clède, Lemos, &c. nearly in the places last cited.

Mohammed Anconi, a man of great wisdom and fidelity, who had always been the advocate of peace with the strangers. With a generosity seldom equalled, Mohammed, though he had sons of his own, caused the son of a former monarch — of one who had been assassinated by the usurper Ibrahim — to be recognised as his successor. Having received, as the representative of dom Manuel, the homage of the new king, erected a fortress to overawe the inhabitants, and destroyed the town of Monbaza, which refused to submit, Almeida hastened to Cananor. There he received an embassy from the king of Bisnagar, who, in admiration at the renown of the Europeans, solicited their alliance. There, too, he built a fortress for the protection of the factory; and there he loaded eight vessels with the richest productions of the Indies, which he despatched to Portugal, and which, in their voyage, discovered the great island of Madagascar. On reaching Cochin, he found that the faithful Trimumpara had resigned in favour of a nephew, who readily renewed the alliance with the Christians. His son, Lourenzo de Almeida, took possession of the Maldive isles, and established factories in Ceylon. The inhabitants of Calicut, who, in the expectation of aid from the soldan of Egypt, and other princes, had made formidable preparations for war, were now assailed and vanquished. The sovereign of Goa, one of the richest and most populous cities of Hindostan, was no less signally humbled. The administration of Almeida was, indeed, glorious for his country. While obtaining these successes in the Peninsula, a squadron of four vessels, equipped by dom Manuel expressly for the purpose, entered into a commercial alliance with the king of Malacca, and formed two commercial establishments on the island of Sumatra. At the same time Alfonso de Albuquerque, who had arrived from Europe to supersede the present viceroy, resolved, before entering on his career of administration, to signalise himself by some memorable exploit. For recovering the permanent possession of

Indian commerce, the Portuguese monarch had instructed his admirals to seize, or to settle in, three other places, Malacca, Ormuz, and Aden. The first of these places had received a factory; the isle of Ormuz was now assailed by Albuquerque. It was defended by 20,000 men, who, headed by the king, Sheifedin II., or rather by his minister, the eunuch Atar. The Portuguese were victorious; Sheifedin consented to pay an annual tribute, and to the erection of a fortress. On the coast of Sofala, another was erected by a Portuguese captain, who compelled the barbarian king to reign as the vassal of dom Manuel. Thus, along the whole of the vast African continent, from the straits of Gibraltar to Abyssinia, and along the Asiatic, from Ormuz to Siam, the Portuguese flag waved triumphant. The success, indeed, was not uniform; it was retarded by the accidents inseparable from human affairs. Thus, the king of Ormuz soon threw off the yoke, and expelled the invaders from the island. In vain did Albuquerque cannonade the capital; finding that his means were inadequate to the conquest, he suspended the enterprise, and proceeded to Malacca, to enter on his charge as viceroy. But Almeida, who had commenced a war with the king of Calicut, refused to resign the dignity until he had brought it to a successful issue. The refusal occasioned a dispute between the two chiefs, which promised to be attended with the most injurious consequences to the new empire. In this dispute Almeida was the only censurable party. Having reduced and consumed Dubal, a fortress belonging to the governor of Goa, he arrested his rival at Cochin. He seems, however, to have repented of the violence; for at the persuasion of a friend he released the prisoners, and left India on his return to Portugal. But his native country he was to see no more: he was killed in a dispute between the Caffres and a portion of his crew, who landed to procure a supply of fresh water. That the man who had trampled over countless thousands of the Asiatics, who had humbled their sovereign princes, and annihilated, in these seas, the powers of the Egyptian soldan, should perish on an obscure strand, by the hands of a few savages, should be a salutary lesson for human ambition.*

Albuquerque commenced his signal administration by the invasion of Goa; as Idalcan, the governor, was absent, the inhabitants unable to oppose a vigorous resistance, consented to receive a Portuguese garrison. This important city the viceroy resolved to make the capital of all Portuguese India. Before, however, he could put his design into execution, the city was recovered by Idalcan, and the Christian garrison expelled. The intelligence afflicted him extremely, and he was anxiously revolving the means of regaining so fair a possession, when he learned that the governor had again departed on a warlike expedition, leaving 3000 men to defend it against the possible hostilities of his soldiers. Without a moment's delay he re-appeared before the place, which he stormed and took, and in which, to inspire the inhabitants with dread, he stained his fame by a horrible revenge. His next care was to expel the forces of Zamorin from Cochin, and to establish the Portuguese domination on the whole western coast of the Peninsula. He now turned his eye towards Malacca, from which he knew his countrymen had been recently expelled through the intrigues of the Moorish merchants. To revenge the indignity he repaired to that country, eluded the designs of the barbarian king, whom he subsequently defeated and dethroned, and whose capital he retained, notwithstanding the efforts of the inhabitants to shake off the yoke, or of their allies in their behalf. This conquest, and the triumphs by which it was followed, inspired many of the neighbouring sovereigns with fear. The viceroy having again visited the coast of Malabar, and increased alike the strength and number of his fortresses, sailed for Aden, in Arabia. On that almost impregnable place,

1509 to 1515.

* Damian à Goes, Barros, Vasconcellos, La Clède, Lemos, with the author of the Vida do Grande Albuquerque.

however, his artillery had little effect, and he was twice compelled to raise the siege. In two years, however, he returned into those seas, less, perhaps, to reduce Aden than to conquer the island of Ormuz. The eunuch Atar was dead, and so was Shiefedin, who had been poisoned. Though a brother of the deceased prince had succeeded, it was the minister who held the reins of power, dependent on the sophi of Persia. As this little kingdom paid tribute also to the Portuguese, the condition of both ruler and subjects was sufficiently humiliating. It was the object of Albuquerque to destroy the homage paid to the sophi, and thereby to secure the undivided superiority of his master; and he was anxious to construct a fortress for the purpose of overawing a people generally prone to novelty. After investing the capital, and establishing a blockade around the island, the viceroy demanded permission for the meditated construction,—a permission which the terrified king hastened to grant. The minister opposed it, and threw every obstacle in the way of its erection. In revenge Albuquerque caused him to be arrested and beheaded,—a measure dictated by that unprincipled ambition and that insolence of power, characteristics of the Portuguese domination in the East. The citadel was soon finished, and thither was transported all the artillery belonging to the city; and the victor sent to Goa thirty princes of the royal house, who had been blinded on the accession of the present king. But for all his splendid services, he was rewarded with envy and ingratitude. His abilities, his bravery, his successful administration, made the courtiers fear or pretend that he aimed at an independent sovereignty in those regions; and by their representations they prevailed on the king to recal him. Don Lope Soares was despatched from Lisbon to supersede him. But before his successor arrived, he felt that his health was worn out in the service of his country; he made his last will, and returned from Ormuz to Goa, to breathe his last sigh. As he proceeded along the coast, he was informed of his supercession—in other words, of his disgrace—and the intelligence sank deep into his mind. This illness so much augmented, that finding his end approach, he wrote a few hasty lines to his sovereign, to whom, as the sole reward of any services he might have performed the state, he recommended the interests of a natural son. He died at sea, within sight of Goa. However violent some of his acts,—none more so than the recent execution of a king in Malacca, for no other crime than an attempt to rescue the peninsula from the avaricious strangers,—his loss was bewailed by both Indians and Portuguese. He certainly administered justice with impartiality; laid no intolerable burdens on the people; restrained the licentiousness of his officers; and introduced unexampled prosperity throughout the wide range of the Portuguese establishments. If to this we add, that the qualities of his mind were of a high order; that he was liberal, affable, and modest, we shall scarcely be surprised that, by his enthusiastic countrymen, he was styled *the Great*. It is probable that no other man would have established the domination of Portugal on so secure a basis: it is certain that no other, in so short a period, could have invested the structure with so much splendour. His remains were magnificently interred at Goa, and his son was laden with honours by the now repentant Manuel,—the only rewards of his great deeds.*

Under the successors of Albuquerque, the administration of India was notorious for its corruption, imbecility and violence, and in the same degree as wisdom and justice were discarded, so did the military spirit decay. The local governors esteemed their offices only so far as ruined fortunes might be repaired or new ones amassed, and their only aim was to extort from the people the greatest possible sum in the shortest given time. One of the most important instructions received by Lope Soares was, to annihilate the armada which the soldan of Egypt had prepared on the Red Sea.

1515 to 1521.

* The same authorities.

With a formidable armament he left Goa, and on reaching Aden found the inhabitants willing to submit with the condition of his defending them against Soliman, the Egyptian admiral. Though this was the most valuable station which the Europeans could have obtained in the Indian seas; though its acquisition had been deemed an object of such moment by preceding viceroys; and, though the famous Albuquerque had failed before it, the viceroy Lope declined the offer, on the pretext that he had no instructions in relation to it. Proceeding through the Straits of Babelmandel, he was assailed by two dreadful tempests, which forced him to retire with loss—a loss increased by sickness and want of provisions. In this emergency he resolved to accept the proposal of the governor of Aden, whither he repaired; but he found the position of affairs greatly changed. While his armament was reduced nearly half, the place had been strengthened by a numerous garrison, and his own incapacity the theme of general ridicule; so that instead of submission, he met with open insults, and was glad to take refuge in Ormuz. From this place he despatched a vessel to Portugal, to acquaint his sovereign with the complete failure of all his designs. During his absence, Goa was nearly lost, through the misconduct of its governor, who, listening to guilty passions instead of a just policy, had drawn a formidable army around it. The siege, however, was at length raised, partly through the valour of two Portuguese captains, who reinforced the garrison, and partly through the concessions made by the governor to the incensed enemy. In Malacca, the death of the governor Brito, occasioned a dispute between two rival candidates for the vacant dignity. Of this, advantage was taken by a neighbouring king, to besiege the city, who, though in the end compelled to retire, had the gratification to know that he had weakened the strangers. In China a settlement was permitted to be made on the coast below Canton, but the violence of the Portuguese soon brought down the wrath of the celestial emperor, and occasioned their temporary expulsion. Factories were also established on the coast of Bengal, and in the Molucca Islands; but from the former the obnoxious strangers were in like manner expelled; and in the latter their footing was insecure. In 1518 the weak and vicious administration of Soares was replaced by that of Siqueira, which was not, however, to prove more fortunate. New troubles broke out in the city of Malacca, which were but imperfectly quelled; an expedition to the Arabian coast, to avenge the late check, was inglorious; in Cananor the people rose against the Portuguese fortress, and were not repulsed without incredible efforts and much loss; in Ceylon the same scenes were exhibited, and with equal loss,—a loss dearly purchased by a temporary calm; and near the port of Diu a Portuguese fleet was defeated by one of Hindoos and Mohammedans. In the last year of dom Manuel's reign, this governor was replaced by dom Duarte de Menezes.*

The celebrated line of demarcation between the right of discovery and conquest was not so clearly understood as to avoid disputes between dom Manuel and his brother sovereign of Castile. His splendid empire in the east had long attracted the jealousy of Fernando, who had frequently attempted, but as frequently been deterred by his remonstrances, to share in the rich commercial advantages thus offered to the sister kingdom. After the death of that prince, a disaffected Portuguese who had served Manuel with distinction both in Æthiopia and India, and who was disgusted with the refusal of his sovereign to reward his services with becoming liberality, fled into Castile, and told the new king, Charles V. of Austria, that the Molucca Islands, in virtue of that line, rightfully belonged to Spain. This

1519 to 1520.

---

* To finish the reign of dom Manuel, we somewhat exceed the limits which we intended to assign Mohammedan Spain. The excess, however, is only five years—viz. from 1516 to 1521.
Authorities: Damian à Goes, Chronica do Rey Manoel, and Barros, Asia, passim. Vasconcellos, p. 265, &c. La Clède, tom iv. liv. 14. Lemos, tom. x. xi. liv. 36, &c.

† See Vol. II. p. 280.

man was Fernando de Magalhanes (Ferdinand Magellan) whose name is immortalised in the annals of maritime discovery. He proposed a shorter route to the Moluccas than the passage by the Cape of Good Hope,—the route by Brazil: he well knew that the American continent must terminate somewhere, and his notion of the earth's rotundity was sufficiently just to convince him that a western voyage would bring him to the same point as the one discovered by Dias and Vasco de Gama. This proposal was submitted to the council of the Indies, which approved it, though Charles himself, on the remonstrances of the Portuguese ambassador, treated, or affected to treat it with indifference. In August, 1519, he embarked at Seville, with five vessels, over the crews of which he was invested with the power of life and death. Directing his course by the Canaries, he doubled Cape de Verde, passed the islands of that name, and plunged into the vast Western Ocean. On reaching the Brazilian coast, he cautiously proceeded southwards, in the expectation that every league would bring him within sight of the final promontory. Nothing but the most ardent zeal, with the most unbending resolution, could have made him persevere, in opposition alike to the elements and the wishes of his crew. The tall stature of the inhabitants of Patagonia, struck him with some surprise, and perhaps magnified the fears of his companions; but he eventually passed this *Land of Giants* and in September, 1520, arriving at a Cape which he called after the Eleven Thousand Virgins, he passed into the dreaded straits which bear his name. The severity of the weather, — weather severer than a northern latitude twenty degrees higher — killed many of his crew. Having cleared the straits, he steered towards the equator, where he knew there was a milder air, and where he hoped to meet with provisions. As the squadrons proceeded through the boundless Pacific, and no signs of land appeared, his crew not merely murmured, but conspired to destroy him, and return to

Spain. A few of the more desperate ringleaders he punished; but his soothing exhortations, and the chances he held forth that their fatigues would soon be over, secured the obedience of the rest. Though the American coast seemed too barren to yield any hopes of provisions, he despatched one of his vessels in quest of them: instead of obeying the order, the captain, in the full conviction that Magellan was leading the crews to inevitable destruction, returned to Europe. At length, considering the absent vessel as for ever lost, the adventurous navigator continued his course to the west; and after a passage of 1500 leagues, unexampled for its boldness, he reached the Philippine Islands. Here closed his extraordinary career. Landing on the isle of Zebu, he was persuaded by the king to join in a warlike expedition against another petty ruler in the same cluster; and he fell, with many of his companions, by the hands of the barbarians. Of the five vessels which had left Spain, two only reached the Moluccas; and of these two, one only returned to Seville. But if the object of the expedition failed, through the catastrophe of its leader, he will be considered by posterity as by far the most undaunted, and in many respects the most extraordinary man, that ever traversed an unknown sea.*

His anxiety to found an empire in the east did not prevent the Portuguese king from attending to the affairs of north-western Africa. In 1501 the king of Fez, at the head of a formidable army, assailed the governor of Tangier, who had just returned from a predatory excursion among the Moors; but he was so valiantly received by that officer, that he turned aside to Arsilla, but with no better success. The excursions, however, of his captain from the fortress of Alcacer-Quibir to the gates of Arsilla were frequent, though, perhaps, less destructive than those of the Christians. In 1506 the city of Saphin recognised the authority of

1501 to 1513.

* "Este Portuguez infiel," and "monstro Lusitano," are epithets lavishly applied to him for prefering a foreign service to that of his country — he has obtained less attention from our biographers than he deserves. — The same authorities.

dom Manuel. An inhabitant of that place, Ali by name, became enamoured of the governor's daughter, and killed the father, who had not only disapproved of the proposed connection, but planned his death. He and his friend Yahia ben Tafut now seized on the vacant government; but, as they had reason to dread the vengeance of their sovereign, the king of Morocco, they implored the aid of dom Manuel, whom, in return, they proposed to recognise as their liege superior. To interest the monarch in his behalf, Yahia visited the Portuguese court, and in his absence Ali assumed the sole authority, and made a similar appeal to the Moorish king. This chief, who afterwards served the Portuguese with unshaken fidelity, was favourably received by Manuel, who ordered him to be provided at first with the command of twenty horsemen, and to be aided in his designs by the governors on the coast. Ali was soon defeated, expelled from the place, and the government intrusted to a Christian knight. This accession to the Christian strength was viewed with great dissatisfaction by the Moors; but the dissensions of their own princes long prevented them from opposing the enemy. Zeilan, king of Mequinez, being expelled by Nassir, brother to the king of Fez, took refuge in Azamor. Thence he applied for aid to the Portuguese king, whom he proposed to recognise as his liege lord, and into whose hands he promised to surrender that city. An armament was immediately equipped to seize the tempting prize; but, on arriving before the city, it was found that the faithless Moor had been reconciled with his brother, had introduced 8000 men into the city, and placed 16,000 in ambush at a short distance from it. The Christian general, dom Joam de Menezes, who had only a handful of troops, though as valiant as his heroic sires, considered a retreat more prudent than the risk of an action, re-embarked, and cruised in the straits. In revenge he took several Moorish vessels; but the perfidy demanded a greater, and he went to Tangier to consult, on the means of obtaining it, with the gallant governor, dom Duarte. They were joined, for the same purpose, by Vasco Coutinho, of Arsilla; but scarcely had their deliberation commenced when intelligence reached them that the king of Fez, with 20,000 cavalry and 120,000 foot[*], was rapidly advancing on the last-named fortress. Dom Vasco immediately hastened to his government, and was fortunate enough to reach it before the arrival of the enemy. It was invested; the walls were furiously assailed, and a breach made sufficiently wide to admit the besiegers, who at length obtained possession of the city, the besieged taking shelter in the citadel. Dom Joam de Menezes, with the armament, hastened from Alcacer-Seguer to relieve this important place; but the attempt, in presence of so numerous a force, was desperate. With a courage, however, which can never be surpassed, some hundreds of the bravest Portuguese immediately forced their way through the hostile squadrons, and threw themselves into the fortress. The Moorish king expressed his joy at the circumstance, saying that the more defenders the more prisoners; but two of his generals, Barraxe and Almanderim, who had been frequently opposed to dom Joam, were far from sharing his exultation. As the citadel continued to be closely invested, aid was solicited from Manuel, and from the Castilian ports of Andalusia. The first who arrived was the corregidor of Xeres, who, with his heavy artillery and 300 men, silenced two of the enemy's batteries: he was followed by an admiral of Castile, with 3500 men. The Christian force, which might now amount to 6000, proposed to give battle; but the Moorish king, having put fire to the city, abandoned it. Before his departure, however, he is said to have sought, in disguise, the tent of dom Joam, for the sake of seeing a hero of whom fame had spoken so loudly; and that the sarcastic observation of the Christian knight, who knew him not, induced him to give orders for extin-

---

[*] As usual, drop a cipher, and read *two* thousand horse, and *twelve* thousand infantry.

guishing the flames. But the defence of these places was not enough for the Portuguese king. Perceiving how much Saphin lay exposed to the assaults of the enemy, he despatched thither a small armament, under Nuno Fernandos de Ataide, one of his most valiant generals, who had orders to remove the Christian frontier in that quarter nearer to the capital of Morocco. This brave officer immediately commenced a series of successful expeditions, not surpassed even by the famous Pedro de Menezes, first governor of Ceuta. They naturally incensed the neighbouring Moors, who combined together for the destruction of Saphin. The force which the barbarians raised against that fortress is estimated by the Portuguese, in their usual manner, at 600,000 foot, besides cavalry. The governor, having solicited and obtained succours from the Christian fortresses on the coast, firmly awaited the advancing tide, which threatened to sweep away both men and fortifications. But it was opposed by a bulwark immoveable as the rocks which bordered the coast. In vain did it dash against the walls: it was soon made to recede with greater rapidity than it had advanced. However exaggerated the Christian accounts of this siege, the defence was, doubtless, as heroic as it was successful, and it covered dom Nuno with glory. But the valiant knight considered it only as the commencement of a long series of victories. From the villages and plains, as far as the foot of Mount Atlas, he succeeded in extorting an annual tribute, as the reward of his forbearance. He was joined by Yahia ben Tafut, who, with unshaken valour and fidelity, aided him in extending the sway, and enriching the coffers, of the Christian king. Saphin became a flourishing town: thither the traders of the desert, the Moors and the Jews, repaired in perfect security. Sometimes, indeed, the tribute was withheld; and, at the instigation of the Moorish kings of Morocco and Fez, new armies were collected to expel the haughty Christians from their strong holds; but through the valour of the latter, and their Mahommedan ally, Aben Tafut, it was speedily regained. But the fidelity of this honourable man was once suspected. To destroy him, a creature of the king of Morocco remarked to Nuno Fernandes, that he held a confidential intercourse with that monarch, and that he was only waiting an opportunity of betraying his allies. Without enquiring into the truth of the charge, and without considering how improbable it was, that one who had done such signal harm to the Moors should be their friend, the governor ordered two Portuguese captains in the squadron of Yahia, to leave his standard. The Moor, deeply affected by this injurious suspicion, after expressing a surprise, that a general so prudent as dom Nuno should so easily credit it, marched to vindicate his honour, or to die. He knew that the king of Morocco was advancing at the head of a formidable army: he instantly put his Moors, amounting to 3000, whom his favour and his liberality had drawn to his standard, in motion, and marched against his reputed ally. Nuno was instantly struck with his own injustice: to repair it he sent a few horsemen to the offended Moor, with the offer of 500 Christians, the following day, in an assault on the enemy. But Yahia was no longer in his encampment; and though the 500 horse were despatched after him, he had attacked and defeated the Moorish king before they could join him. His fidelity, no less than his valour, was now the theme of universal admiration. By the repentant Nuno he was soon invested with the important government of Almedina, which he made to flourish by a just and liberal administration. In 1513 the Portuguese king equipped a more powerful armament than he had before raised, for the African coast. It consisted of 400 sail, carrying about 23,000 horse and foot; its destination was Azamor; and the command confided to the king's nephew, the duke of Braganza. The expedition was crowned with complete success; the place was stormed and taken with little loss; and though the Moorish inhabitants fled, yet as the Christians entered they were soon allured to their habitations by the promises of the duke. Success so signal and so sudden, surprised the Portuguese themselves, who loudly declared, that nothing now remained to prevent them from marching on the city of Morocco. But the prudent general turned a deaf ear to their voices, on the ground that he could not exceed the tenour of his instructions; his chief reason, doubtless, was, that he would not risk the glory of his recent enterprise. To change his purpose, the nobles prevailed on his chaplain, the friar Joam de Chaves, to expatiate, in a studied sermon, on the glory of the prepared enterprise; on the certainty of its success: and on the duty of every Christian knight to engage in it. The words of the preacher had so great an effect on the audience, that the duke was compelled to rise in his place, and to justify his refusal; and this he did in terms weighty enough to silence both friar and congregation. Soon afterwards he embarked his troops and returned.*

1510 to 1519. About this time a family arose in Africa, destined, in the process of time, to act a momentous part in the revolutions of these regions. The chief of a small village, in the province of Dara, Mohammed ben Hamed by name, seeing the divisions of the Moors, and their consequent inability to resist the Europeans, formed the magnificent design of founding a new empire. As his state was obscure, and his possessions scanty, his object would only be effected, by exciting and concentrating the fanaticism of the people. He boasted of his descent from the prophet, and changed his name into Xerif. His first step was to send his two sons on the pilgrimage to Mecca, an infallible road to reputation, and consequently to power. On their return they were regarded as oracles by their credulous countrymen; by their pretensions to sanctity, and their reported exemptions from worldly passions, they aspired to the character, if not of prophets, at least of holy doctors.

* Vasconcellos, p. 270, &c. Damian à Goes, Chron. passim. La Clède, tom. iv. 14. Lemos, tom. xi. liv. 40, &c.

The everlasting burden of their complaint, was the degeneracy of the faithful; and their constant encouragement that Allah would speedily raise up some chosen one to emancipate his people. In 1510, by the desire of their father, they repaired to the court of the king of Fez and offered to fight for the ancient law of their prophet. The offer was readily accepted; a squadron of horse was placed at their disposal, and with the title of royal alcaldes, they commenced their career as missionaries and heroes. With the consecrated standard of the prophet borne before them, they proceeded through the country, to persuade or to compel the Moorish vassals of dom Manuel to throw off his authority, and fight for the faith of Islam. It was owing more to their preaching than to the valour of their countrymen, that this faith was not banished from this angle of Africa. When they began their orthodox labours, the Portuguese were every where triumphant; and there was evidently no native Mahommedan prince capable of resisting their rapid progress. At first, indeed, the success of the two prophets did not correspond with their pretensions: they could not collect a force sufficiently resolute to withstand the brunt of the infidels; and they were compelled to retreat on Morocco. About the same time, too, a Christian detachment, under Ataide, moved on Tednest, where the father of the two saints had taken up his abode. They flew to his succour; and all three, with 4000 horse, ventured to arrest the Portuguese chief, and his ally, Yahia ben Tafut. But their presumption was repaid by a precipitate flight before the victorious enemy, and by the loss of Tednest, with abundant spoil. The check caused by this defeat brought the eldest Xerif to the grave. If, at this crisis, the conquerors had united their forces, and marched on Morocco, that capital would certainly have been theirs; but the jealousies of the local governors prevented them from acting in concert. Had such an expedition marched, it must have been headed by dom Juan de Menezes, and his must consequently have been the glory of the success,—a consideration which determined Ataide not to share in it. The Christians penetrated indeed within three leagues of the city, and then sacked a village; but no remonstrances could draw the chief nearer. They were compelled to retire, indignant at his base jealousy. Through the efforts of the two Xerifs, the kings of Fez, Morocco, and Mequinez, prepared to combine their forces, and to march on Azamor; and to oppose this dreaded union, the Christians and Aben Tafut effected a junction, and succeeded in destroying a considerable body of the enemy. The kings of Mequinez and Fez, however, with an army too powerful to be assailed or withstood by the Christians, proceeded towards the coast; but the former, who was destitute of military talents, unexpectedly turned off to pillage Almedina and the adjoining country. Yahia retired into Saphin, but his activity would not allow him to remain; he soon sisued from the gates, hovered about the flanks of the king, annihilated one of the detachments, forced Nassir to retire, and persuaded a considerable body of the Moors to forsake him, and renew their homage to Manuel. When Nassir saw that a portion of his own army assailed his camp, he precipitately fled to the mountains. The king of Fez, with more valour, soon afterwards advanced against Ceuta, but he effected nothing. Yahia, who for his great services received a flattering letter from the Portuguese king, and was appointed captain-general of three powerful Moorish tribes submitted to the Christians, again advanced to the walls of Morocco, and took immense spoils in his ceaseless hostile incursions into the neighbouring towns. — But these triumphs were more than counterbalanced by an unsuccessful attempt to construct a citadel at the mouth of the river Mamora. An armament of 8000 men, under dom Antonio de Noronha, disembarked, and commenced the work; but an immense host of Moors, under the kings of Mequinez and Fez, suddenly fell on them, and annihilated one half of the number. This was the heaviest loss ever sustained by the army of dom Manuel.

The various warlike transactions which followed this failure, are too uniform, alike in character and results, to to merit detailing. As usual, the governors of the several fortresses, in emulation of each other, and in the hope of plunder, made their destructive irruptions into the neighbouring country: as usual, too, the Moorish inhabitants perpetually changed masters, transferring their allegiance from one to the other according to the fortune of arms. It was the lot of this unfortunate people to be the continued prey of either Moors or Christians, according to the sovereign they appeared at the time to acknowledge. The king of Fez no less frequently advanced with great armies against the Christian possessions, always with the same want of success. At length, the illustrious Yahia ben Tafut was treacherously slain, while attending the funeral of a friend, and accompanied by no more than three attendants. His troops, being assailed by the hostile Moors, were compelled to retreat on Saphin. The equally intrepid Ataide had been before killed by a Moor, in one of his numerous inroads among the savage tribes bordering on mount Atlas.*

In the mean time the Xerifs were not idle: if their designs were impeded for a season, they were not always unsuccessful. They sometimes made destructive irruptions into the territory of the Christians; and, if sometimes made to retreat, they had the consolation of knowing that they had thinned the ranks of their prophet's enemies, and that they were enriched by plunder. They had soon the glory of aiding the inhabitants of Morocco to repel an assault on that city by the too confident Christians. But their zeal was not always equalled by their valour, nor their merit by their rewards. Perceiving how slow their progress towards their

* Authorities — Damian à Goes, Vasconcellos, La Clède, Lemos, &c.

great object, they abandoned the capital, and resolved to fight for themselves. A valley in the kingdom of Fez, about sixty square leagues in extent, yet with no other population than the village of Tarudante, seemed a fit situation for the foundation of an empire. There they settled, and the little village soon became a great city. At the same time they seized on cape Aguer, and a fort at the mouth of the Aguz,—a position which they were resolved to render impregnable. Apprehensive of the consequences, which with men so ambitious and restless as the two brothers, might result from these usurpations, some counsellors of the Morocco king advised him to pluck up the growing evil by the roots — to annihilate the new candidates for power; but they advice was in vain: succours both of men and money were sent to the Xerifs. From thence they were attentive observers of passing events, and prominent actors in them. It was probably at their instigation that the dreaded Yahia was removed by assassination. The consternation produced by this event, and the notorious weakness of the court of Morocco, emboldened them to attempt the execution of their long meditated design. They proposed to the Moorish king the siege of Saphin; and offered for the enterprise both their troops and their personal service. The offer was eagerly accepted: they repaired to the capital with royal pomp, were received with suitable magnificence, and lodged in the palace. On the pretext of arranging the plan of the projected expedition, the elder Xerif requested a private interview with the king, to which three of the royal domestics were admitted. At that interview, Muley fell under the poniards of the assassins, and the Xerif was proclaimed that very night king of Morocco. How fatal this revolution proved to the Portuguese empire in southern Africa, will be seen in the next book.

Dom Manuel did not long survive this change of dynasty: he died at the close of the year 1521, after one of the most glorious reigns on record. Of his public administration enough has been said; and of his private character what little we know is chiefly in his favour. He administered justice with impartiality; and had regulated hours when he received his subjects without distinction: nay, such was his anxiety to do them justice, that if at the expiration of the appointed period complaints remained unredressed, he would sacrifice the hours sacred to enjoyment or repose. One night a lady demanded an audience as he was laying down to rest: he calmly put on his clothes, and ordered her to be introduced. The manner of her address was not less extraordinary than the tone: — "Would your serene highness pardon my husband if he caught me in adultery and killed me?"—" Certainly I would!" replied the monarch. " Then, by the same justice, your highness, must pardon me; for I have just killed both my husband, and a female slave, whom I detected in the crime!" Manuel acknowledged the reasonableness of her request; and ordered the instrument of her justification to be expedited. But the persecution of the unfortunate Jews is a deep stain on his memory.* In a popular insurrection, however, headed by two monks, who stimulated the mob to murder that unfortunate race, he showed more justice. He caused the monks to be degraded, strangled, and burnt; and the ringleaders, who were many in number, to be no less publicly executed. He also dismissed and fined the judges, who, in alarm at the massacre, had forsaken their posts. In every respect he was a great monarch, and his fame filled the world as much as his enlightened policy enriched his kingdom. He despatched ambassadors to all the potentates of his time, — to the king of England, and the ruler of Abyssinia; to the royal chief of Congou, and the soldan of Egypt; to the sultan of Persia, and the emperor of China. Some of them, — that for instance,

* See Vol. II. p. 274.

in which he displayed before the astonished pope and cardinals a Persian panther, and an Indian elephant, with their native attendants, — were distinguished by a magnificence suitable to the lord of so many regions.*

* Authorities the same as have been so frequently quoted.

APPENDIX A. Page 14.

DIVISION OF SANCHO'S DOMINIONS.

On this subject there is a fable in Rodrigo of Toledo, which is here abridged.

Sancho had a very valuable horse, which he would allow no one to mount but himself. On the eve of an expedition against the Moors of Cordova, he strictly enjoined his queen to see that his prohibition was observed. After his departure, however, don Garcia, his eldest son, so earnestly petitioned for leave to mount this noble steed, that she could not deny him; but a cavalier, don Pedro Sese by name, so strongly remonstrated with her on her imprudence that she revoked the permission. In revenge, the enraged Garcia prevailed on his brother, the infante Fernando, to accuse her of adultery with the cavalier. The accusation was credulously believed by don Sancho, who arrested his queen, and brought her to trial in the cortes of the kingdom. There it was resolved, that unless a champion came forward in her behalf, and overcame the infantes, she should be burned alive. The humane nobles were either afraid or unwilling to encounter the princes, and she was about to be resigned to her fate, when don Ramiro, a bastard of Sancho, espoused her cause. The repentant princes, however, would not appear in the lists, and confessed to a monk of Najera that the accusation was false. At the monk's and his queen's request, Sancho pardoned Garcia, but resolved that he should not inherit Castile; and to Ramiro, who had so nobly defended her innocence, he bequeathed the lordship of Aragon, which was her patrimony.

APPENDIX B. Page 14.

FABLE RESPECTING THE REBUILDING OF PALENCIA.

(Abridged from Moret, Anales de Navarre, 1—601).

The ancient city of Palencia had been so ruined by the Moors, and, perhaps, by Alfonso the Catholic, in the fear that they should inhabit it, that nothing covered its site beyond grass and brambles, which afforded good shelter to the wild beasts. One day, while Sancho was absent on an expedition against king Bermudo of Leon, being in the vicinity of this once noble city, he resolved to hunt in the mountains. His attendants soon raised a wild boar, which Sancho pursued with great heat, until it took refuge in a cave, that had once been a hermitage. He dismounted, and pursued the beast into the cave: it had sought an altar, which appeared in one corner, half in ruins. Without thinking of the sanctity of the place, he raised his arm to dart his hunting spear, when suddenly his arm stiffened so that he could not move it. In great surprise, he enquired what place this was, and hearing that it had been a hermitage of the holy martyr San Antonino, he fell down on his knees, and devoutly asked pardon of the saint for the sacrilege he had been about to commit; and if the holy saint would restore the use of his arm, he vowed to rebuild, in his honour, the church of Palencia. The vow was heard, for his arm was immediately restored to its right use: and the king royally fulfilled his pledge.

Moret (who follows the archbishop Rodrigo) relates this legend with becoming gravity.

APPENDIX C. Page 69.

THE POSSESSED PRINCESS.

(Abridged from Diago, Historia de las Victoriosissimos Antiguos Condes de Barcelona, liv. ii. cap. 14.)

About the year 888, the devil entered into the body of a daughter of the count, a young girl of about twelve years of age; and she was carried about to all the holy places, and was exorcised by the priests; but the demon replied, that he would not leave her for any one's command, except that of Juan Garin, a great servant of God, who lived in a solitary cave on Montserrat; and the man of God prayed over her, and the evil spirit left her! Yet how powerful is opportunity with the best of us! The rich viands sent by the count to this hermit stimulated the flesh, and the councils of another hermit, his confessor, who was in sooth a devil in disguise, urged him to commit a great sin: for he had a carnal knowledge of the damsel, whom, through fear of detection, he killed and buried. And so enormous were the two crimes he had committed, that Satan would have him to despair of mercy, but in vain. For, through our Lord's help, and that of heaven's glorious Queen, he went to Rome, confessed his crimes to the pope, and was appointed a penance suitable to their enormity. So he returned to his cave, and for seven years saw no human being; living in so penitential a manner, that he seemed more like a savage or wild beast than a man. And one day, the count's huntsmen following the chace in the mountains, fell in with him; and so strange was his appearance, that thinking him some wild animal, they took him with them to the court of their master. And one day, when the count was rejoicing with his friends, he ordered the animal to be brought forth to divert them all by its tricks. But God would not suffer his image to be thus defiled, but loosened the tongue of Miro, the count's child, then only three months old, and in its nurse's arms. And the child cried out, "Juan Garin, arise; for God has forgiven thee!" Then the saint knelt down, and praised the Lord for so signal a mercy.

Diago receives the Legend with full assurance of faith. We have somewhere seen an eastern tale extremely like it.

APPENDIX D. Page 76.

CHIVALRY OF COUNT RAYMUNDO.

(Abridged from Diago and from Lucius Marineus Siculus.)

There was an emperor of Germany, who married a daughter of the king of Bohemia. And by some principal courtier of the count, she was accused of being in love with a certain noble page. And the emperor shut her up in an apartment like a prison, saying that if in a year and a day no knight came forward to do battle in her behalf, she should be burnt to death in sight of the whole people. And never could the afflicted empress find any one to do battle for her, so great was the power of her accusers. Howbeit one of her servants pitied her so much, that he came all the way to Barcelona, and related the affair to the count. And hearing that there was no one in Germany who would fight for so noble a lady, he resolved to go in person and do her need. And the champion of the accusers was a gentleman of Provence. So the count reached the emperor's court only three days before the battle; and he obtained permission to see the empress, and she proved her innocence to him. So when the day arrived, a great fire was made, and a great company gathered together; and the count prepared himself for the battle, but the champion fled. Then the count engaged to fight the two chief accusers one after the other: and when he had killed one, the other feared to come forth, and owned himself vanquished. And the false testimony was confessed, and the queen declared innocent. And the count, after his victory, immediately stole from Germany, as if to avoid the praises and rewards. And the empress followed him with a noble suite and brought him back; and right nobly was he used by the emperor, who gave him the marquisate of Provenæ.

APPENDIX E. Page 91.

ORIGIN OF THE WORD ÆRA.

There has been much dispute about the origin and meaning of the word *æra* or *era*, the use of which was confined to the Peninsula.

" St. Isidore thinks it originated from the tribute imposed by Augustus, and that the word was literally *Aera*,— brazen money. Brito says that this is confirmed by a manuscript of Eusebius at Alcobaça, in which these words are found: Hoc tempore, edicto Augusti Cæsaris, aes in tributum et census dari jubetur, ex quo *æra* collecta est.

" Sepulveda says it is a corruption of *annus erat Augusti*, and from this abbreviation of *erat Augusti* comes era. Resende and Morales assert that era was a well known word in this acceptation before the age of Augustus.

" Of these opinions, says Bernardo de Brito, the reader may choose which he likes best. For my part, I judge St. Isidore's to be very likely, Sepulveda's very ingenious, and

Resende's very true, — till some better shall be discovered. Certain it is that this date is peculiar to Spain."— *Southey's Chronicle of the Cid*, note 1.

The system of Resende is, *ab exordio regni Augusti*, the initial letters of which make *aera*.

Of these systems few readers will embrace any other than St. Isidore's.

APPENDIX F.   Page 187.

MIRACULOUS ESCAPE OF DOM FUAS ROUPINHO.

" In the days of Affonso Henriquez, the first king of Portugal, this part of the country was governed by D. Fuas Roupinho, a knight famous in the Portuguese chronicles, who resided in the castle at Porto de Mos. This Dom Fuas, " when he saw the land secure from enemies, used often to go out hunting among the sands and thickets between the town and the sea, where, in those days, there used to be great store of game, and even now, though the land is so populous, there is still some; and as he followed this exercise, the proper pastime of noble and spirited men, and came sometimes to the sea-shore, he came upon that remarkable rock, which being level on the side of the north, and on a line with the flat country, ends towards the south in a precipice over the waves of the sea, of a prodigious height, causing the greater admiration to him who, going over the plain country without finding any irregularity, finds himself, when least expecting it, suddenly on the summit of such a height. And as he was curiously regarding this natural wonder, he perceived between the two biggest cliffs which stand out from the ground and project over the sea, a sort of house built of loose stones, which, from its form and antiquity, made him go himself and examine it; and descending by the chasm between the two rocks, he entered into a low cavern, where, upon a little altar, he saw the venerable Image of the Virgin Mary of Nazareth, being of such perfection and modesty as are found in very few images of that size. The catholic knight venerated it with all submission, and would have removed it to his castle of Porto de Mos, to have it held in more veneration, but that he feared to offend it if he should move it from a habitation where it had abode for so many years. This consideration made him leave it for the present in the same place and manner in which he found it; and although he visited it afterwards when in course of the chase he came to those parts, nevertheless he never took in hand to improve the poor hermitage in which it was, nor would he have done it, if the Virgin had not saved him from a notorious danger of death, which, peradventure, God permitted, as a punishment for his negligence, and in this manner to make the virtue of the Holy Image manifest to the world. It was thus, that going to his ordinary exercise of the chase, in the month of September, in the year of Christ 1182, and on the 14th of the month, being the day on which the church celebrates the festival of the Exaltation of the Cross, upon the which Christ redeemed the human race, as the day rose thick with clouds, which ordinarily arise from the sea, and the country round about could not be seen by reason of the clouds, save for a little space, it befell that the dogs put up a stag, (if indeed it were one) and Dom Fuas pressing his horse in pursuit, without fear of any danger, because he thought it was all plain ground, and the mist hindered him from seeing where he was, found himself upon the very edge of the rock on a precipice, two hundred fathoms above the sea, at a moment when it was no longer in his power to turn the reins, nor could he do any thing more than invoke the succours of the Virgin Mary, whose image was in that place; and she succoured him in such a manner, that less than two palms from the edge of the rock, on a long and narrow point thereof, the horse stopt as if it had been made of stone, the marks of his hoofs remaining in proof of the miracle imprinted in the living rock, such as at this day they are seen by all strangers and persons on pilgrimages, who go to visit the Image of Our Lady; and it is a notable thing, and deserving of serious consideration, to see that in the midst of this rock, upon which the miracle happened, and on the side towards the east, and in a part where, because it is suspended in the air, it is not possible that any human being could reach, Nature herself has impressed a cross as if nailed to the hardness of the rock, as though she had sanctified that cliff therewith, and marked it with that holy sign, to be the theatre in which the miraculous circumstance was to be celebrated ; which, by reason that it took place on the day of the Exaltation of the Cross, seemed as if it showed the honour and glory which should from thence redound to the Lord who redeemed us thereon. Dom Fuas seeing himself delivered from so great danger, and knowing from whence the grace had come to him, went to the little hermitage, where, with the great devotion which the presence of the miracle occasioned, he gave infinite thanks to the Lady, accusing himself before her of having neglected to repair the house, and promising all the amends which his possibility permitted. His huntsmen afterwards arrived, following the track of the horse, and knowing the marvel which had occurred, they prostrated themselves before the Image of the Lady, adding with their astonishment to the devotion of Dom Fuas, who hearing that the stag had not been seen, and that the dogs had found no track of him in any part, though one had been represented before him to draw him on, understood that it was an illusion of the devil, seeking by that means to make him perish miserably. All these considerations enhanced the greatness of the miracle, and the obligations of Dom Fuas, who, tarrying there some days, made workmen come from Leyria and Porto de Mos, to make another hermitage, in which the Lady should be more venerated; and as they were demolishing the first, they found placed between the stones of the altar, a little box of ivory, and and within it relicks of St. Bras, St. Bartholomew, and other saints, with a parchment, wherein a relation was given of how, and at what time those relicks and the image were brought there, according as has been aforesaid. A vaulted chapel was soon made, after a good form for times so ancient, over the very place where the Lady had been ; and to the end that it might be seen from all sides, they left it open with four arches, which in process of time were closed, to prevent the damage which the rains and storms did within the chapel, and in this manner it remains in our days. The Lady remained in her place, being soon known and visited by the faithful, who flocked there upon the fame of her appearance : the valiant and holy king D. Affonso Henriquez, being one of the first whom Dom Fuas advised of what had happened, and he, accompanied with the great persons of his court, and with his son, D. Sancho, came to visit the Image of the Lady, and see with his own eyes the marks of so rare a miracle as that which had taken place; and with his consent, D. Fuas made a donation to The Lady of a certain quantity of land round about, which was at that time a wild thicket, and for the greater part is so still, being well nigh all wild sands incapable of giving fruit, and would produce nothing more than heath and some wild pine-trees."

"This legend," continues Southey, "cannot have been invented before Emanuel's reign, for Duarte Galvam says nothing of it in his Chronicle of Affonso Henriquez, though he relates the exploits and death of D. Fuas Roupinho. I believe there is no earlier authority for it than. Bernardo de Brito himself. It is one of many articles of the same kind from the great manufactory at Alcobaça, and is at this day as firmly believed by the people of Portugal as any article of the Christian faith. How indeed should they fail to believe it? I have a print, it is one of the most popular devotional prints in Portugal, which represents the miracle. The diabolical stag is flying down the precipice, and looking back with a wicked turn of the head, in hopes of seeing Dom Fuas follow him; the horse is rearing up with his hind feet upon the brink of the precipice; the knight has dropt his hunting-spear, his cocked hat is falling behind him, and an exclamation to the Virgin is coming out of his mouth. The Virgin with a crown upon her head, and the Babe with a crown upon his, at her breast, appear in the sky amidst clouds of glory. *N. S. de Nazarée*, is written above this precious print, and this more precious information below it, — *O. Emo. Snr. Cardeal Patriarcha concede 50 dias de Indulga. a qm. rezar huma have ma. diante desta Image.* His Eminency the Cardinal Patriarch grants fifty days' indulgence to whosoever shall say an Ave-Maria before this Image. The print is included, and plenty of Ave-Marias are said before it in full faith, for this *nossa senhora* is in high vogue. Before the French invasion, this famous Image used annually to be escorted by the court to Cape Espichel. In 1796 I happened to be upon the Tagus at the time of her embarkation